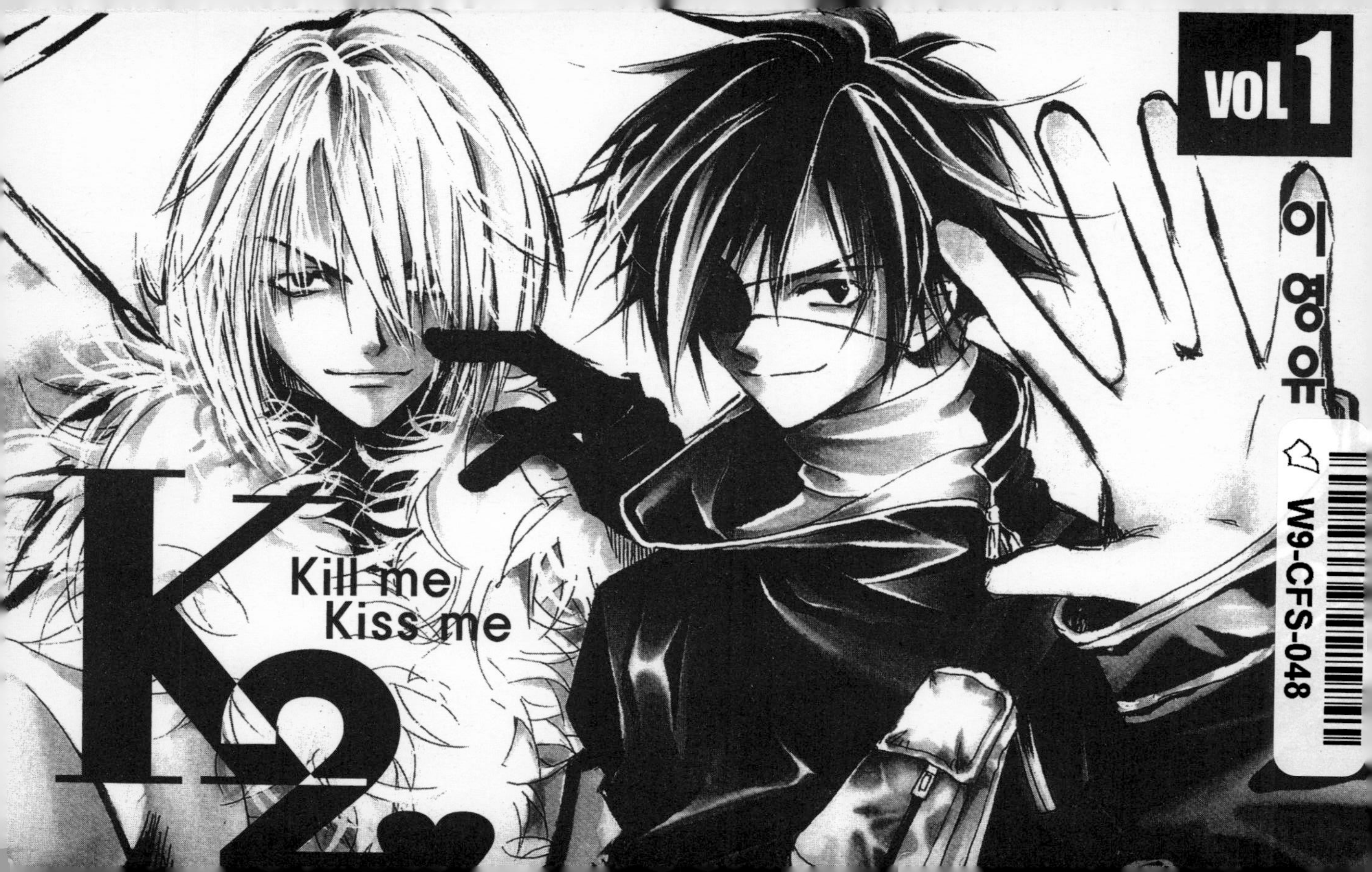
VOL 1
이영유
K2
Kill me
Kiss me
W9-CFS-048

Translator - Jihae Hong
English Adaptation - Paul Morrissey
Retouch and Lettering - William Suh
Cover Layout - Anna Kernbaum

Editor - Luis Reyes
Managing Editor - Jill Freshney
Production Coordinator - Antonio DePietro
Production Manager - Jennifer Miller, Mutsumi Miyazaki
Art Director - Matt Alford
Editorial Director - Jeremy Ross
VP of Production - Ron Klamert
President & C.O.O. - John Parker
Publisher & C.E.O. - Stuart Levy

Email: editor@TOKYOPOP.com
Come visit us online at www.TOKYOPOP.com

A  Manga

TOKYOPOP Inc.
5900 Wilshire Blvd. Suite 2000
Los Angeles, CA 90036

Kill Me Kiss Me Vol. 1

ISBN: 1-59182-593-8

First TOKYOPOP printing: February 2004

10 9 8 7 6 5 4 3 2 1
Printed in the USA

KILL ME Kiss Me

Volume 1

by Lee Young Yuu

TOKYOPOP
Los Angeles • Tokyo • London

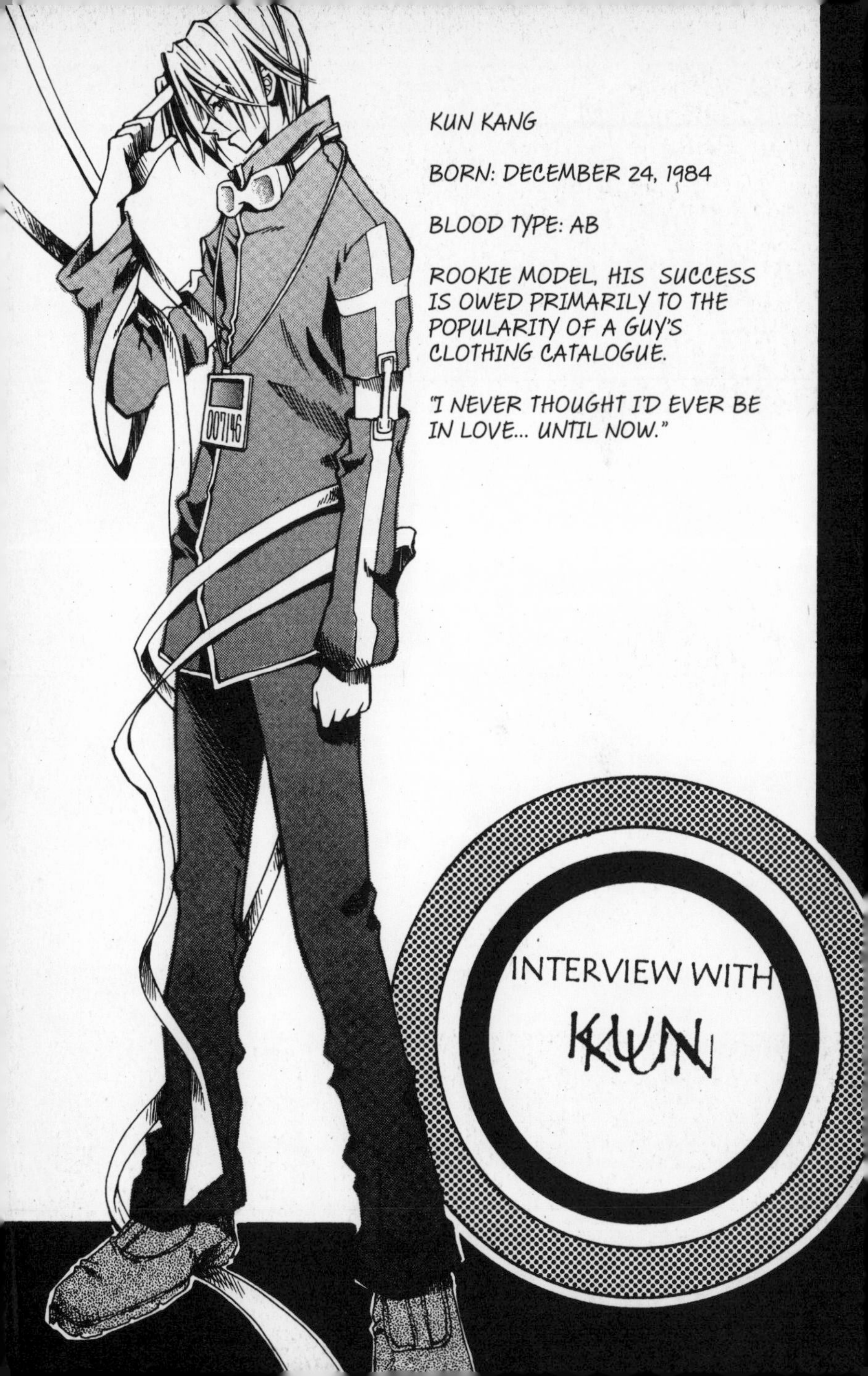
007146

KUN KANG

BORN: DECEMBER 24, 1984

BLOOD TYPE: AB

ROOKIE MODEL, HIS SUCCESS IS OWED PRIMARILY TO THE POPULARITY OF A GUY'S CLOTHING CATALOGUE.

"I NEVER THOUGHT I'D EVER BE IN LOVE... UNTIL NOW."

INTERVIEW WITH KUN

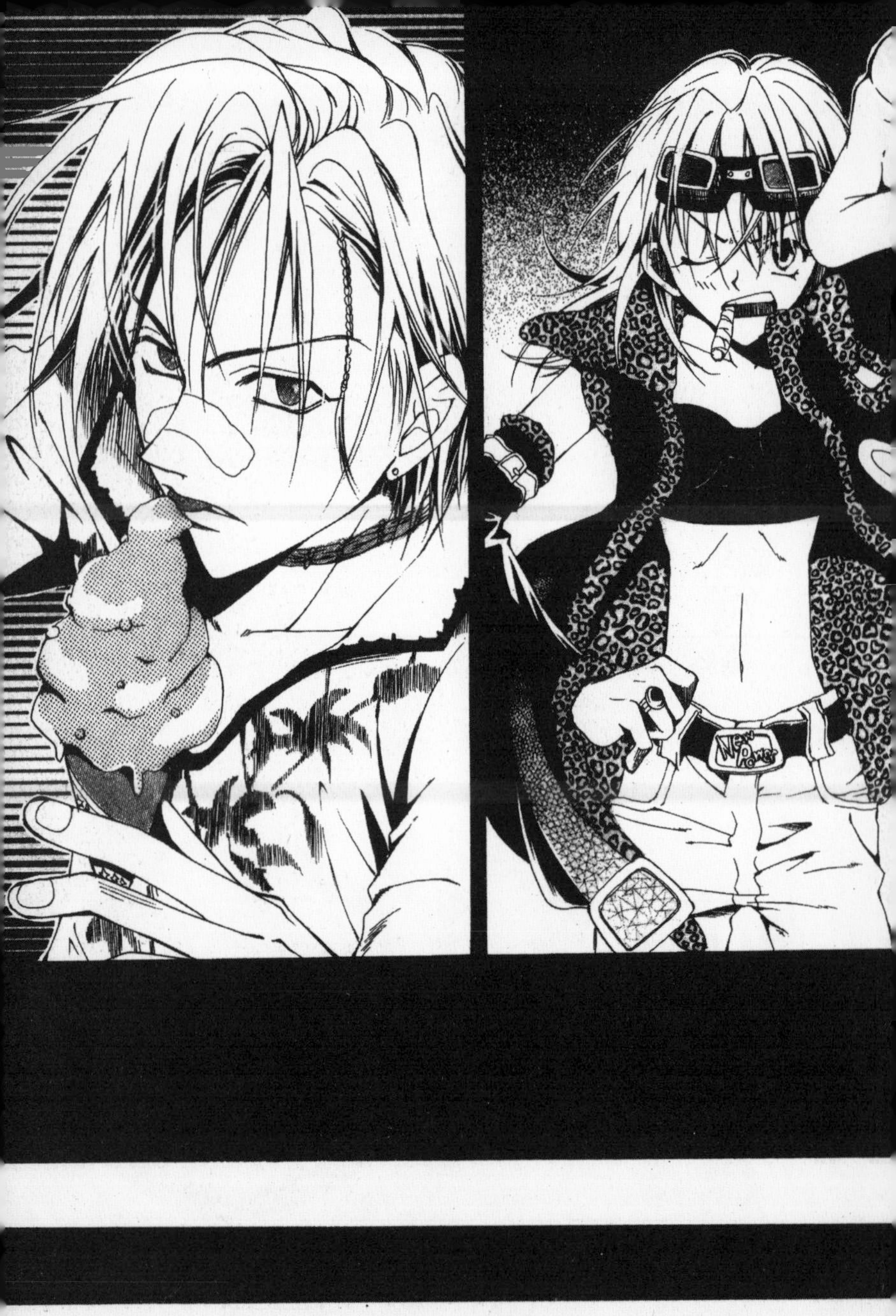
New Power

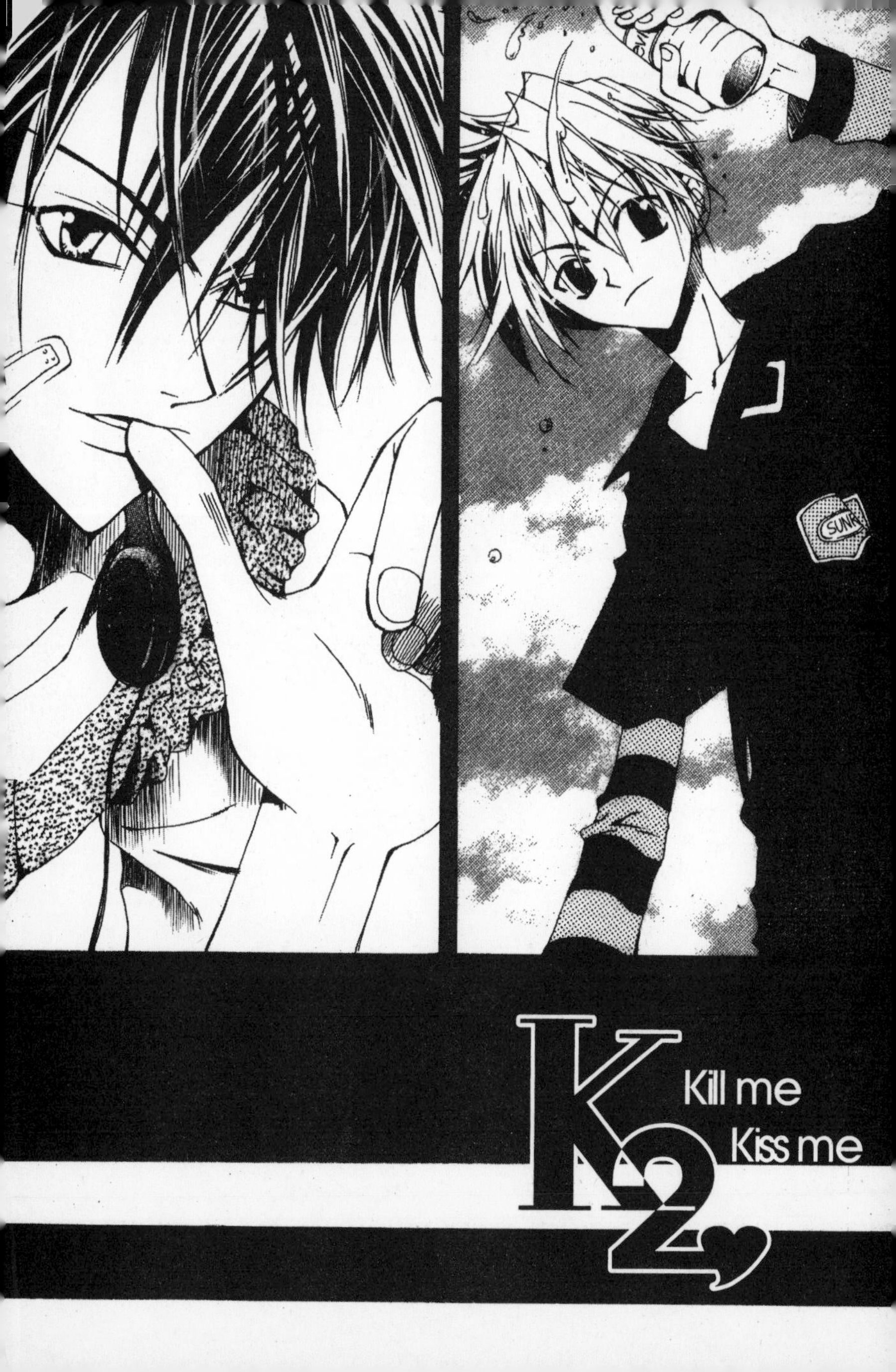
SUNK
K2
Kill me
Kiss me

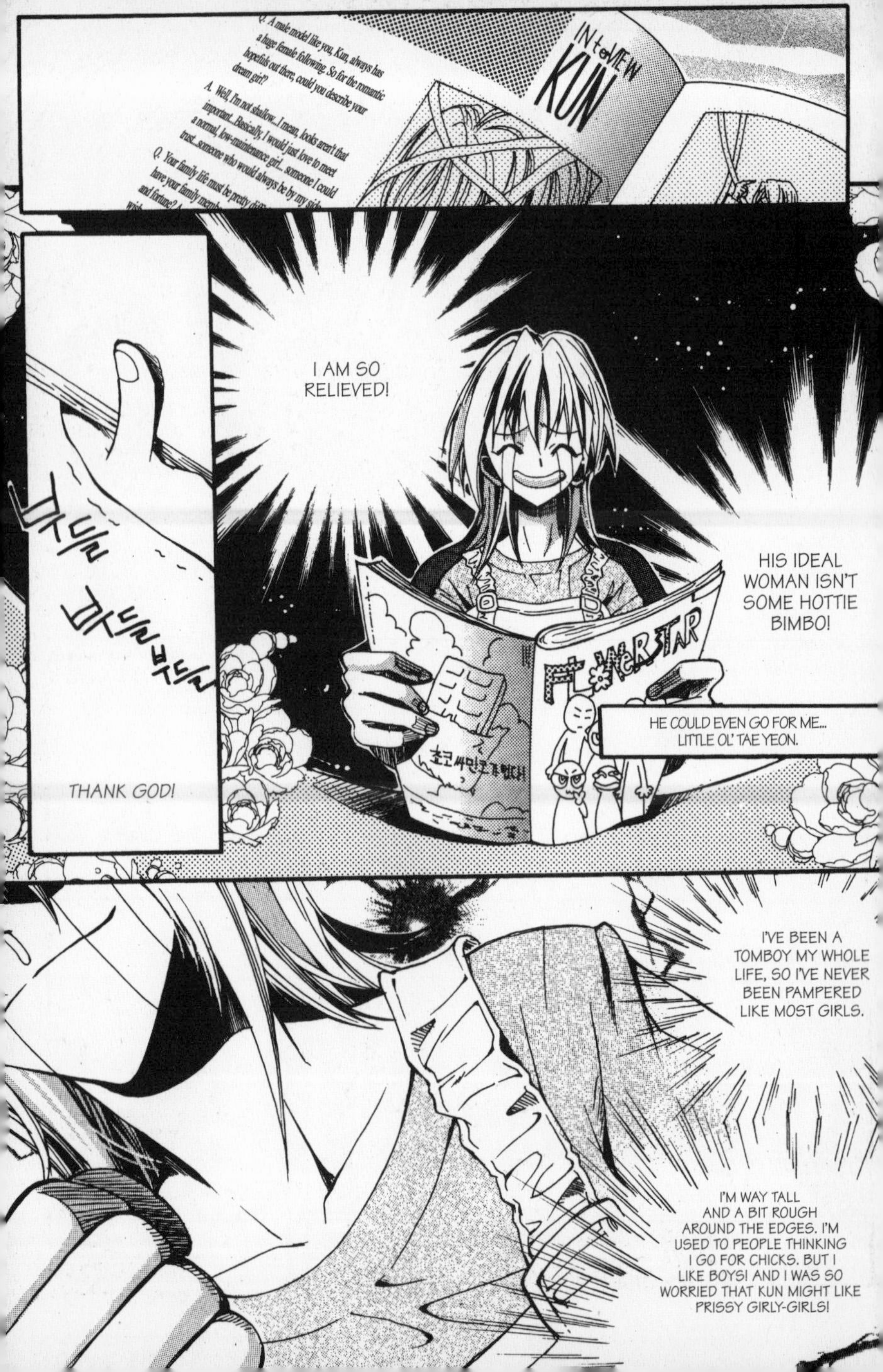
INTERVIEW KUN
Q. A male model like you, Kun, always has a huge female following. So for the romantic hopefuls out there, could you describe your dream girl?
A. Well, I'm not shallow...I mean, looks aren't that important...Basically, I would just love to meet a normal, low-maintenance girl... someone I could trust...someone who would always be by my side
Q. Your family life must be pretty
부들
부들부들
THANK GOD!
I AM SO RELIEVED!
HIS IDEAL WOMAN ISN'T SOME HOTTIE BIMBO!
HE COULD EVEN GO FOR ME... LITTLE OL' TAE YEON.
I'VE BEEN A TOMBOY MY WHOLE LIFE, SO I'VE NEVER BEEN PAMPERED LIKE MOST GIRLS.
I'M WAY TALL AND A BIT ROUGH AROUND THE EDGES. I'M USED TO PEOPLE THINKING I GO FOR CHICKS. BUT I LIKE BOYS! AND I WAS SO WORRIED THAT KUN MIGHT LIKE PRISSY GIRLY-GIRLS!

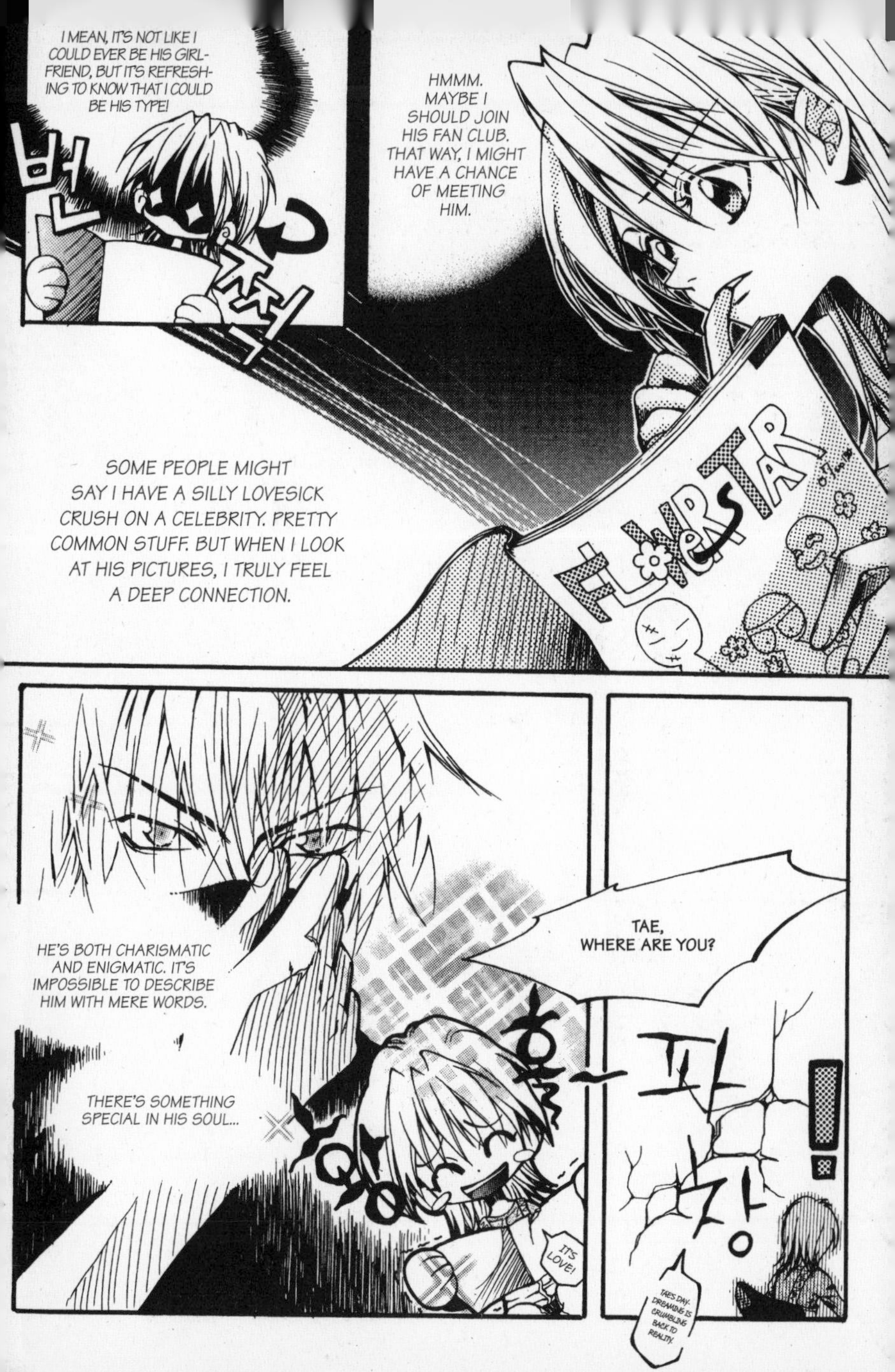
I MEAN, IT'S NOT LIKE I COULD EVER BE HIS GIRL-FRIEND, BUT IT'S REFRESH-ING TO KNOW THAT I COULD BE HIS TYPE!
HMMM. MAYBE I SHOULD JOIN HIS FAN CLUB. THAT WAY, I MIGHT HAVE A CHANCE OF MEETING HIM.
FLOWERSTAR
SOME PEOPLE MIGHT SAY I HAVE A SILLY LOVESICK CRUSH ON A CELEBRITY. PRETTY COMMON STUFF. BUT WHEN I LOOK AT HIS PICTURES, I TRULY FEEL A DEEP CONNECTION.
HE'S BOTH CHARISMATIC AND ENIGMATIC. IT'S IMPOSSIBLE TO DESCRIBE HIM WITH MERE WORDS.
THERE'S SOMETHING SPECIAL IN HIS SOUL...
IT'S LOVE!
TAE, WHERE ARE YOU?
TAE'S DAY-DREAMING IS CRUMBLING BACK TO REALITY.

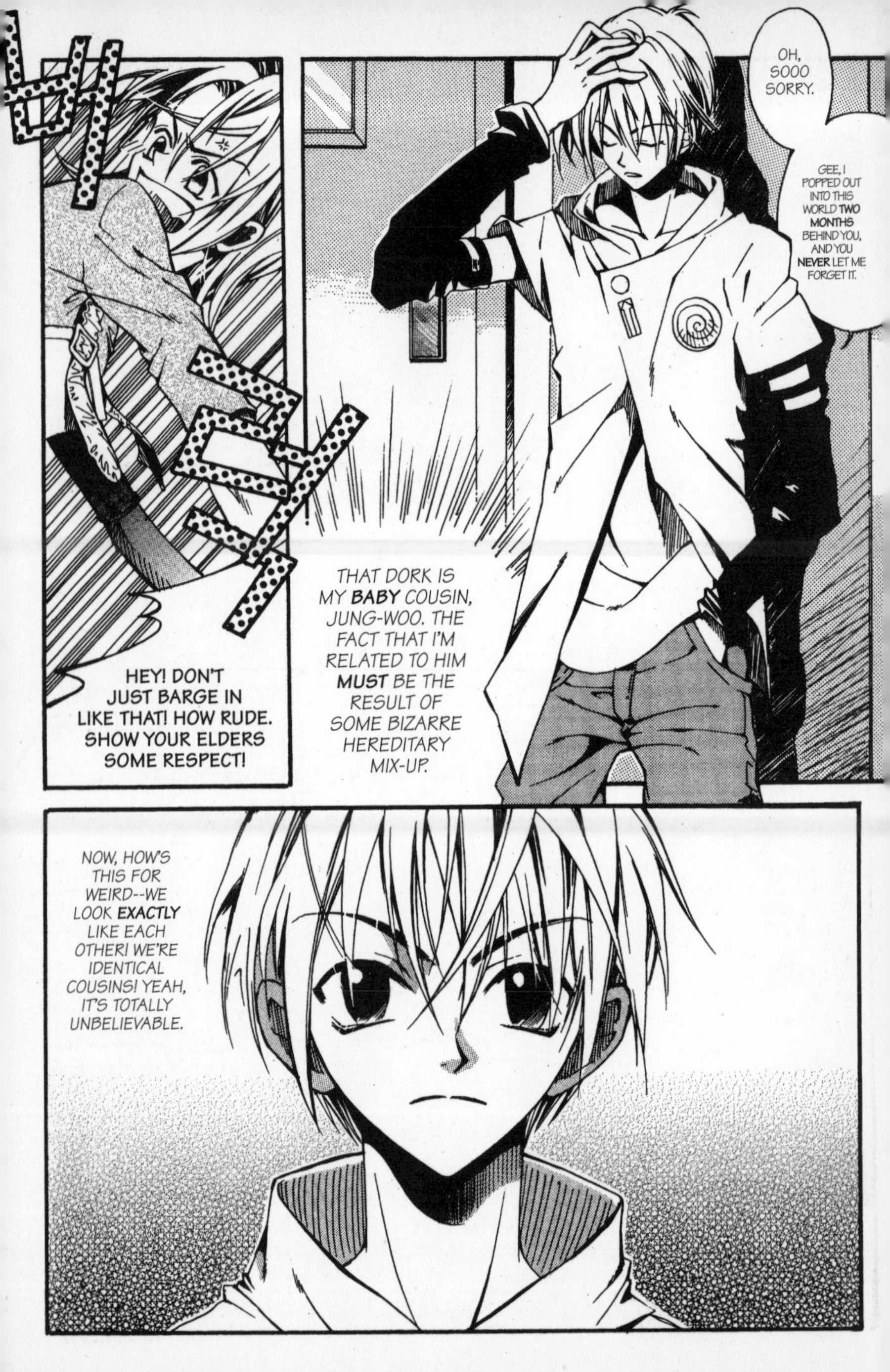
HEY! DON'T JUST BARGE IN LIKE THAT! HOW RUDE. SHOW YOUR ELDERS SOME RESPECT!
OH, SOOO SORRY.
GEE, I POPPED OUT INTO THIS WORLD TWO MONTHS BEHIND YOU, AND YOU NEVER LET ME FORGET IT.
THAT DORK IS MY BABY COUSIN, JUNG-WOO. THE FACT THAT I'M RELATED TO HIM MUST BE THE RESULT OF SOME BIZARRE HEREDITARY MIX-UP.
NOW, HOW'S THIS FOR WEIRD--WE LOOK EXACTLY LIKE EACH OTHER! WE'RE IDENTICAL COUSINS! YEAH, IT'S TOTALLY UNBELIEVABLE.

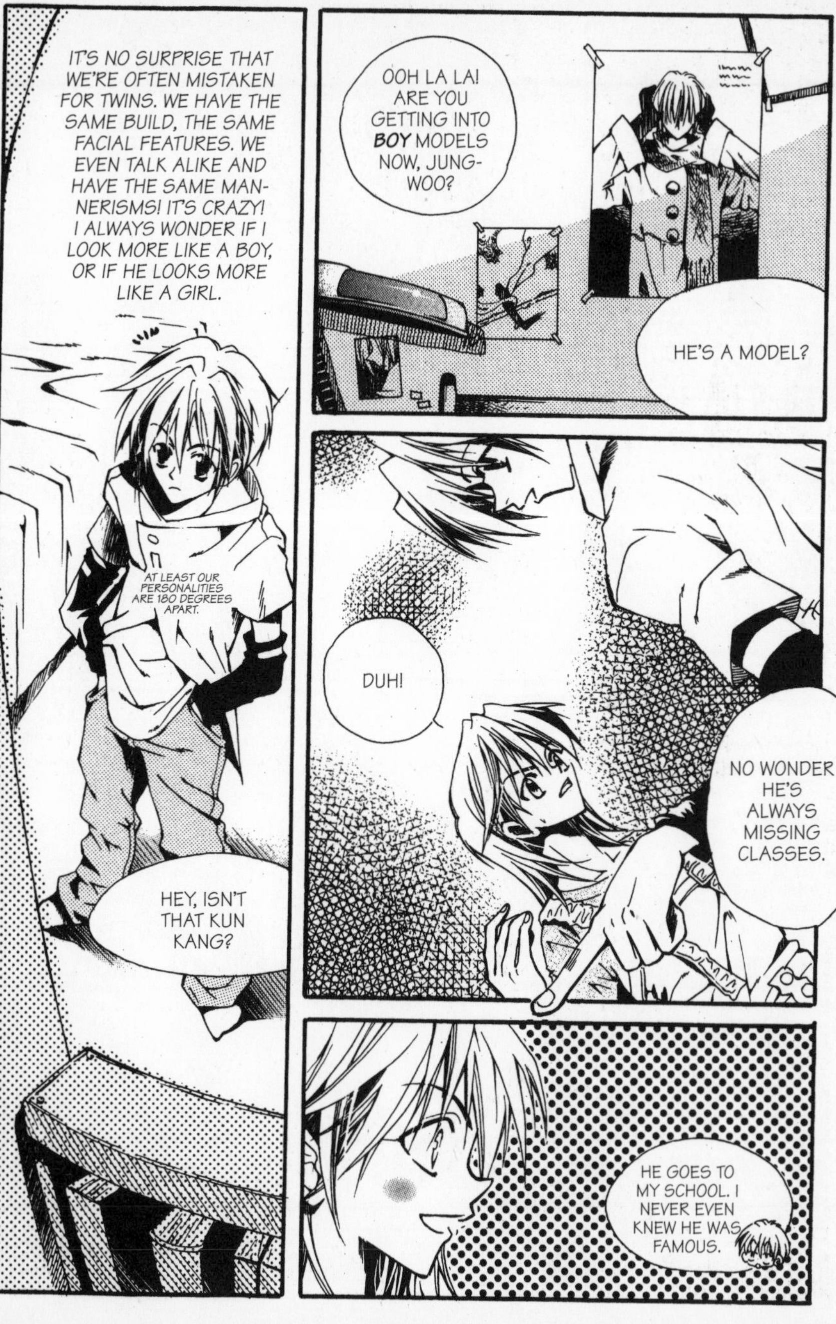
IT'S NO SURPRISE THAT WE'RE OFTEN MISTAKEN FOR TWINS. WE HAVE THE SAME BUILD, THE SAME FACIAL FEATURES. WE EVEN TALK ALIKE AND HAVE THE SAME MANNERISMS! IT'S CRAZY! I ALWAYS WONDER IF I LOOK MORE LIKE A BOY, OR IF HE LOOKS MORE LIKE A GIRL.
AT LEAST OUR PERSONALITIES ARE 180 DEGREES APART.
HEY, ISN'T THAT KUN KANG?
OOH LA LA! ARE YOU GETTING INTO **BOY** MODELS NOW, JUNG-WOO?
HE'S A MODEL?
DUH!
NO WONDER HE'S ALWAYS MISSING CLASSES.
HE GOES TO MY SCHOOL. I NEVER EVEN KNEW HE WAS FAMOUS.

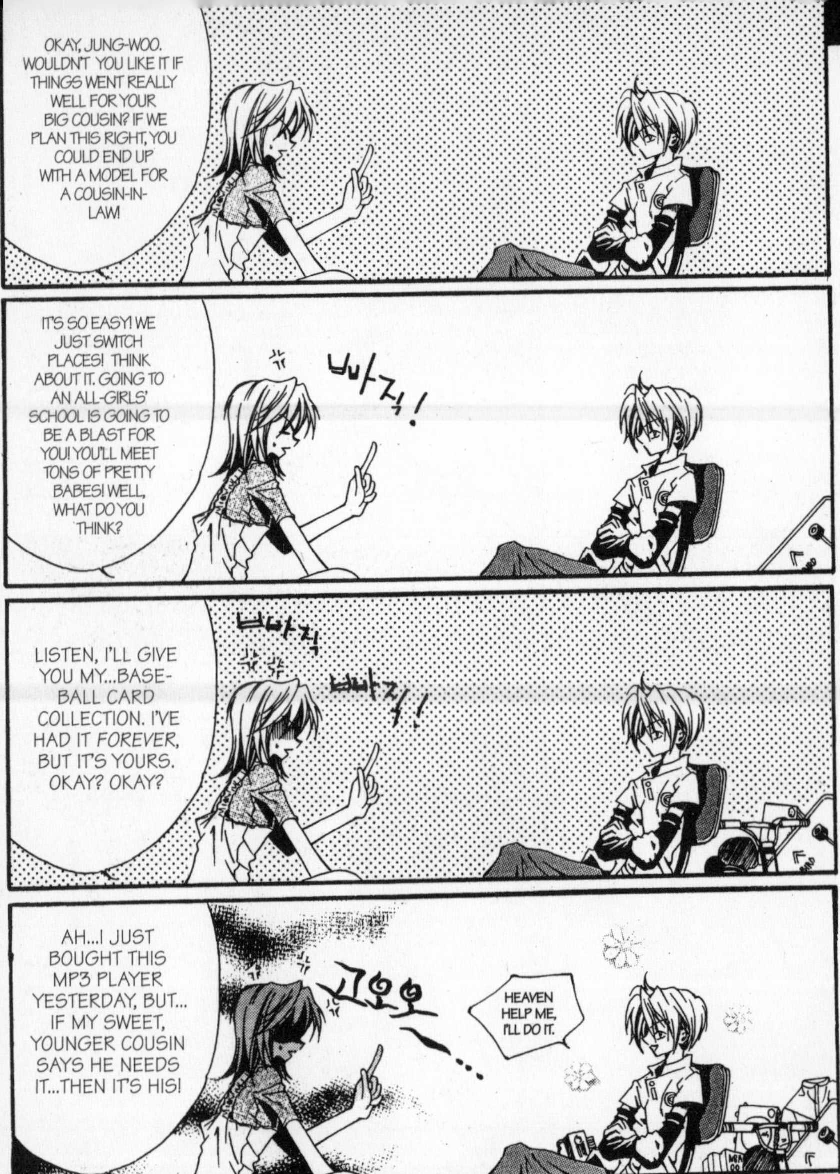
OKAY, JUNG-WOO. WOULDN'T YOU LIKE IT IF THINGS WENT REALLY WELL FOR YOUR BIG COUSIN? IF WE PLAN THIS RIGHT, YOU COULD END UP WITH A MODEL FOR A COUSIN-IN-LAW!
IT'S SO EASY! WE JUST SWITCH PLACES! THINK ABOUT IT. GOING TO AN ALL-GIRLS' SCHOOL IS GOING TO BE A BLAST FOR YOU! YOU'LL MEET TONS OF PRETTY BABES! WELL, WHAT DO YOU THINK?
빠직!
LISTEN, I'LL GIVE YOU MY...BASE-BALL CARD COLLECTION. I'VE HAD IT *FOREVER*, BUT IT'S YOURS. OKAY? OKAY?
빠직
빠직!
AH...I JUST BOUGHT THIS MP3 PLAYER YESTERDAY, BUT... IF MY SWEET, YOUNGER COUSIN SAYS HE NEEDS IT...THEN IT'S HIS!
고오오~...
HEAVEN HELP ME, I'LL DO IT.

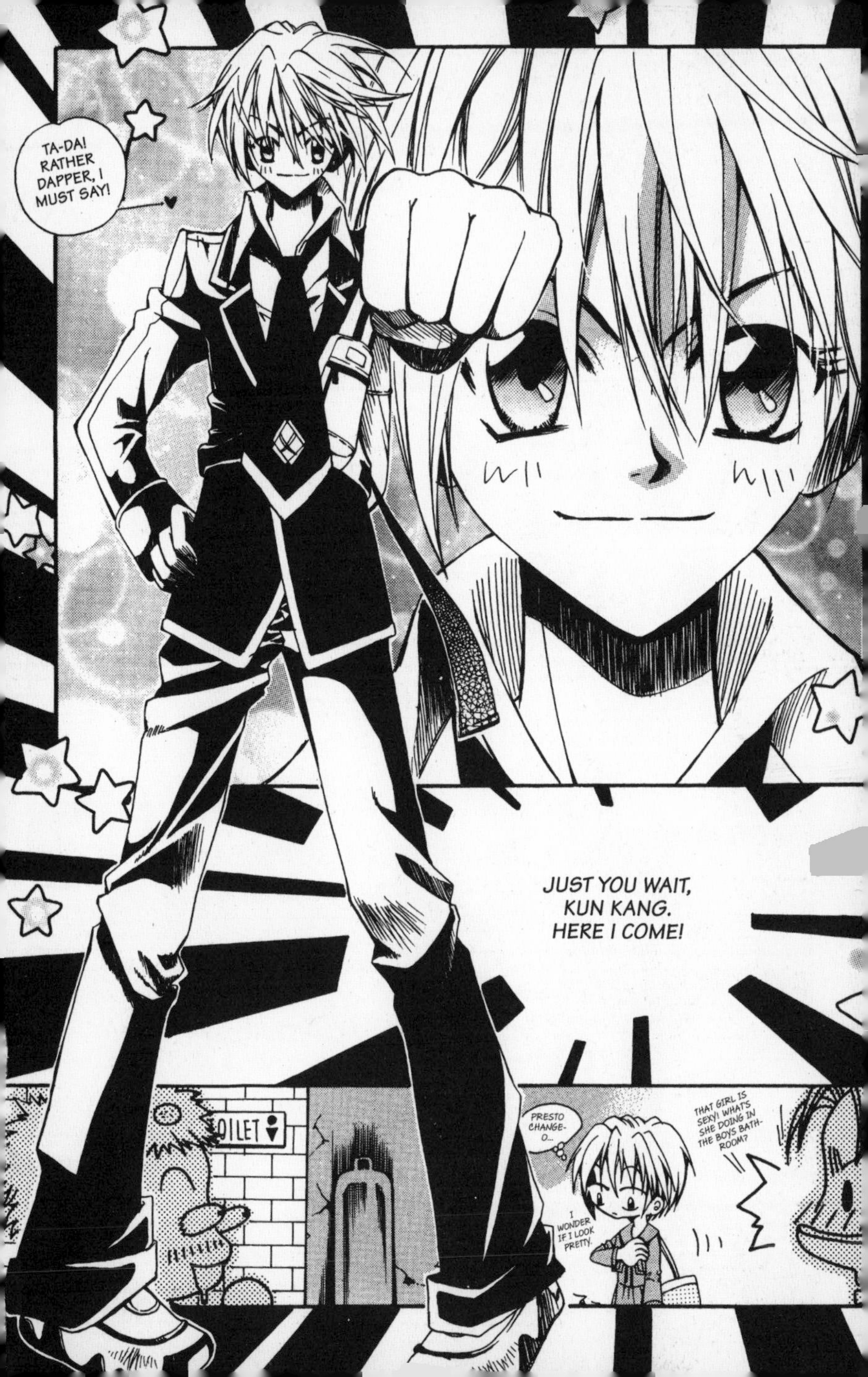
TA-DA! RATHER DAPPER, I MUST SAY!
JUST YOU WAIT, KUN KANG. HERE I COME!
OILET
PRESTO CHANGE-O...
I WONDER IF I LOOK PRETTY.
THAT GIRL IS SEXY! WHAT'S SHE DOING IN THE BOYS BATH-ROOM?

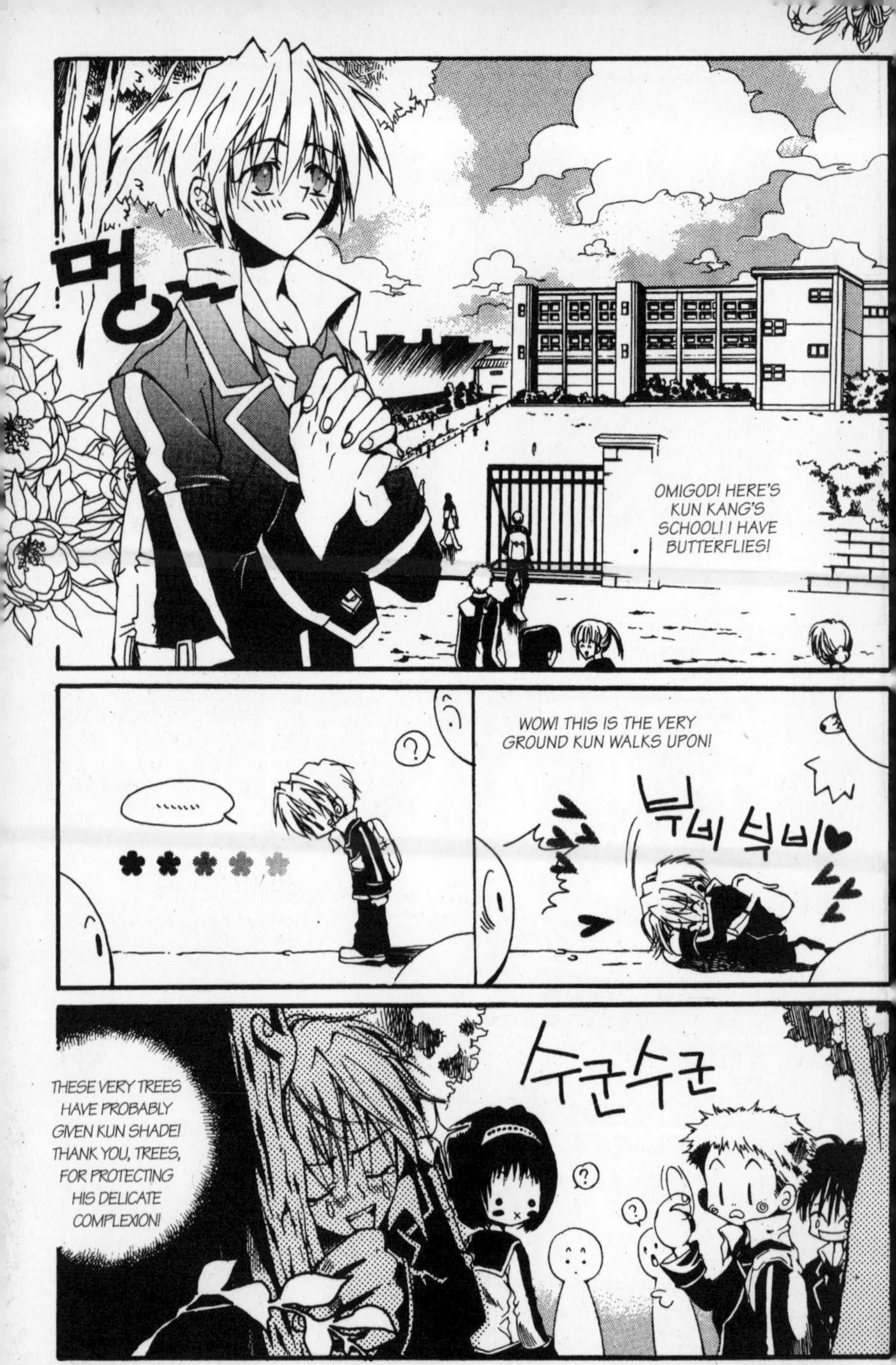

멍~
OMIGOD! HERE'S KUN KANG'S SCHOOL! I HAVE BUTTERFLIES!
......
?
WOW! THIS IS THE VERY GROUND KUN WALKS UPON!
부비 부비♥
THESE VERY TREES HAVE PROBABLY GIVEN KUN SHADE! THANK YOU, TREES, FOR PROTECTING HIS DELICATE COMPLEXION!
수군수군
?
?

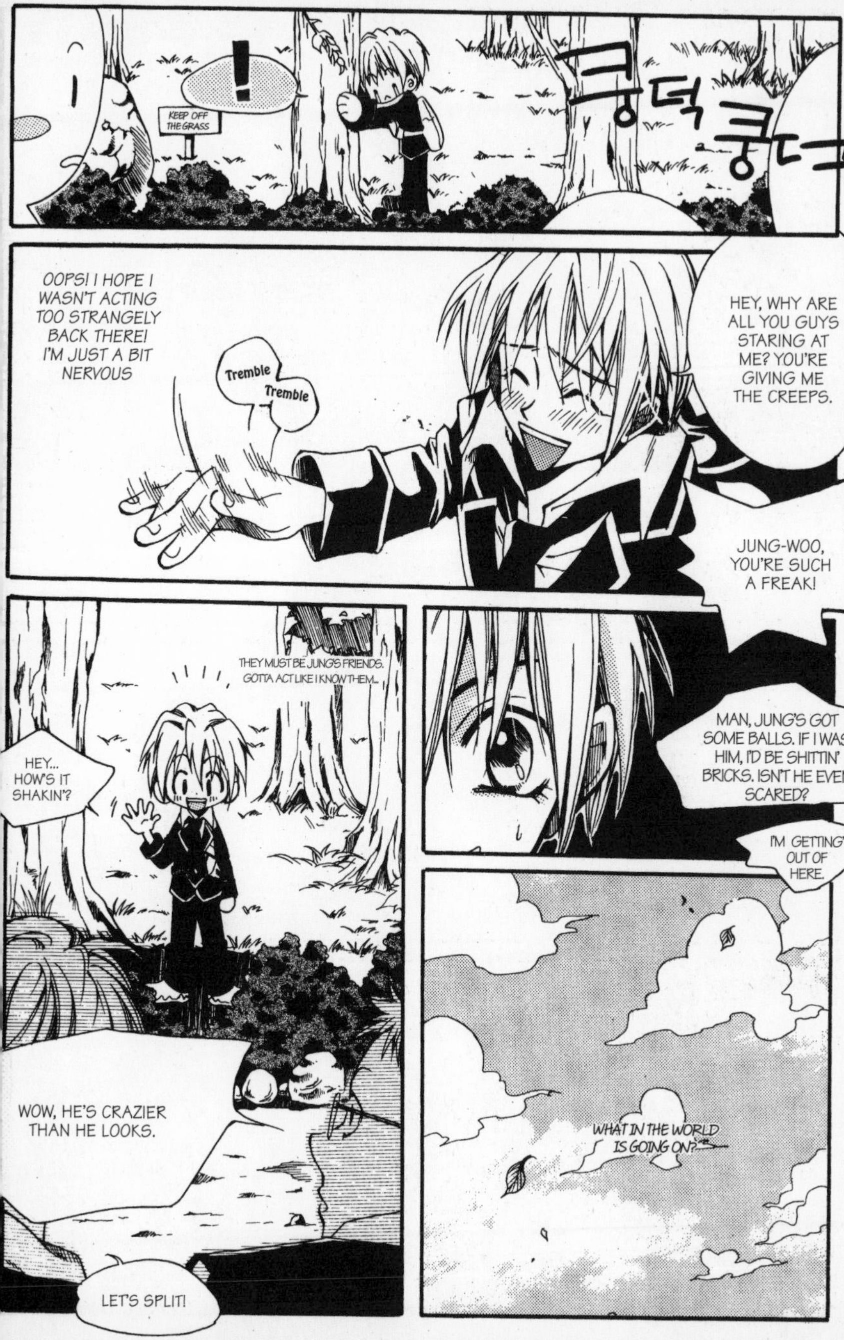
!
KEEP OFF THE GRASS
쿵덕 쿵덕
OOPS! I HOPE I WASN'T ACTING TOO STRANGELY BACK THERE! I'M JUST A BIT NERVOUS
Tremble Tremble
HEY, WHY ARE ALL YOU GUYS STARING AT ME? YOU'RE GIVING ME THE CREEPS.
JUNG-WOO, YOU'RE SUCH A FREAK!
THEY MUST BE JUNG'S FRIENDS. GOTTA ACT LIKE I KNOW THEM...
HEY... HOW'S IT SHAKIN'?
WOW, HE'S CRAZIER THAN HE LOOKS.
LET'S SPLIT!
MAN, JUNG'S GOT SOME BALLS. IF I WAS HIM, I'D BE SHITTIN' BRICKS. ISN'T HE EVEN SCARED?
I'M GETTING' OUT OF HERE.
WHAT IN THE WORLD IS GOING ON?

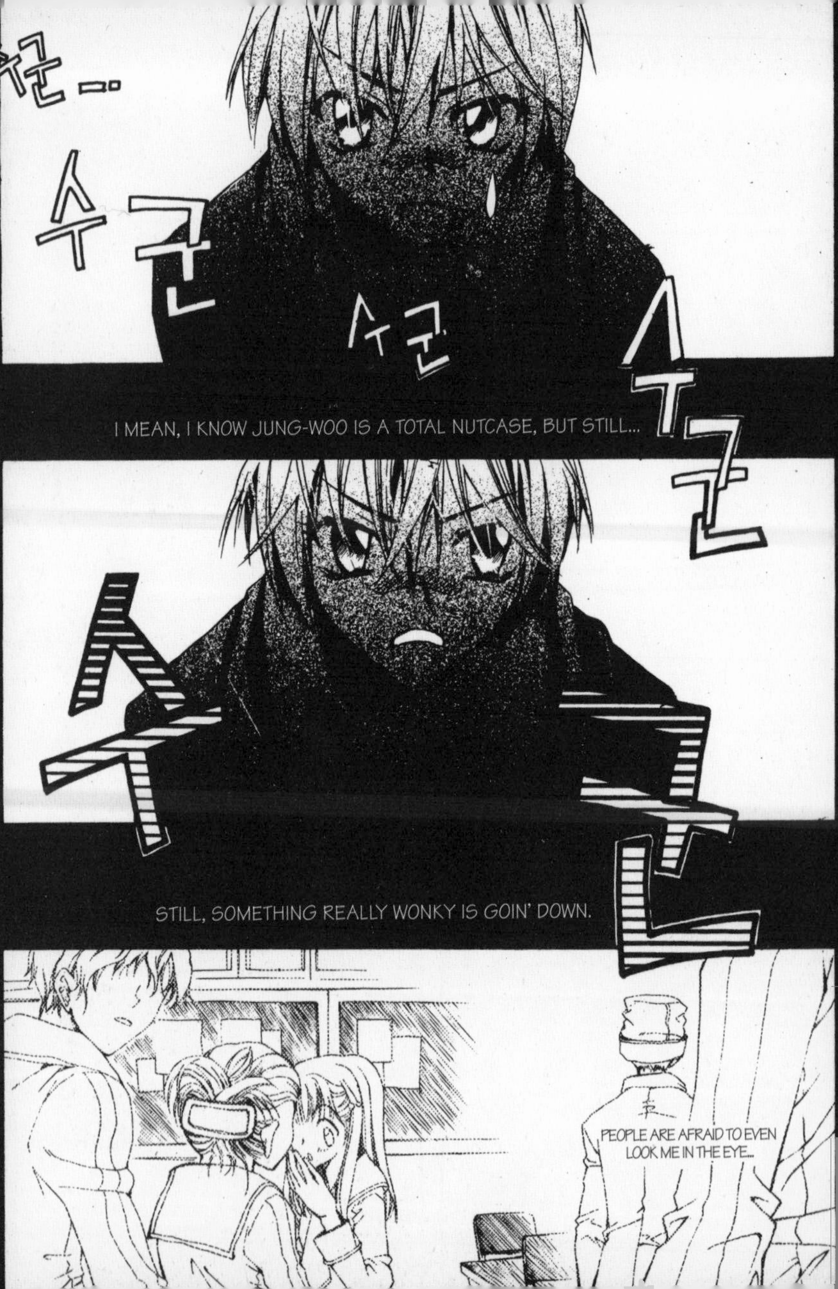
수군
수군
수군
I MEAN, I KNOW JUNG-WOO IS A TOTAL NUTCASE, BUT STILL...
수군
STILL, SOMETHING REALLY WONKY IS GOIN' DOWN.
PEOPLE ARE AFRAID TO EVEN LOOK ME IN THE EYE...

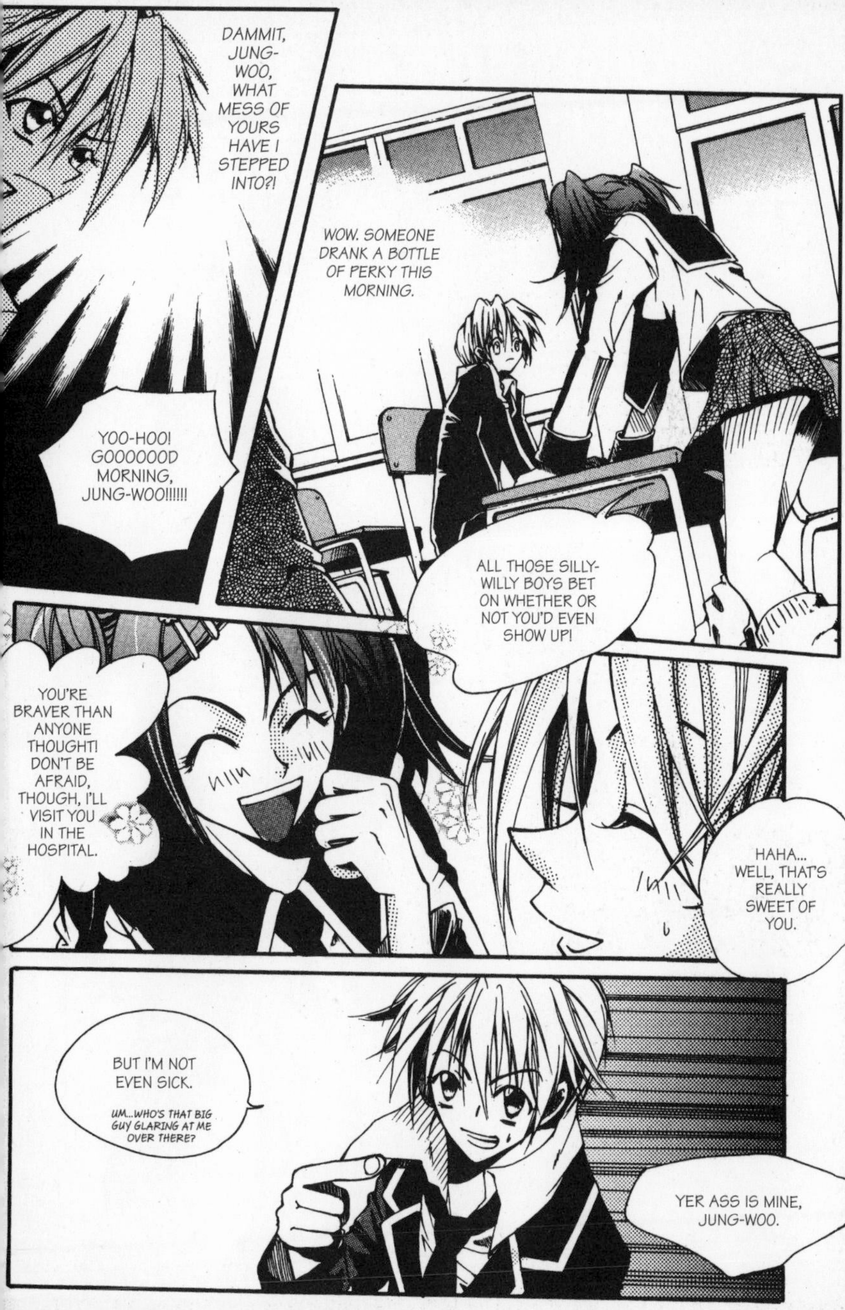
DAMMIT, JUNG-WOO, WHAT MESS OF YOURS HAVE I STEPPED INTO?!
YOO-HOO! GOOOOOOD MORNING, JUNG-WOO!!!!!!
WOW. SOMEONE DRANK A BOTTLE OF PERKY THIS MORNING.
ALL THOSE SILLY-WILLY BOYS BET ON WHETHER OR NOT YOU'D EVEN SHOW UP!
YOU'RE BRAVER THAN ANYONE THOUGHT! DON'T BE AFRAID, THOUGH, I'LL VISIT YOU IN THE HOSPITAL.
HAHA... WELL, THAT'S REALLY SWEET OF YOU.
BUT I'M NOT EVEN SICK.
UM...WHO'S THAT BIG GUY GLARING AT ME OVER THERE?
YER ASS IS MINE, JUNG-WOO.

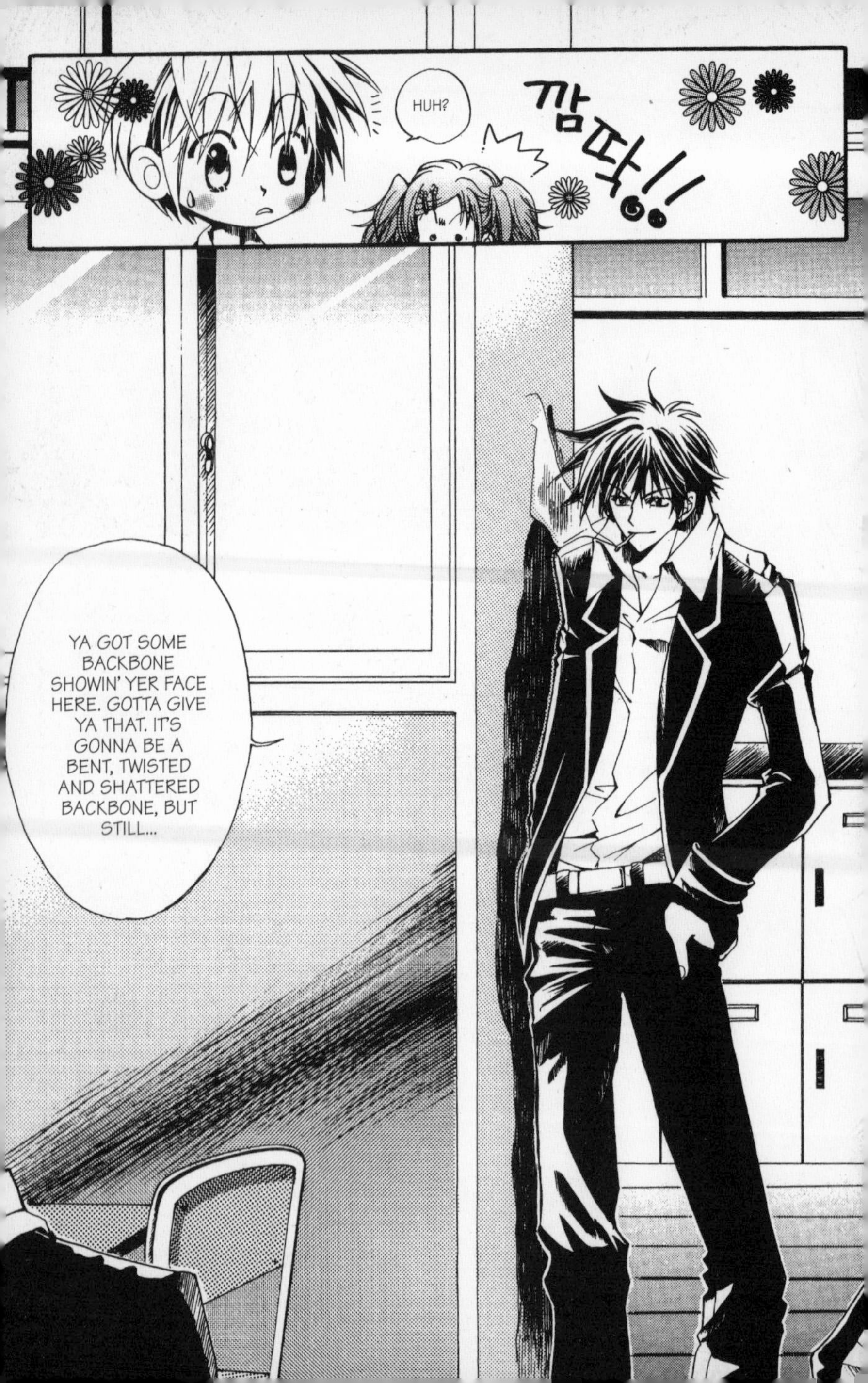
HUH?
깜짝!!
YA GOT SOME BACKBONE SHOWIN' YER FACE HERE. GOTTA GIVE YA THAT. IT'S GONNA BE A BENT, TWISTED AND SHATTERED BACKBONE, BUT STILL...

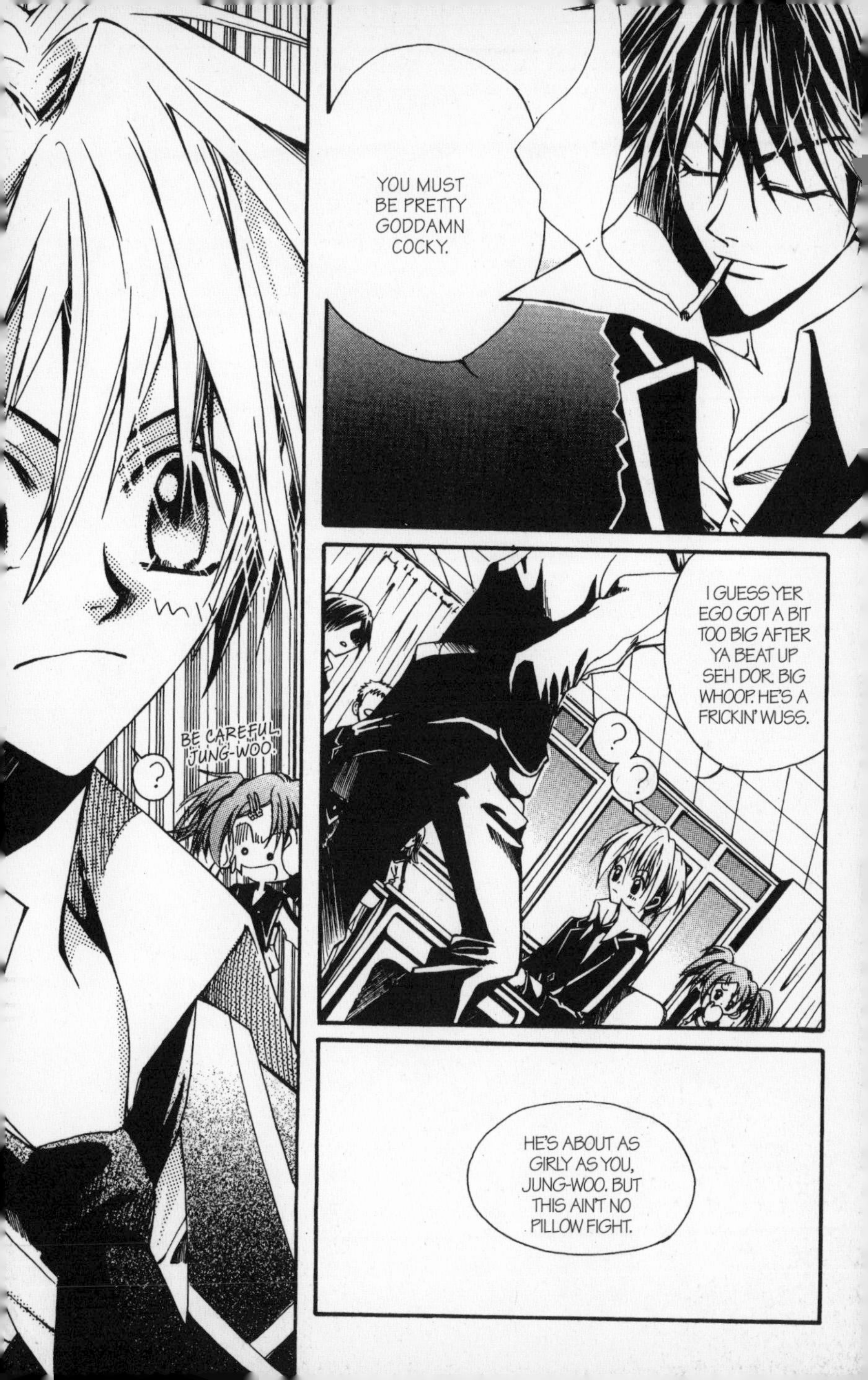
BE CAREFUL, JUNG-WOO.
?
YOU MUST BE PRETTY GODDAMN COCKY.
I GUESS YER EGO GOT A BIT TOO BIG AFTER YA BEAT UP SEH DOR. BIG WHOOP. HE'S A FRICKIN' WUSS.
? ?
HE'S ABOUT AS GIRLY AS YOU, JUNG-WOO. BUT THIS AIN'T NO PILLOW FIGHT.

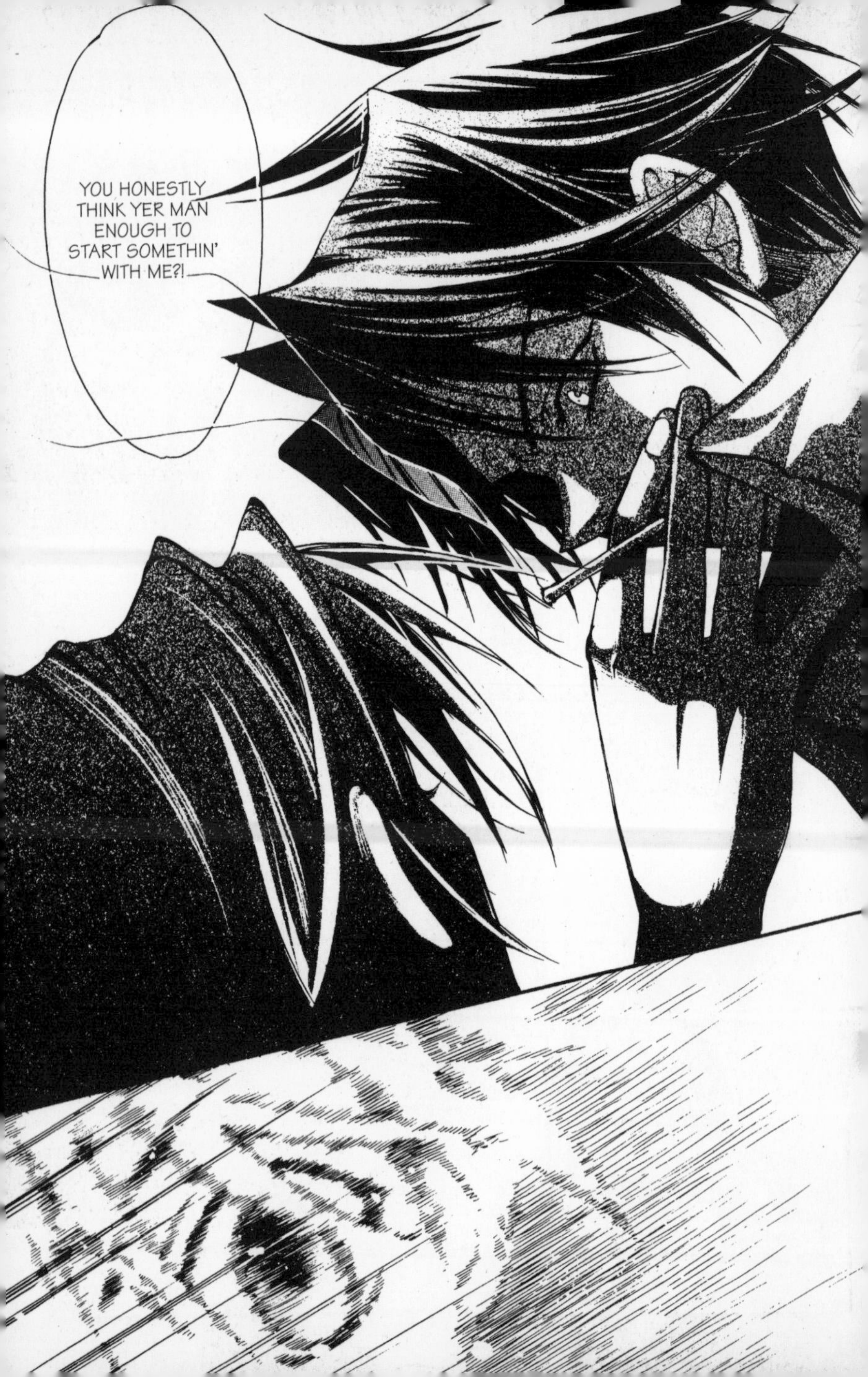
YOU HONESTLY THINK YER MAN ENOUGH TO START SOMETHIN' WITH ME?!

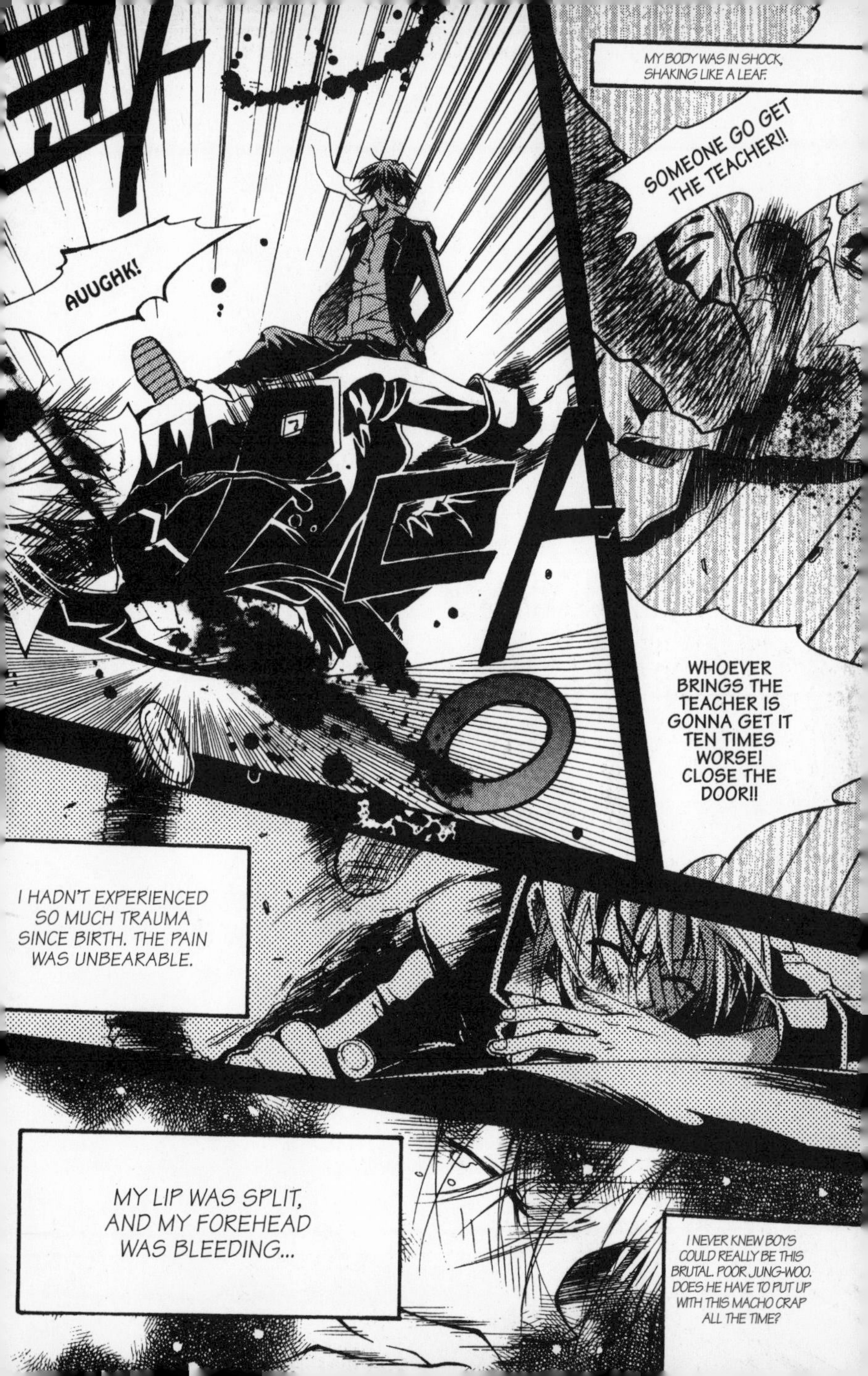
AUUGHK!
MY BODY WAS IN SHOCK, SHAKING LIKE A LEAF.
SOMEONE GO GET THE TEACHER!!
WHOEVER BRINGS THE TEACHER IS GONNA GET IT TEN TIMES WORSE! CLOSE THE DOOR!!
I HADN'T EXPERIENCED SO MUCH TRAUMA SINCE BIRTH. THE PAIN WAS UNBEARABLE.
MY LIP WAS SPLIT, AND MY FOREHEAD WAS BLEEDING...
I NEVER KNEW BOYS COULD REALLY BE THIS BRUTAL. POOR JUNG-WOO. DOES HE HAVE TO PUT UP WITH THIS MACHO CRAP ALL THE TIME?

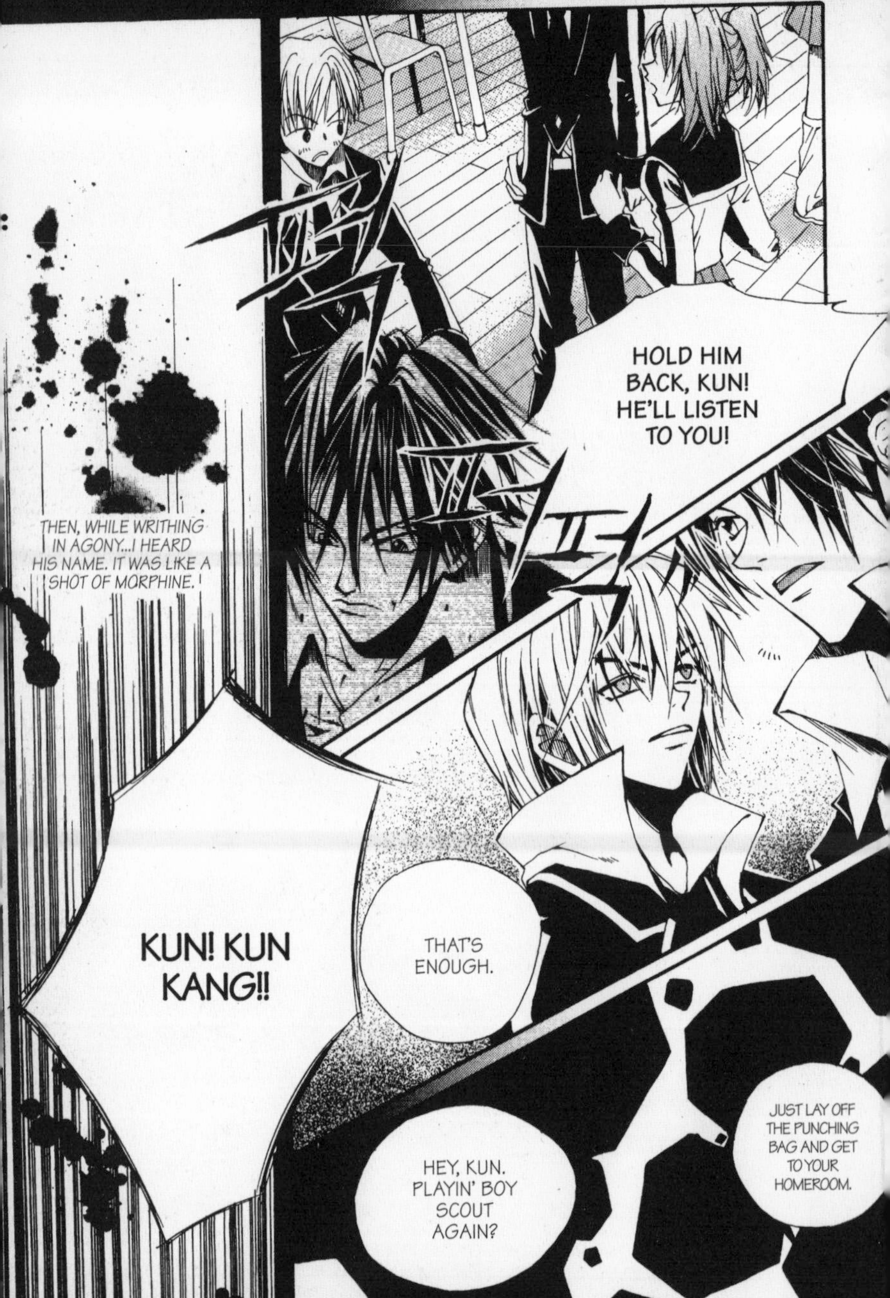
THEN, WHILE WRITHING IN AGONY...I HEARD HIS NAME. IT WAS LIKE A SHOT OF MORPHINE.
KUN! KUN KANG!!
HOLD HIM BACK, KUN! HE'LL LISTEN TO YOU!
THAT'S ENOUGH.
HEY, KUN. PLAYIN' BOY SCOUT AGAIN?
JUST LAY OFF THE PUNCHING BAG AND GET TO YOUR HOMEROOM.

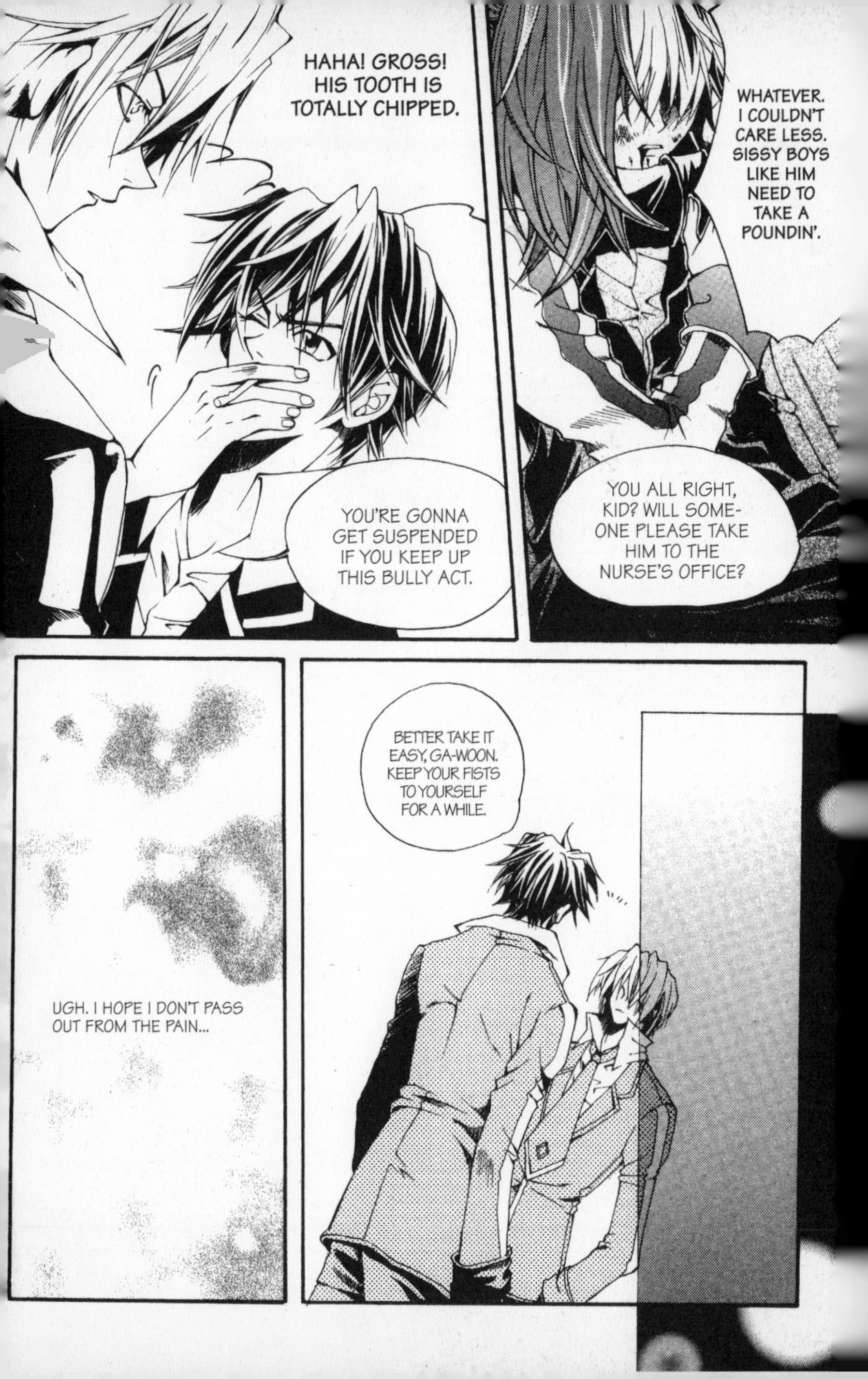
HAHA! GROSS! HIS TOOTH IS TOTALLY CHIPPED.
YOU'RE GONNA GET SUSPENDED IF YOU KEEP UP THIS BULLY ACT.
WHATEVER. I COULDN'T CARE LESS. SISSY BOYS LIKE HIM NEED TO TAKE A POUNDIN'.
YOU ALL RIGHT, KID? WILL SOME-ONE PLEASE TAKE HIM TO THE NURSE'S OFFICE?
UGH. I HOPE I DON'T PASS OUT FROM THE PAIN...
BETTER TAKE IT EASY, GA-WOON. KEEP YOUR FISTS TO YOURSELF FOR A WHILE.

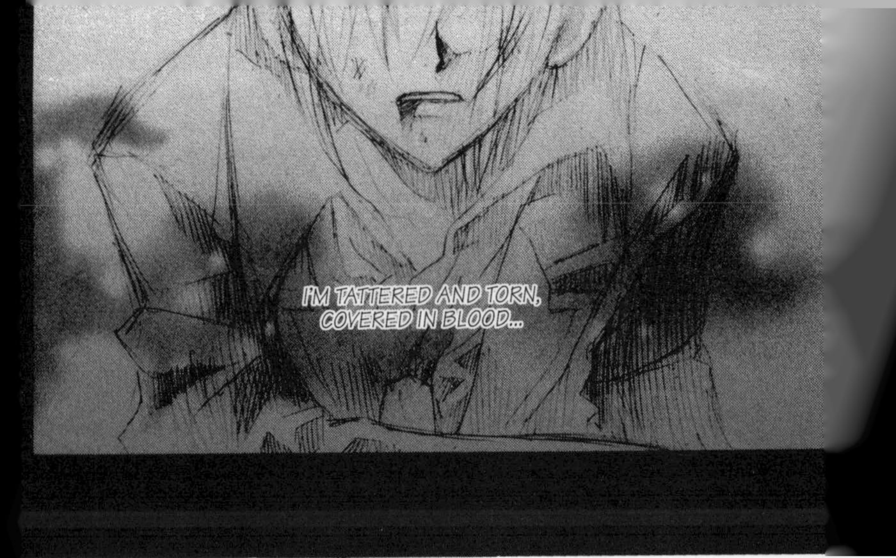
I'M TATTERED AND TORN,
COVERED IN BLOOD...

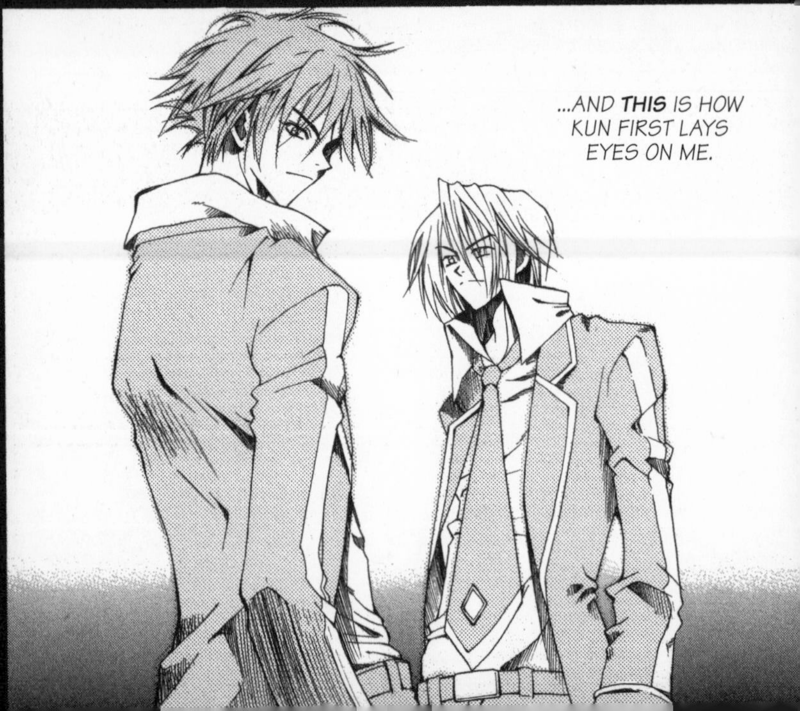
...AND THIS IS HOW KUN FIRST LAYS EYES ON ME.

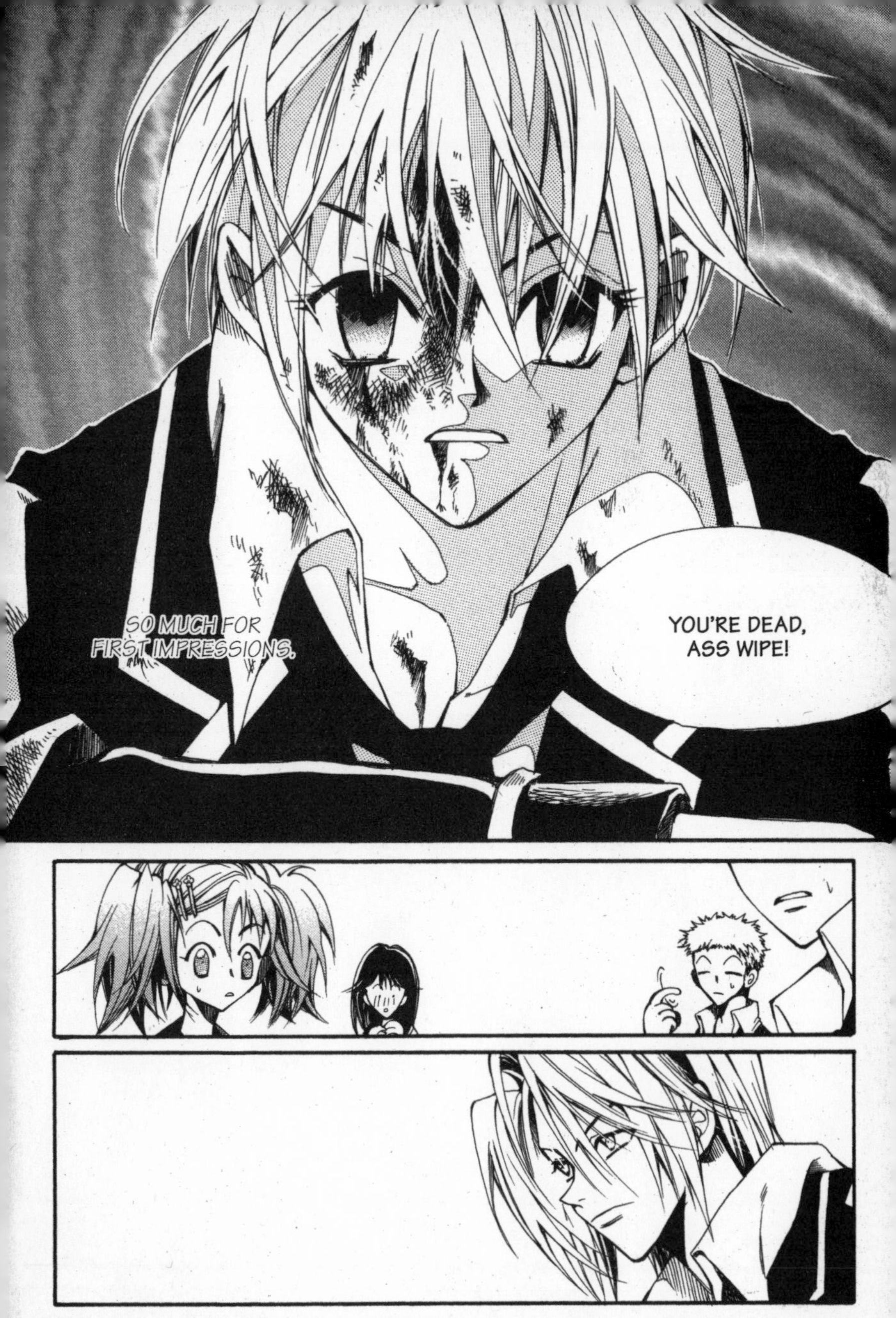
SO MUCH FOR FIRST IMPRESSIONS.
YOU'RE DEAD, ASS WIPE!

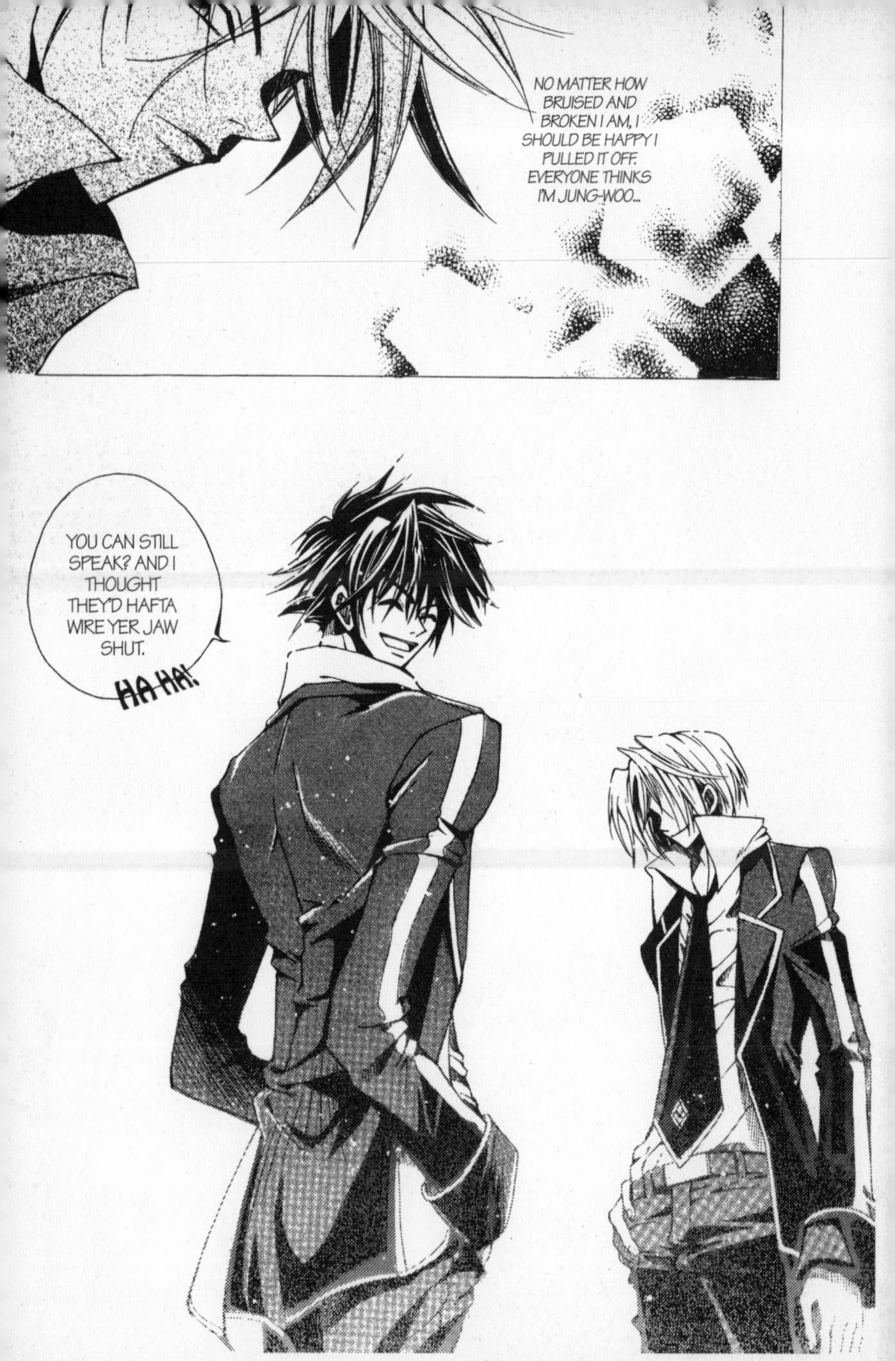
NO MATTER HOW BRUISED AND BROKEN I AM, I SHOULD BE HAPPY I PULLED IT OFF. EVERYONE THINKS I'M JUNG-WOO...
YOU CAN STILL SPEAK? AND I THOUGHT THEY'D HAFTA WIRE YER JAW SHUT.
HA HA!

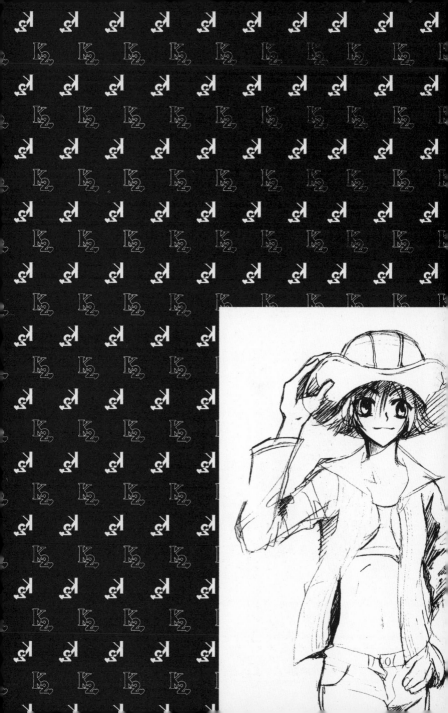

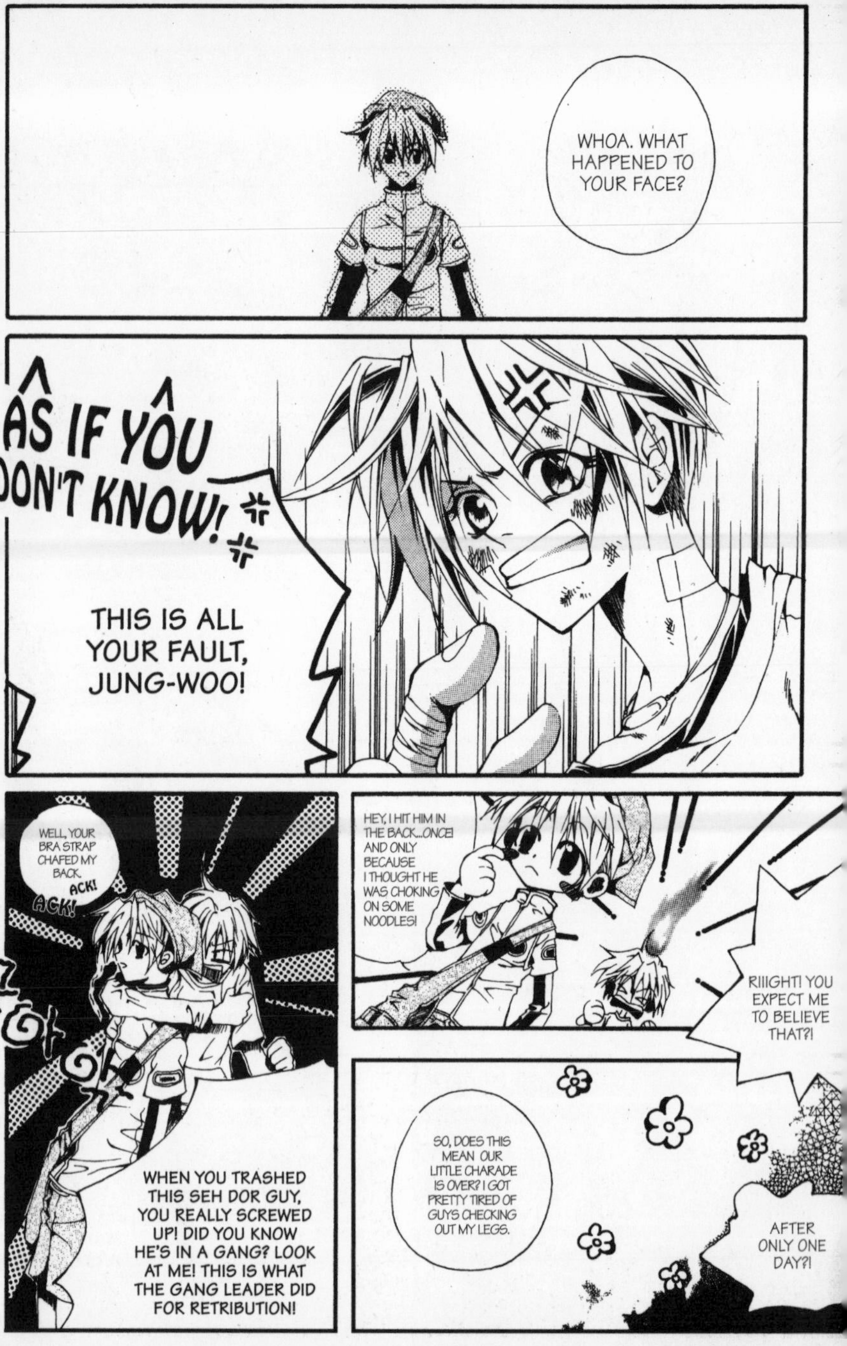
WHOA. WHAT HAPPENED TO YOUR FACE?
AS IF YOU DON'T KNOW!
THIS IS ALL YOUR FAULT, JUNG-WOO!
WELL, YOUR BRA STRAP CHAFED MY BACK.
ACK!
ACK!
WHEN YOU TRASHED THIS SEH DOR GUY, YOU REALLY SCREWED UP! DID YOU KNOW HE'S IN A GANG? LOOK AT ME! THIS IS WHAT THE GANG LEADER DID FOR RETRIBUTION!
HEY, I HIT HIM IN THE BACK...ONCE! AND ONLY BECAUSE I THOUGHT HE WAS CHOKING ON SOME NOODLES!
RIIIGHT! YOU EXPECT ME TO BELIEVE THAT?!
SO, DOES THIS MEAN OUR LITTLE CHARADE IS OVER? I GOT PRETTY TIRED OF GUYS CHECKING OUT MY LEGS.
AFTER ONLY ONE DAY?!

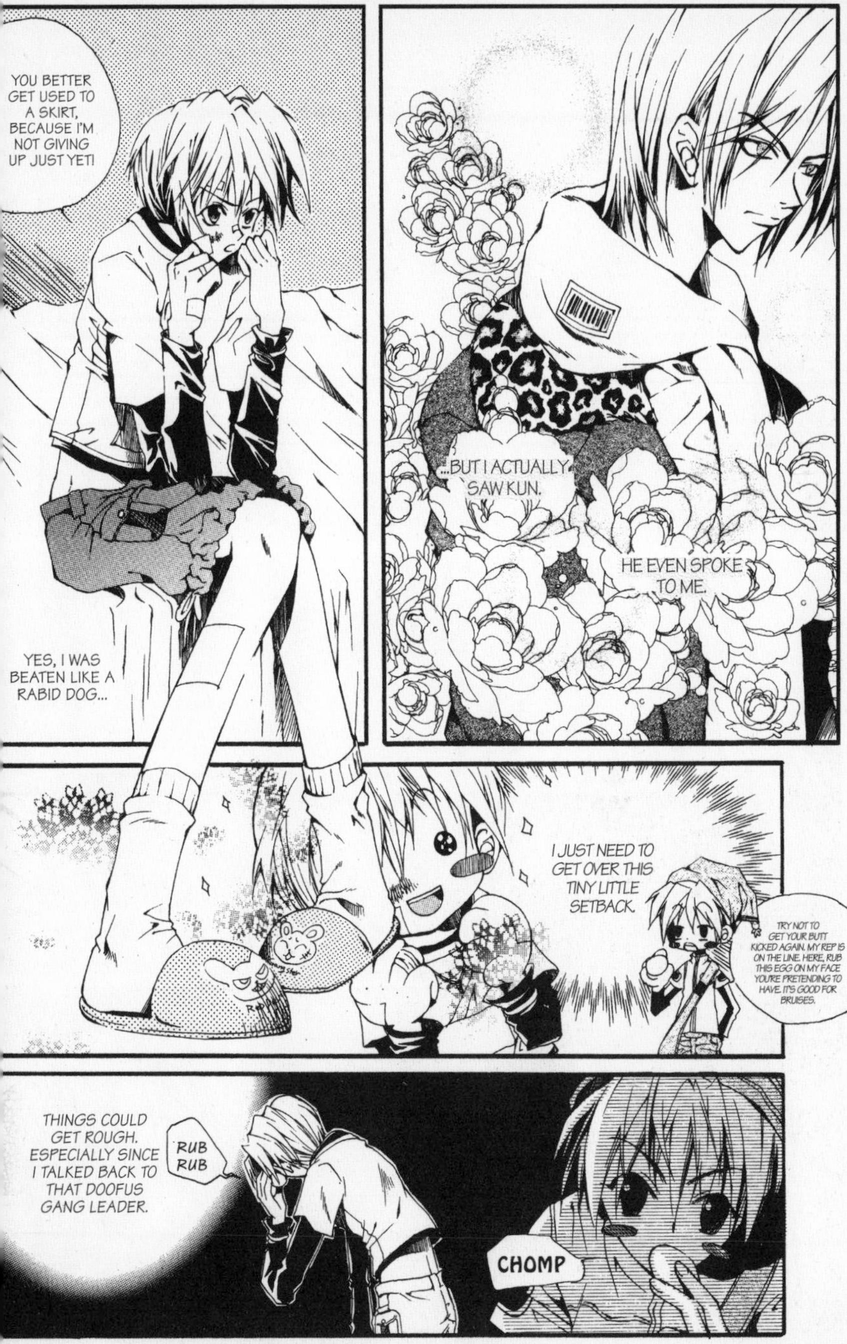
YOU BETTER GET USED TO A SKIRT, BECAUSE I'M NOT GIVING UP JUST YET!
YES, I WAS BEATEN LIKE A RABID DOG...
...BUT I ACTUALLY SAW KUN.
HE EVEN SPOKE TO ME.
I JUST NEED TO GET OVER THIS TINY LITTLE SETBACK.
TRY NOT TO GET YOUR BUTT KICKED AGAIN. MY REP IS ON THE LINE. HERE, RUB THIS EGG ON MY FACE YOU'RE PRETENDING TO HAVE. IT'S GOOD FOR BRUISES.
THINGS COULD GET ROUGH. ESPECIALLY SINCE I TALKED BACK TO THAT DOOFUS GANG LEADER.
RUB RUB
CHOMP

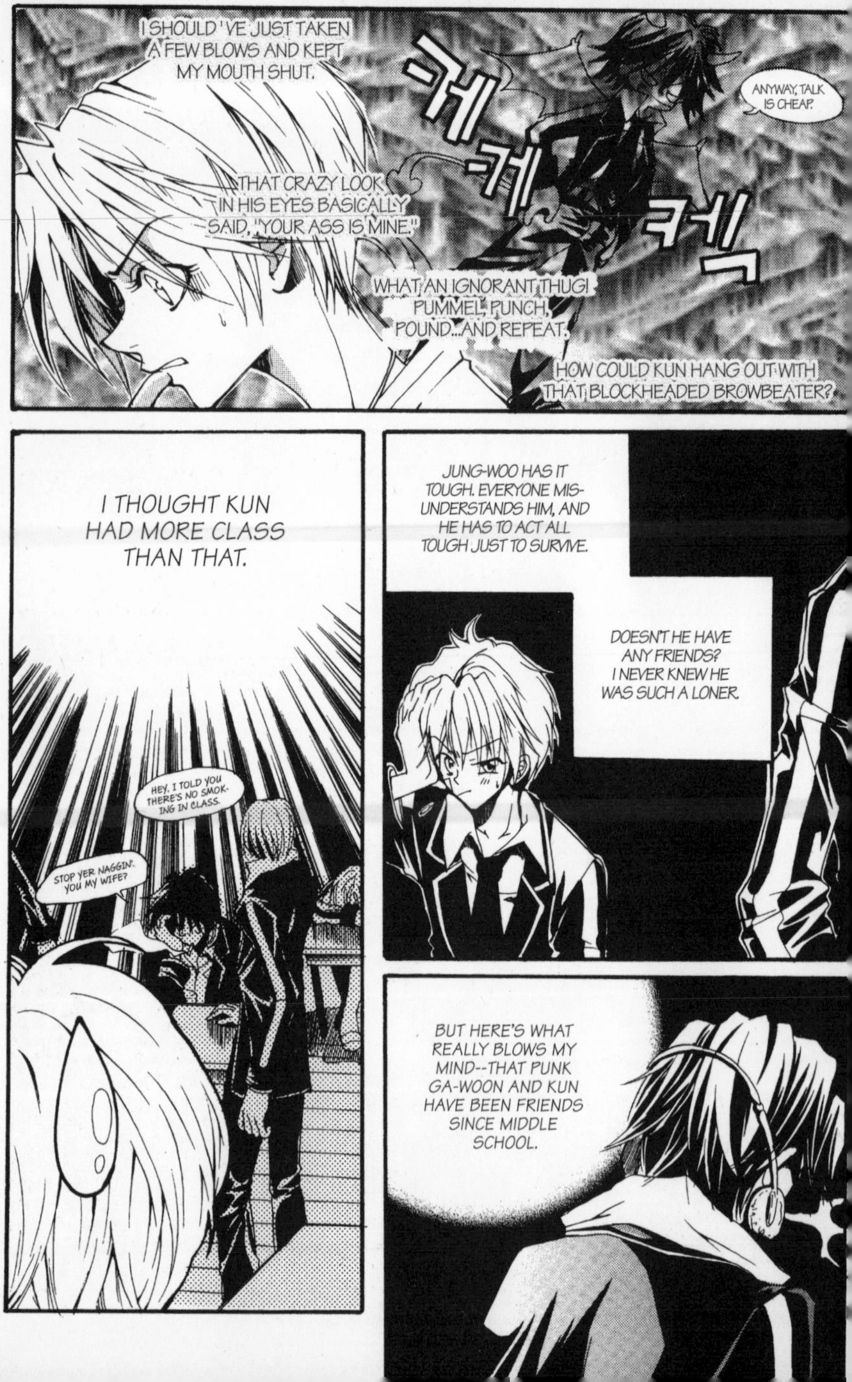
I SHOULD'VE JUST TAKEN A FEW BLOWS AND KEPT MY MOUTH SHUT.
ANYWAY, TALK IS CHEAP.
THAT CRAZY LOOK IN HIS EYES BASICALLY SAID, "YOUR ASS IS MINE."
WHAT AN IGNORANT THUG! PUMMEL, PUNCH, POUND...AND REPEAT.
HOW COULD KUN HANG OUT WITH THAT BLOCKHEADED BROWBEATER?
I THOUGHT KUN HAD MORE CLASS THAN THAT.
HEY, I TOLD YOU THERE'S NO SMOKING IN CLASS.
STOP YER NAGGIN'. YOU MY WIFE?
JUNG-WOO HAS IT TOUGH. EVERYONE MISUNDERSTANDS HIM, AND HE HAS TO ACT ALL TOUGH JUST TO SURVIVE.
DOESN'T HE HAVE ANY FRIENDS? I NEVER KNEW HE WAS SUCH A LONER.
BUT HERE'S WHAT REALLY BLOWS MY MIND--THAT PUNK GA-WOON AND KUN HAVE BEEN FRIENDS SINCE MIDDLE SCHOOL.

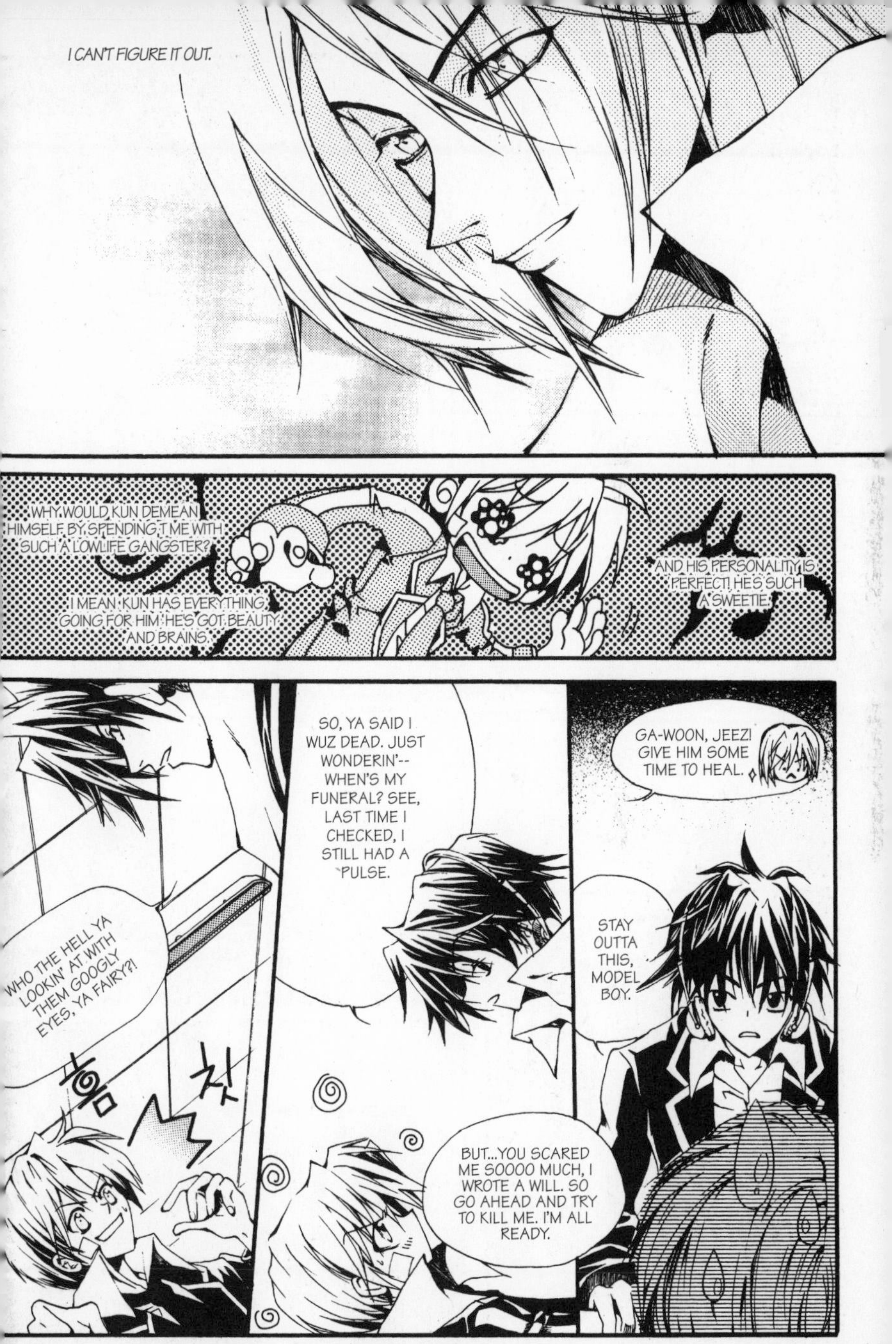
I CAN'T FIGURE IT OUT.
WHY WOULD KUN DEMEAN HIMSELF BY SPENDING TIME WITH SUCH A LOWLIFE GANGSTER?
I MEAN, KUN HAS EVERYTHING GOING FOR HIM. HE'S GOT BEAUTY AND BRAINS.
AND HIS PERSONALITY IS PERFECT! HE'S SUCH A SWEETIE!
WHO THE HELL YA LOOKIN' AT WITH THEM GOOGLY EYES, YA FAIRY?!
SO, YA SAID I WUZ DEAD. JUST WONDERIN'-- WHEN'S MY FUNERAL? SEE, LAST TIME I CHECKED, I STILL HAD A PULSE.
BUT...YOU SCARED ME SOOOO MUCH, I WROTE A WILL. SO GO AHEAD AND TRY TO KILL ME. I'M ALL READY.
GA-WOON, JEEZ! GIVE HIM SOME TIME TO HEAL.
STAY OUTTA THIS, MODEL BOY.

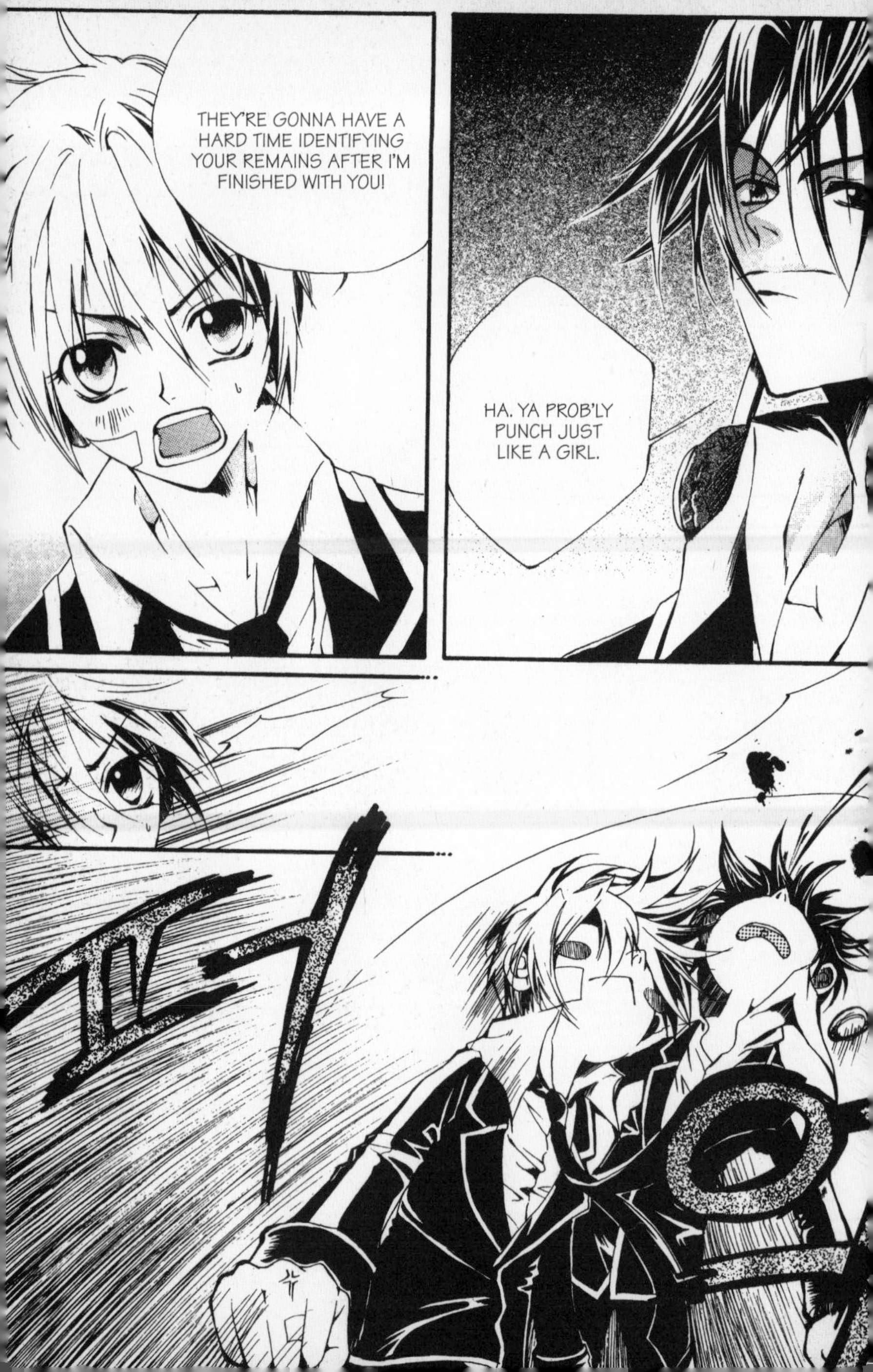
THEY'RE GONNA HAVE A HARD TIME IDENTIFYING YOUR REMAINS AFTER I'M FINISHED WITH YOU!
HA. YA PROB'LY PUNCH JUST LIKE A GIRL.

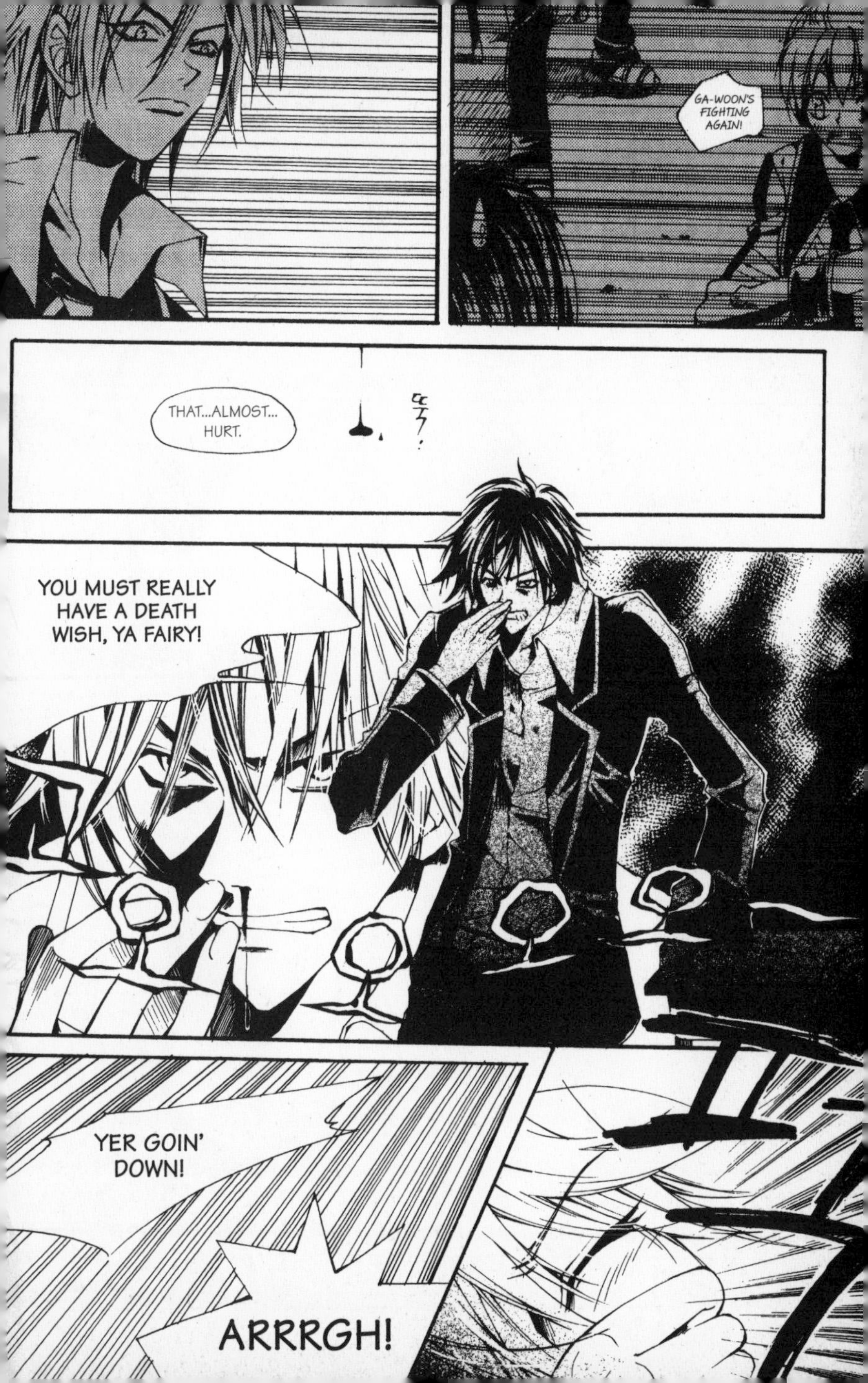
GA-WOON'S FIGHTING AGAIN!
THAT...ALMOST... HURT.
YOU MUST REALLY HAVE A DEATH WISH, YA FAIRY!
YER GOIN' DOWN!
ARRRGH!

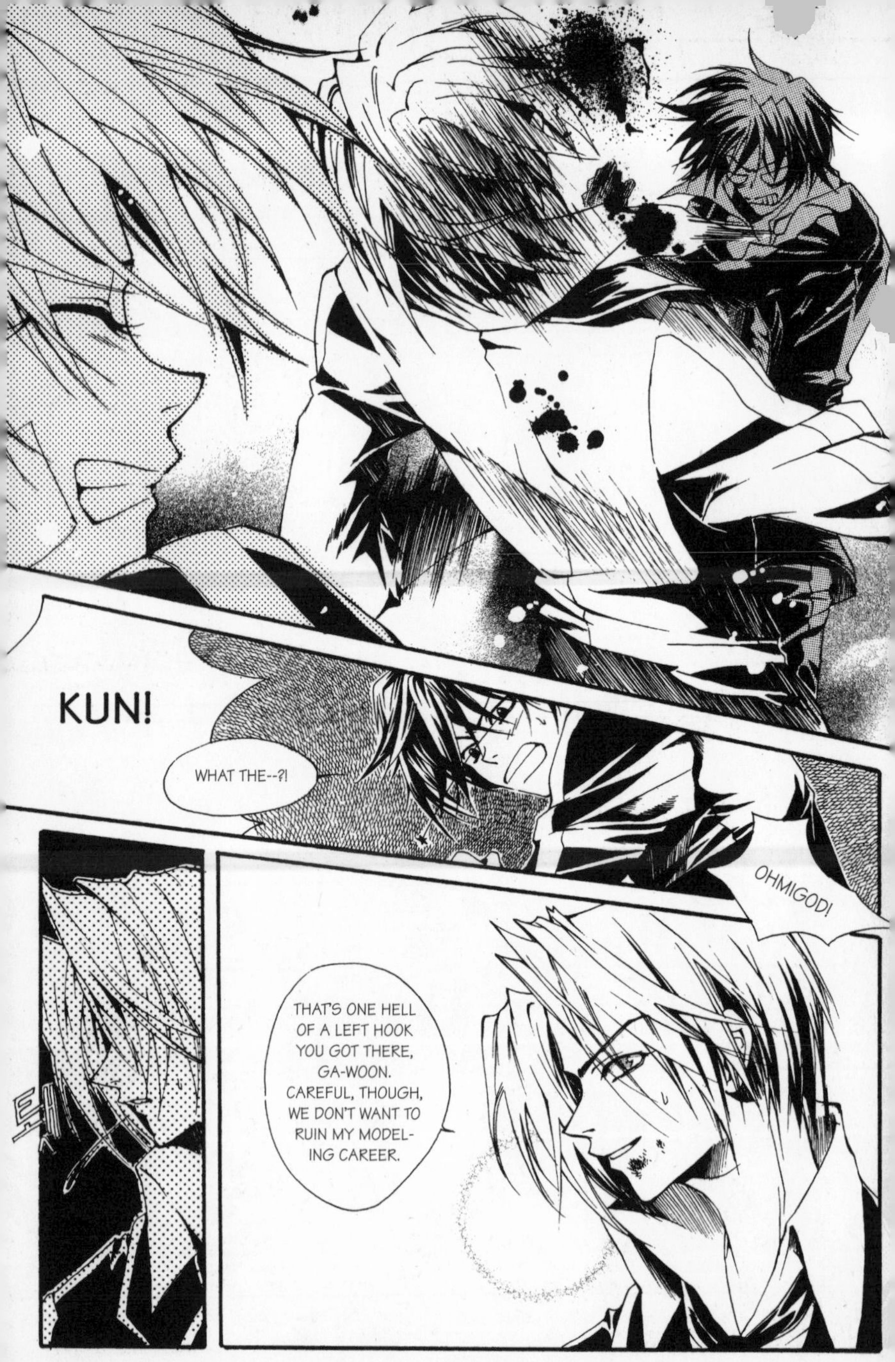
KUN!
WHAT THE--?!
OHMIGOD!
THAT'S ONE HELL OF A LEFT HOOK YOU GOT THERE, GA-WOON. CAREFUL, THOUGH, WE DON'T WANT TO RUIN MY MODEL-ING CAREER.

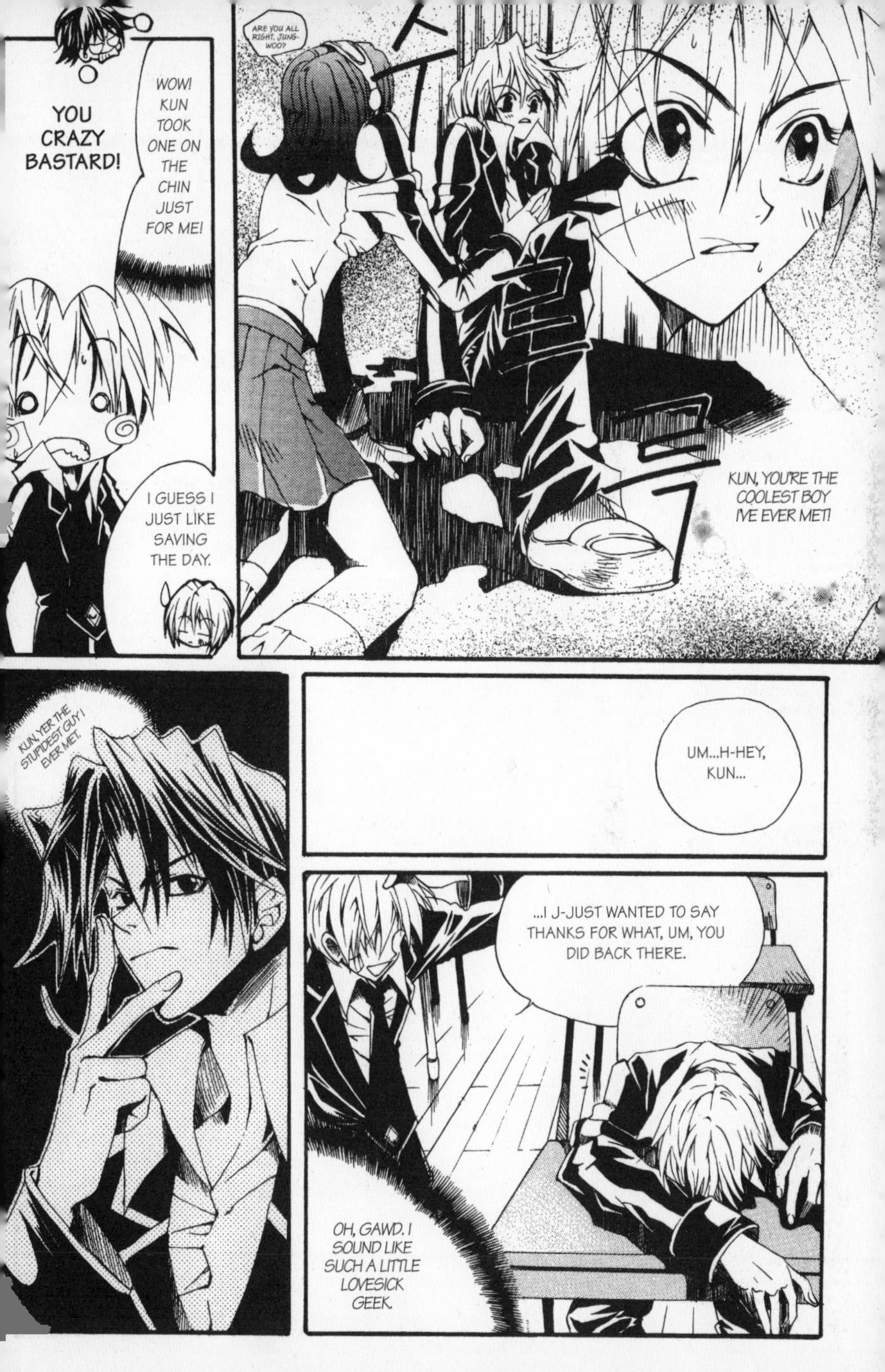
YOU CRAZY BASTARD!
WOW! KUN TOOK ONE ON THE CHIN JUST FOR ME!
I GUESS I JUST LIKE SAVING THE DAY.
ARE YOU ALL RIGHT, JUNG-WOO?
KUN, YOU'RE THE COOLEST BOY I'VE EVER MET!
KUN, YER THE STUPIDEST GUY I EVER MET.
UM...H-HEY, KUN...
...I J-JUST WANTED TO SAY THANKS FOR WHAT, UM, YOU DID BACK THERE.
OH, GAWD. I SOUND LIKE SUCH A LITTLE LOVESICK GEEK.

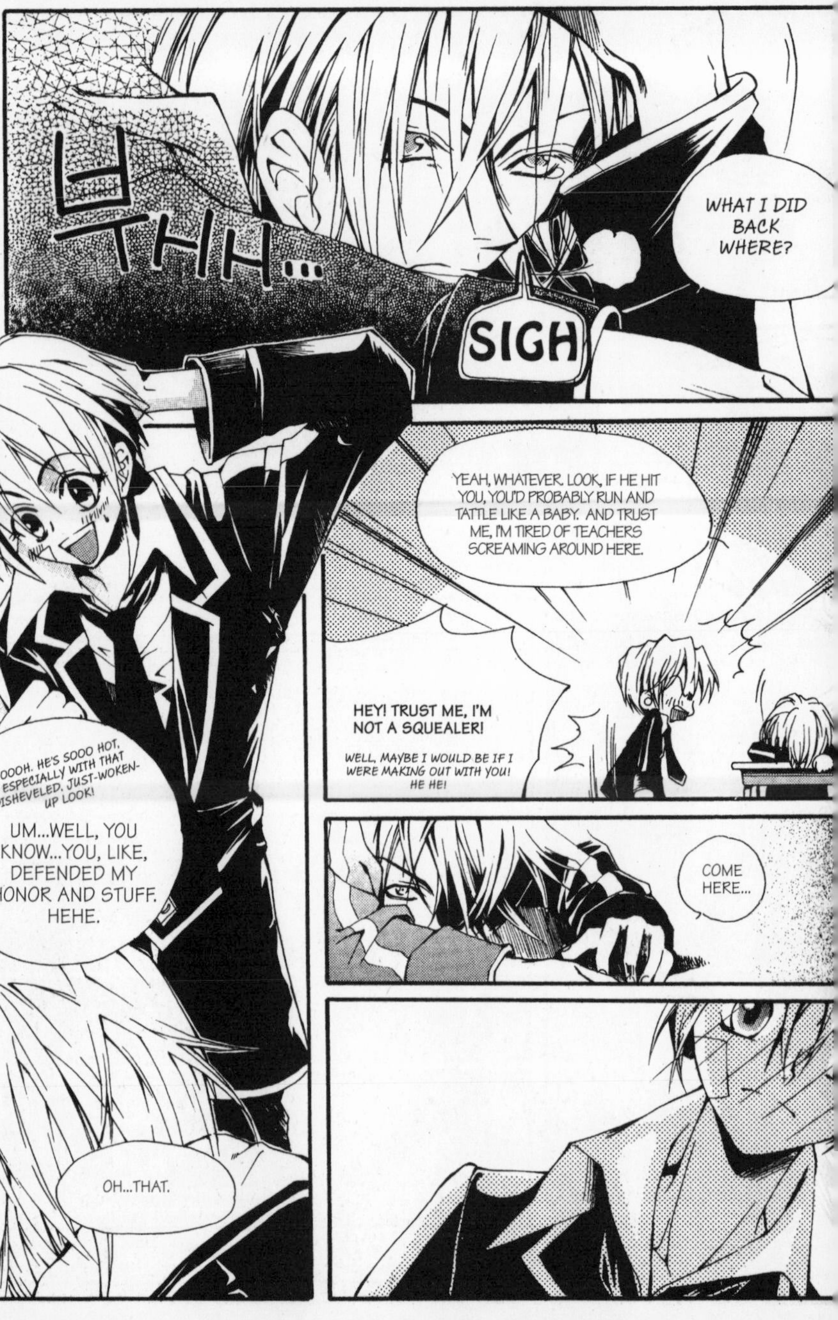
FTHH...
SIGH
WHAT I DID BACK WHERE?
OOOH. HE'S SOOO HOT, ESPECIALLY WITH THAT DISHEVELED, JUST-WOKEN-UP LOOK!
UM...WELL, YOU KNOW...YOU, LIKE, DEFENDED MY HONOR AND STUFF. HEHE.
OH...THAT.
YEAH, WHATEVER. LOOK, IF HE HIT YOU, YOU'D PROBABLY RUN AND TATTLE LIKE A BABY. AND TRUST ME, I'M TIRED OF TEACHERS SCREAMING AROUND HERE.
HEY! TRUST ME, I'M NOT A SQUEALER!
WELL, MAYBE I WOULD BE IF I WERE MAKING OUT WITH YOU! HE HE!
COME HERE...

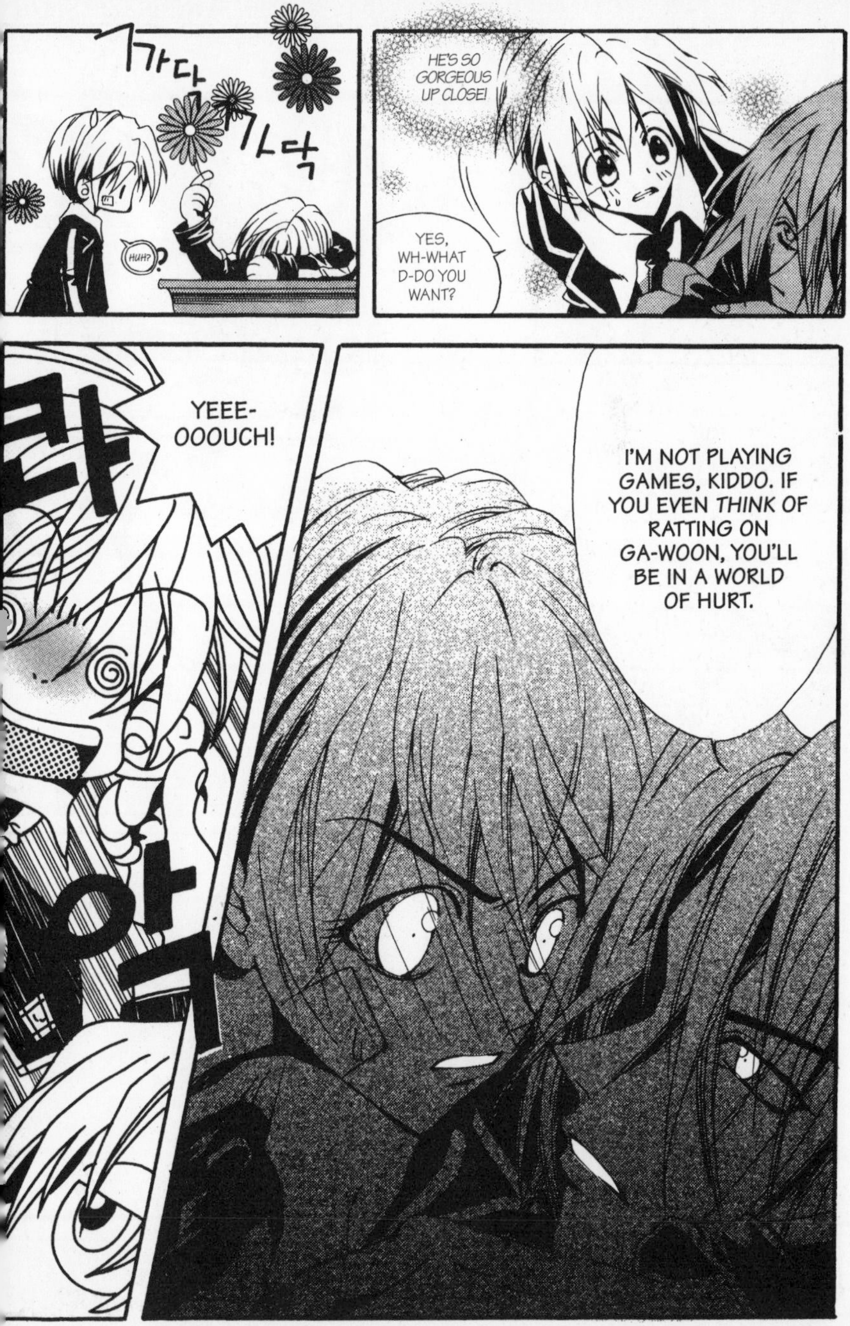
HUH?
HE'S SO GORGEOUS UP CLOSE!
YES, WH-WHAT D-DO YOU WANT?
YEEE-OOOUCH!
I'M NOT PLAYING GAMES, KIDDO. IF YOU EVEN *THINK* OF RATTING ON GA-WOON, YOU'LL BE IN A WORLD OF HURT.

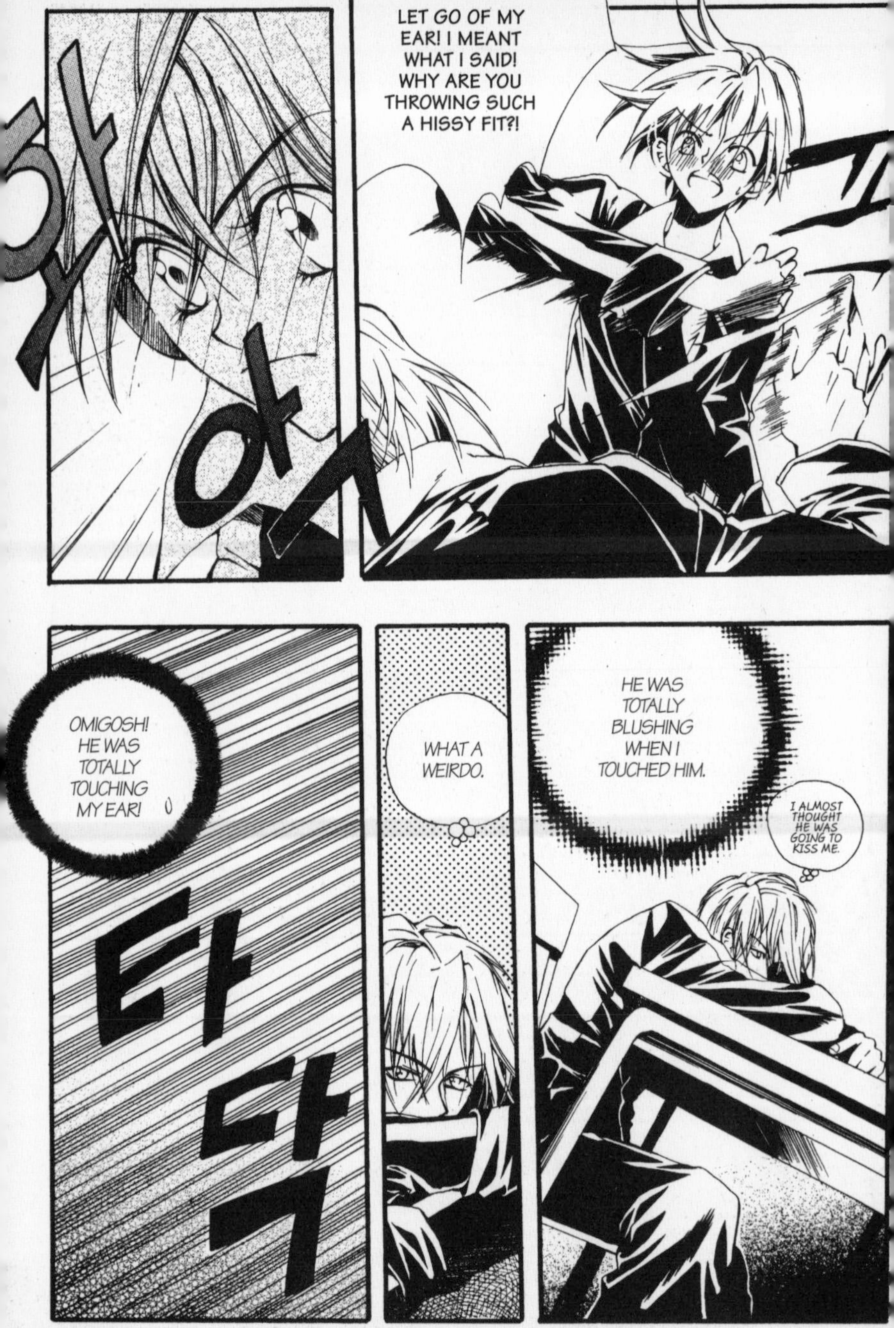
LET GO OF MY EAR! I MEANT WHAT I SAID! WHY ARE YOU THROWING SUCH A HISSY FIT?!
OMIGOSH! HE WAS TOTALLY TOUCHING MY EAR!
타닥
WHAT A WEIRDO.
HE WAS TOTALLY BLUSHING WHEN I TOUCHED HIM.
I ALMOST THOUGHT HE WAS GOING TO KISS ME.

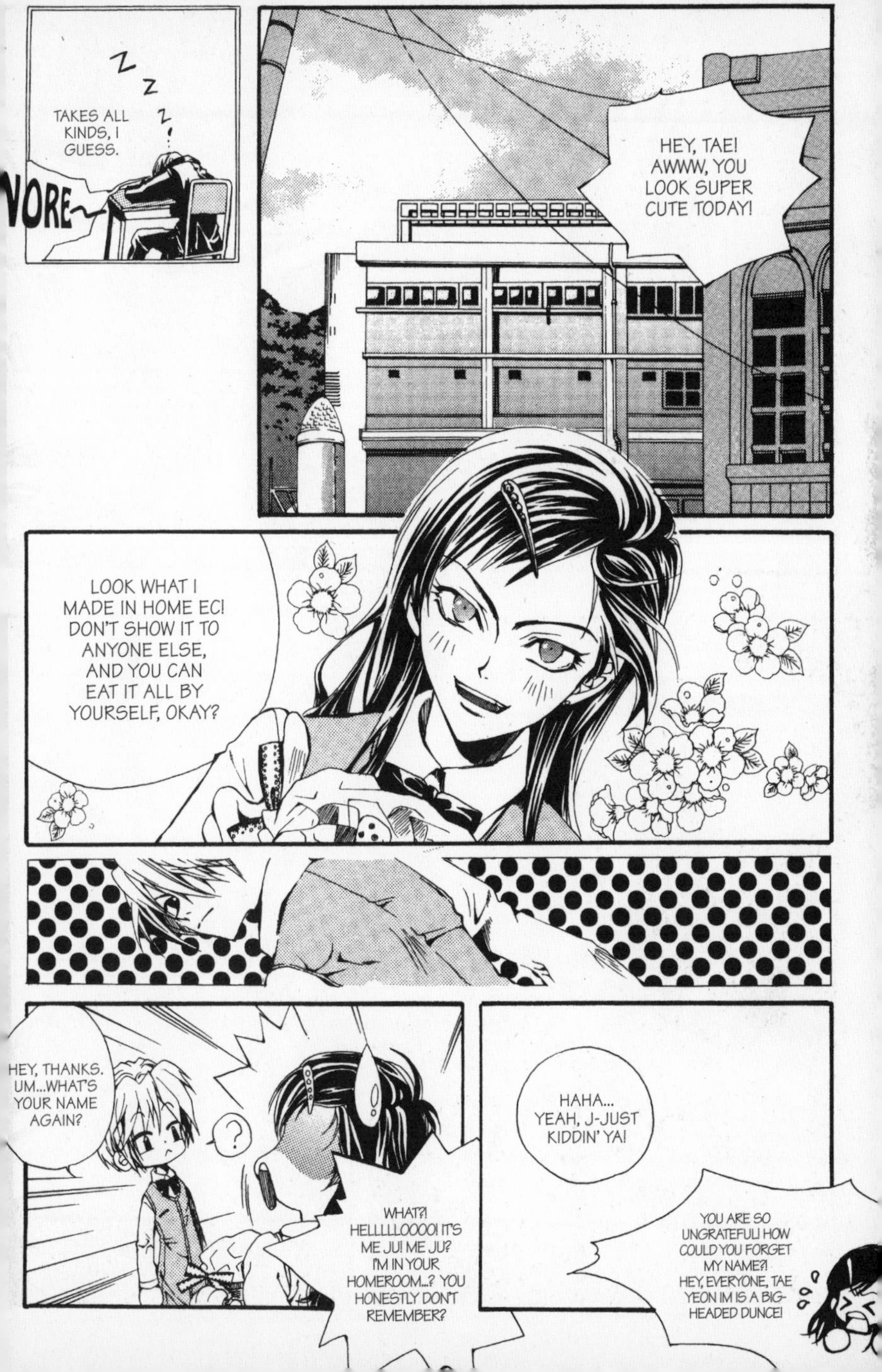
Z
Z
Z
TAKES ALL KINDS, I GUESS.
SNORE~
HEY, TAE! AWWW, YOU LOOK SUPER CUTE TODAY!
LOOK WHAT I MADE IN HOME EC! DON'T SHOW IT TO ANYONE ELSE, AND YOU CAN EAT IT ALL BY YOURSELF, OKAY?
HEY, THANKS. UM...WHAT'S YOUR NAME AGAIN?
?
WHAT?! HELLLLLOOOO! IT'S ME JU! ME JU? I'M IN YOUR HOMEROOM...? YOU HONESTLY DON'T REMEMBER?
HAHA... YEAH, J-JUST KIDDIN' YA!
YOU ARE SO UNGRATEFUL! HOW COULD YOU FORGET MY NAME?! HEY, EVERYONE, TAE YEON IM IS A BIG-HEADED DUNCE!

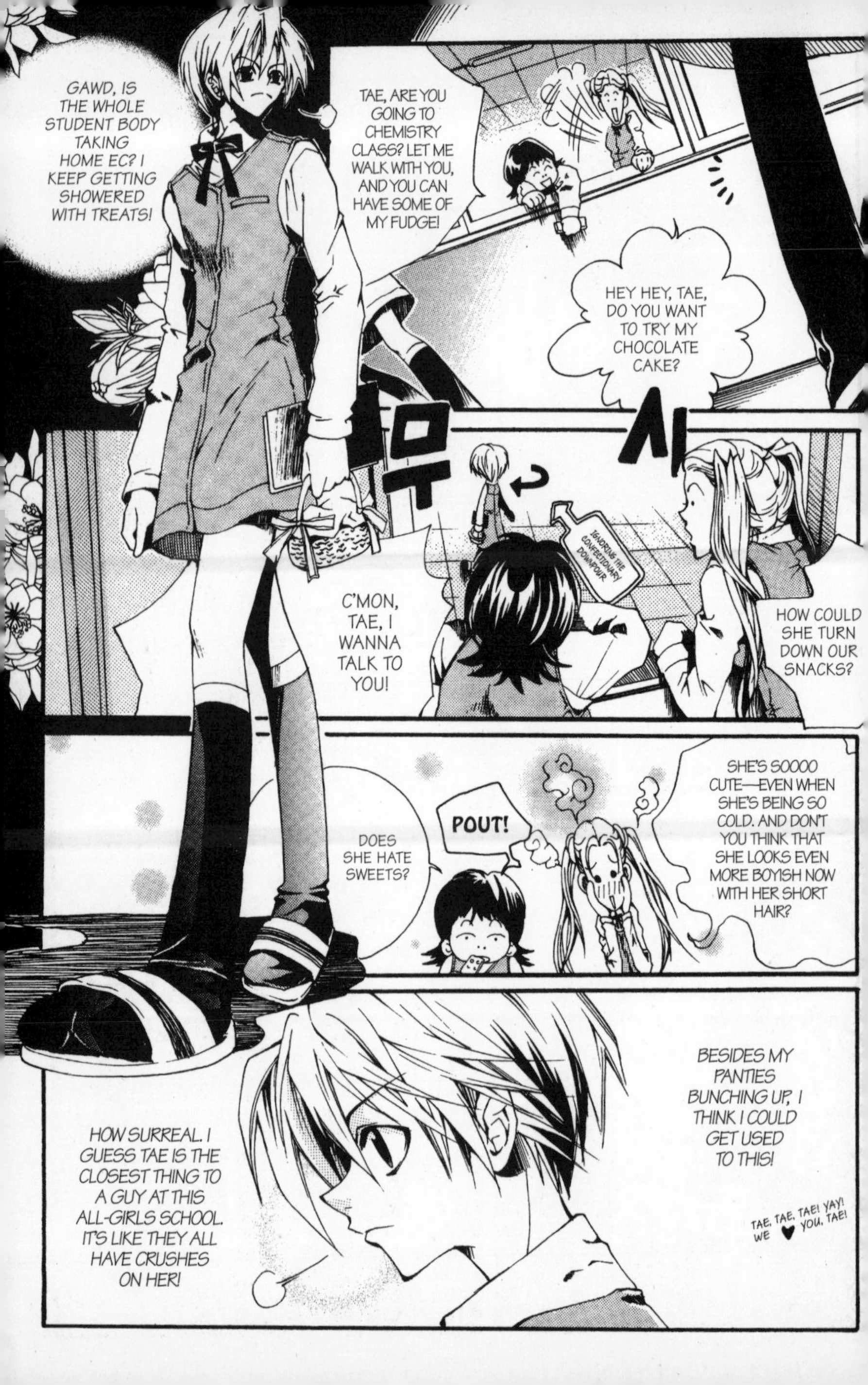
GAWD, IS THE WHOLE STUDENT BODY TAKING HOME EC? I KEEP GETTING SHOWERED WITH TREATS!
TAE, ARE YOU GOING TO CHEMISTRY CLASS? LET ME WALK WITH YOU, AND YOU CAN HAVE SOME OF MY FUDGE!
HEY HEY, TAE, DO YOU WANT TO TRY MY CHOCOLATE CAKE?
C'MON, TAE, I WANNA TALK TO YOU!
IGNORING THE CONFECTIONARY DOWNPOUR
HOW COULD SHE TURN DOWN OUR SNACKS?
DOES SHE HATE SWEETS?
POUT!
SHE'S SOOOO CUTE—EVEN WHEN SHE'S BEING SO COLD. AND DON'T YOU THINK THAT SHE LOOKS EVEN MORE BOYISH NOW WITH HER SHORT HAIR?
HOW SURREAL. I GUESS TAE IS THE CLOSEST THING TO A GUY AT THIS ALL-GIRLS SCHOOL. IT'S LIKE THEY ALL HAVE CRUSHES ON HER!
BESIDES MY PANTIES BUNCHING UP, I THINK I COULD GET USED TO THIS!
TAE, TAE, TAE! YAY! WE ♥ YOU, TAE!

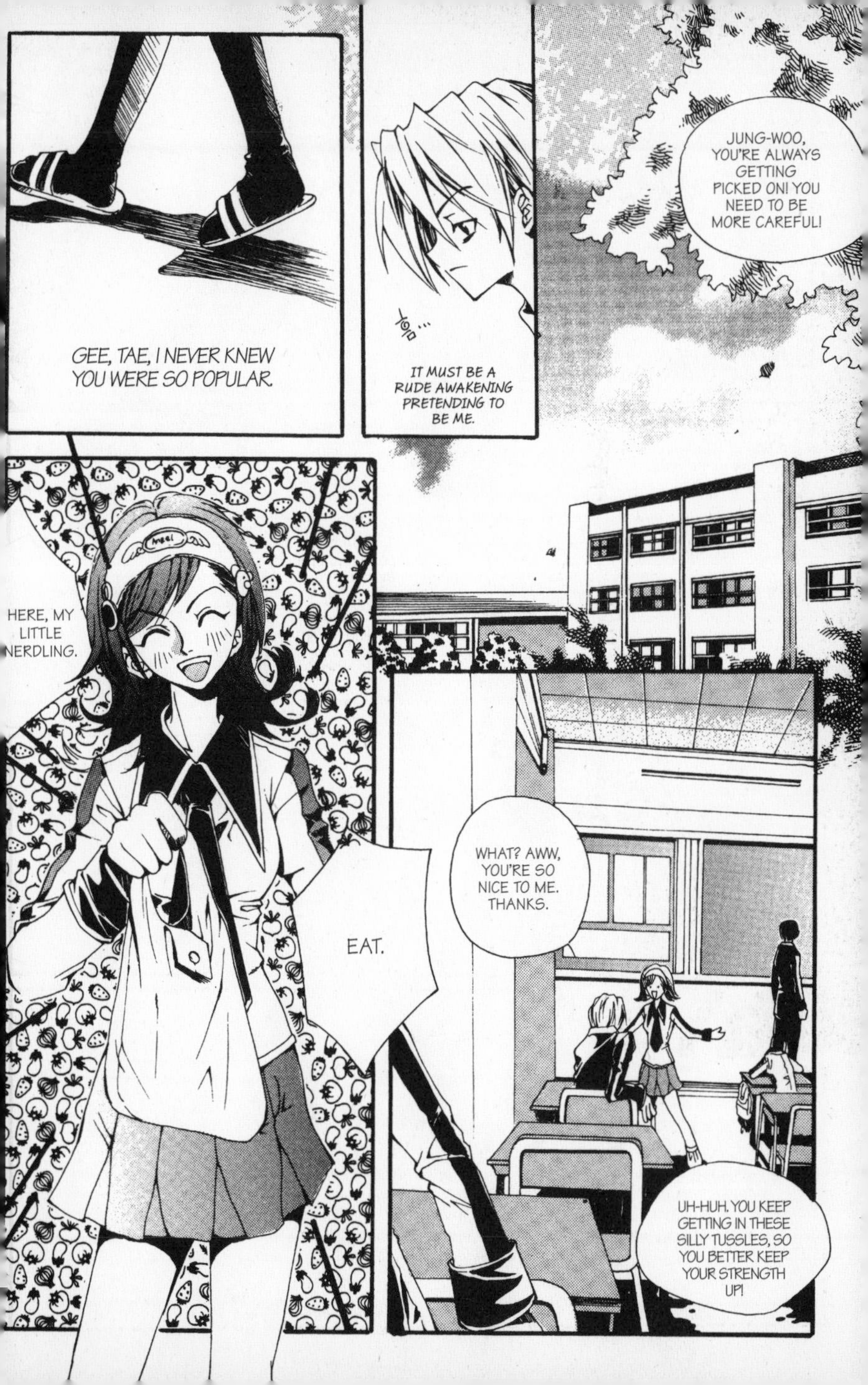
GEE, TAE, I NEVER KNEW YOU WERE SO POPULAR.
IT MUST BE A RUDE AWAKENING PRETENDING TO BE ME.
JUNG-WOO, YOU'RE ALWAYS GETTING PICKED ON! YOU NEED TO BE MORE CAREFUL!
HERE, MY LITTLE NERDLING.
EAT.
WHAT? AWW, YOU'RE SO NICE TO ME. THANKS.
UH-HUH. YOU KEEP GETTING IN THESE SILLY TUSSLES, SO YOU BETTER KEEP YOUR STRENGTH UP!

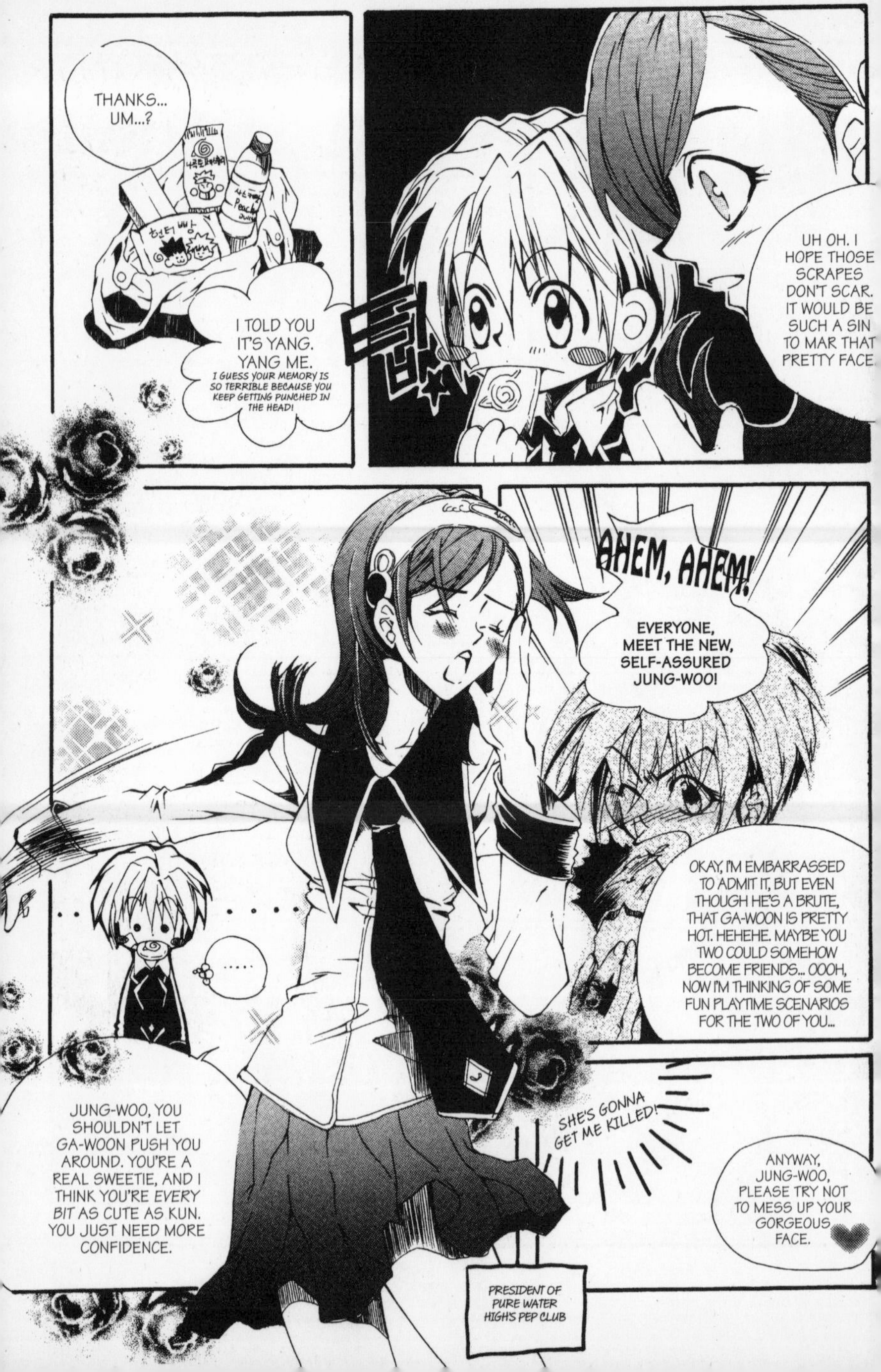

THANKS... UM...?
I TOLD YOU IT'S YANG. YANG ME.
I GUESS YOUR MEMORY IS SO TERRIBLE BECAUSE YOU KEEP GETTING PUNCHED IN THE HEAD!
UH OH. I HOPE THOSE SCRAPES DON'T SCAR. IT WOULD BE SUCH A SIN TO MAR THAT PRETTY FACE.
AHEM, AHEM!
EVERYONE, MEET THE NEW, SELF-ASSURED JUNG-WOO!
OKAY, I'M EMBARRASSED TO ADMIT IT, BUT EVEN THOUGH HE'S A BRUTE, THAT GA-WOON IS PRETTY HOT. HEHEHE. MAYBE YOU TWO COULD SOMEHOW BECOME FRIENDS... OOOH, NOW I'M THINKING OF SOME FUN PLAYTIME SCENARIOS FOR THE TWO OF YOU...
. . . .
......
JUNG-WOO, YOU SHOULDN'T LET GA-WOON PUSH YOU AROUND. YOU'RE A REAL SWEETIE, AND I THINK YOU'RE *EVERY BIT* AS CUTE AS KUN. YOU JUST NEED MORE CONFIDENCE.
SHE'S GONNA GET ME KILLED!
ANYWAY, JUNG-WOO, PLEASE TRY NOT TO MESS UP YOUR GORGEOUS FACE.
PRESIDENT OF PURE WATER HIGH'S PEP CLUB

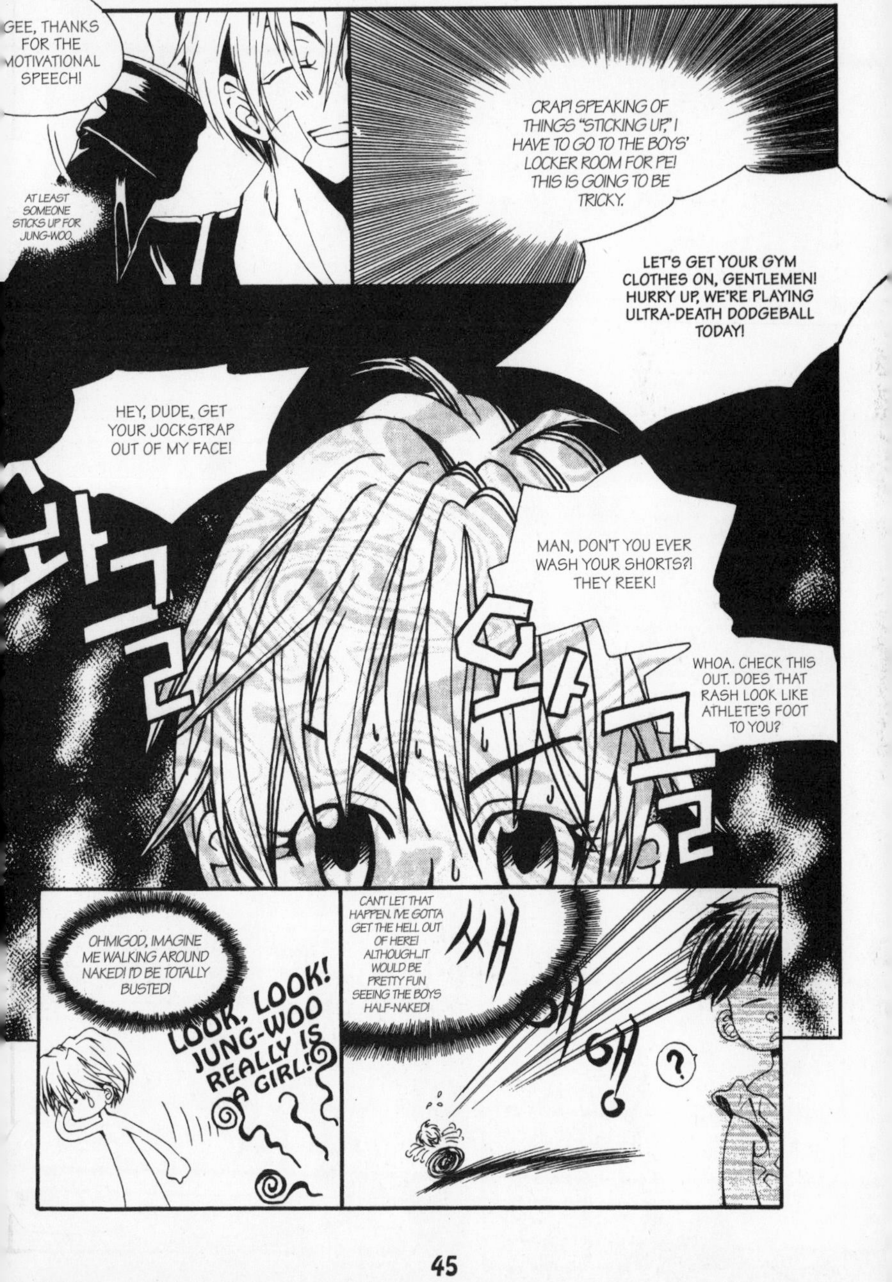
GEE, THANKS FOR THE MOTIVATIONAL SPEECH!
AT LEAST SOMEONE STICKS UP FOR JUNG-WOO.
CRAP! SPEAKING OF THINGS "STICKING UP," I HAVE TO GO TO THE BOYS' LOCKER ROOM FOR PE! THIS IS GOING TO BE TRICKY.
LET'S GET YOUR GYM CLOTHES ON, GENTLEMEN! HURRY UP, WE'RE PLAYING ULTRA-DEATH DODGEBALL TODAY!
HEY, DUDE, GET YOUR JOCKSTRAP OUT OF MY FACE!
와그르
MAN, DON'T YOU EVER WASH YOUR SHORTS?! THEY REEK!
와그르
WHOA. CHECK THIS OUT. DOES THAT RASH LOOK LIKE ATHLETE'S FOOT TO YOU?
OHMIGOD, IMAGINE ME WALKING AROUND NAKED! I'D BE TOTALLY BUSTED!
LOOK, LOOK! JUNG-WOO REALLY IS A GIRL!
CAN'T LET THAT HAPPEN. I'VE GOTTA GET THE HELL OUT OF HERE! ALTHOUGH...IT WOULD BE PRETTY FUN SEEING THE BOYS HALF-NAKED!
?

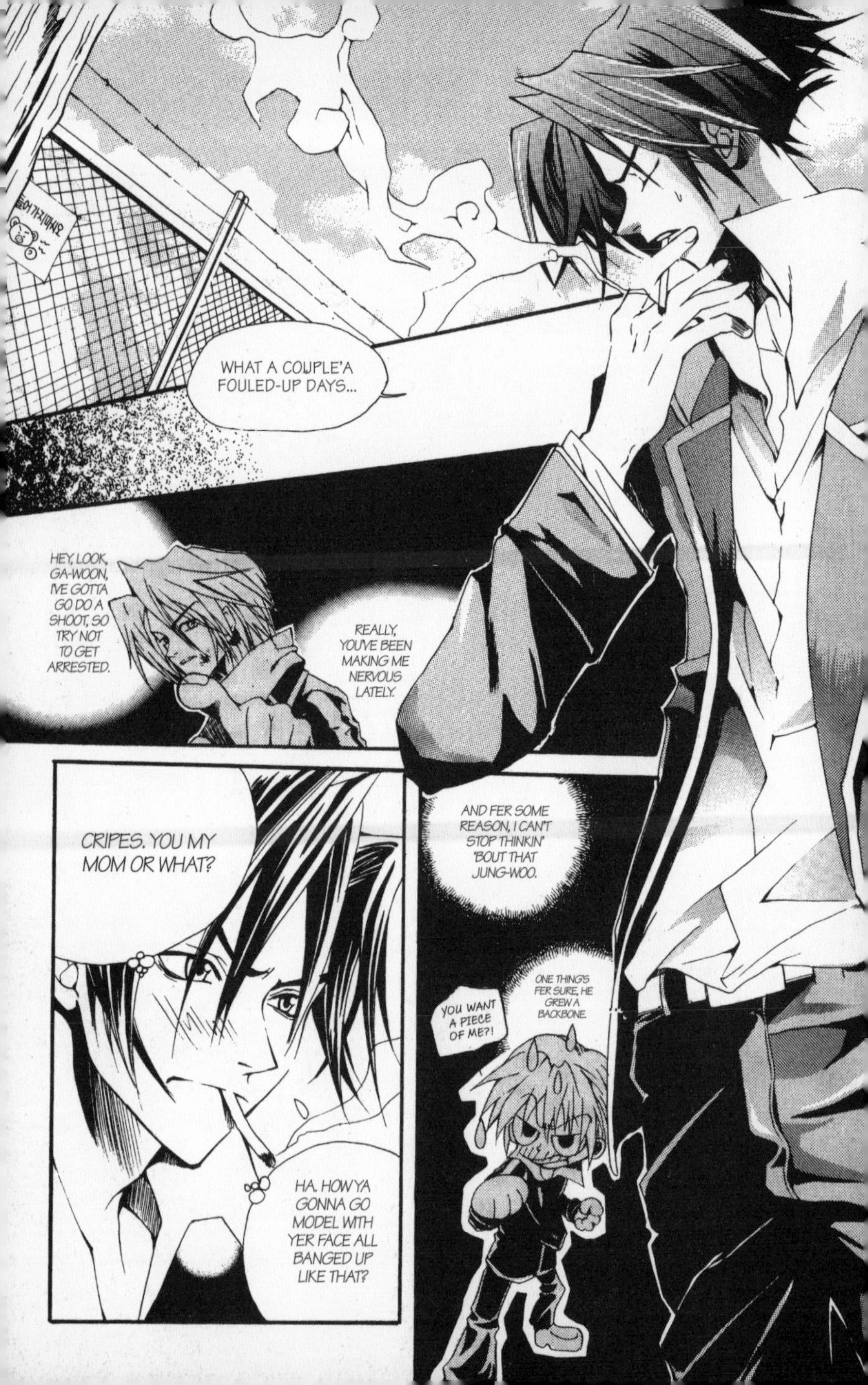
WHAT A COUPLE'A FOULED-UP DAYS...
HEY, LOOK, GA-WOON, I'VE GOTTA GO DO A SHOOT, SO TRY NOT TO GET ARRESTED.
REALLY, YOU'VE BEEN MAKING ME NERVOUS LATELY.
CRIPES. YOU MY MOM OR WHAT?
HA. HOW YA GONNA GO MODEL WITH YER FACE ALL BANGED UP LIKE THAT?
AND FER SOME REASON, I CAN'T STOP THINKIN' 'BOUT THAT JUNG-WOO.
ONE THING'S FER SURE, HE GREW A BACKBONE.
YOU WANT A PIECE OF ME?!

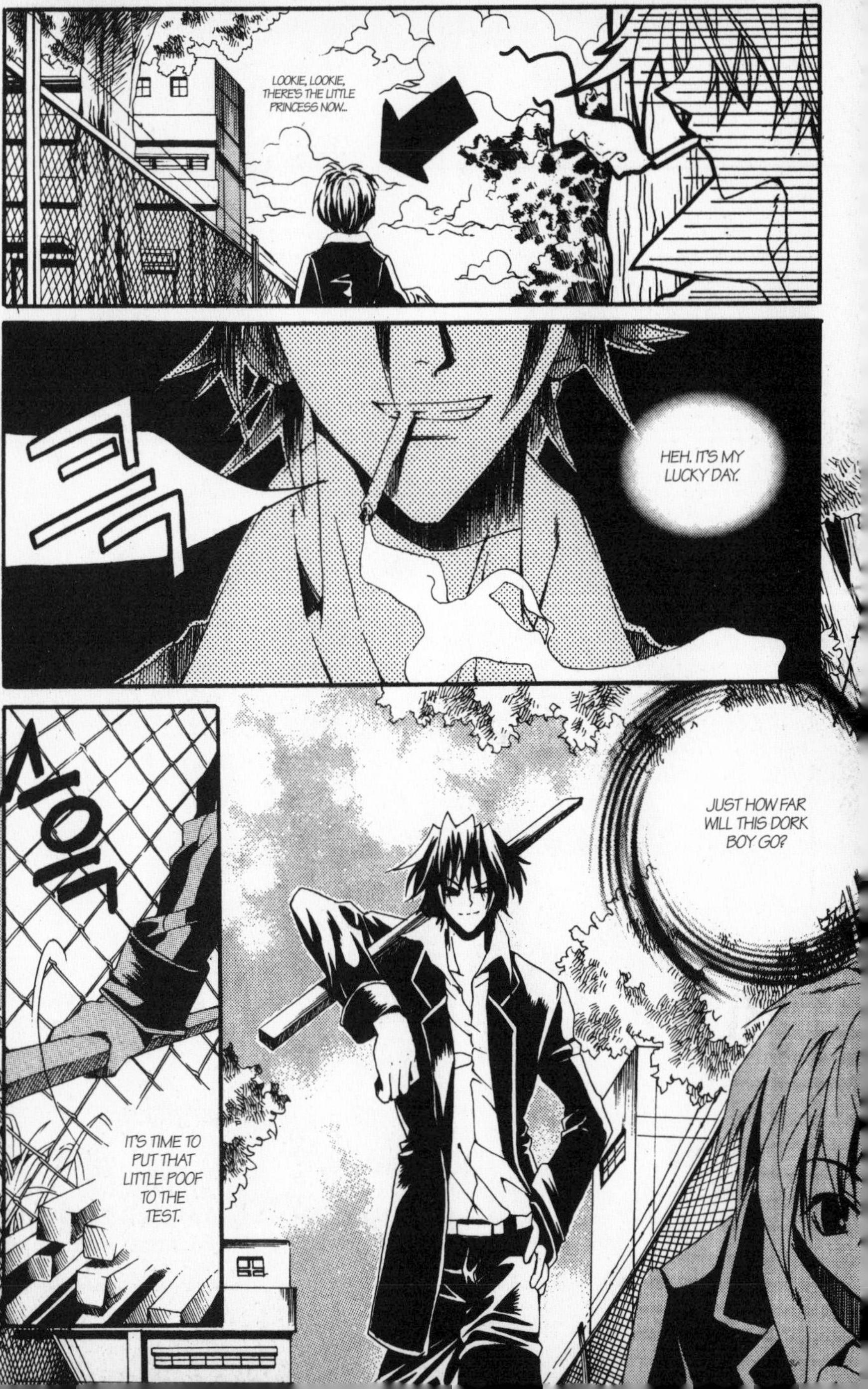
LOOKIE, LOOKIE, THERE'S THE LITTLE PRINCESS NOW...
HEH. IT'S MY LUCKY DAY.
IT'S TIME TO PUT THAT LITTLE POOF TO THE TEST.
JUST HOW FAR WILL THIS DORK BOY GO?

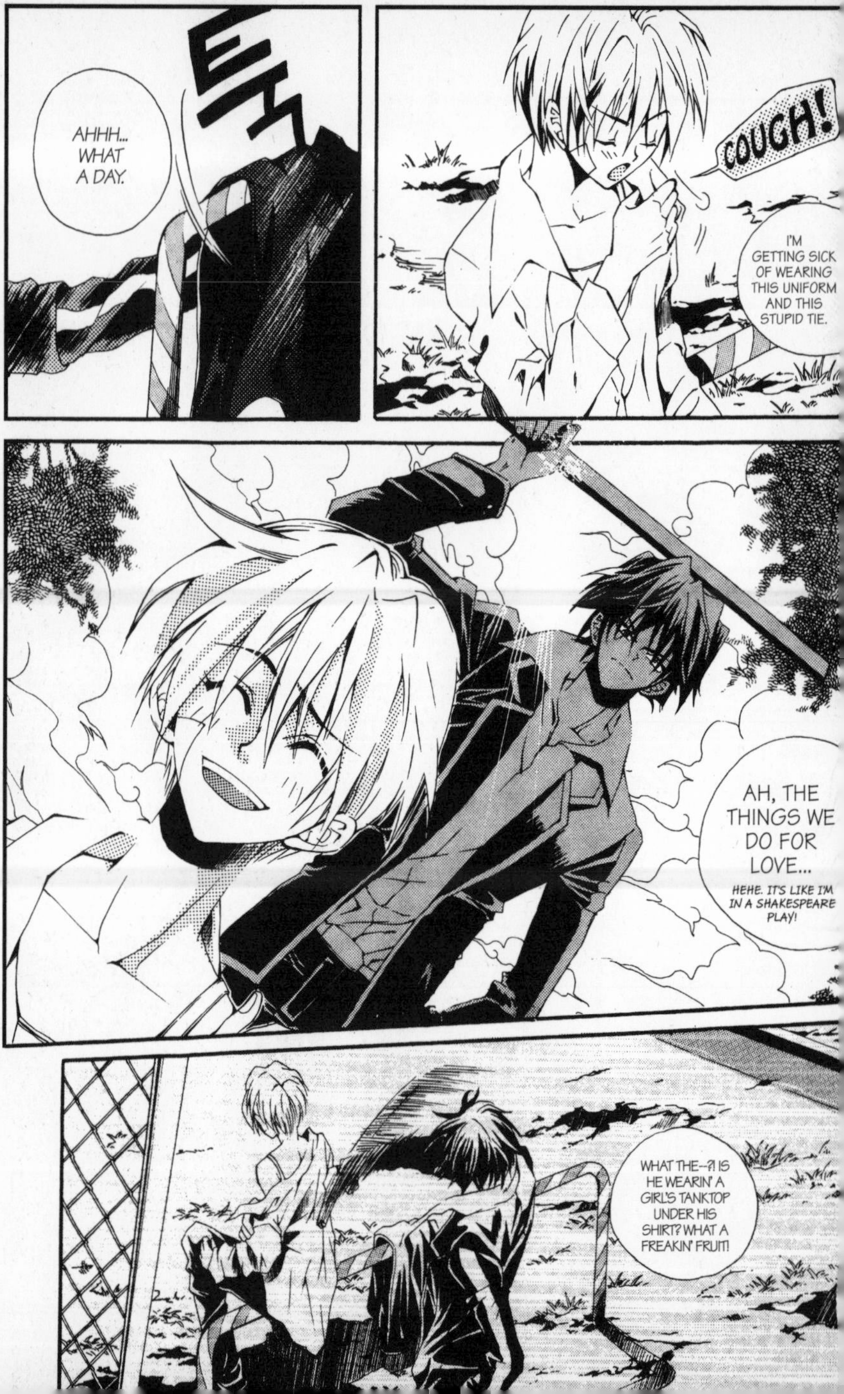
AHHH... WHAT A DAY.
COUGH!
I'M GETTING SICK OF WEARING THIS UNIFORM AND THIS STUPID TIE.
AH, THE THINGS WE DO FOR LOVE...
HEHE. IT'S LIKE I'M IN A SHAKESPEARE PLAY!
WHAT THE--?! IS HE WEARIN' A GIRL'S TANKTOP UNDER HIS SHIRT? WHAT A FREAKIN' FRUIT!

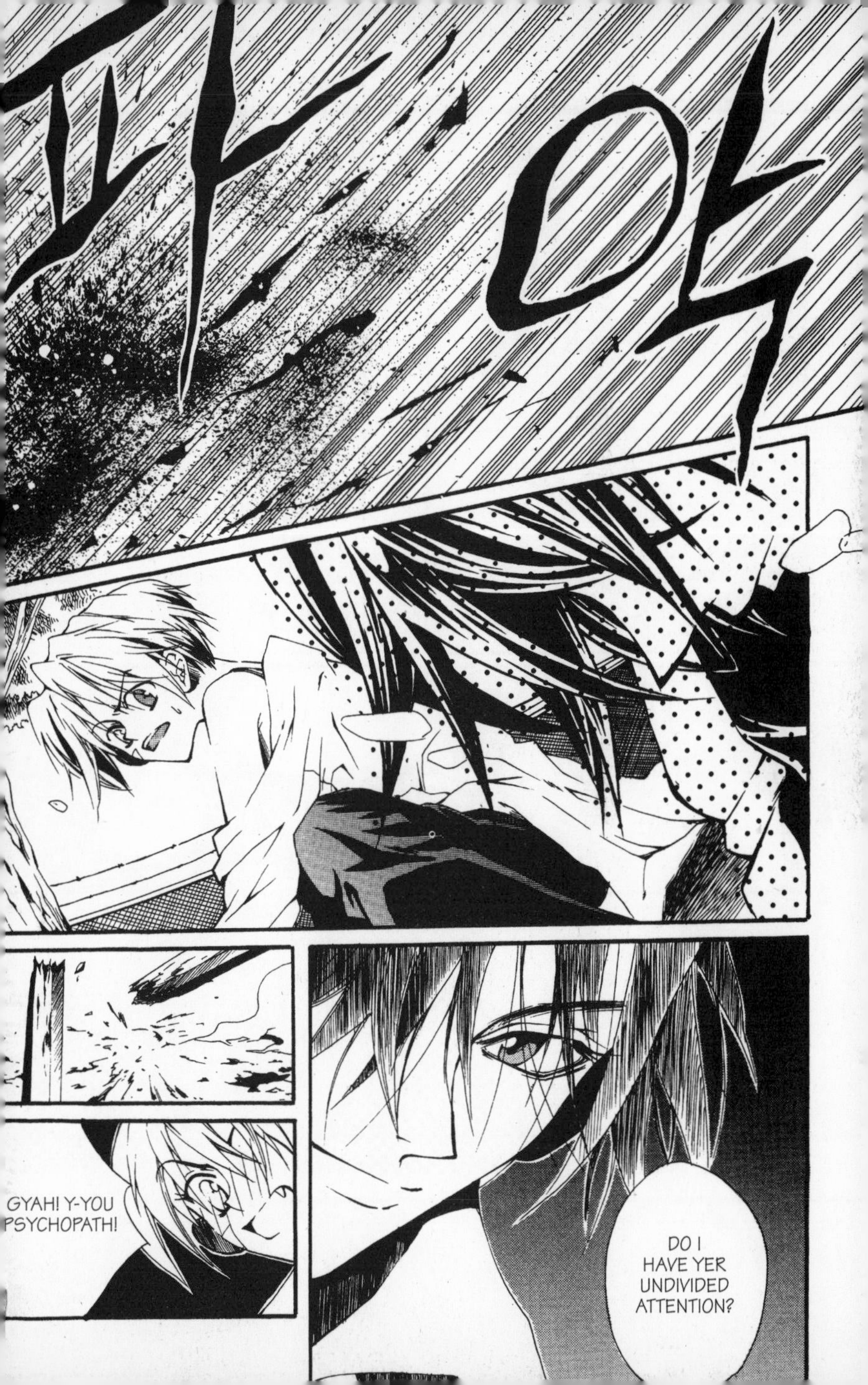
GYAH! Y-YOU PSYCHOPATH!
DO I HAVE YER UNDIVIDED ATTENTION?

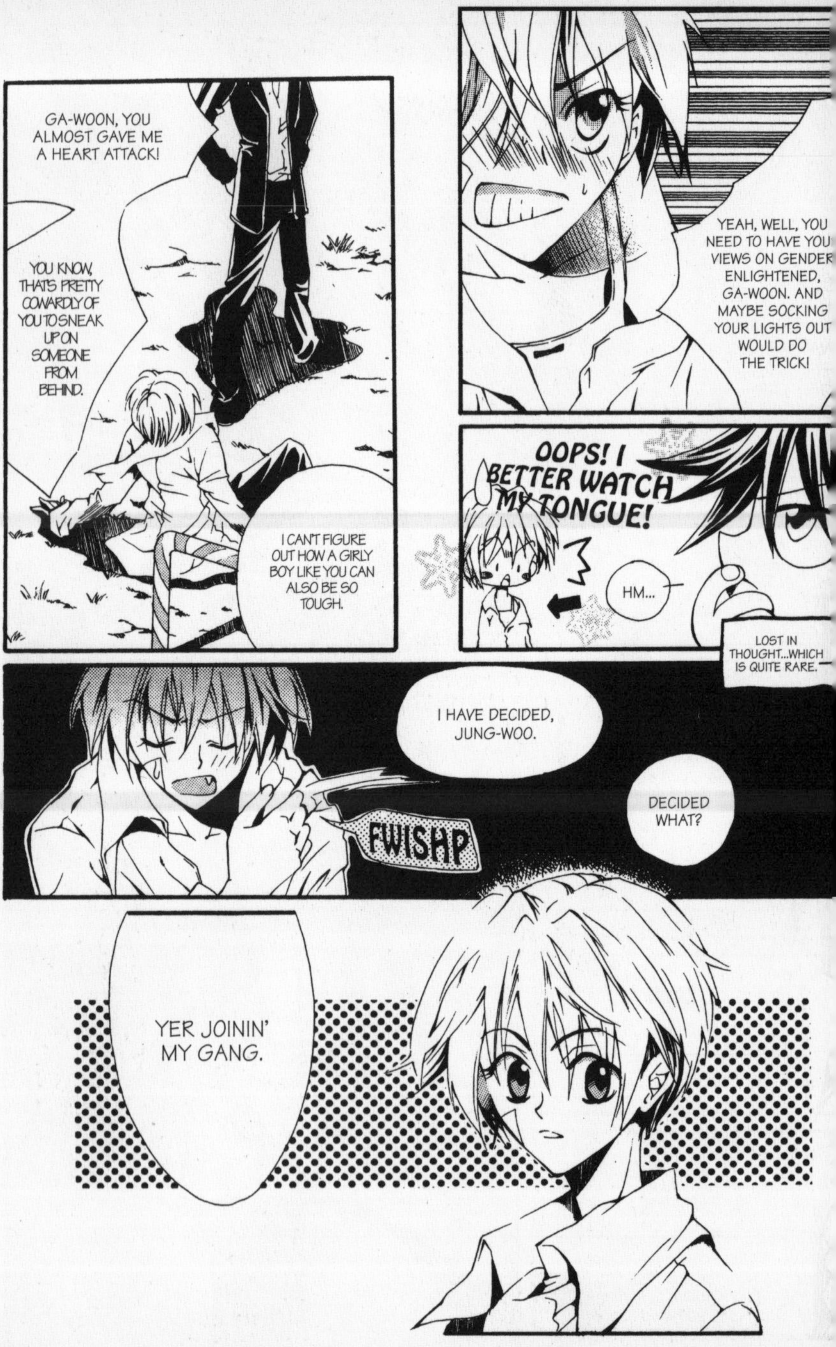
GA-WOON, YOU ALMOST GAVE ME A HEART ATTACK!
YOU KNOW, THAT'S PRETTY COWARDLY OF YOU TO SNEAK UP ON SOMEONE FROM BEHIND.
I CAN'T FIGURE OUT HOW A GIRLY BOY LIKE YOU CAN ALSO BE SO TOUGH.
YEAH, WELL, YOU NEED TO HAVE YOU VIEWS ON GENDER ENLIGHTENED, GA-WOON. AND MAYBE SOCKING YOUR LIGHTS OUT WOULD DO THE TRICK!
OOPS! I BETTER WATCH MY TONGUE!
HM...
LOST IN THOUGHT...WHICH IS QUITE RARE.
I HAVE DECIDED, JUNG-WOO.
FWISHP
DECIDED WHAT?
YER JOININ' MY GANG.

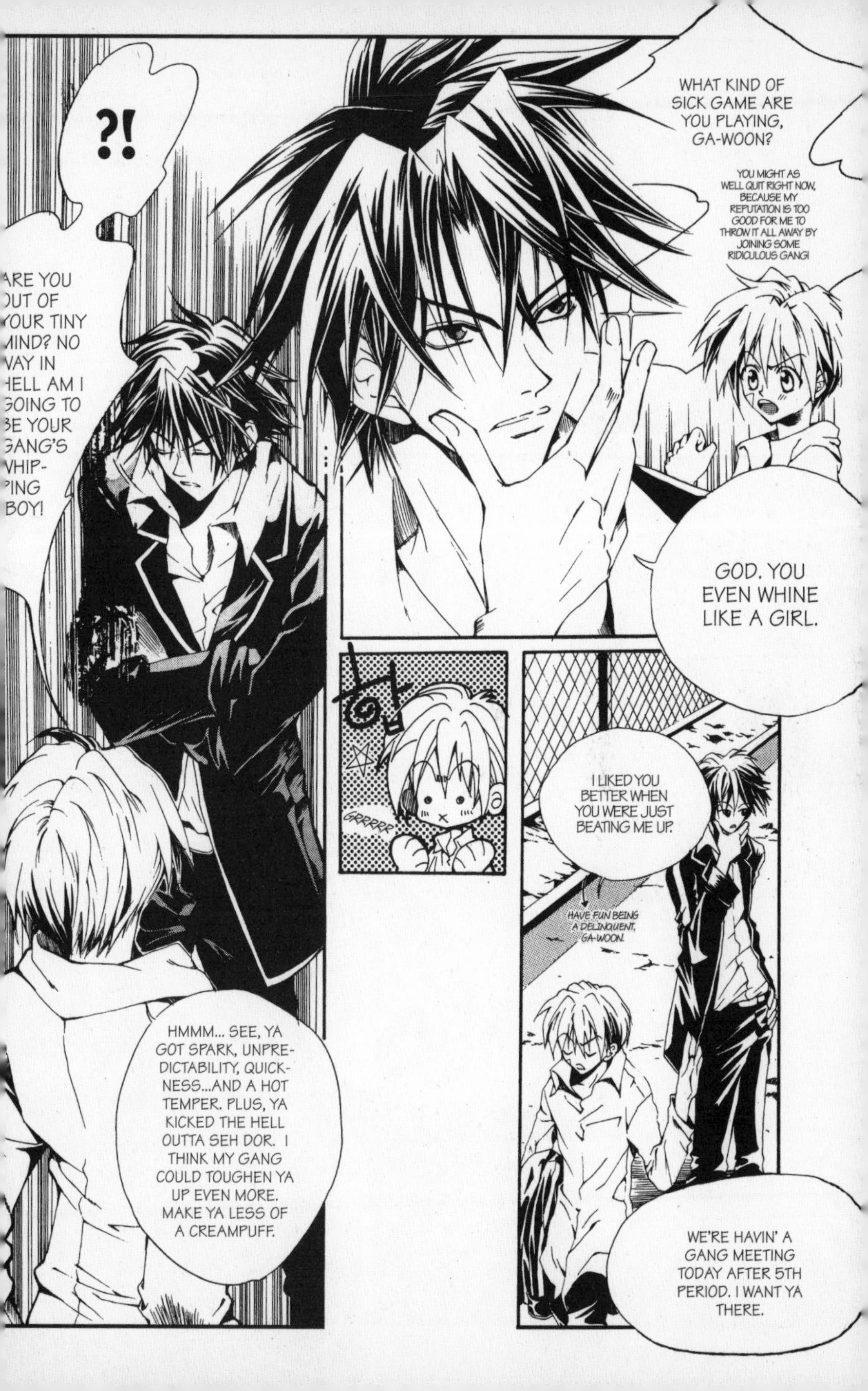
?!
ARE YOU OUT OF YOUR TINY MIND? NO WAY IN HELL AM I GOING TO BE YOUR GANG'S WHIP-PING BOY!
HMMM... SEE, YA GOT SPARK, UNPRE-DICTABILITY, QUICK-NESS...AND A HOT TEMPER. PLUS, YA KICKED THE HELL OUTTA SEH DOR. I THINK MY GANG COULD TOUGHEN YA UP EVEN MORE. MAKE YA LESS OF A CREAMPUFF.
WHAT KIND OF SICK GAME ARE YOU PLAYING, GA-WOON?
YOU MIGHT AS WELL QUIT RIGHT NOW, BECAUSE MY REPUTATION IS TOO GOOD FOR ME TO THROW IT ALL AWAY BY JOINING SOME RIDICULOUS GANG!
GOD. YOU EVEN WHINE LIKE A GIRL.
GRRRRR
I LIKED YOU BETTER WHEN YOU WERE JUST BEATING ME UP.
HAVE FUN BEING A DELINQUENT, GA-WOON.
WE'RE HAVIN' A GANG MEETING TODAY AFTER 5TH PERIOD. I WANT YA THERE.

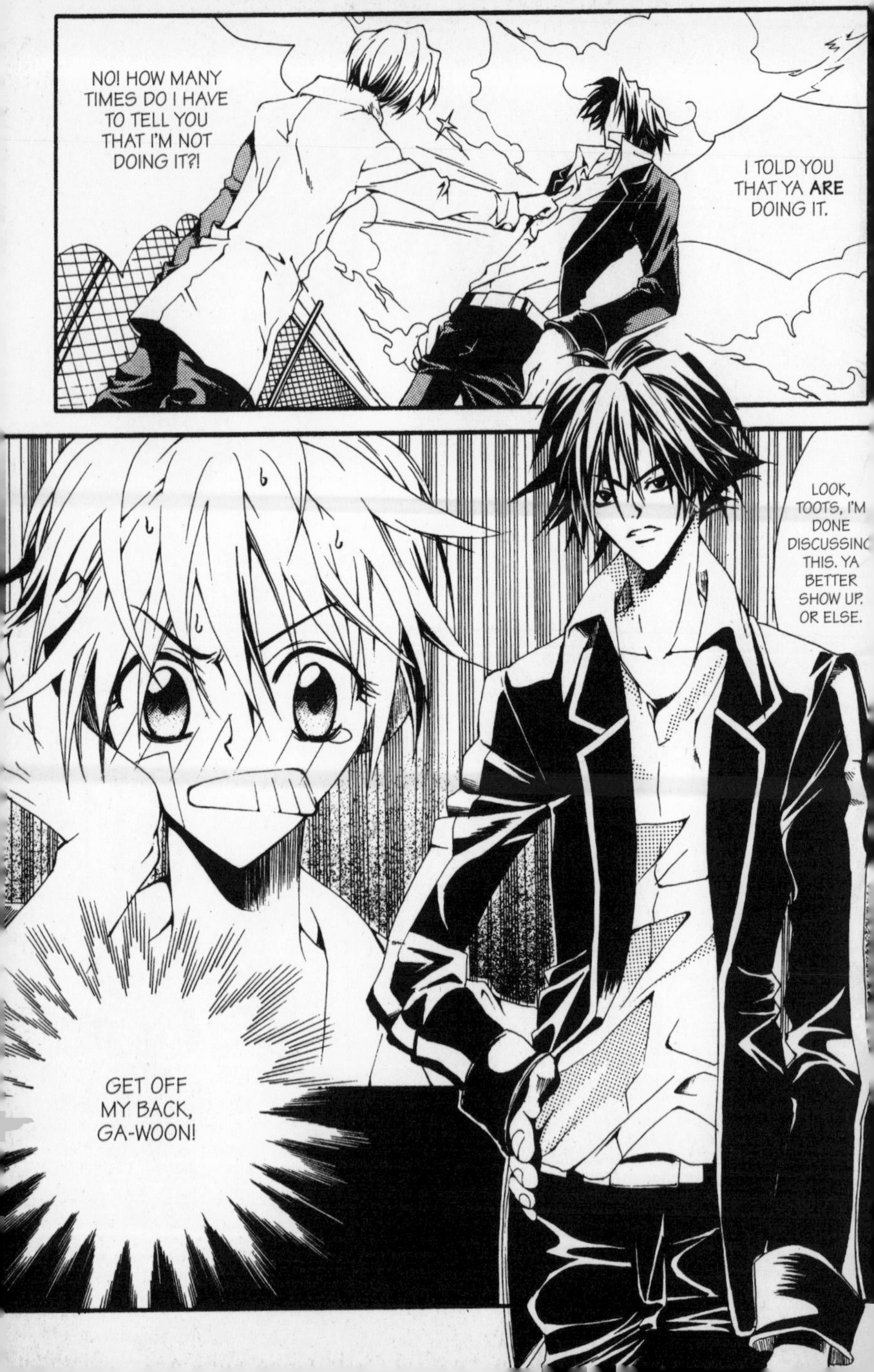

NO! HOW MANY TIMES DO I HAVE TO TELL YOU THAT I'M NOT DOING IT?!
I TOLD YOU THAT YA **ARE** DOING IT.
LOOK, TOOTS, I'M DONE DISCUSSING THIS. YA BETTER SHOW UP. OR ELSE.
GET OFF MY BACK, GA-WOON!

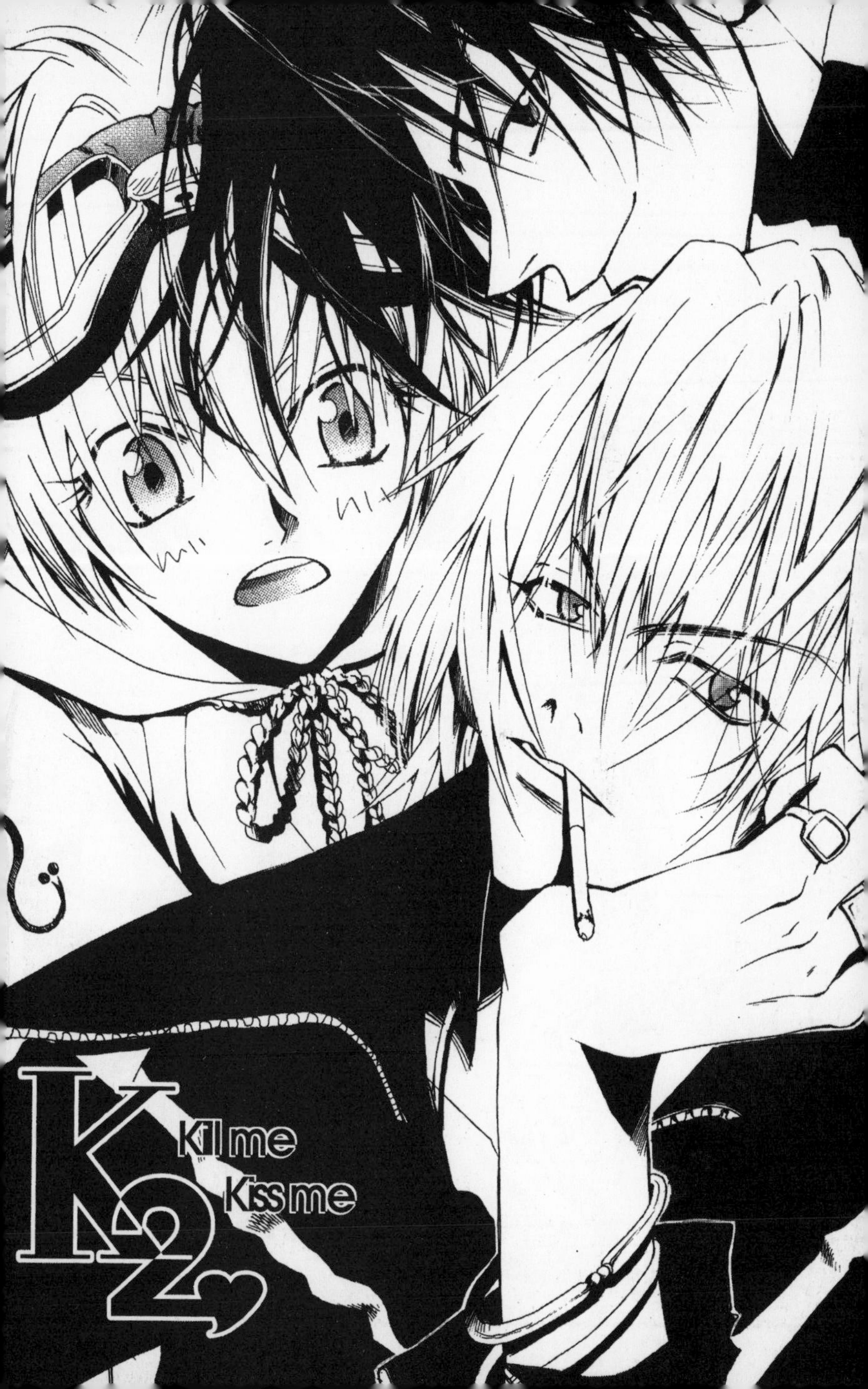
K2
Kill me
Kiss me

FOR FOUR DAYS, I'VE BEEN PRETENDING TO BE MY COUSIN JUNG-WOO AT PURE WATER HIGH SCHOOL. I THINK BEING AROUND ALL THIS TESTOSTERONE HAS MADE ME CRAZY.

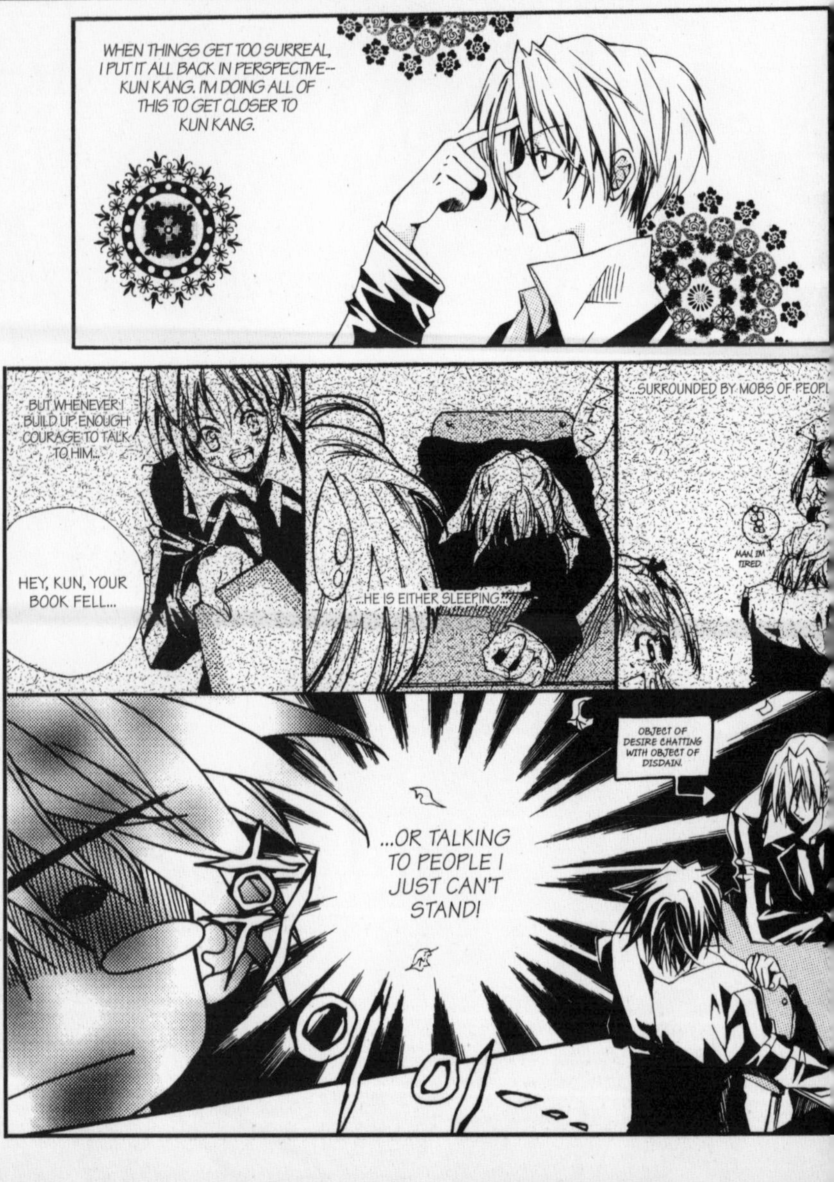
WHEN THINGS GET TOO SURREAL, I PUT IT ALL BACK IN PERSPECTIVE-- KUN KANG. I'M DOING ALL OF THIS TO GET CLOSER TO KUN KANG.
BUT WHENEVER I BUILD UP ENOUGH COURAGE TO TALK TO HIM...
HEY, KUN, YOUR BOOK FELL...
...HE IS EITHER SLEEPING...
...SURROUNDED BY MOBS OF PEOPL
MAN, I'M TIRED.
...OR TALKING TO PEOPLE I JUST CAN'T STAND!
OBJECT OF DESIRE CHATTING WITH OBJECT OF DISDAIN.

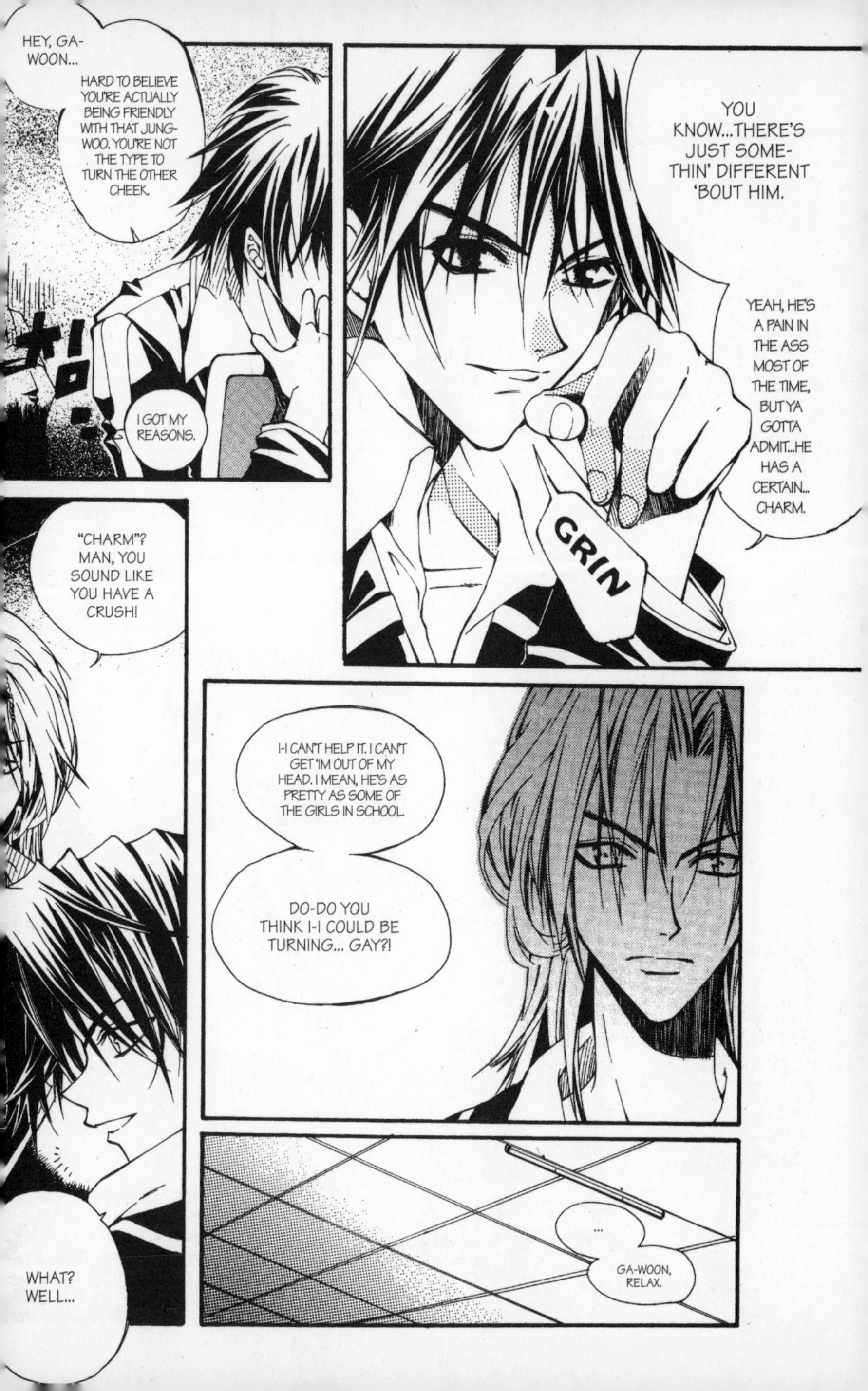
HEY, GA-WOON...
HARD TO BELIEVE YOU'RE ACTUALLY BEING FRIENDLY WITH THAT JUNG-WOO. YOU'RE NOT THE TYPE TO TURN THE OTHER CHEEK.
I GOT MY REASONS.
YOU KNOW...THERE'S JUST SOME-THIN' DIFFERENT 'BOUT HIM.
YEAH, HE'S A PAIN IN THE ASS MOST OF THE TIME, BUT YA GOTTA ADMIT...HE HAS A CERTAIN... CHARM.
GRIN
"CHARM"? MAN, YOU SOUND LIKE YOU HAVE A CRUSH!
WHAT? WELL...
I-I CAN'T HELP IT. I CAN'T GET 'IM OUT OF MY HEAD. I MEAN, HE'S AS PRETTY AS SOME OF THE GIRLS IN SCHOOL.
DO-DO YOU THINK I-I COULD BE TURNING... GAY?!
...
GA-WOON, RELAX.

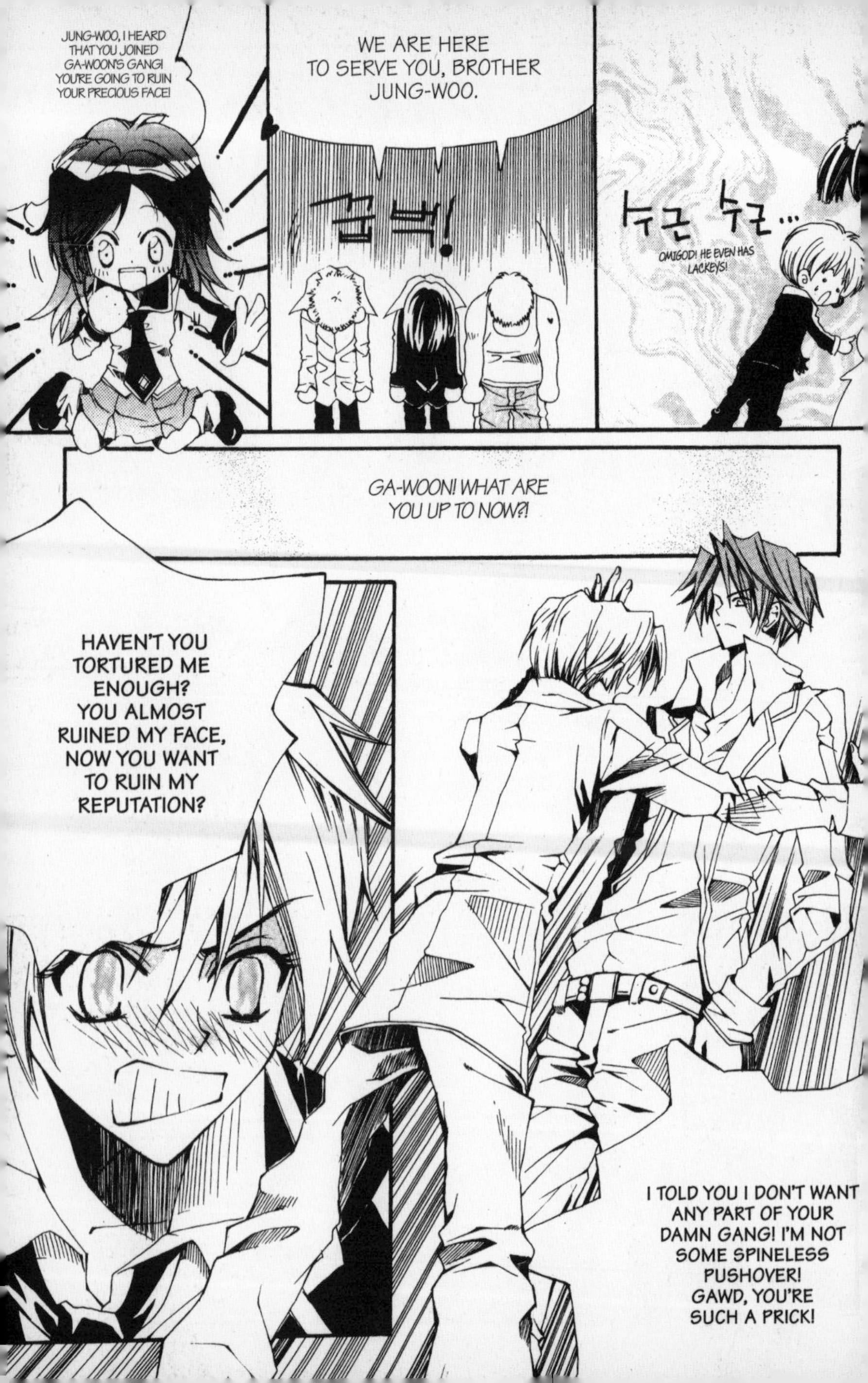
JUNG-WOO, I HEARD THAT YOU JOINED GA-WOON'S GANG! YOU'RE GOING TO RUIN YOUR PRECIOUS FACE!
WE ARE HERE TO SERVE YOU, BROTHER JUNG-WOO.
굽벅!
수군 수군...
OMIGOD! HE EVEN HAS LACKEYS!
GA-WOON! WHAT ARE YOU UP TO NOW?!
HAVEN'T YOU TORTURED ME ENOUGH? YOU ALMOST RUINED MY FACE, NOW YOU WANT TO RUIN MY REPUTATION?
I TOLD YOU I DON'T WANT ANY PART OF YOUR DAMN GANG! I'M NOT SOME SPINELESS PUSHOVER! GAWD, YOU'RE SUCH A PRICK!

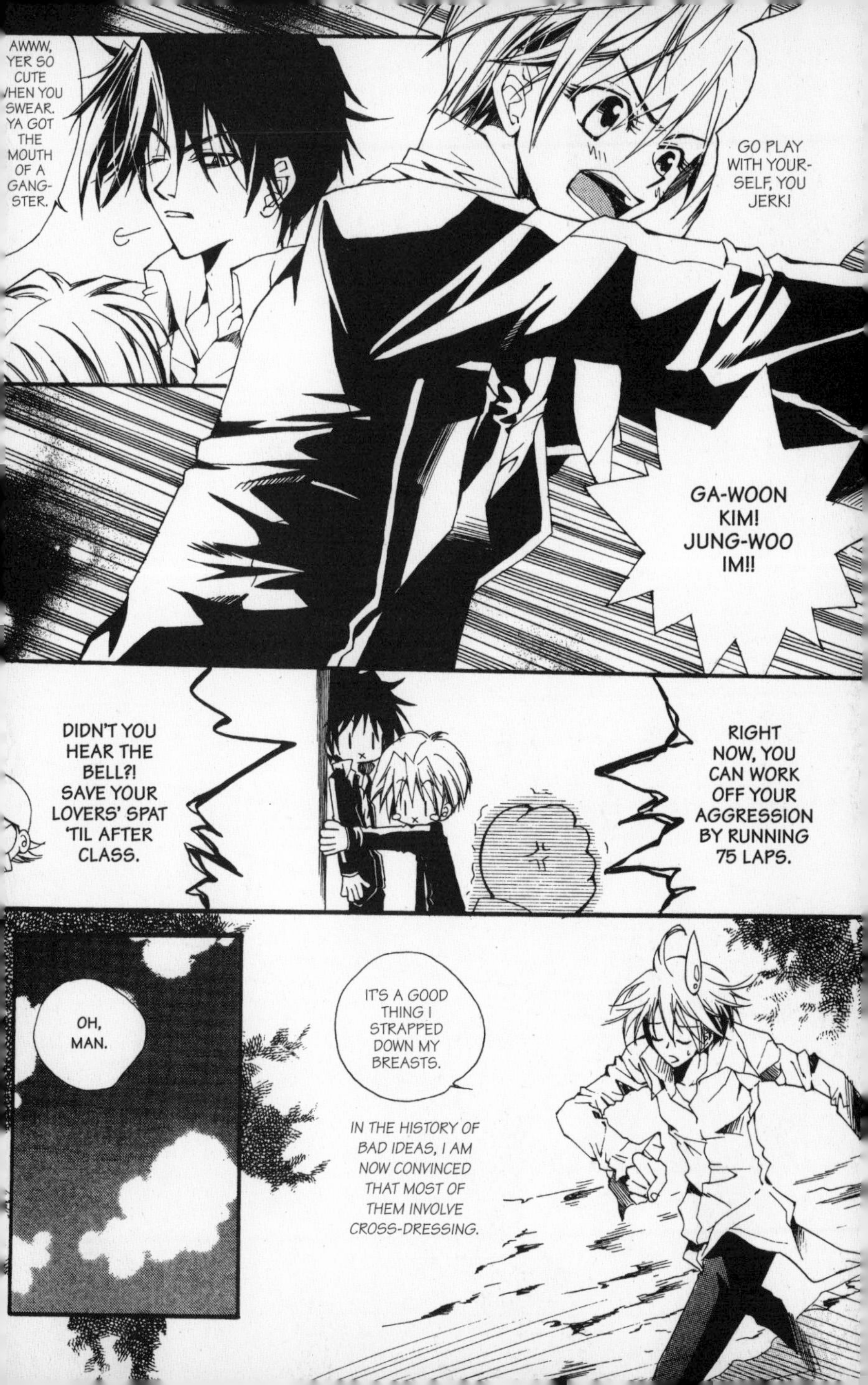
AWWW, YER SO CUTE WHEN YOU SWEAR. YA GOT THE MOUTH OF A GANG-STER.
GO PLAY WITH YOUR-SELF, YOU JERK!
GA-WOON KIM! JUNG-WOO IM!!
DIDN'T YOU HEAR THE BELL?! SAVE YOUR LOVERS' SPAT 'TIL AFTER CLASS.
RIGHT NOW, YOU CAN WORK OFF YOUR AGGRESSION BY RUNNING 75 LAPS.
OH, MAN.
IT'S A GOOD THING I STRAPPED DOWN MY BREASTS.
IN THE HISTORY OF BAD IDEAS, I AM NOW CONVINCED THAT MOST OF THEM INVOLVE CROSS-DRESSING.

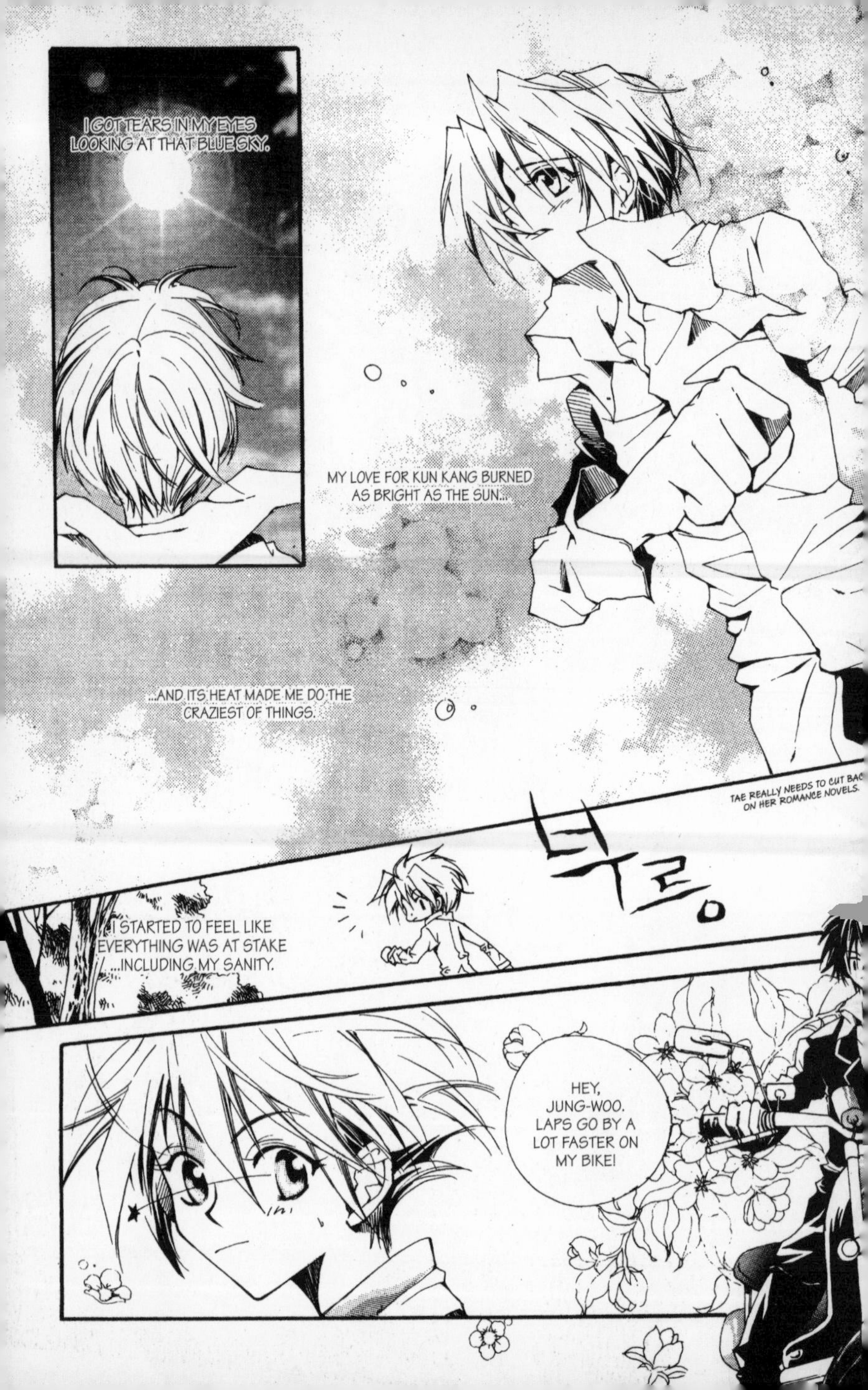
I GOT TEARS IN MY EYES LOOKING AT THAT BLUE SKY.
MY LOVE FOR KUN KANG BURNED AS BRIGHT AS THE SUN...
...AND ITS HEAT MADE ME DO THE CRAZIEST OF THINGS.
TAE REALLY NEEDS TO CUT BAC ON HER ROMANCE NOVELS.
I STARTED TO FEEL LIKE EVERYTHING WAS AT STAKE ...INCLUDING MY SANITY.
HEY, JUNG-WOO. LAPS GO BY A LOT FASTER ON MY BIKE!

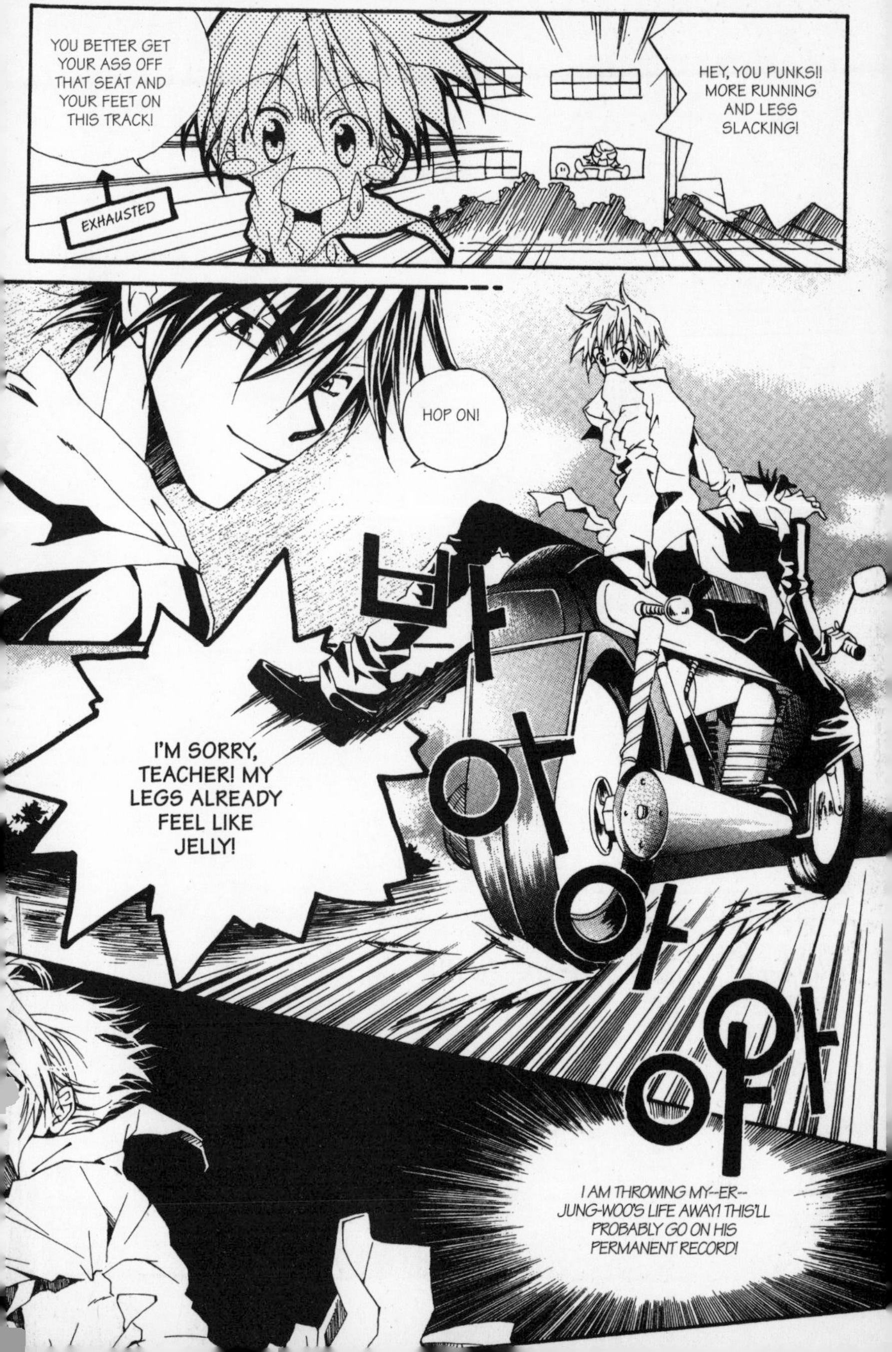
YOU BETTER GET YOUR ASS OFF THAT SEAT AND YOUR FEET ON THIS TRACK!
EXHAUSTED
HEY, YOU PUNKS!! MORE RUNNING AND LESS SLACKING!
HOP ON!
I'M SORRY, TEACHER! MY LEGS ALREADY FEEL LIKE JELLY!
I AM THROWING MY--ER-- JUNG-WOO'S LIFE AWAY! THIS'LL PROBABLY GO ON HIS PERMANENT RECORD!

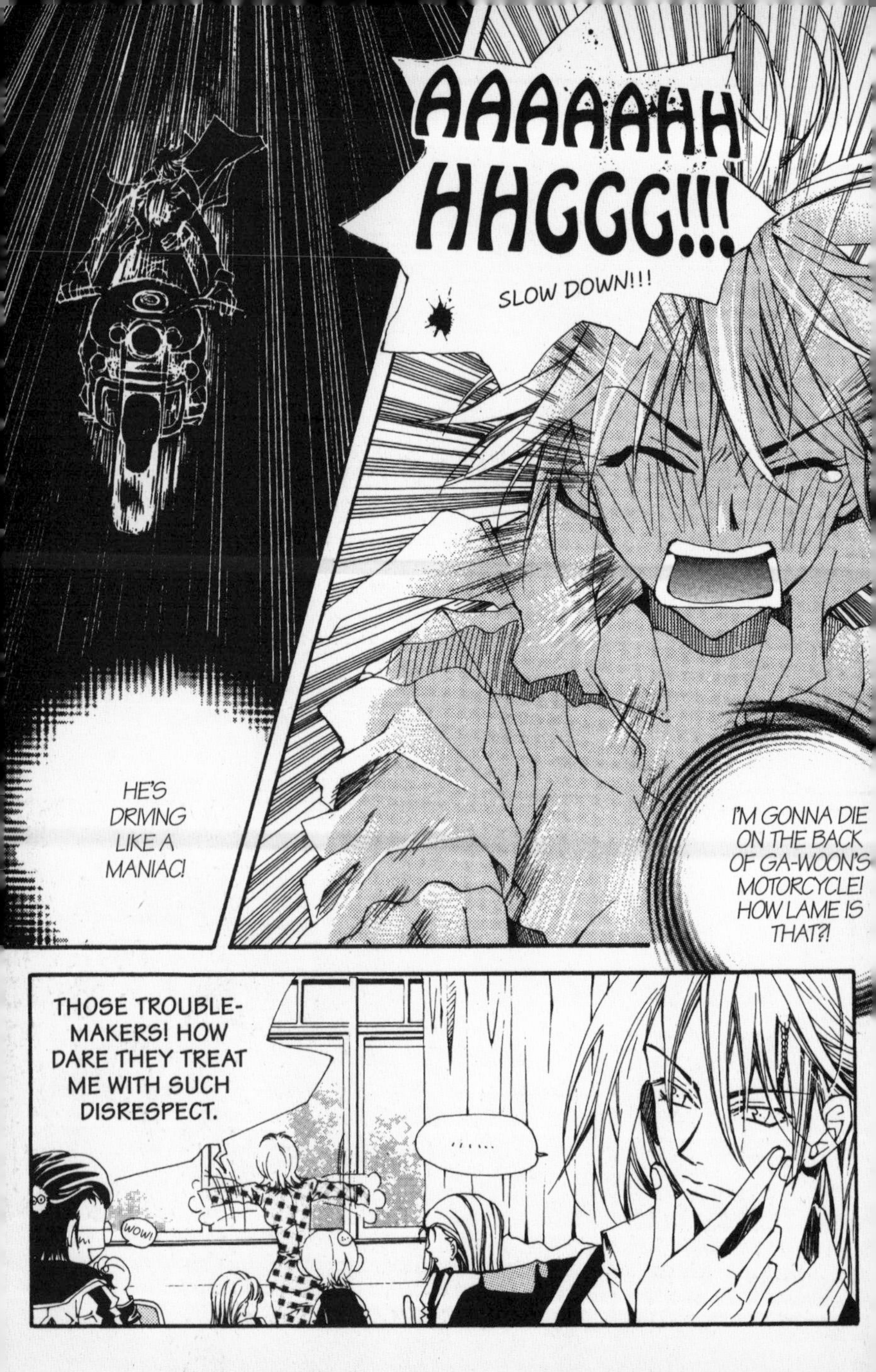
HE'S DRIVING LIKE A MANIAC!
AAAAAHHHGGG!!!
SLOW DOWN!!!
I'M GONNA DIE ON THE BACK OF GA-WOON'S MOTORCYCLE! HOW LAME IS THAT?!
THOSE TROUBLE-MAKERS! HOW DARE THEY TREAT ME WITH SUCH DISRESPECT.
WOW!
......

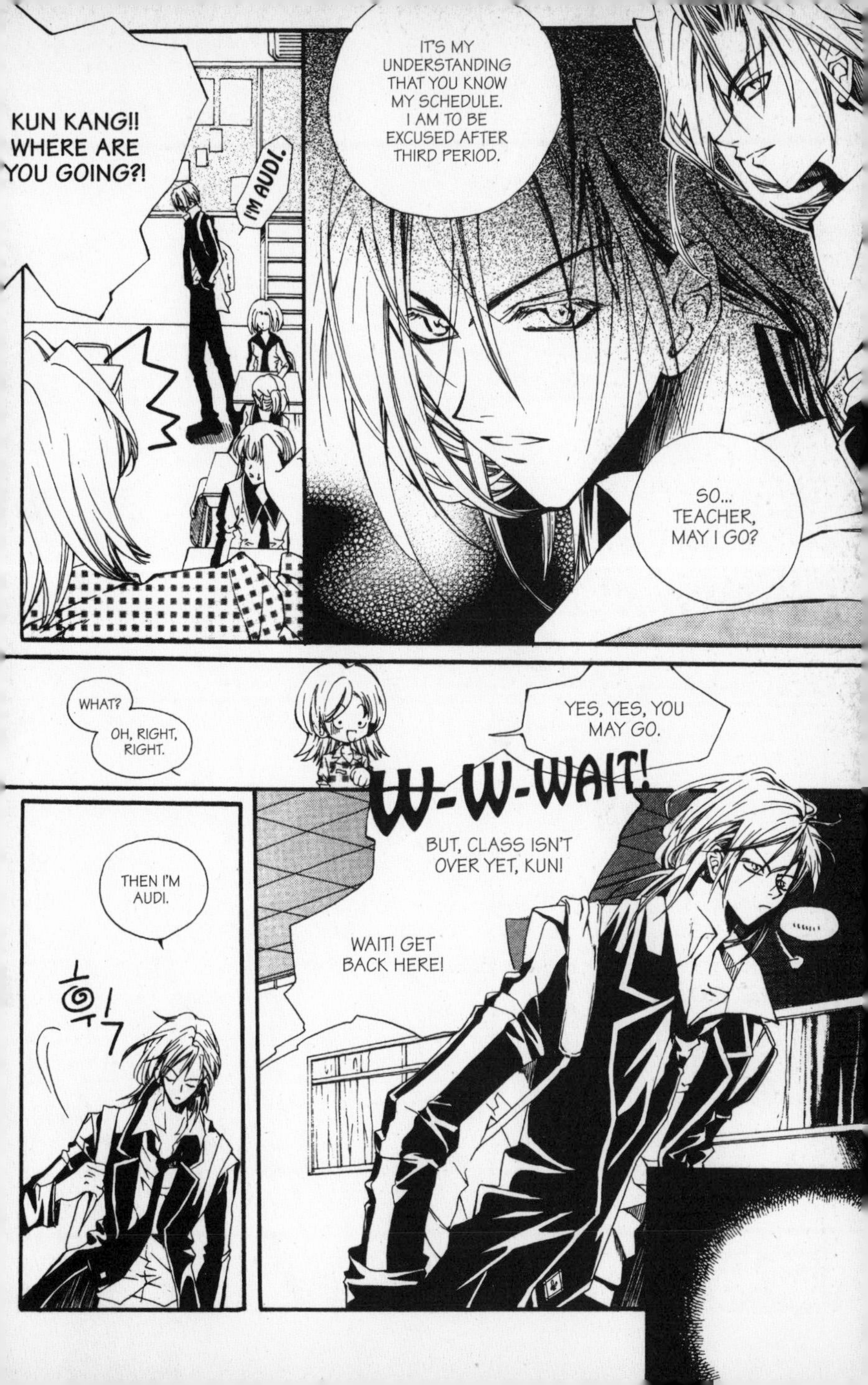
KUN KANG!! WHERE ARE YOU GOING?!
I'M AUDI.
IT'S MY UNDERSTANDING THAT YOU KNOW MY SCHEDULE. I AM TO BE EXCUSED AFTER THIRD PERIOD.
SO... TEACHER, MAY I GO?
WHAT?
OH, RIGHT, RIGHT.
YES, YES, YOU MAY GO.
THEN I'M AUDI.
W-W-WAIT!
BUT, CLASS ISN'T OVER YET, KUN!
WAIT! GET BACK HERE!
......

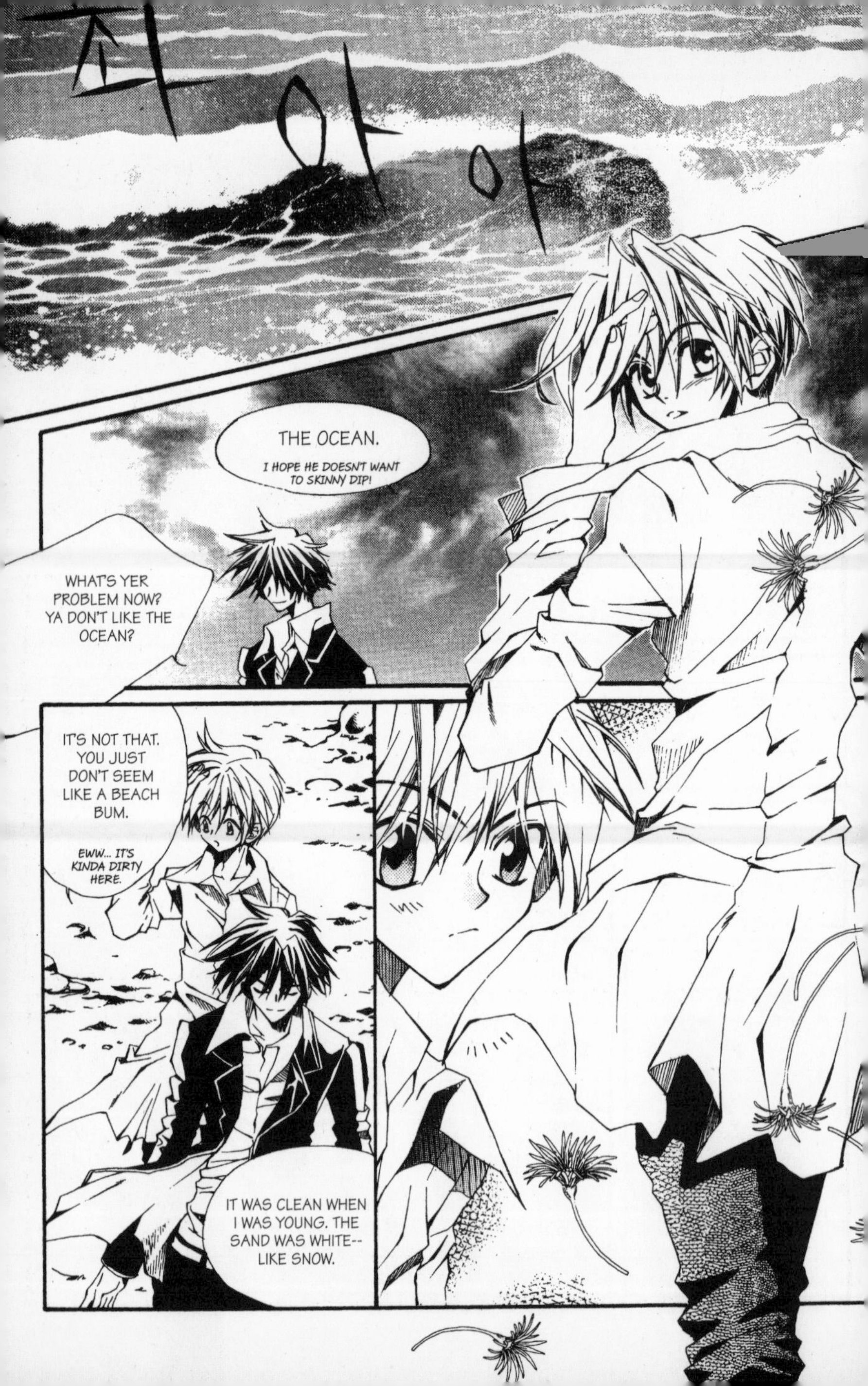
THE OCEAN.
I HOPE HE DOESN'T WANT TO SKINNY DIP!
WHAT'S YER PROBLEM NOW? YA DON'T LIKE THE OCEAN?
IT'S NOT THAT. YOU JUST DON'T SEEM LIKE A BEACH BUM.
EWW... IT'S KINDA DIRTY HERE.
IT WAS CLEAN WHEN I WAS YOUNG. THE SAND WAS WHITE--LIKE SNOW.

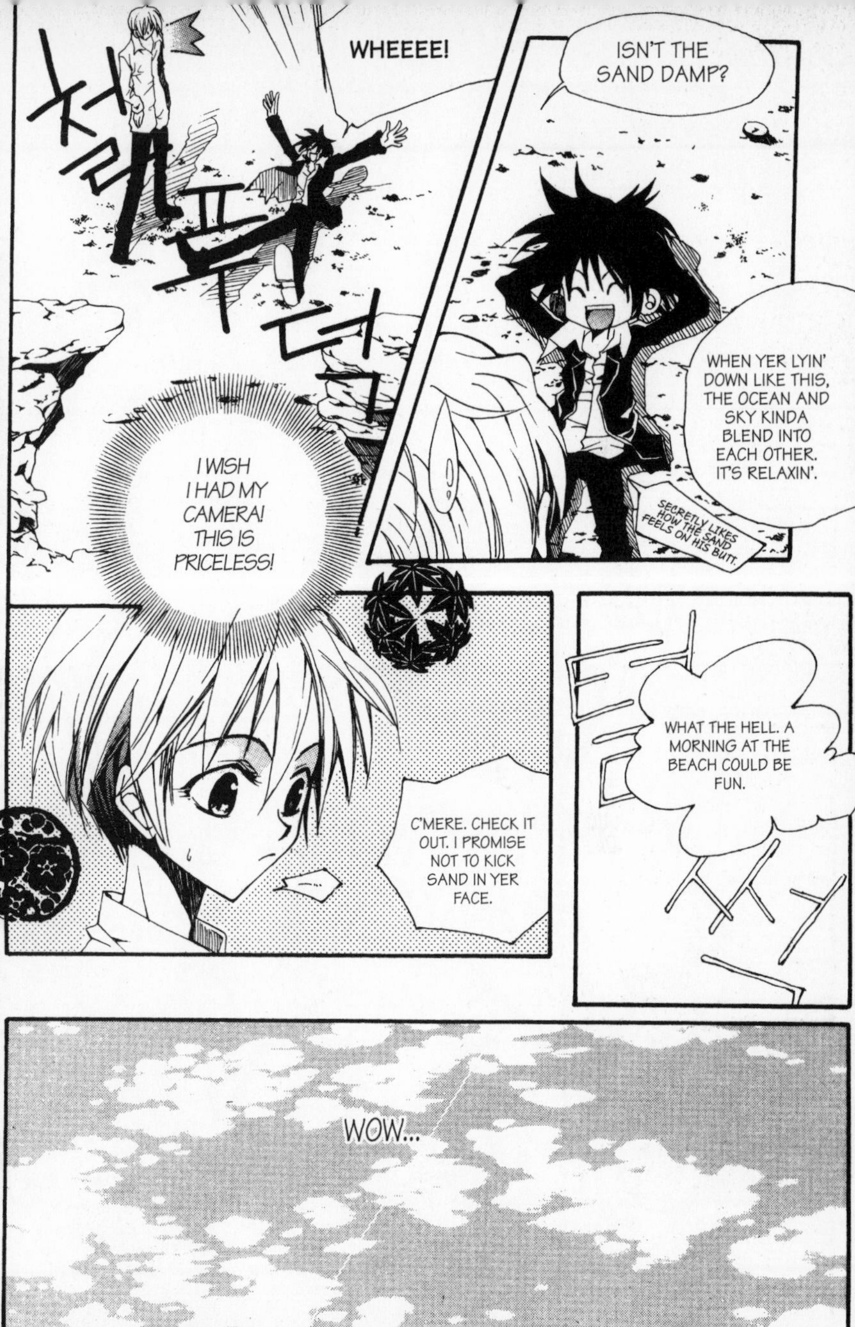
WHEEEE!
철퍼덕
I WISH I HAD MY CAMERA! THIS IS PRICELESS!
ISN'T THE SAND DAMP?
WHEN YER LYIN' DOWN LIKE THIS, THE OCEAN AND SKY KINDA BLEND INTO EACH OTHER. IT'S RELAXIN'.
SECRETLY LIKES HOW THE SAND FEELS ON HIS BUTT.
C'MERE. CHECK IT OUT. I PROMISE NOT TO KICK SAND IN YER FACE.
WHAT THE HELL. A MORNING AT THE BEACH COULD BE FUN.
WOW...

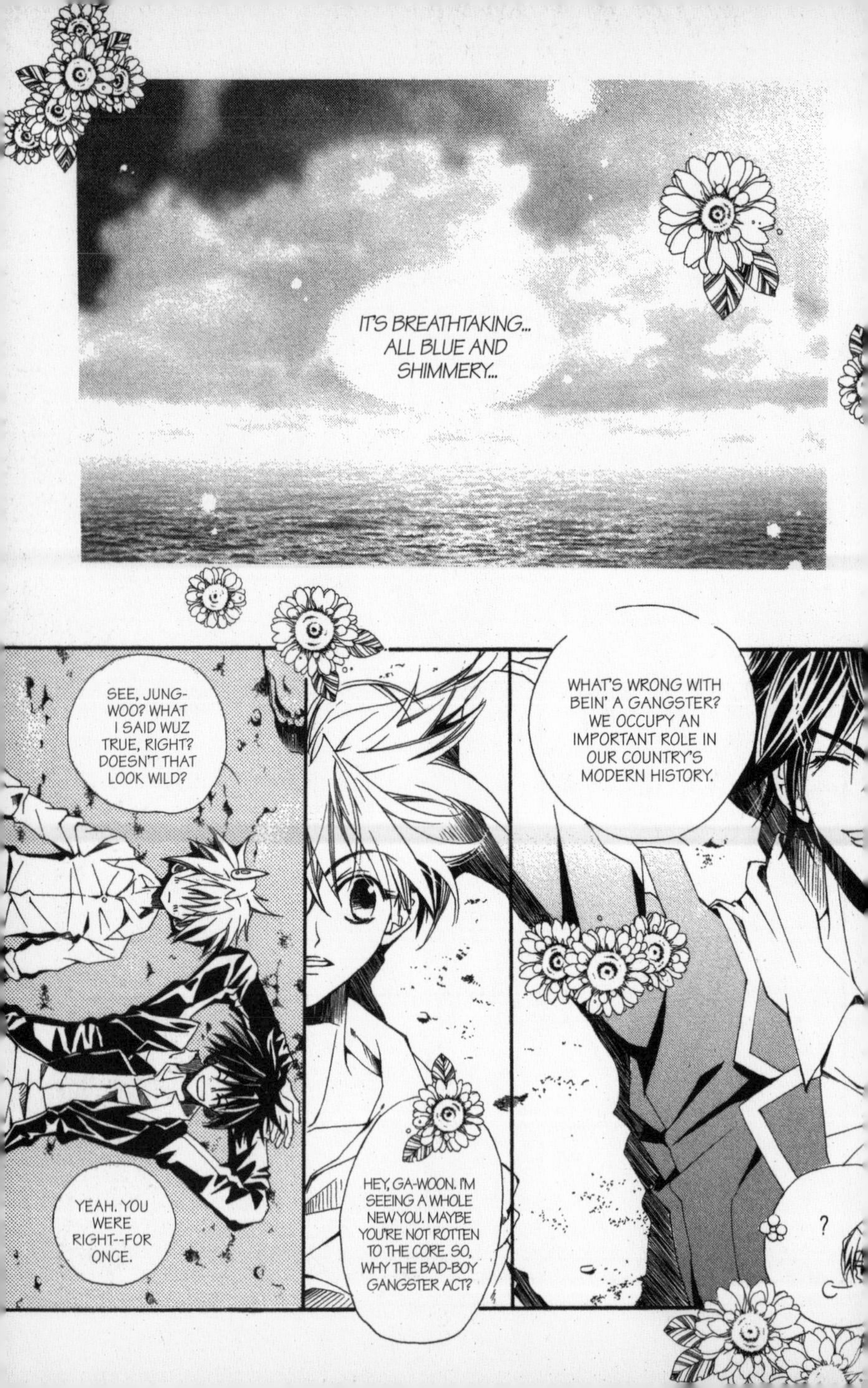
IT'S BREATHTAKING... ALL BLUE AND SHIMMERY...
SEE, JUNG-WOO? WHAT I SAID WUZ TRUE, RIGHT? DOESN'T THAT LOOK WILD?
YEAH. YOU WERE RIGHT--FOR ONCE.
HEY, GA-WOON. I'M SEEING A WHOLE NEW YOU. MAYBE YOU'RE NOT ROTTEN TO THE CORE. SO, WHY THE BAD-BOY GANGSTER ACT?
WHAT'S WRONG WITH BEIN' A GANGSTER? WE OCCUPY AN IMPORTANT ROLE IN OUR COUNTRY'S MODERN HISTORY.
?

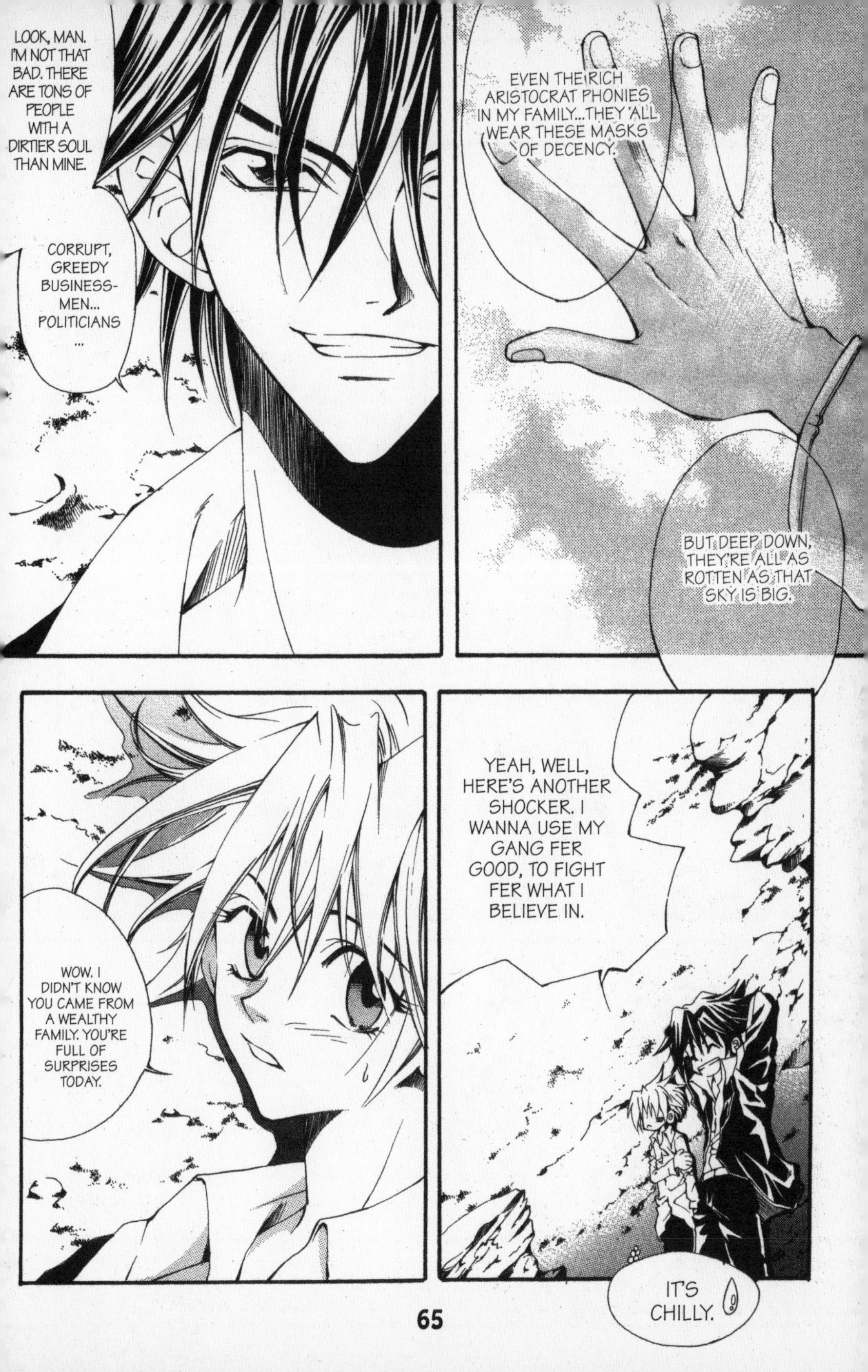
LOOK, MAN. I'M NOT THAT BAD. THERE ARE TONS OF PEOPLE WITH A DIRTIER SOUL THAN MINE.
CORRUPT, GREEDY BUSINESS-MEN... POLITICIANS ...
EVEN THE RICH ARISTOCRAT PHONIES IN MY FAMILY...THEY ALL WEAR THESE MASKS OF DECENCY.
BUT DEEP DOWN, THEY'RE ALL AS ROTTEN AS THAT SKY IS BIG.
WOW. I DIDN'T KNOW YOU CAME FROM A WEALTHY FAMILY. YOU'RE FULL OF SURPRISES TODAY.
YEAH, WELL, HERE'S ANOTHER SHOCKER. I WANNA USE MY GANG FER GOOD, TO FIGHT FER WHAT I BELIEVE IN.
IT'S CHILLY.

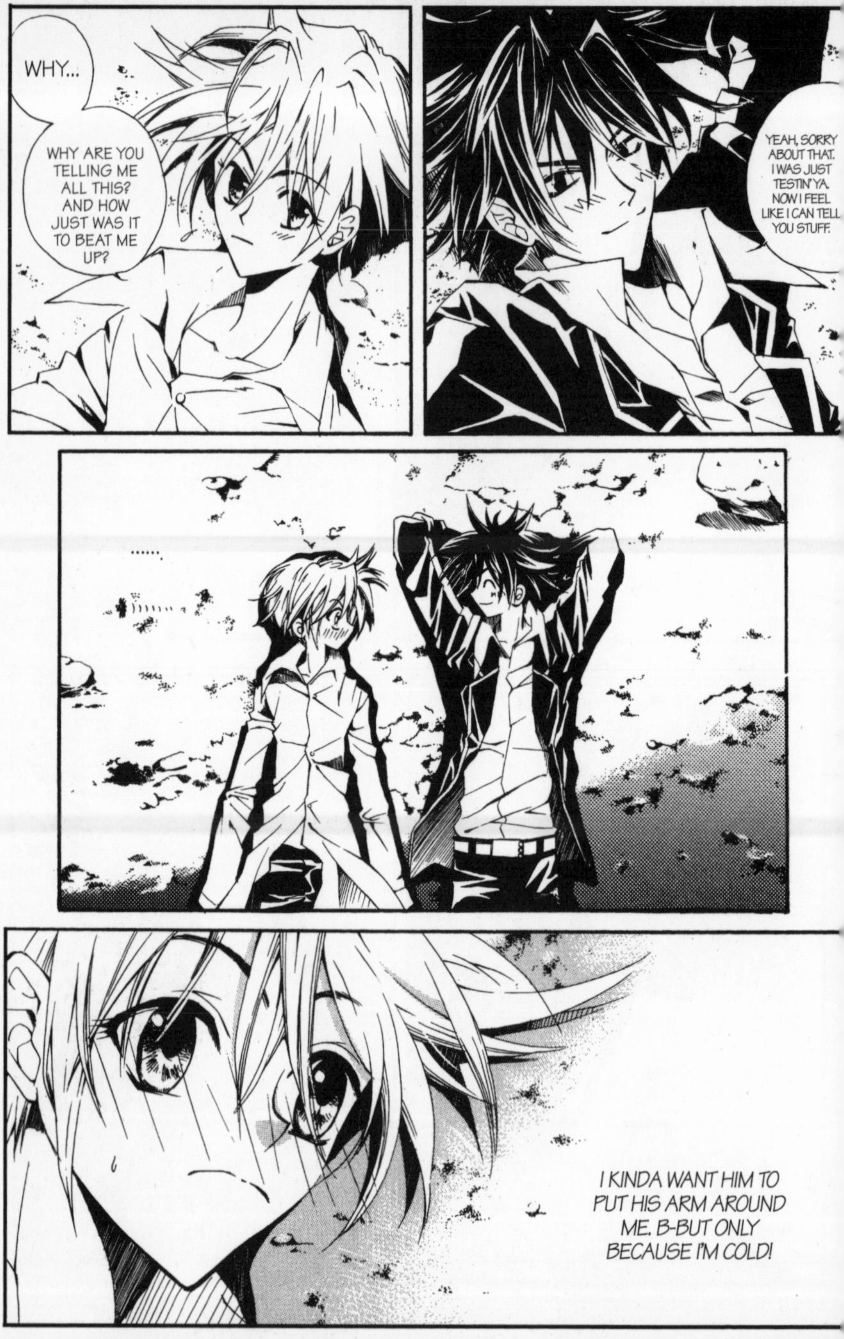
WHY...
WHY ARE YOU TELLING ME ALL THIS? AND HOW JUST WAS IT TO BEAT ME UP?
YEAH, SORRY ABOUT THAT. I WAS JUST TESTIN' YA. NOW I FEEL LIKE I CAN TELL YOU STUFF.
......
I KINDA WANT HIM TO PUT HIS ARM AROUND ME. B-BUT ONLY BECAUSE I'M COLD!

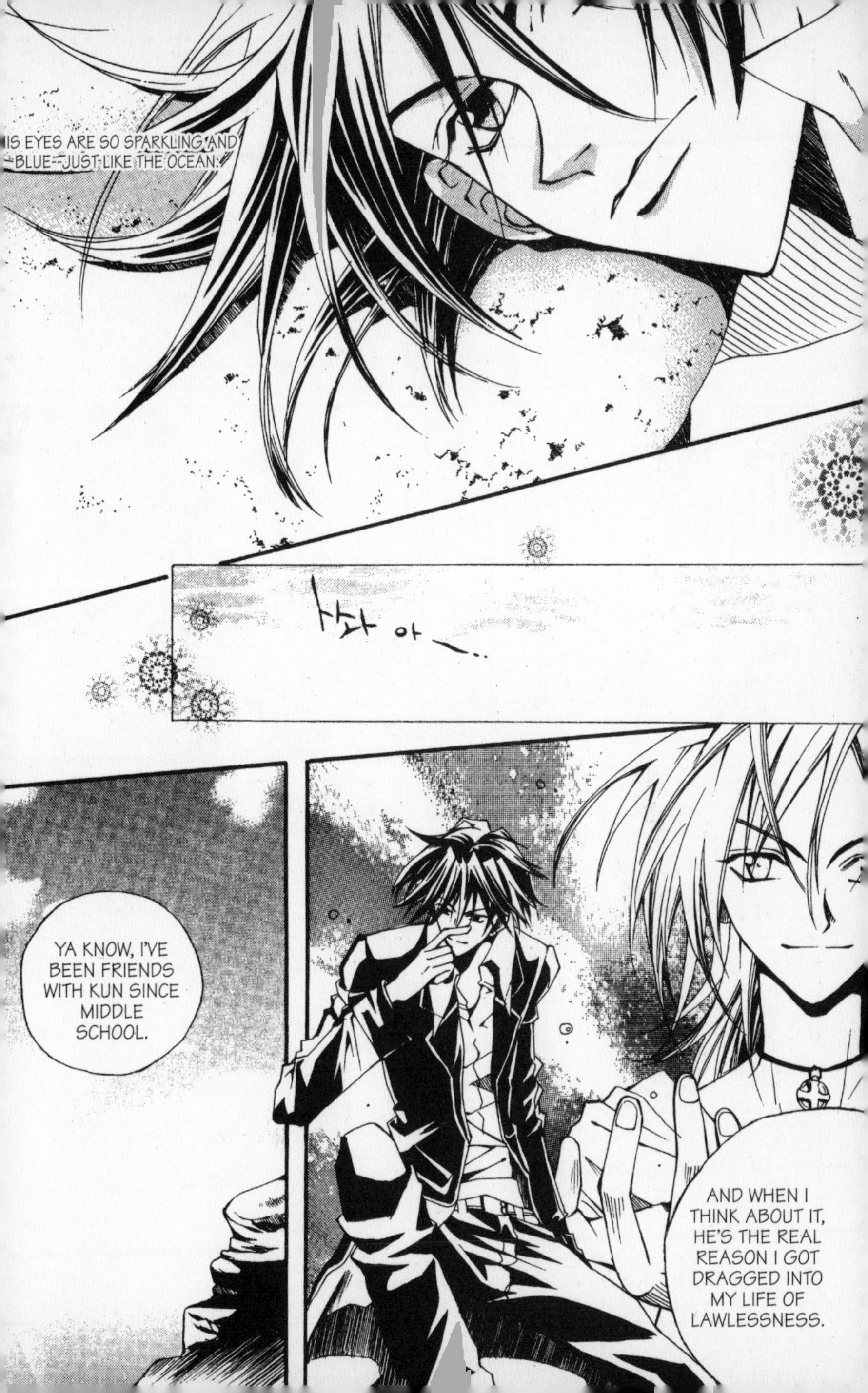
IS EYES ARE SO SPARKLING AND BLUE--JUST LIKE THE OCEAN.
YA KNOW, I'VE BEEN FRIENDS WITH KUN SINCE MIDDLE SCHOOL.
AND WHEN I THINK ABOUT IT, HE'S THE REAL REASON I GOT DRAGGED INTO MY LIFE OF LAWLESSNESS.

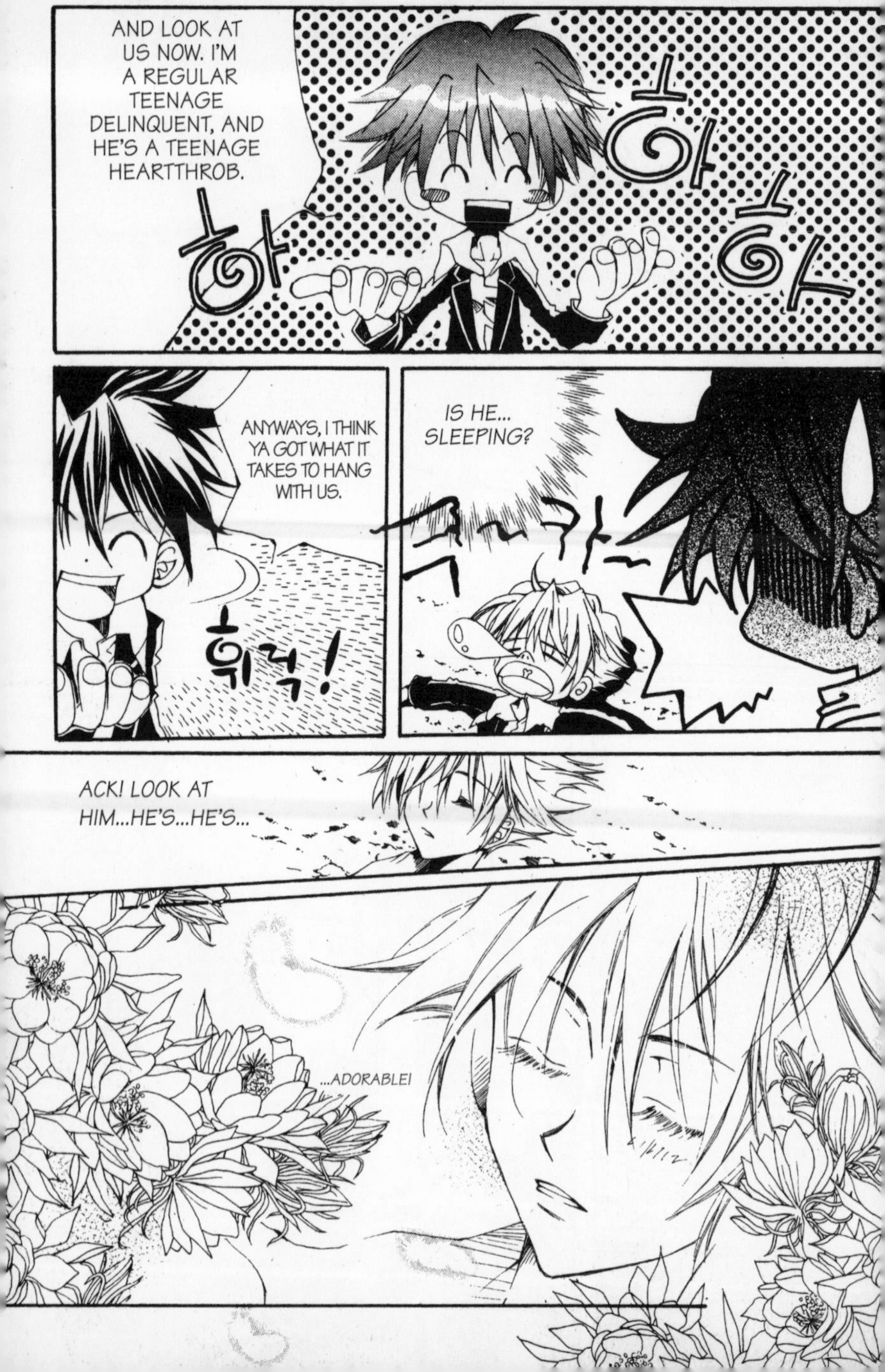
AND LOOK AT US NOW. I'M A REGULAR TEENAGE DELINQUENT, AND HE'S A TEENAGE HEARTTHROB.
하 하 하
ANYWAYS, I THINK YA GOT WHAT IT TAKES TO HANG WITH US.
휘릭!
IS HE... SLEEPING?
ACK! LOOK AT HIM...HE'S...HE'S...
...ADORABLE!

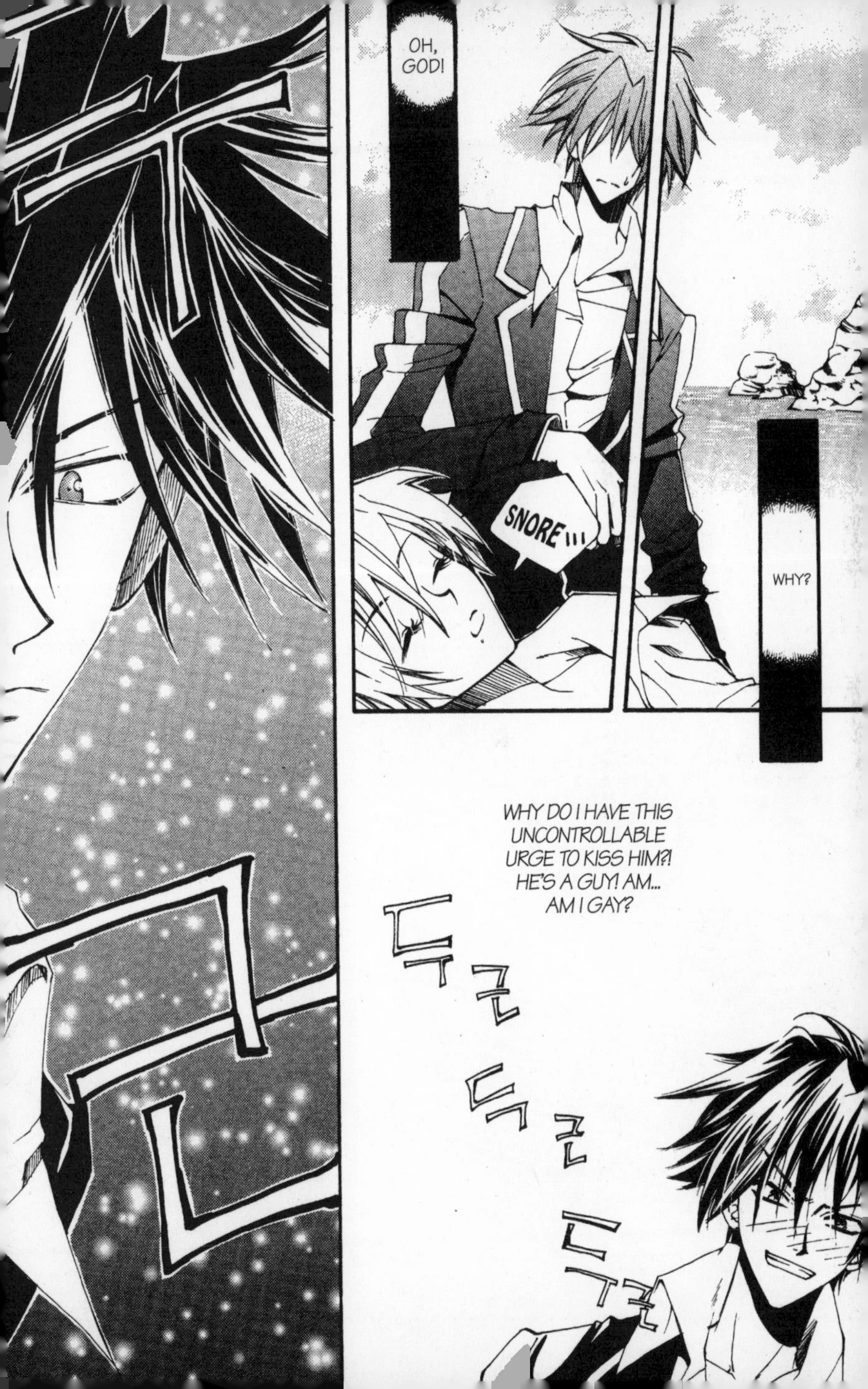
OH, GOD!
SNORE
WHY?
WHY DO I HAVE THIS UNCONTROLLABLE URGE TO KISS HIM?! HE'S A GUY! AM... AM I GAY?

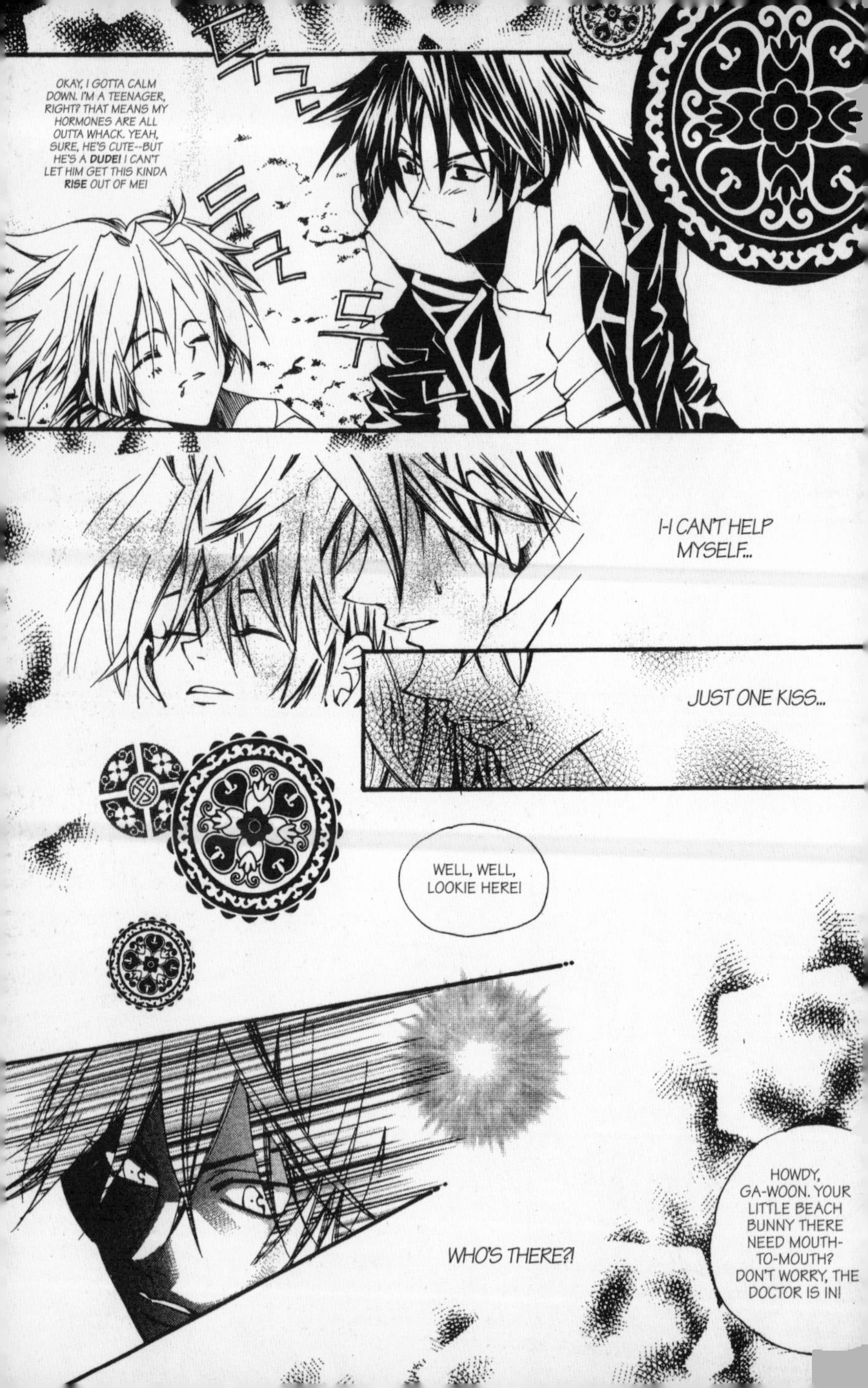
OKAY, I GOTTA CALM DOWN. I'M A TEENAGER, RIGHT? THAT MEANS MY HORMONES ARE ALL OUTTA WHACK. YEAH, SURE, HE'S CUTE--BUT HE'S A **DUDE!** I CAN'T LET HIM GET THIS KINDA **RISE** OUT OF ME!
I-I CAN'T HELP MYSELF...
JUST ONE KISS...
WELL, WELL, LOOKIE HERE!
WHO'S THERE?!
HOWDY, GA-WOON. YOUR LITTLE BEACH BUNNY THERE NEED MOUTH-TO-MOUTH? DON'T WORRY, THE DOCTOR IS IN!

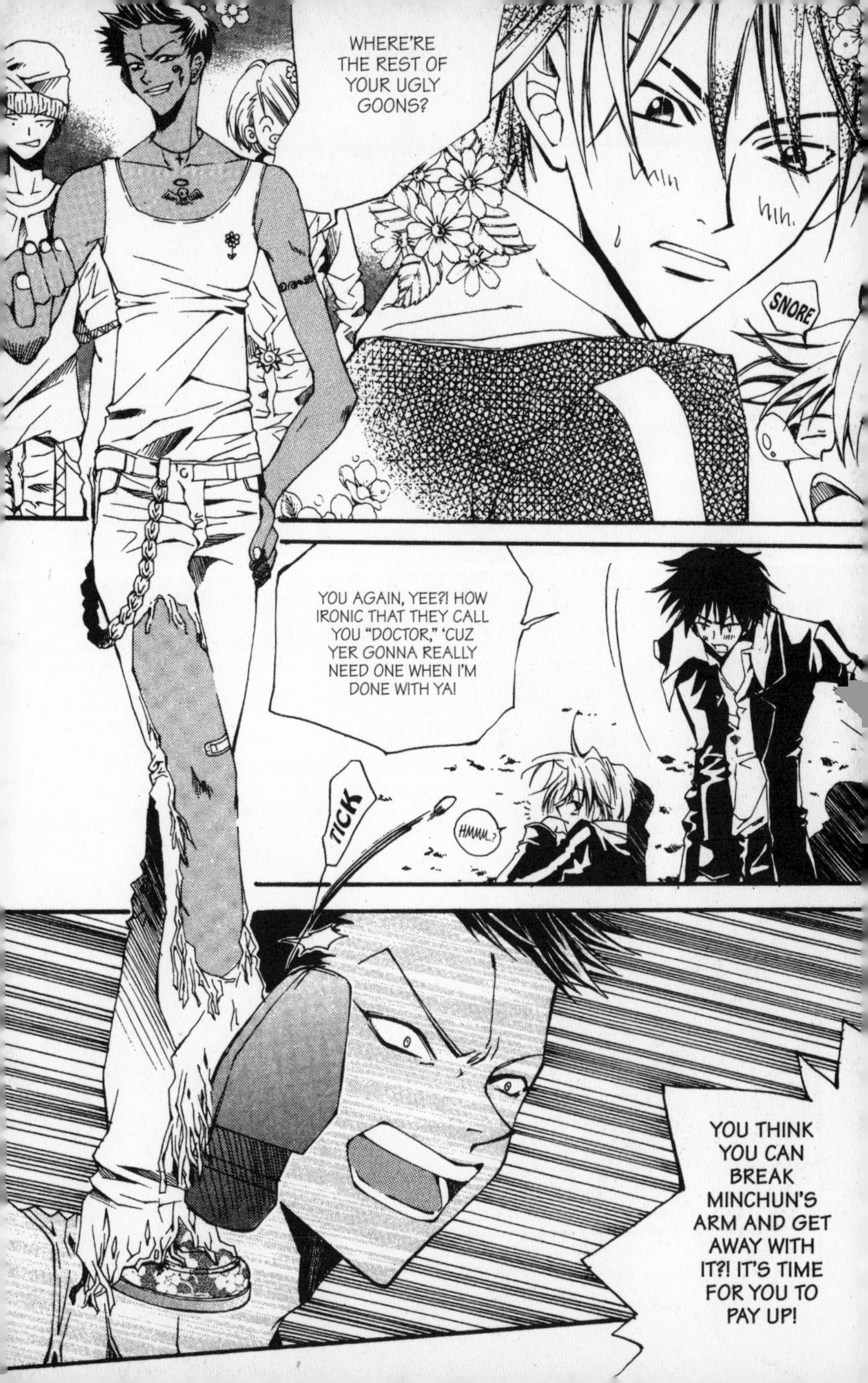
WHERE'RE THE REST OF YOUR UGLY GOONS?
SNORE
YOU AGAIN, YEE?! HOW IRONIC THAT THEY CALL YOU "DOCTOR," 'CUZ YER GONNA REALLY NEED ONE WHEN I'M DONE WITH YA!
TICK
HMMM..?
YOU THINK YOU CAN BREAK MINCHUN'S ARM AND GET AWAY WITH IT?! IT'S TIME FOR YOU TO PAY UP!

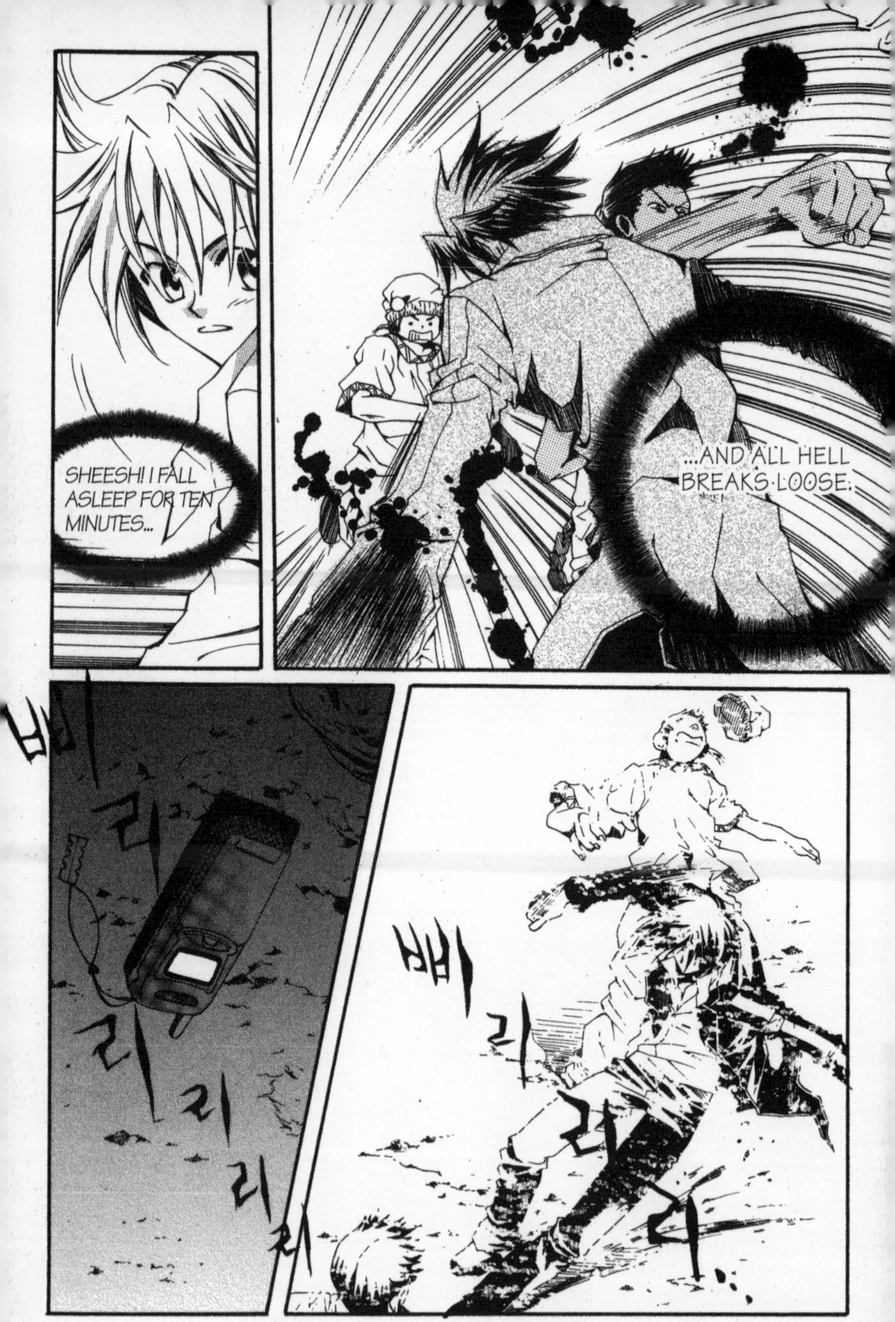
SHEESH! I FALL ASLEEP FOR TEN MINUTES...
...AND ALL HELL BREAKS LOOSE.
삐리리리리리
삐리리리

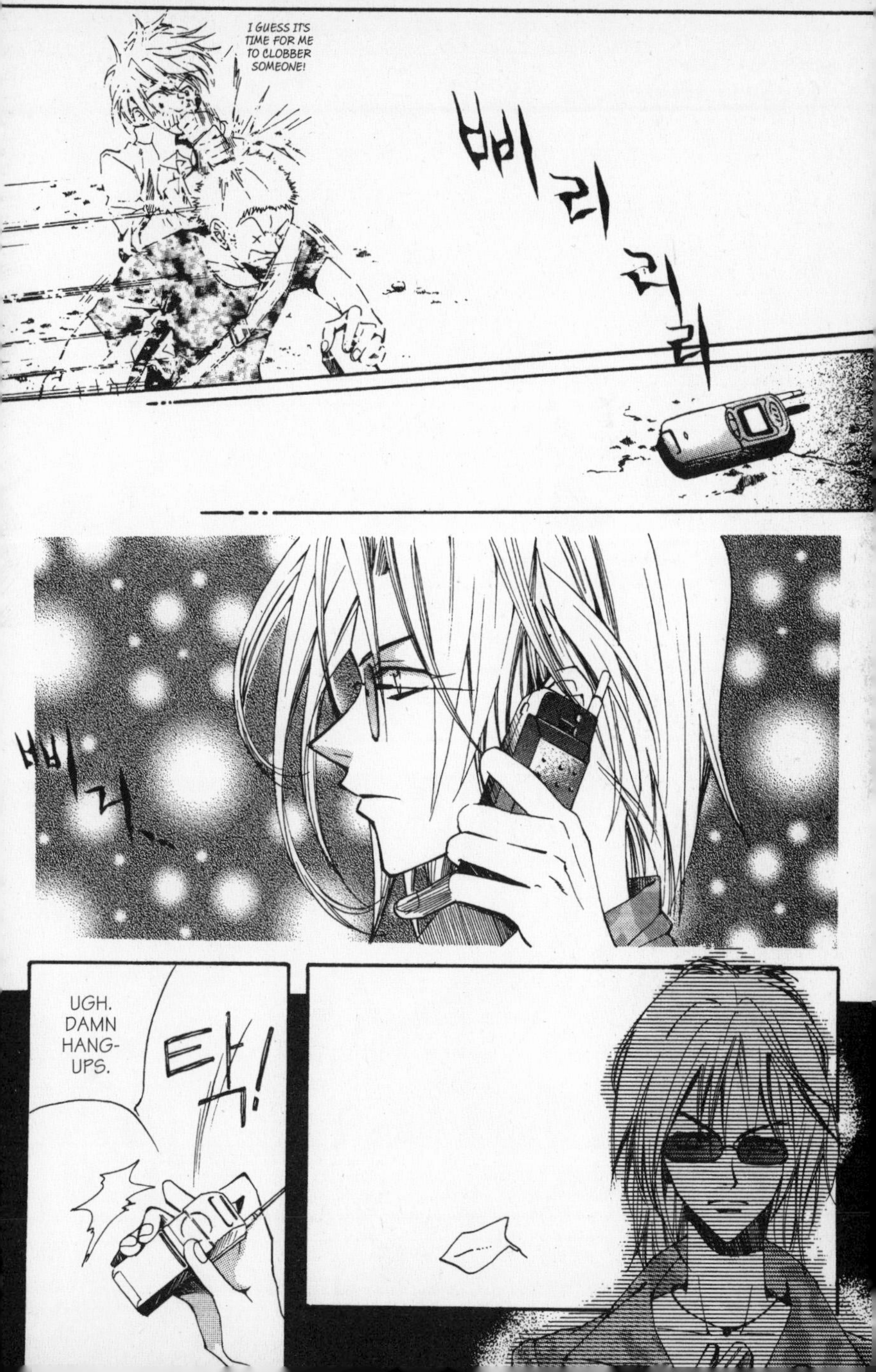
I GUESS IT'S TIME FOR ME TO CLOBBER SOMEONE!
삐리리리
삐리...
UGH. DAMN HANG-UPS.
탁!

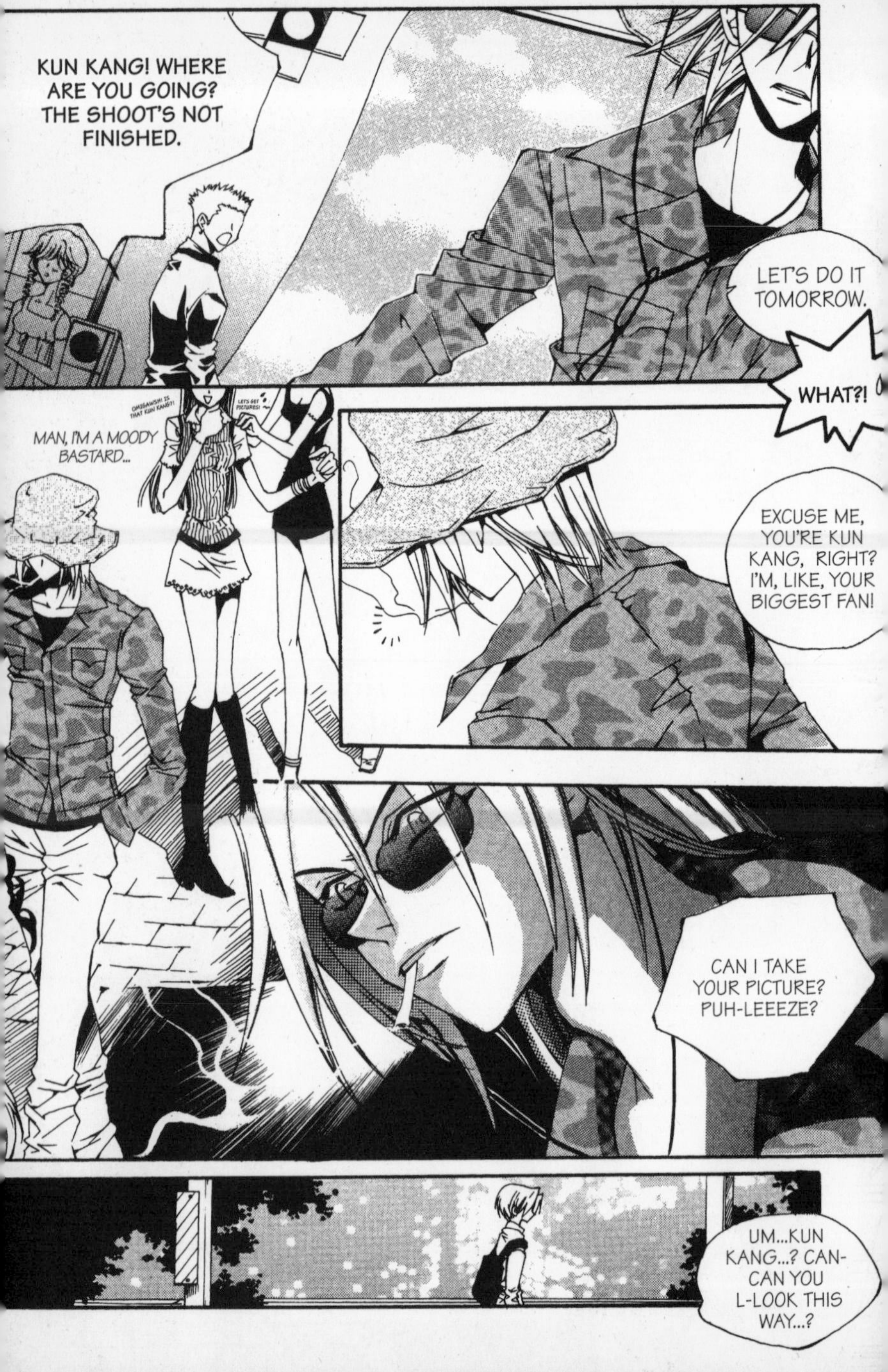
KUN KANG! WHERE ARE YOU GOING? THE SHOOT'S NOT FINISHED.
LET'S DO IT TOMORROW.
WHAT?!
MAN, I'M A MOODY BASTARD...
OMIGAWSH! IS THAT KUN KANG?!
LET'S GET PICTURES!
EXCUSE ME, YOU'RE KUN KANG, RIGHT? I'M, LIKE, YOUR BIGGEST FAN!
CAN I TAKE YOUR PICTURE? PUH-LEEEZE?
UM...KUN KANG...? CAN-CAN YOU L-LOOK THIS WAY...?

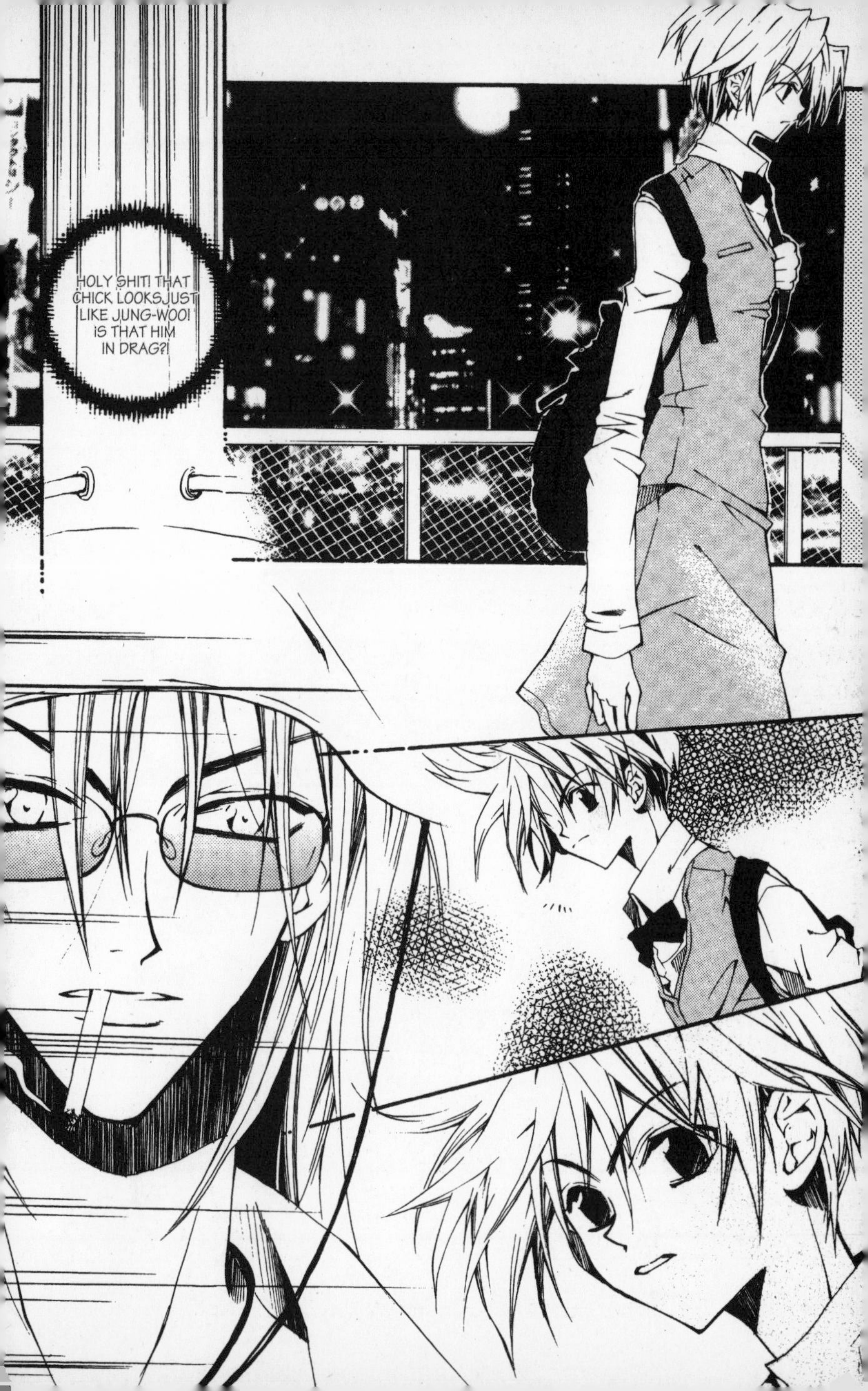
HOLY SHIT! THAT CHICK LOOKS JUST LIKE JUNG-WOO! IS THAT HIM IN DRAG?!

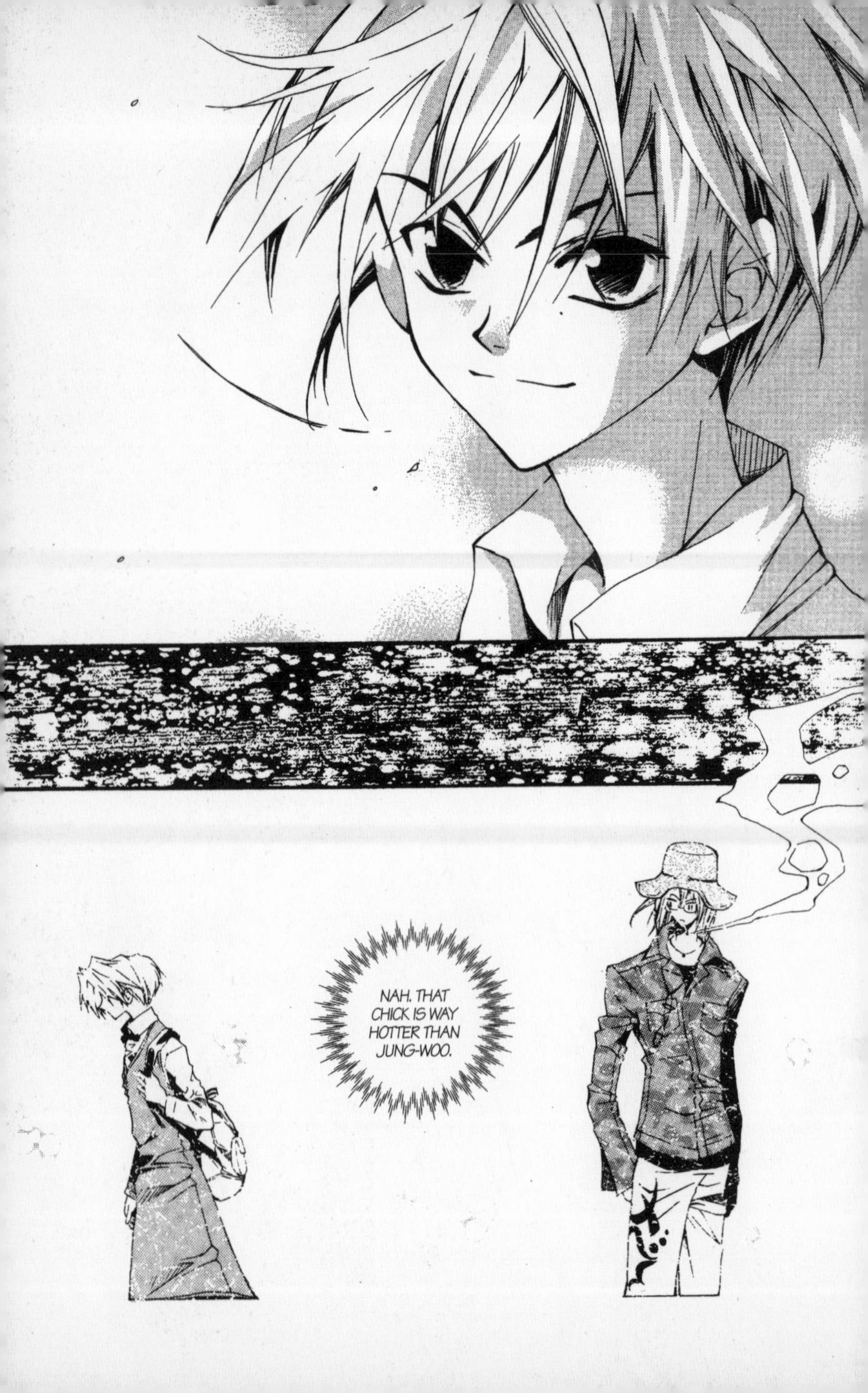
NAH. THAT CHICK IS WAY HOTTER THAN JUNG-WOO.

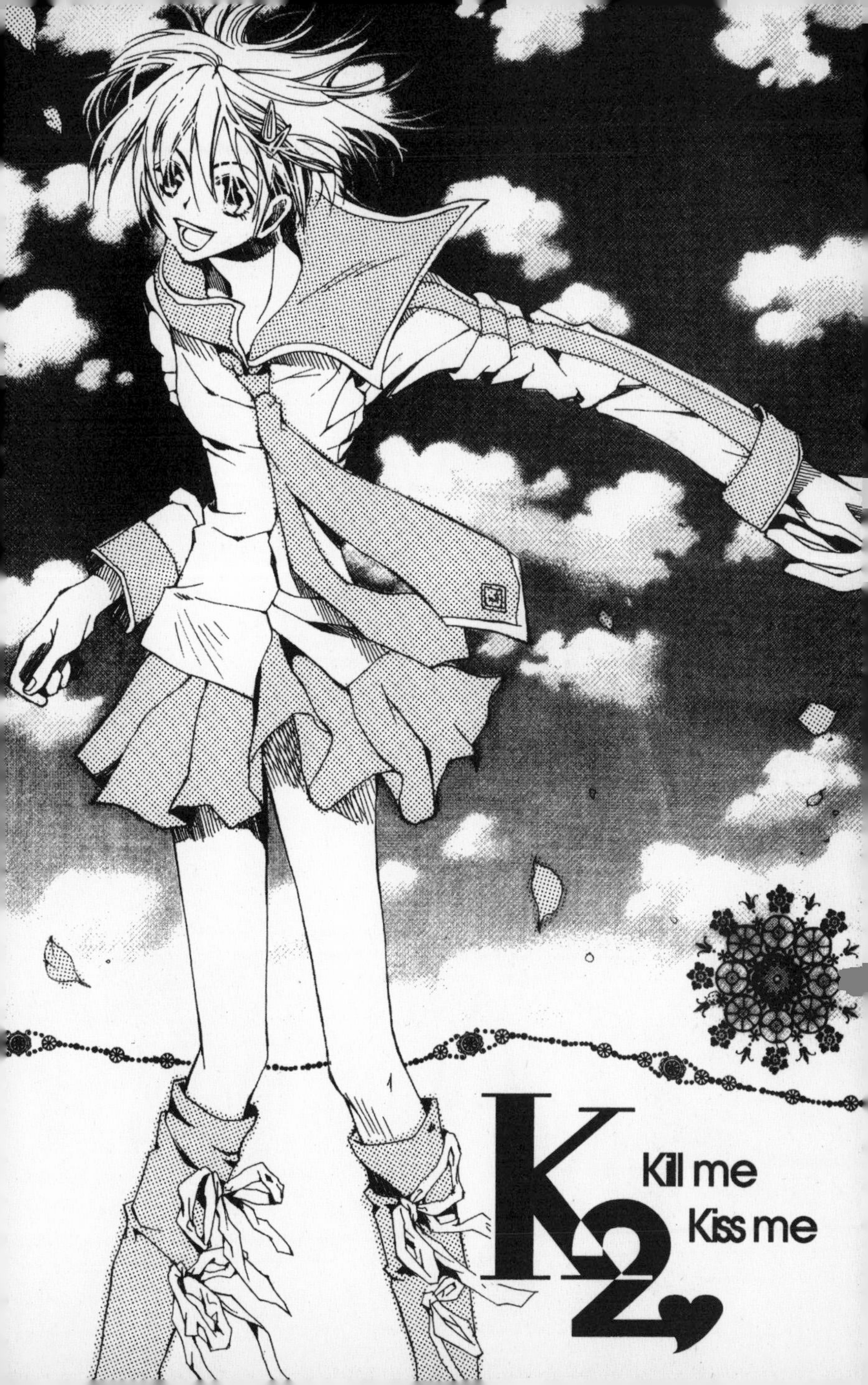
K2
Kill me
Kiss me

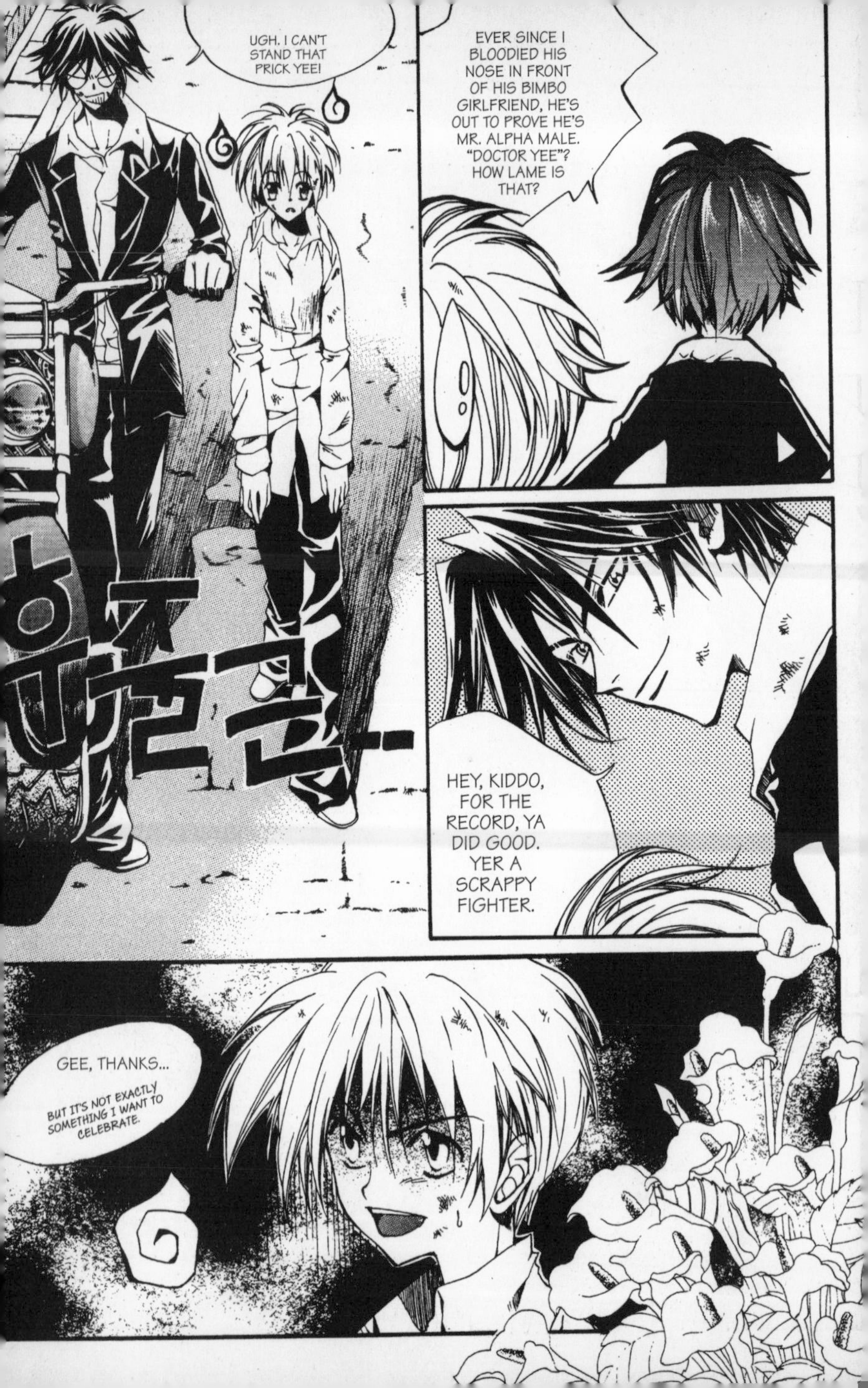
UGH. I CAN'T STAND THAT PRICK YEE!
EVER SINCE I BLOODIED HIS NOSE IN FRONT OF HIS BIMBO GIRLFRIEND, HE'S OUT TO PROVE HE'S MR. ALPHA MALE. "DOCTOR YEE"? HOW LAME IS THAT?
HEY, KIDDO, FOR THE RECORD, YA DID GOOD. YER A SCRAPPY FIGHTER.
GEE, THANKS...
BUT IT'S NOT EXACTLY SOMETHING I WANT TO CELEBRATE.

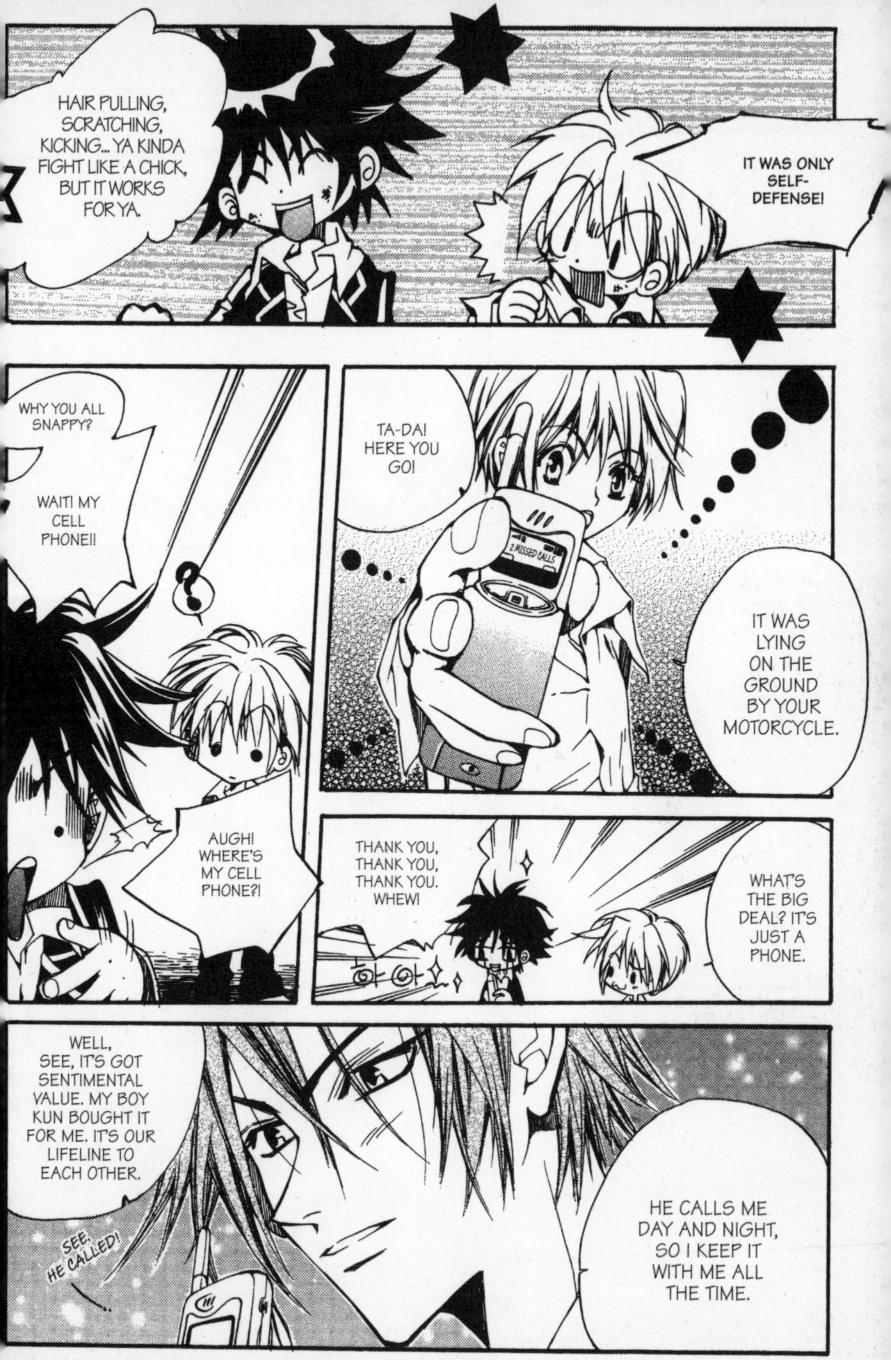

HAIR PULLING, SCRATCHING, KICKING... YA KINDA FIGHT LIKE A CHICK, BUT IT WORKS FOR YA.
IT WAS ONLY SELF-DEFENSE!
WHY YOU ALL SNAPPY?
WAIT! MY CELL PHONE!!
AUGH! WHERE'S MY CELL PHONE?!
TA-DA! HERE YOU GO!
2 MISSED CALLS
IT WAS LYING ON THE GROUND BY YOUR MOTORCYCLE.
THANK YOU, THANK YOU, THANK YOU. WHEW!
WHAT'S THE BIG DEAL? IT'S JUST A PHONE.
WELL, SEE, IT'S GOT SENTIMENTAL VALUE. MY BOY KUN BOUGHT IT FOR ME. IT'S OUR LIFELINE TO EACH OTHER.
SEE, HE CALLED!
HE CALLS ME DAY AND NIGHT, SO I KEEP IT WITH ME ALL THE TIME.

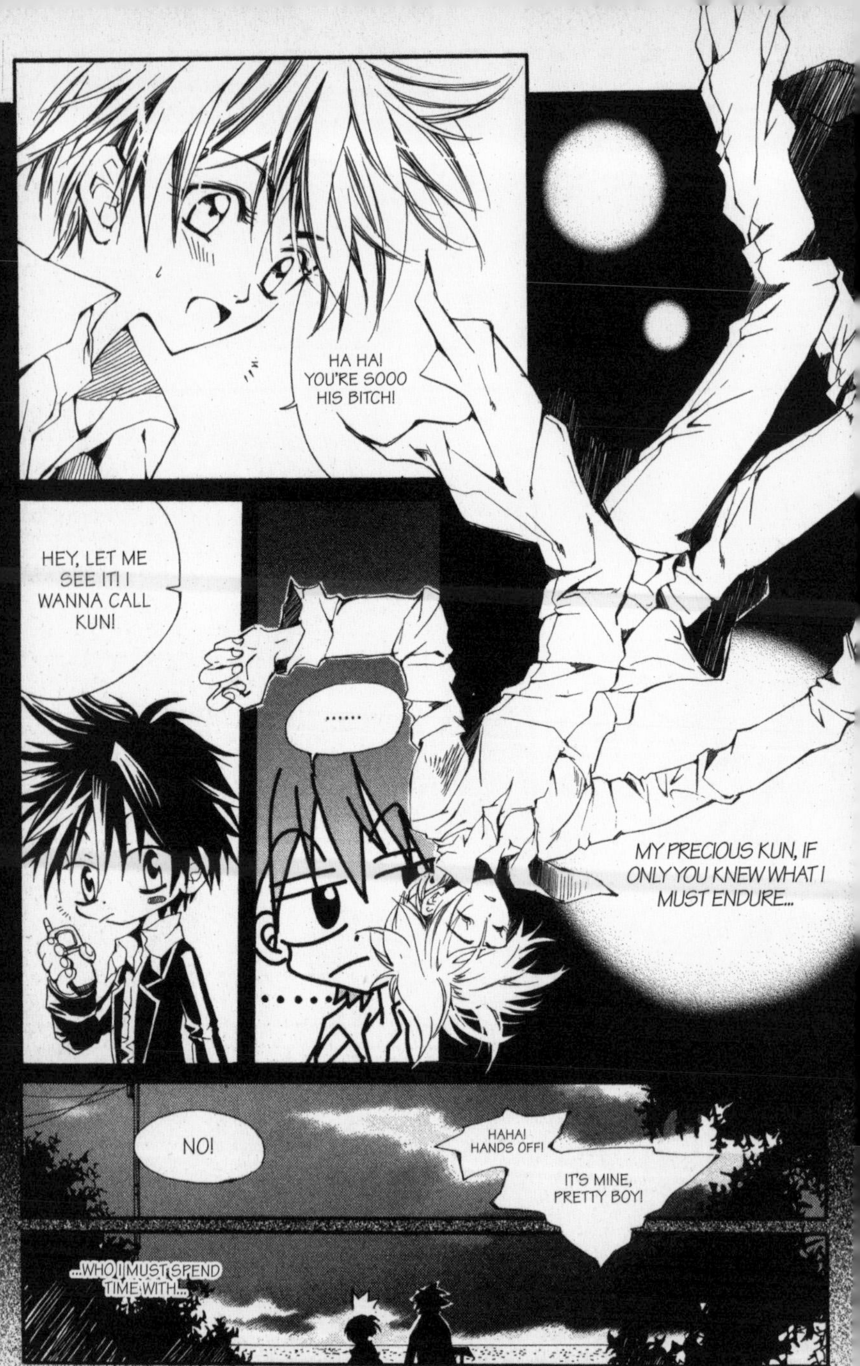
HA HA! YOU'RE SOOO HIS BITCH!
HEY, LET ME SEE IT! I WANNA CALL KUN!
......
....
MY PRECIOUS KUN, IF ONLY YOU KNEW WHAT I MUST ENDURE...
NO!
HAHA! HANDS OFF!
IT'S MINE, PRETTY BOY!
...WHO I MUST SPEND TIME WITH...

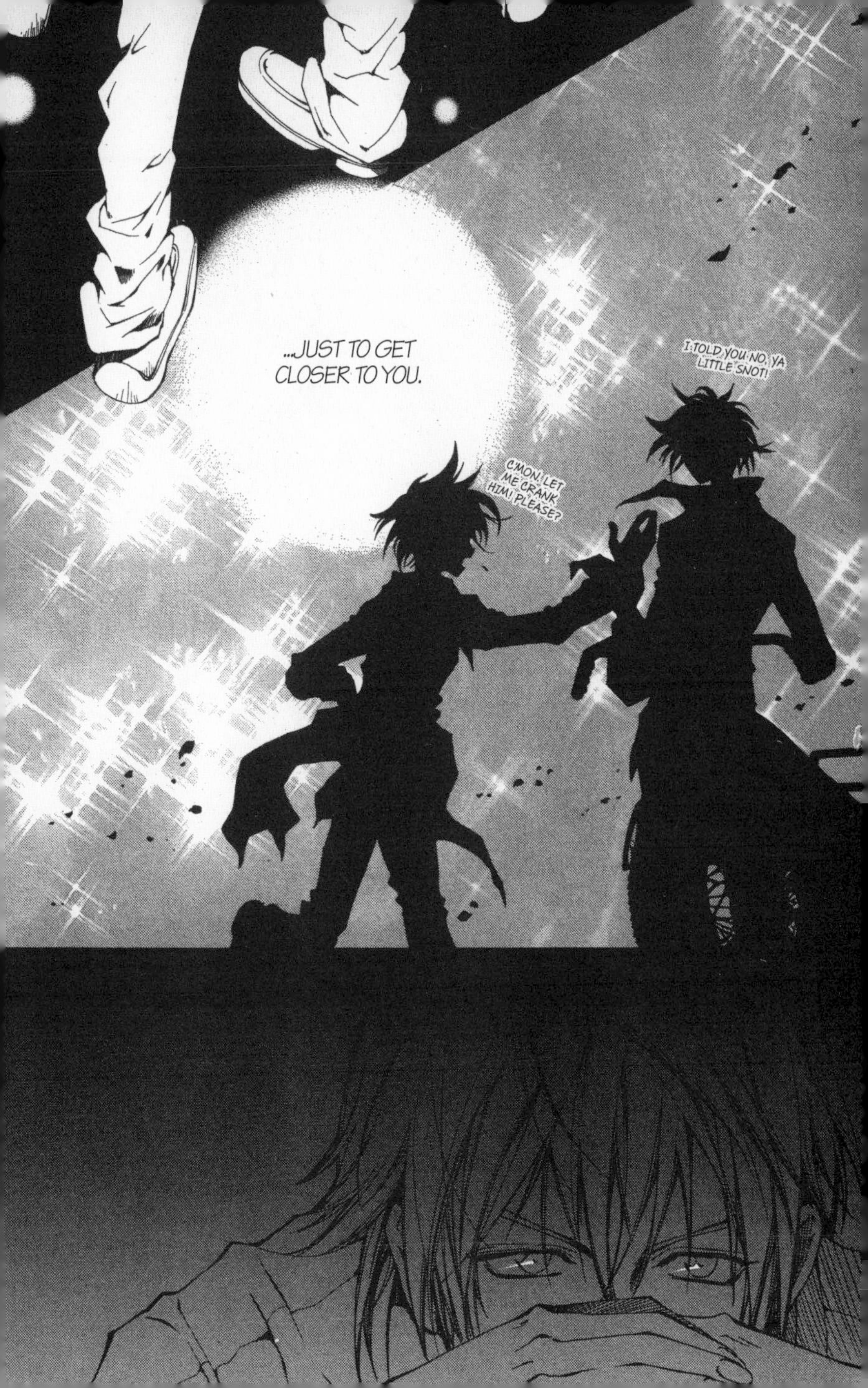
...JUST TO GET CLOSER TO YOU.
C'MON, LET ME CRANK HIM! PLEASE?
I TOLD YOU NO, YA LITTLE SNOT!

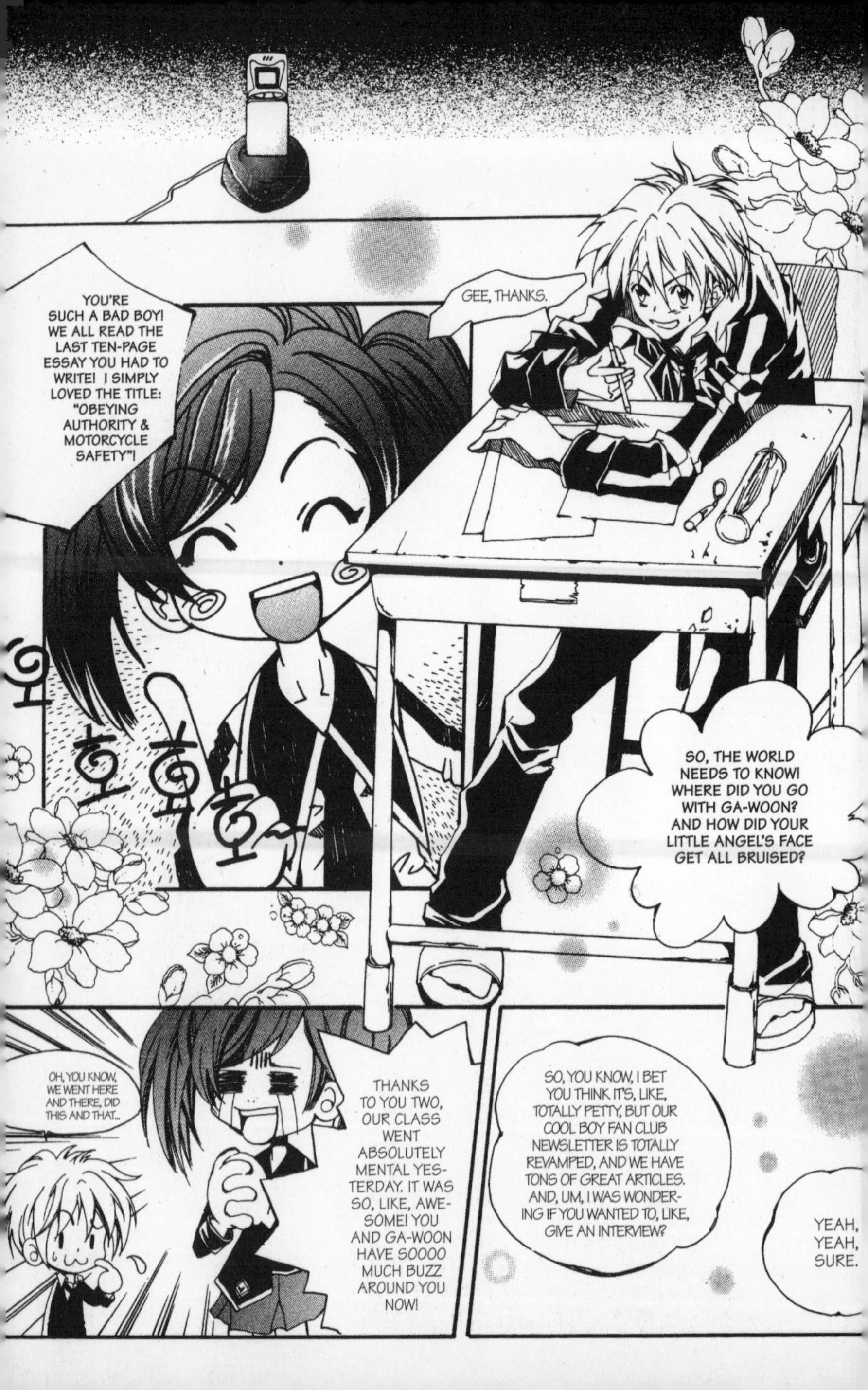
YOU'RE SUCH A BAD BOY! WE ALL READ THE LAST TEN-PAGE ESSAY YOU HAD TO WRITE! I SIMPLY LOVED THE TITLE: "OBEYING AUTHORITY & MOTORCYCLE SAFETY"!
GEE, THANKS.
SO, THE WORLD NEEDS TO KNOW! WHERE DID YOU GO WITH GA-WOON? AND HOW DID YOUR LITTLE ANGEL'S FACE GET ALL BRUISED?
OH, YOU KNOW, WE WENT HERE AND THERE, DID THIS AND THAT...
THANKS TO YOU TWO, OUR CLASS WENT ABSOLUTELY MENTAL YESTERDAY. IT WAS SO, LIKE, AWESOME! YOU AND GA-WOON HAVE SOOOO MUCH BUZZ AROUND YOU NOW!
SO, YOU KNOW, I BET YOU THINK IT'S, LIKE, TOTALLY PETTY, BUT OUR COOL BOY FAN CLUB NEWSLETTER IS TOTALLY REVAMPED, AND WE HAVE TONS OF GREAT ARTICLES. AND, UM, I WAS WONDERING IF YOU WANTED TO, LIKE, GIVE AN INTERVIEW?
YEAH, YEAH, SURE.

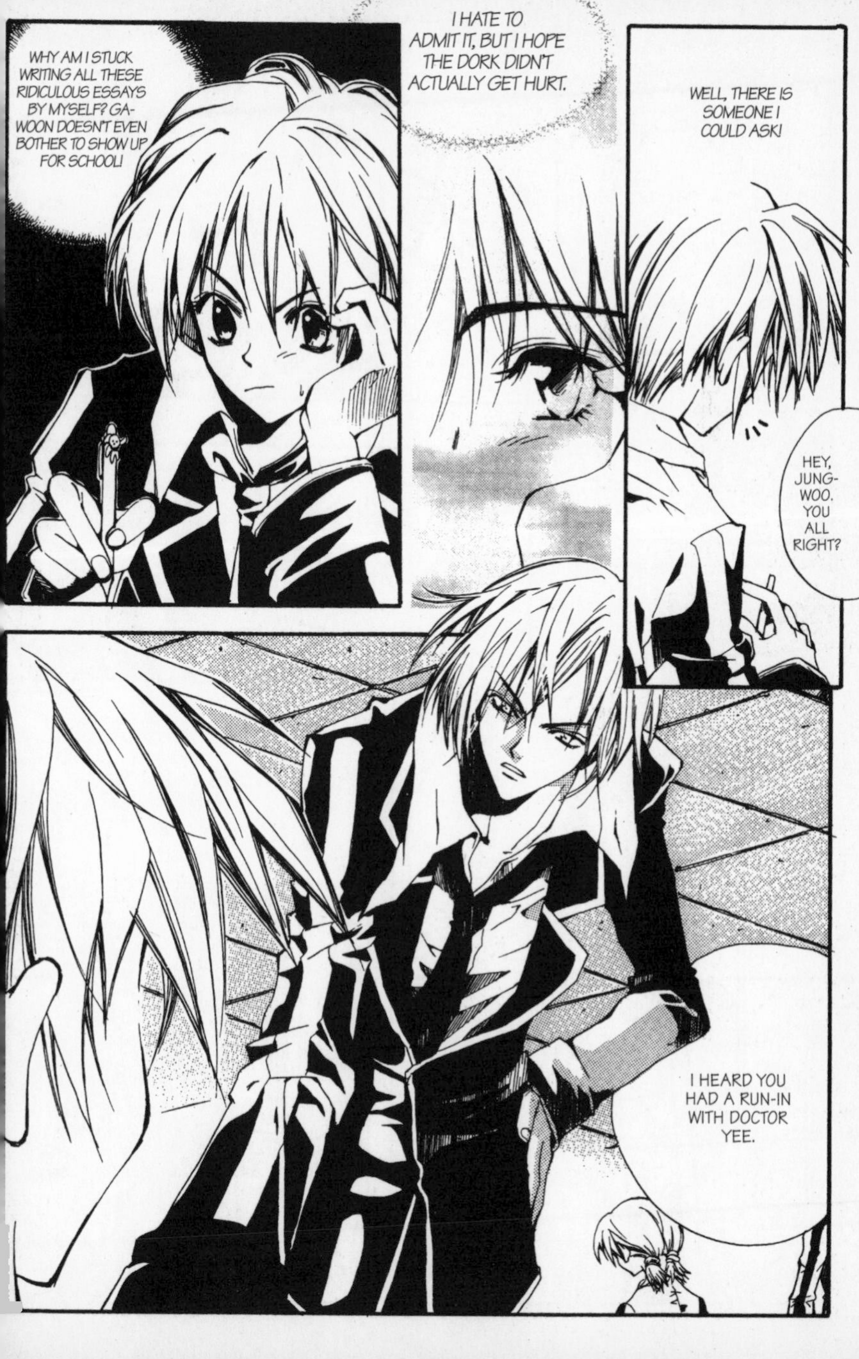
WHY AM I STUCK WRITING ALL THESE RIDICULOUS ESSAYS BY MYSELF? GA-WOON DOESN'T EVEN BOTHER TO SHOW UP FOR SCHOOL!
I HATE TO ADMIT IT, BUT I HOPE THE DORK DIDN'T ACTUALLY GET HURT.
WELL, THERE IS SOMEONE I COULD ASK!
HEY, JUNG-WOO. YOU ALL RIGHT?
I HEARD YOU HAD A RUN-IN WITH DOCTOR YEE.

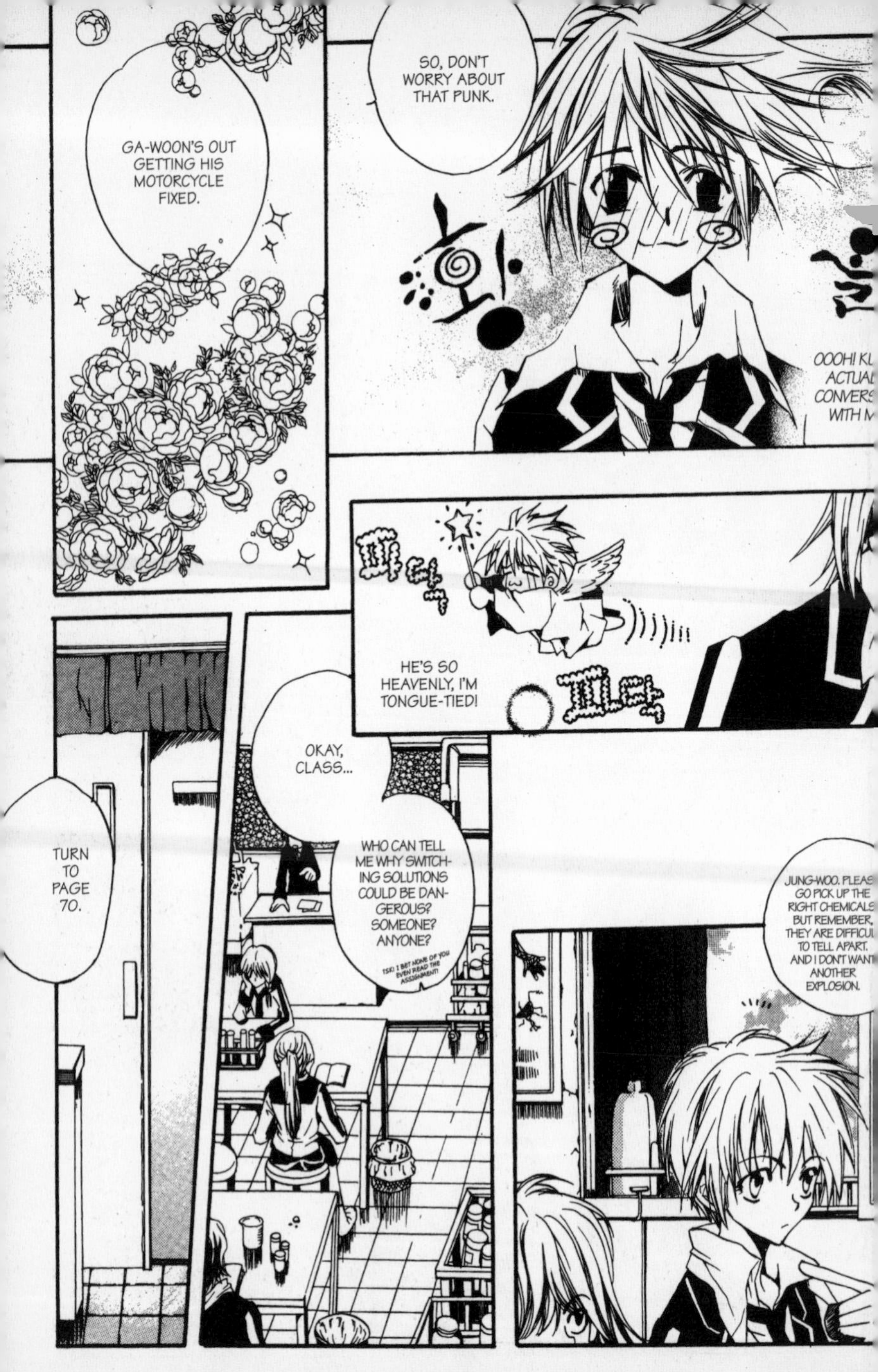
GA-WOON'S OUT GETTING HIS MOTORCYCLE FIXED.
SO, DON'T WORRY ABOUT THAT PUNK.
HE'S SO HEAVENLY, I'M TONGUE-TIED!
TURN TO PAGE 70.
OKAY, CLASS...
WHO CAN TELL ME WHY SWITCHING SOLUTIONS COULD BE DANGEROUS? SOMEONE? ANYONE?
TSK! I BET NONE OF YOU EVEN READ THE ASSIGNMENT!

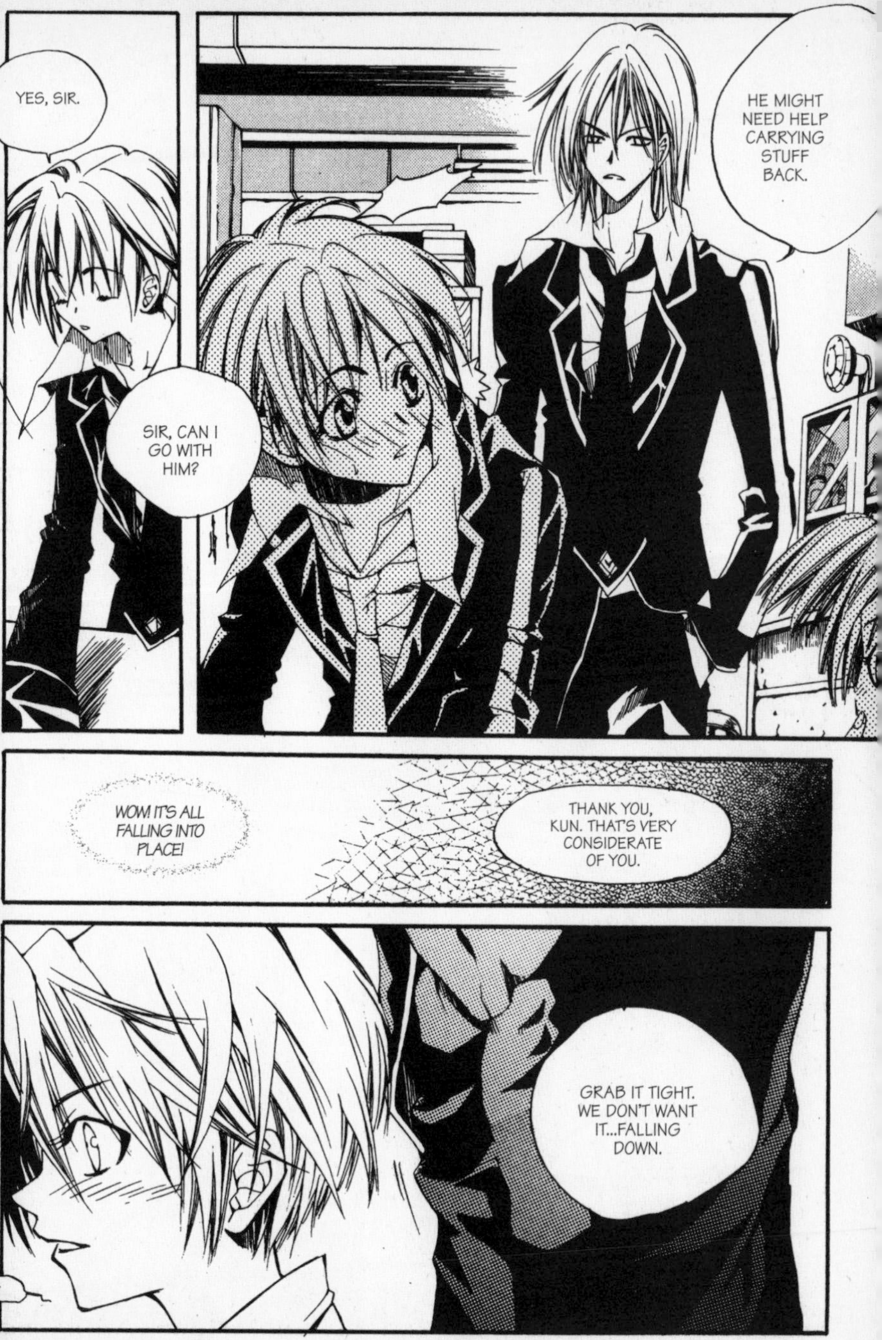
HE MIGHT NEED HELP CARRYING STUFF BACK.
SIR, CAN I GO WITH HIM?
YES, SIR.
THANK YOU, KUN. THAT'S VERY CONSIDERATE OF YOU.
WOW! IT'S ALL FALLING INTO PLACE!
GRAB IT TIGHT. WE DON'T WANT IT...FALLING DOWN.

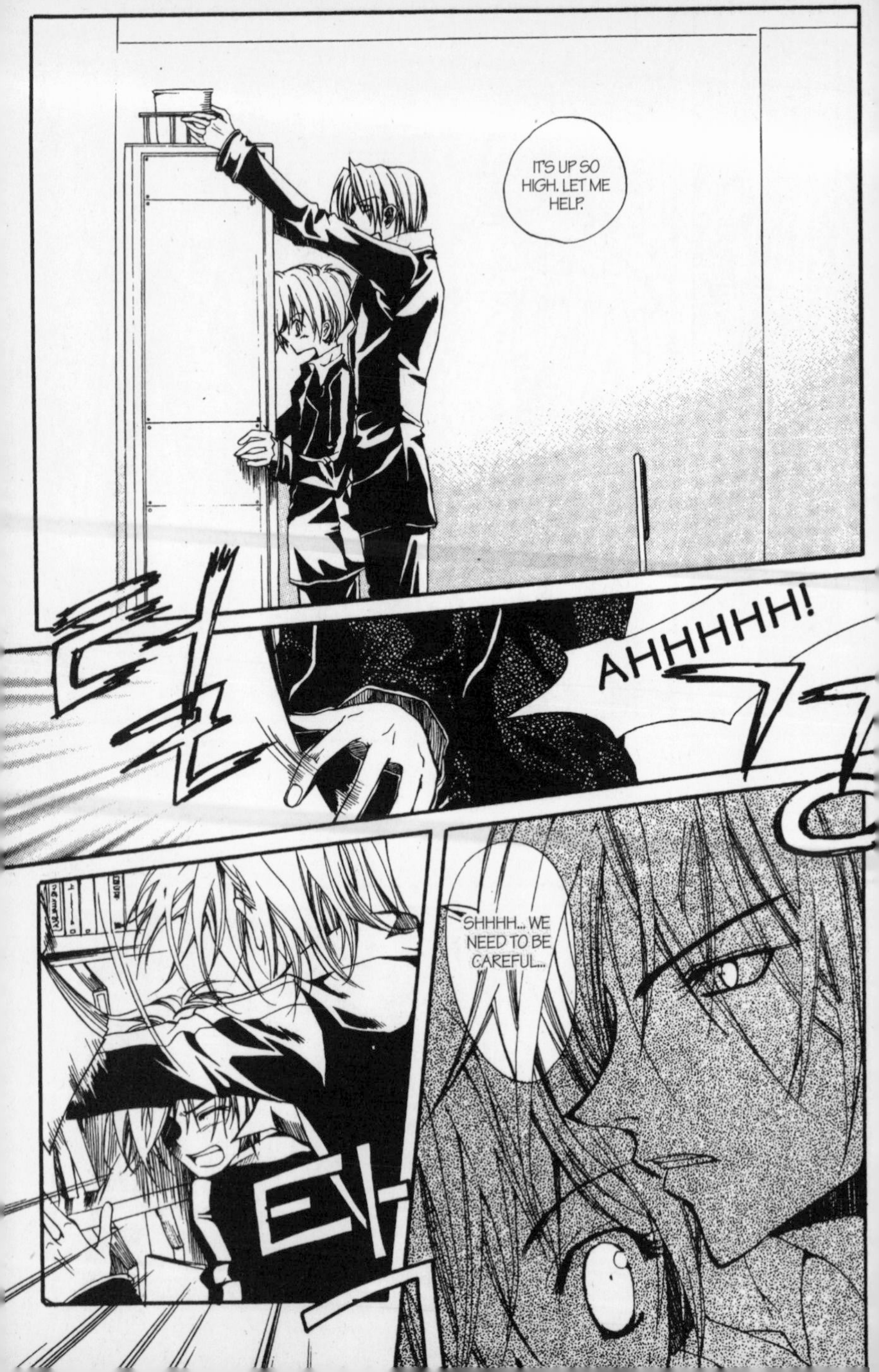
IT'S UP SO HIGH. LET ME HELP.
AHHHHH!
SHHHH... WE NEED TO BE CAREFUL...

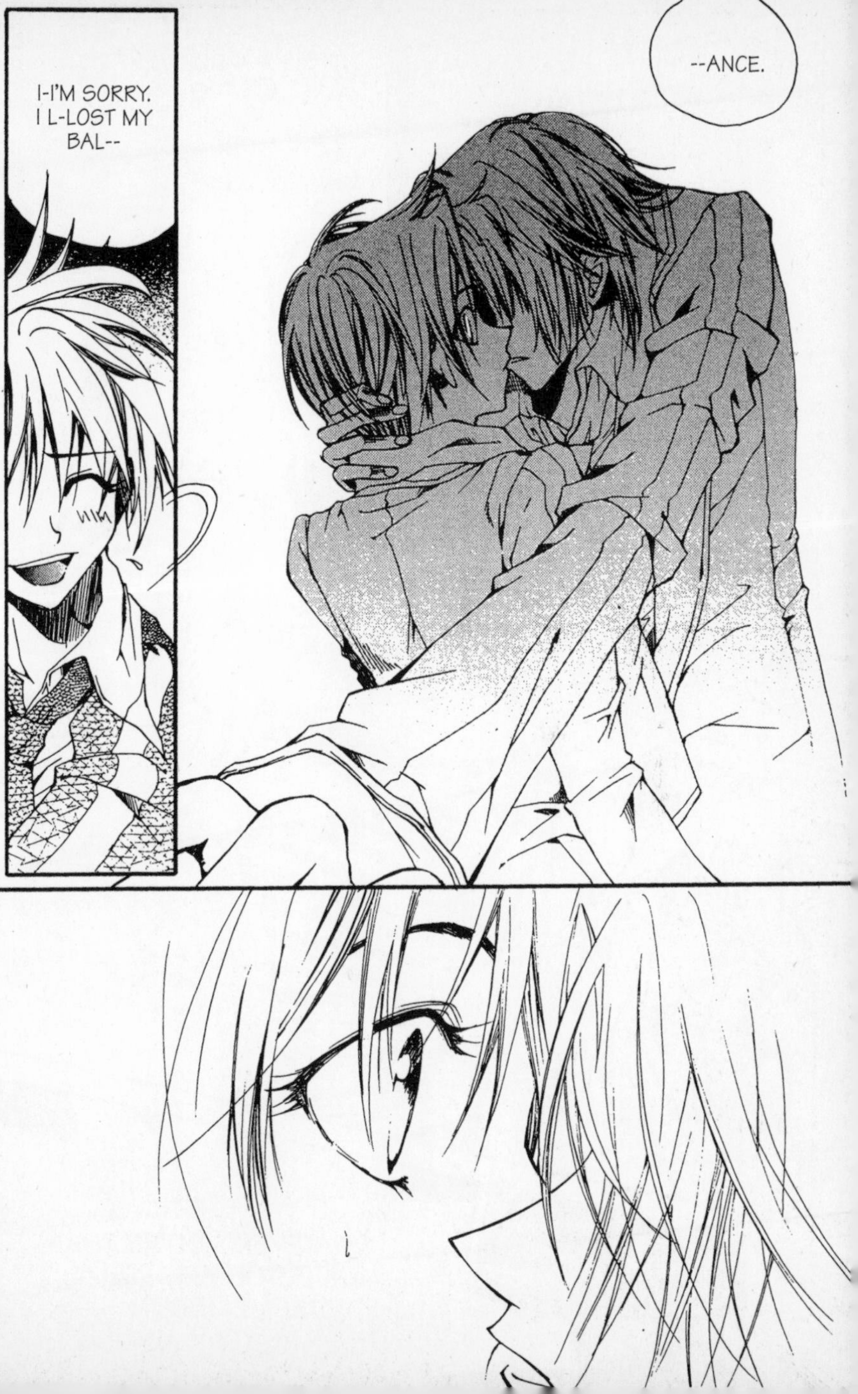
I-I'M SORRY. I L-LOST MY BAL--
--ANCE.

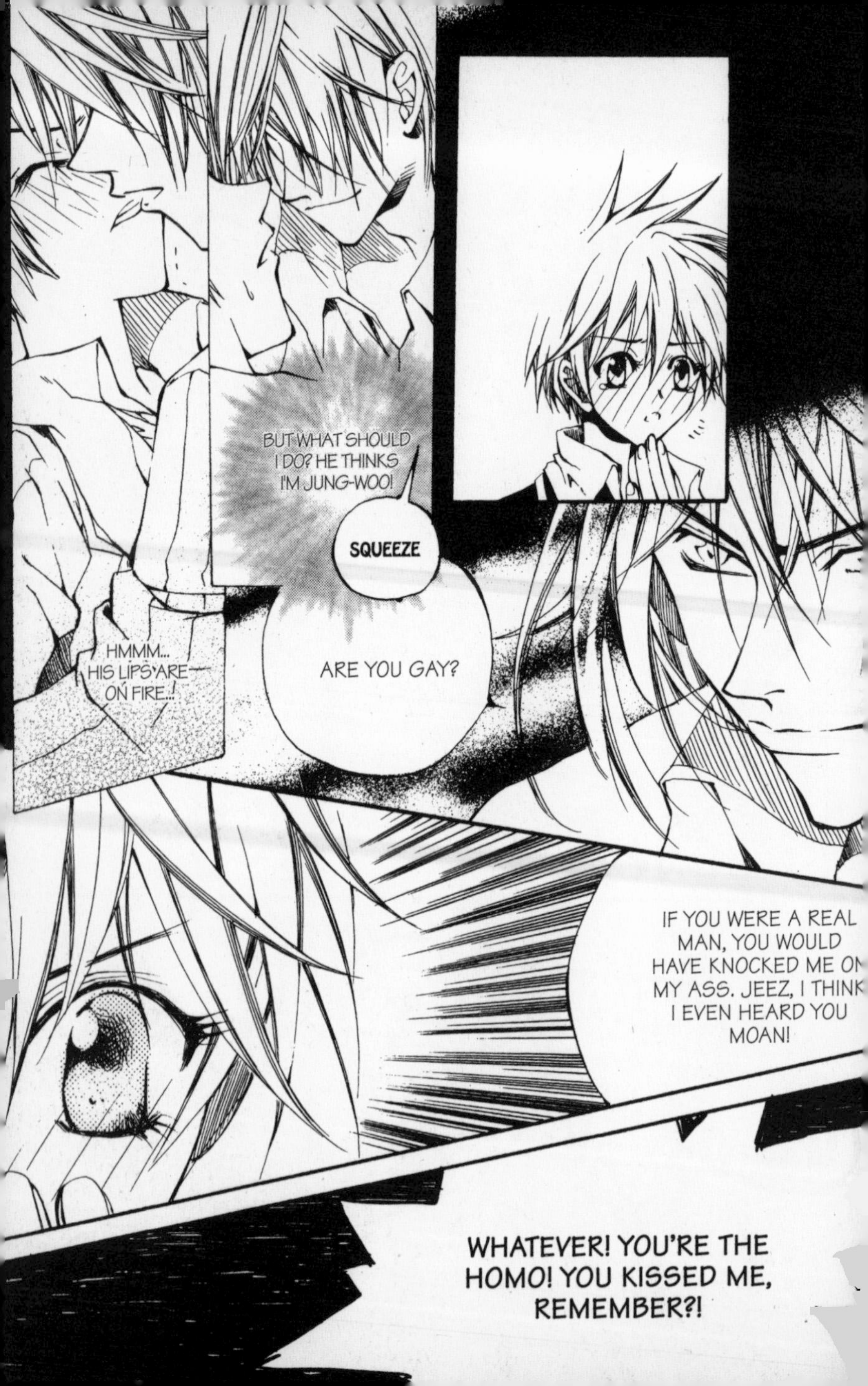
HMMM... HIS LIPS ARE ON FIRE..!
BUT WHAT SHOULD I DO? HE THINKS I'M JUNG-WOO!
SQUEEZE
ARE YOU GAY?
IF YOU WERE A REAL MAN, YOU WOULD HAVE KNOCKED ME ON MY ASS. JEEZ, I THINK I EVEN HEARD YOU MOAN!
WHATEVER! YOU'RE THE HOMO! YOU KISSED ME, REMEMBER?!

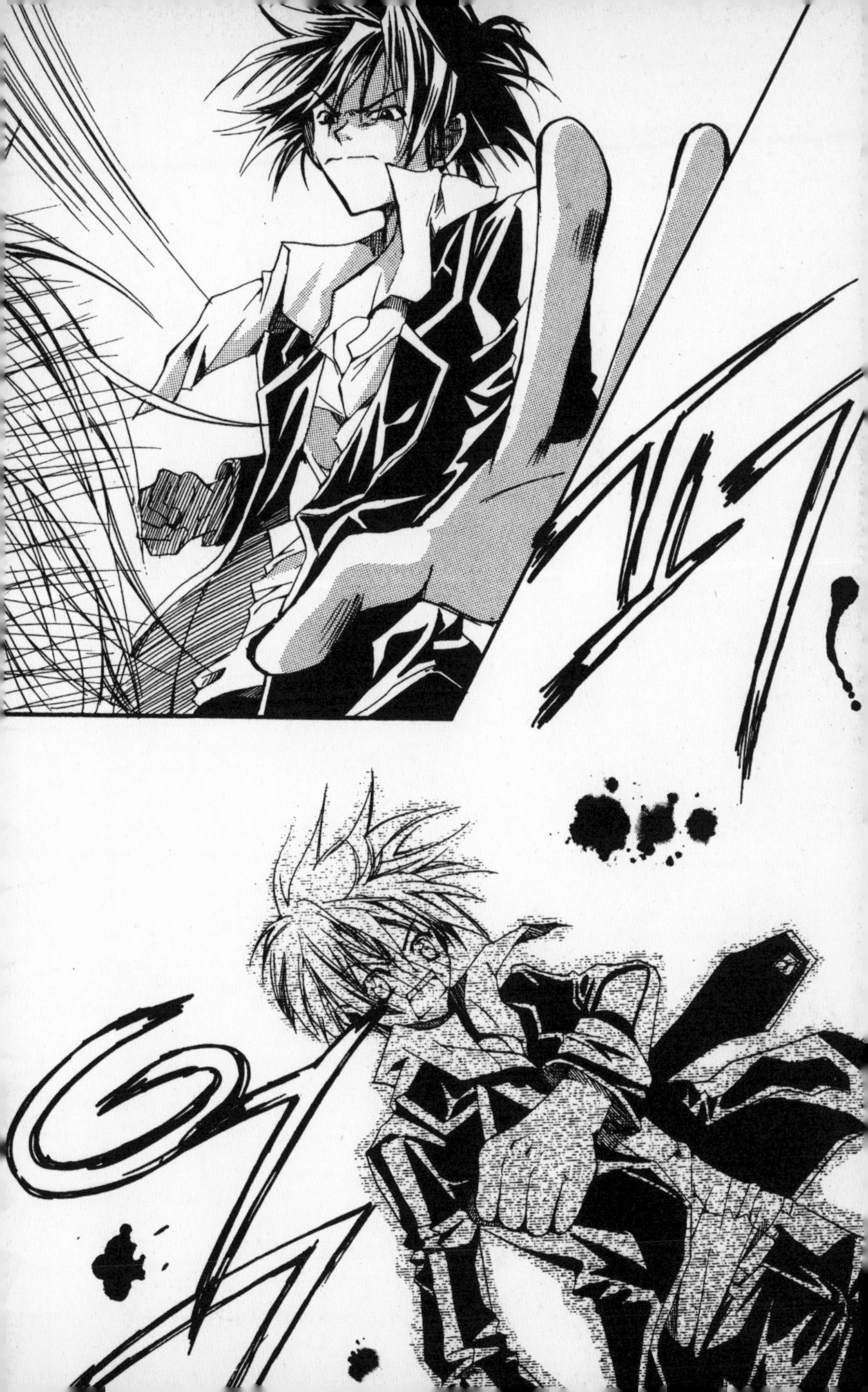

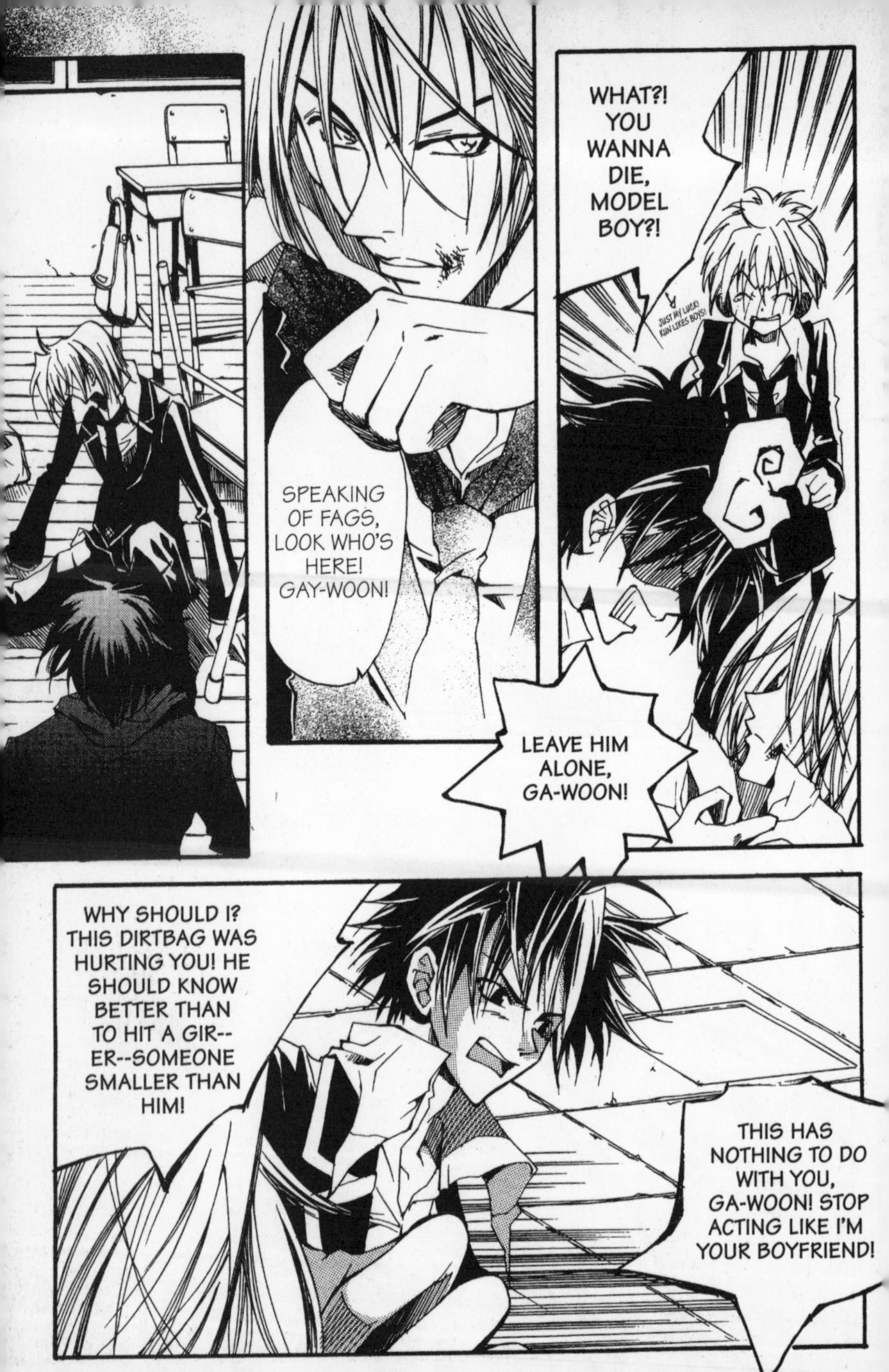
SPEAKING OF FAGS, LOOK WHO'S HERE! GAY-WOON!
WHAT?! YOU WANNA DIE, MODEL BOY?!
JUST MY LUCK! KUN LIKES BOYS!
LEAVE HIM ALONE, GA-WOON!
WHY SHOULD I? THIS DIRTBAG WAS HURTING YOU! HE SHOULD KNOW BETTER THAN TO HIT A GIR-- ER--SOMEONE SMALLER THAN HIM!
THIS HAS NOTHING TO DO WITH YOU, GA-WOON! STOP ACTING LIKE I'M YOUR BOYFRIEND!

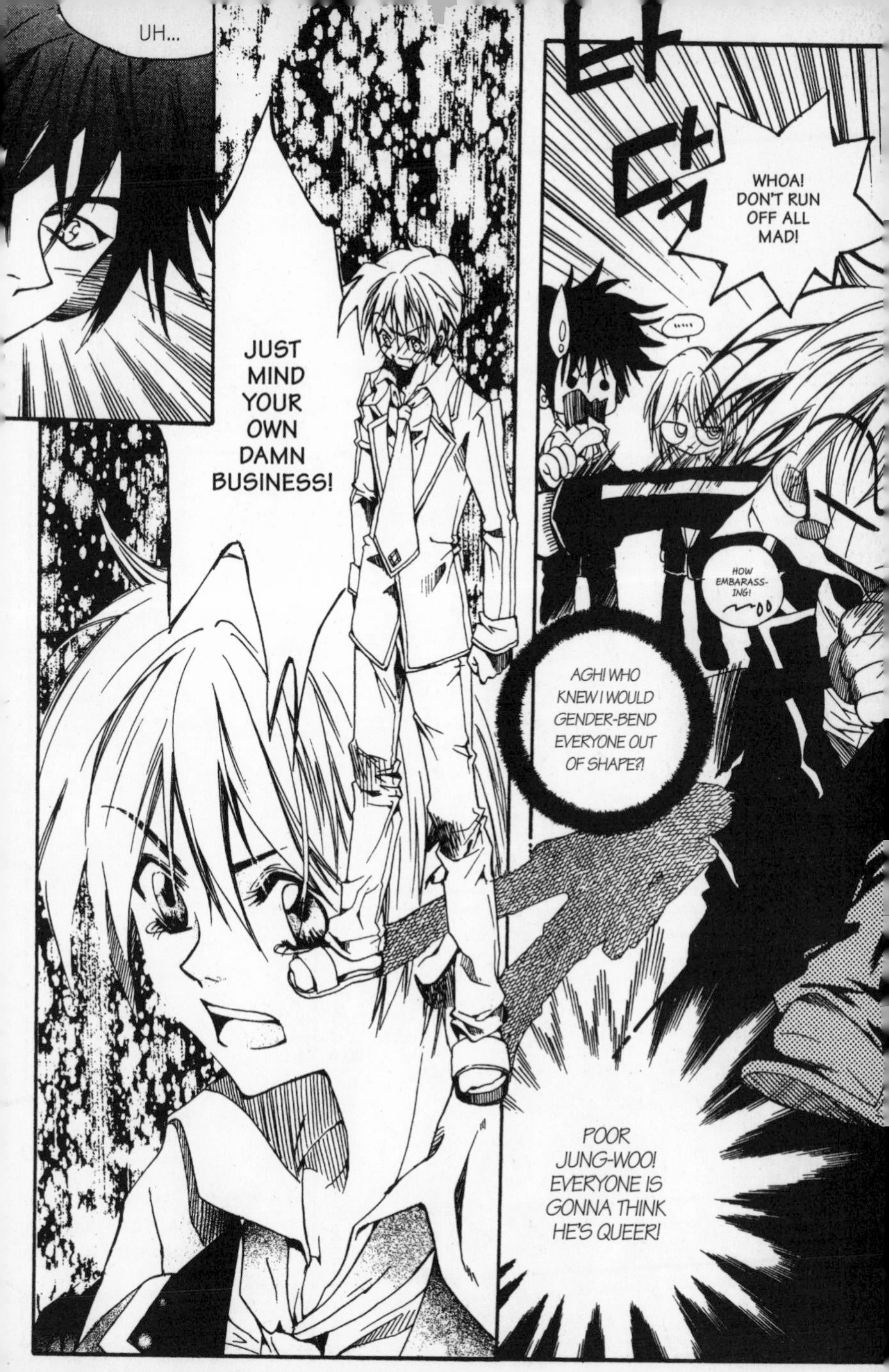
UH...
JUST MIND YOUR OWN DAMN BUSINESS!
WHOA! DON'T RUN OFF ALL MAD!
.....
HOW EMBARASS-ING!
AGH! WHO KNEW I WOULD GENDER-BEND EVERYONE OUT OF SHAPE?!
POOR JUNG-WOO! EVERYONE IS GONNA THINK HE'S QUEER!

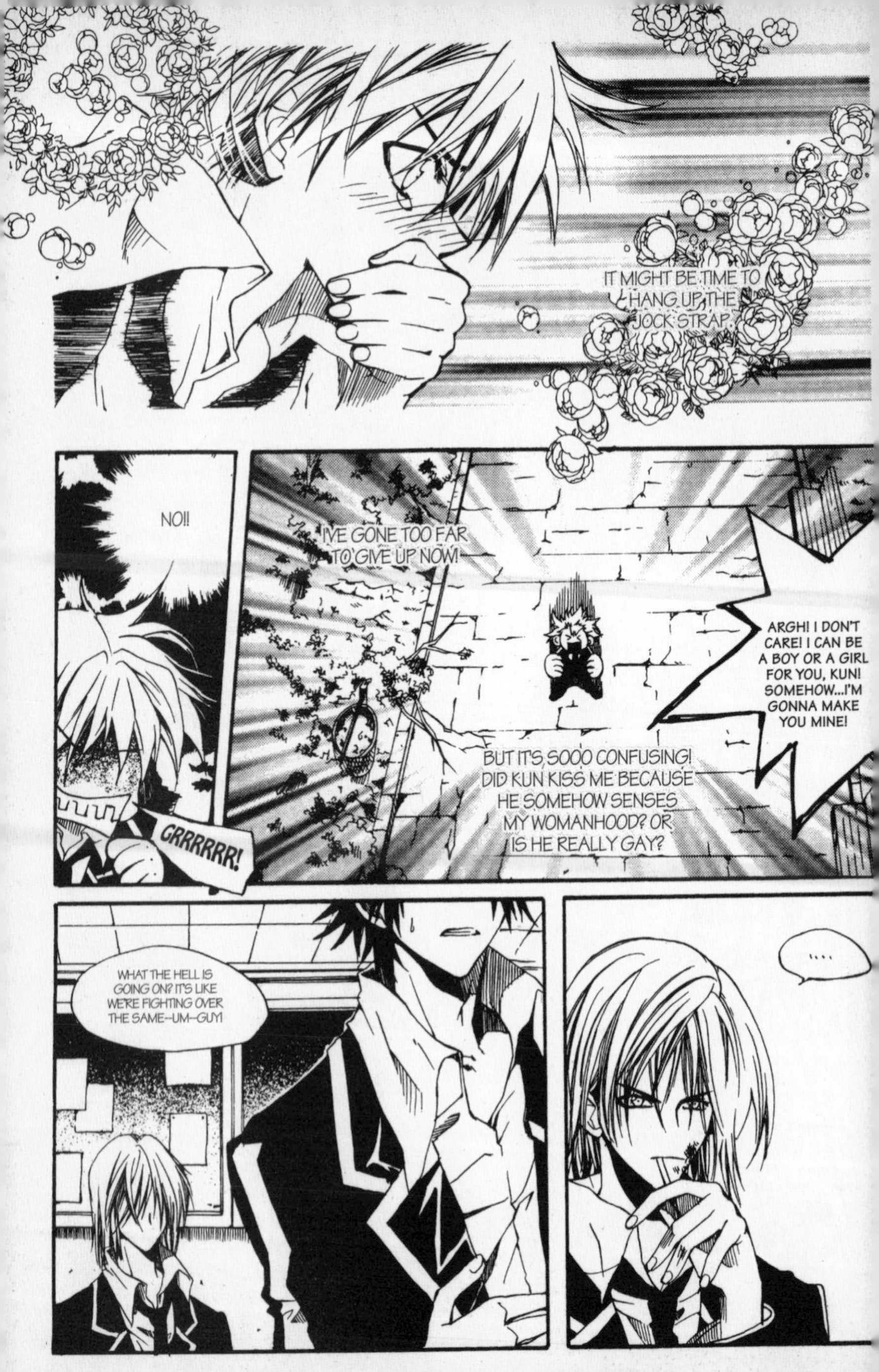
IT MIGHT BE TIME TO HANG UP THE JOCK STRAP.
NO!!
GRRRRRR!
I'VE GONE TOO FAR TO GIVE UP NOW!
BUT IT'S SOOO CONFUSING! DID KUN KISS ME BECAUSE HE SOMEHOW SENSES MY WOMANHOOD? OR IS HE REALLY GAY?
ARGH! I DON'T CARE! I CAN BE A BOY OR A GIRL FOR YOU, KUN! SOMEHOW...I'M GONNA MAKE YOU MINE!
WHAT THE HELL IS GOING ON? IT'S LIKE WE'RE FIGHTING OVER THE SAME--UM--GUY!
....

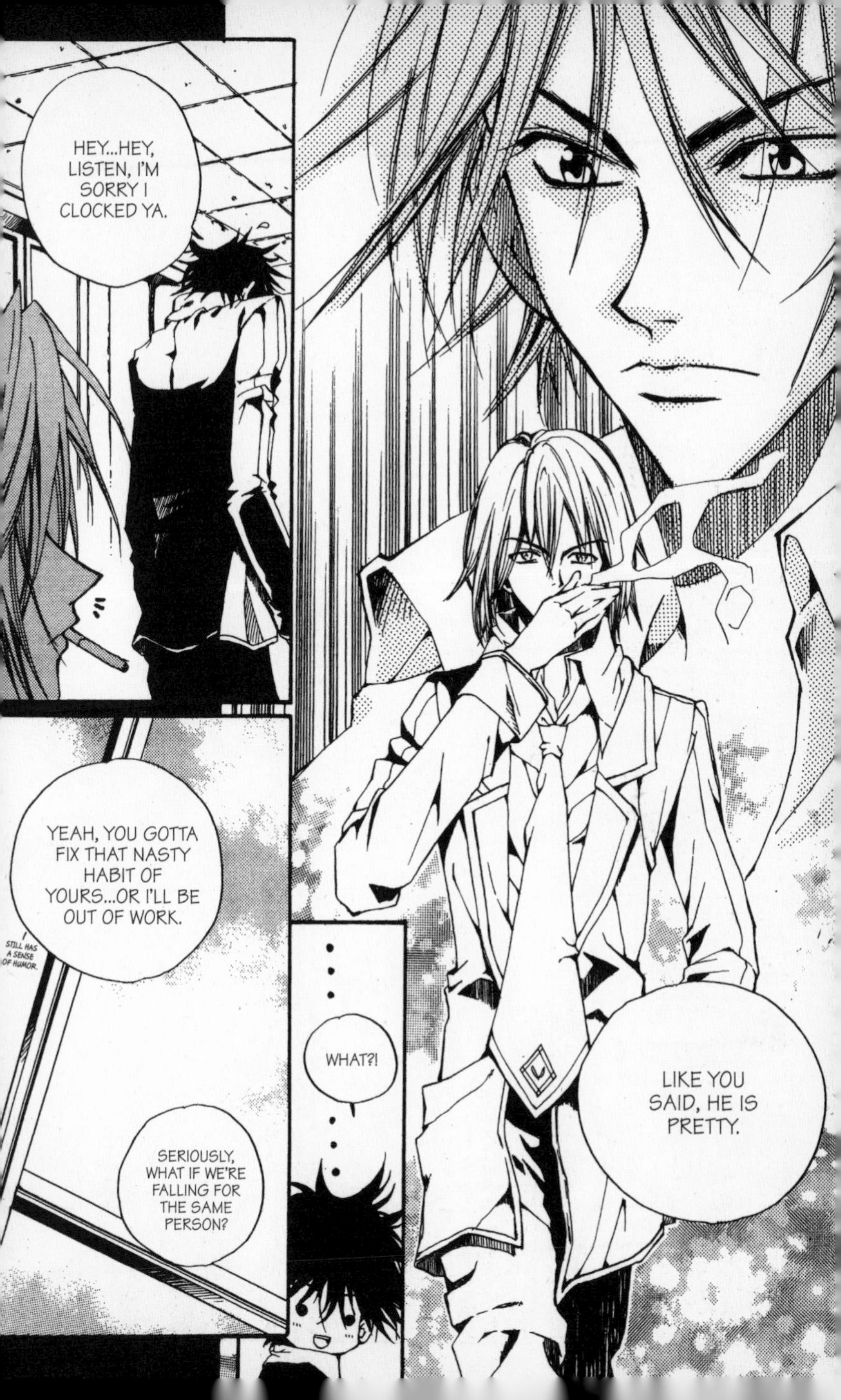
HEY...HEY, LISTEN, I'M SORRY I CLOCKED YA.
YEAH, YOU GOTTA FIX THAT NASTY HABIT OF YOURS...OR I'LL BE OUT OF WORK.
I STILL HAS A SENSE OF HUMOR.
SERIOUSLY, WHAT IF WE'RE FALLING FOR THE SAME PERSON?
...
WHAT?!
...
LIKE YOU SAID, HE IS PRETTY.

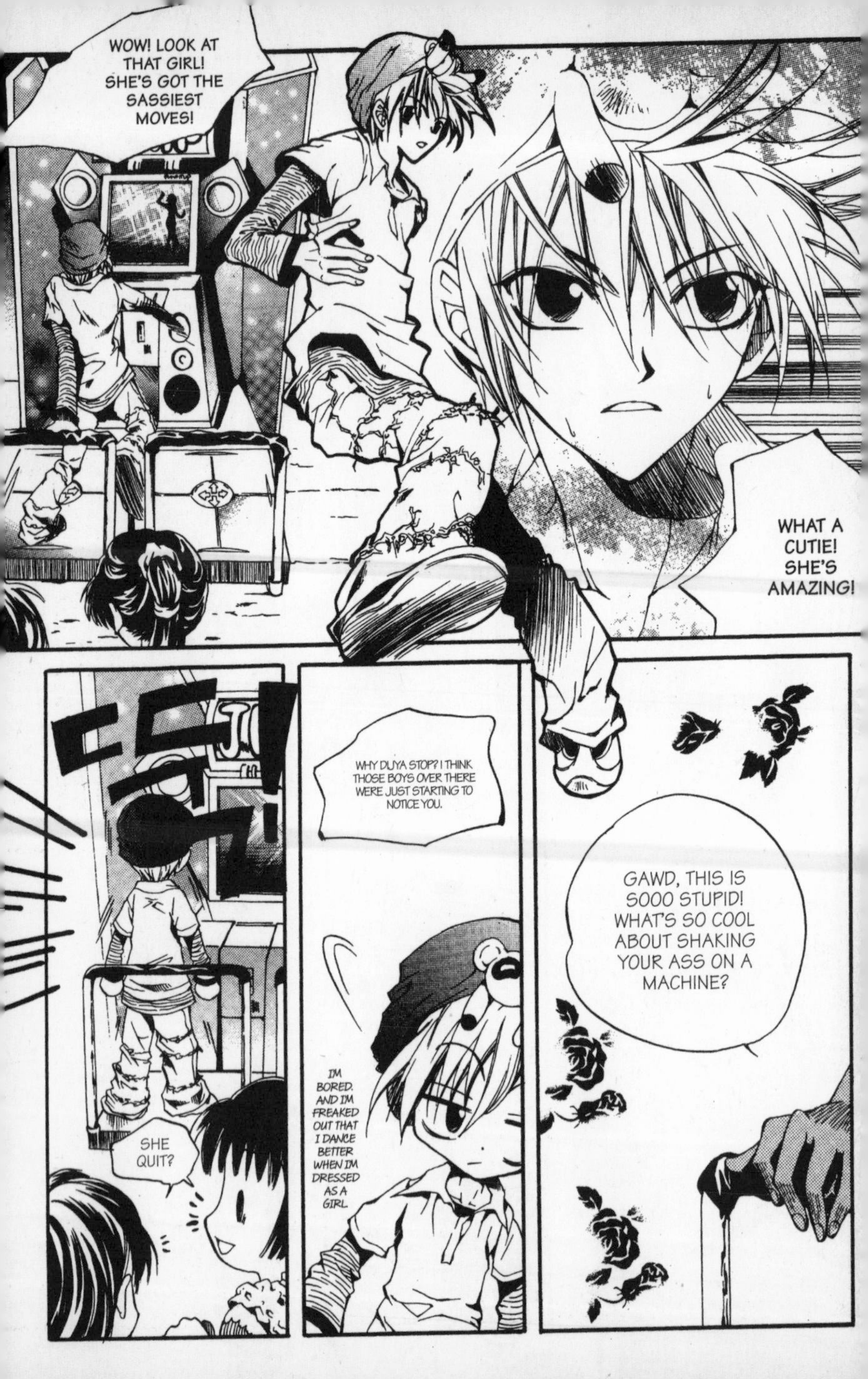
WOW! LOOK AT THAT GIRL! SHE'S GOT THE SASSIEST MOVES!
WHAT A CUTIE! SHE'S AMAZING!
SHE QUIT?
WHY DUYA STOP? I THINK THOSE BOYS OVER THERE WERE JUST STARTING TO NOTICE YOU.
I'M BORED. AND I'M FREAKED OUT THAT I DANCE BETTER WHEN I'M DRESSED AS A GIRL
GAWD, THIS IS SOOO STUPID! WHAT'S SO COOL ABOUT SHAKING YOUR ASS ON A MACHINE?

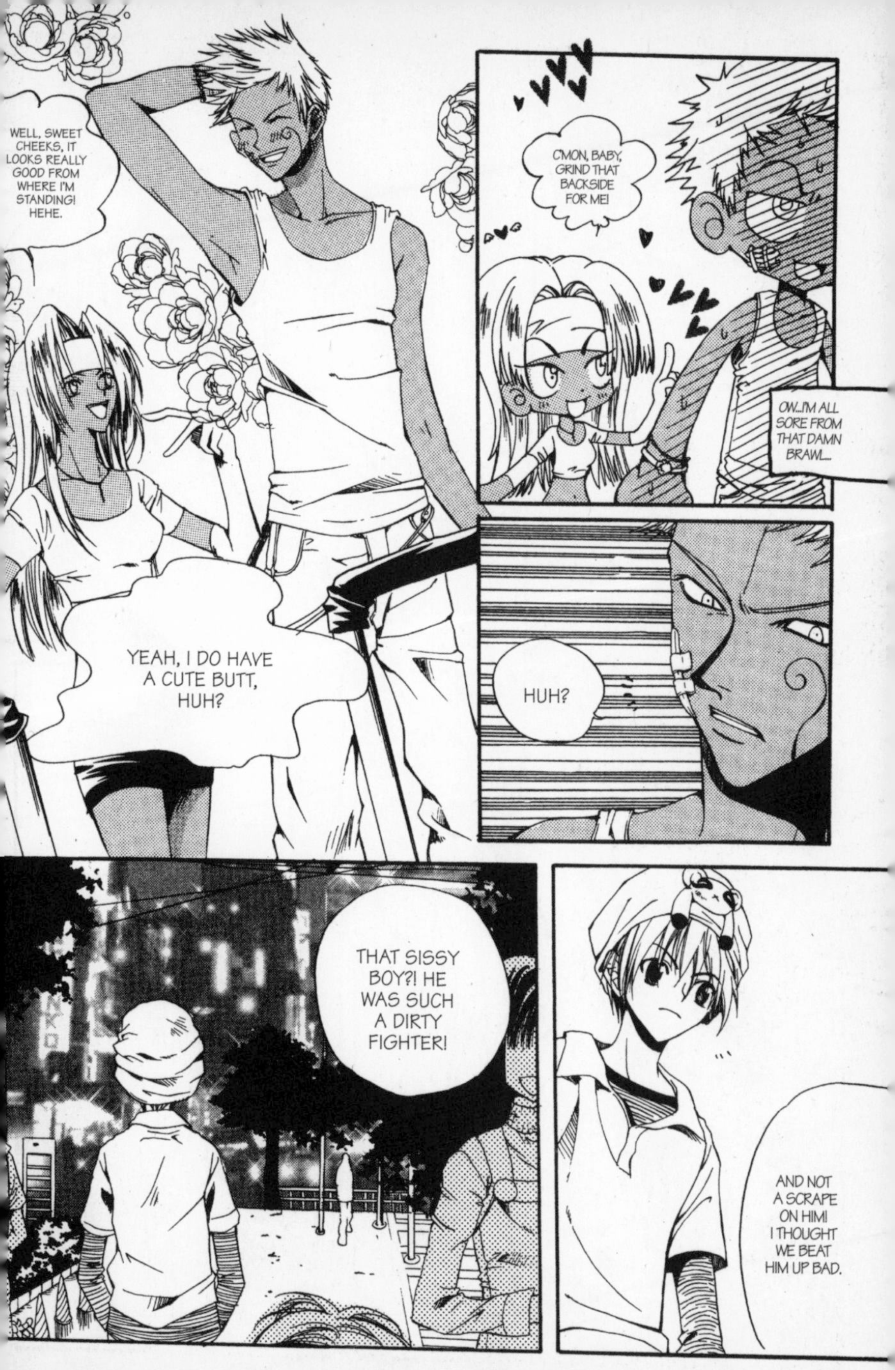
WELL, SWEET CHEEKS, IT LOOKS REALLY GOOD FROM WHERE I'M STANDING! HEHE.
YEAH, I DO HAVE A CUTE BUTT, HUH?
C'MON, BABY, GRIND THAT BACKSIDE FOR ME!
OW...I'M ALL SORE FROM THAT DAMN BRAWL...
HUH?
THAT SISSY BOY?! HE WAS SUCH A DIRTY FIGHTER!
AND NOT A SCRAPE ON HIM! I THOUGHT WE BEAT HIM UP BAD.

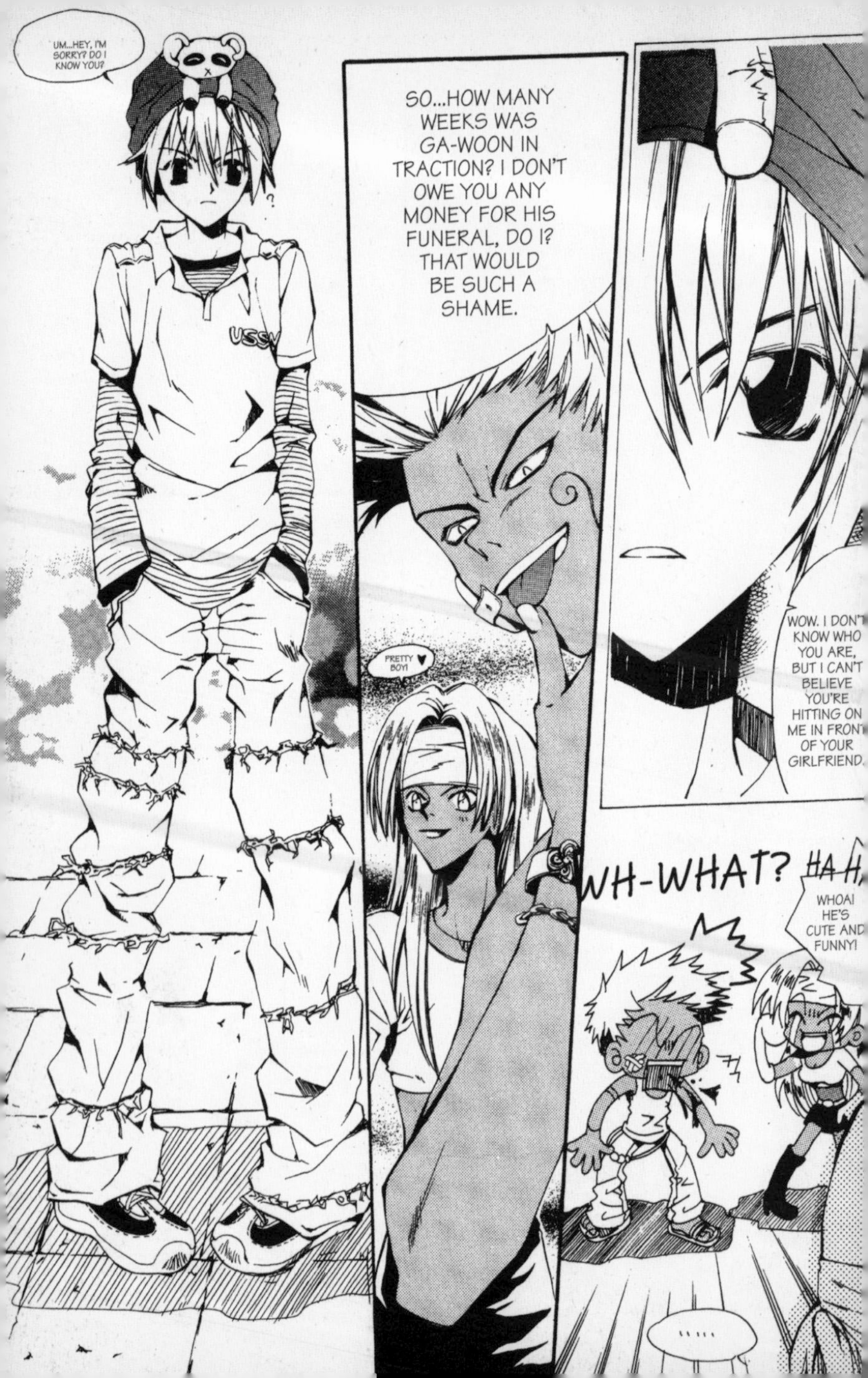
UM...HEY, I'M SORRY? DO I KNOW YOU?
SO...HOW MANY WEEKS WAS GA-WOON IN TRACTION? I DON'T OWE YOU ANY MONEY FOR HIS FUNERAL, DO I? THAT WOULD BE SUCH A SHAME.
PRETTY BOY! ♥
WOW. I DON'T KNOW WHO YOU ARE, BUT I CAN'T BELIEVE YOU'RE HITTING ON ME IN FRONT OF YOUR GIRLFRIEND.
WH-WHAT?
HA H
WHOA! HE'S CUTE AND FUNNY!

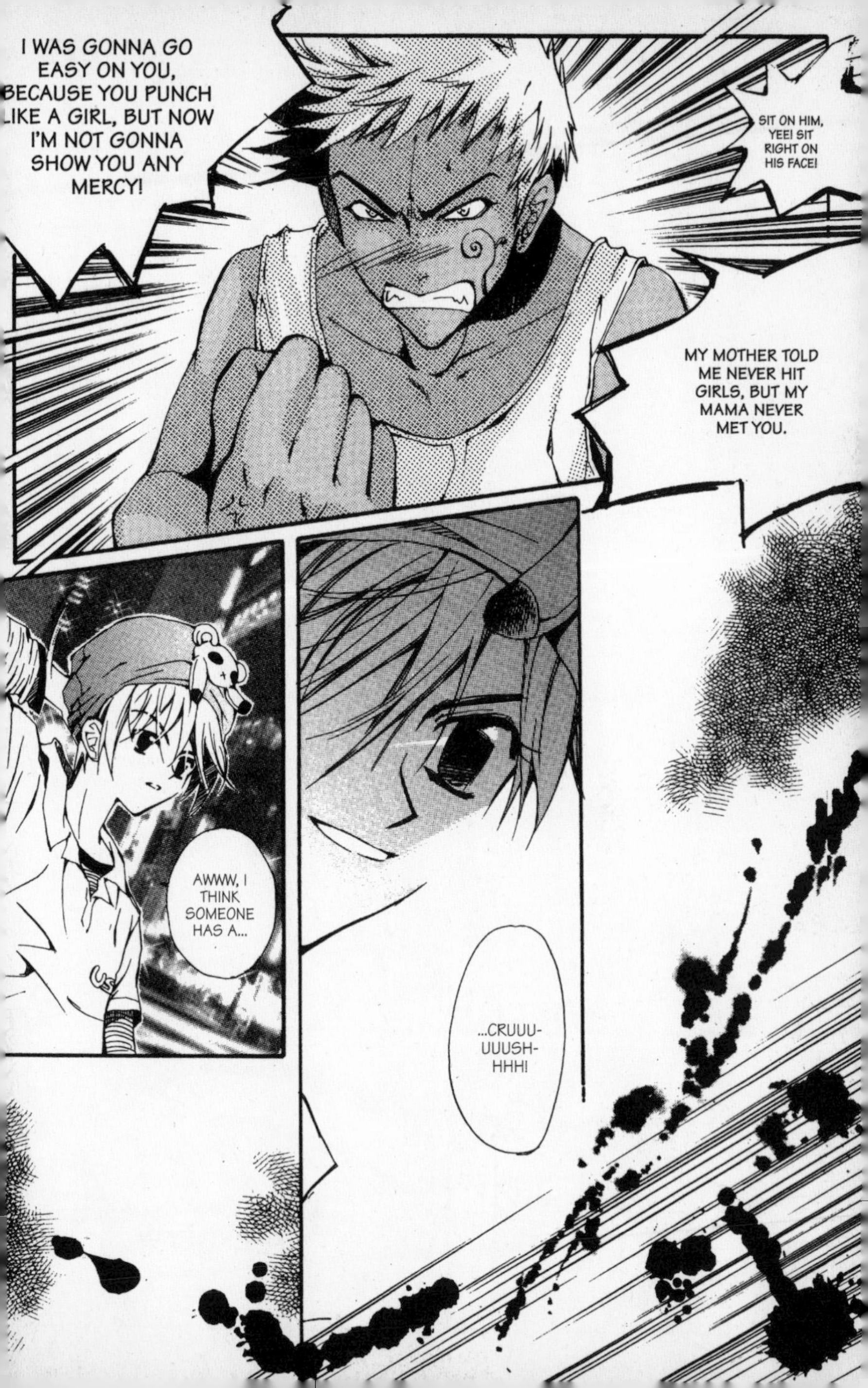
I WAS GONNA GO EASY ON YOU, BECAUSE YOU PUNCH LIKE A GIRL, BUT NOW I'M NOT GONNA SHOW YOU ANY MERCY!
SIT ON HIM, YEE! SIT RIGHT ON HIS FACE!
MY MOTHER TOLD ME NEVER HIT GIRLS, BUT MY MAMA NEVER MET YOU.
AWWW, I THINK SOMEONE HAS A...
...CRUUU-UUUSH-HHH!

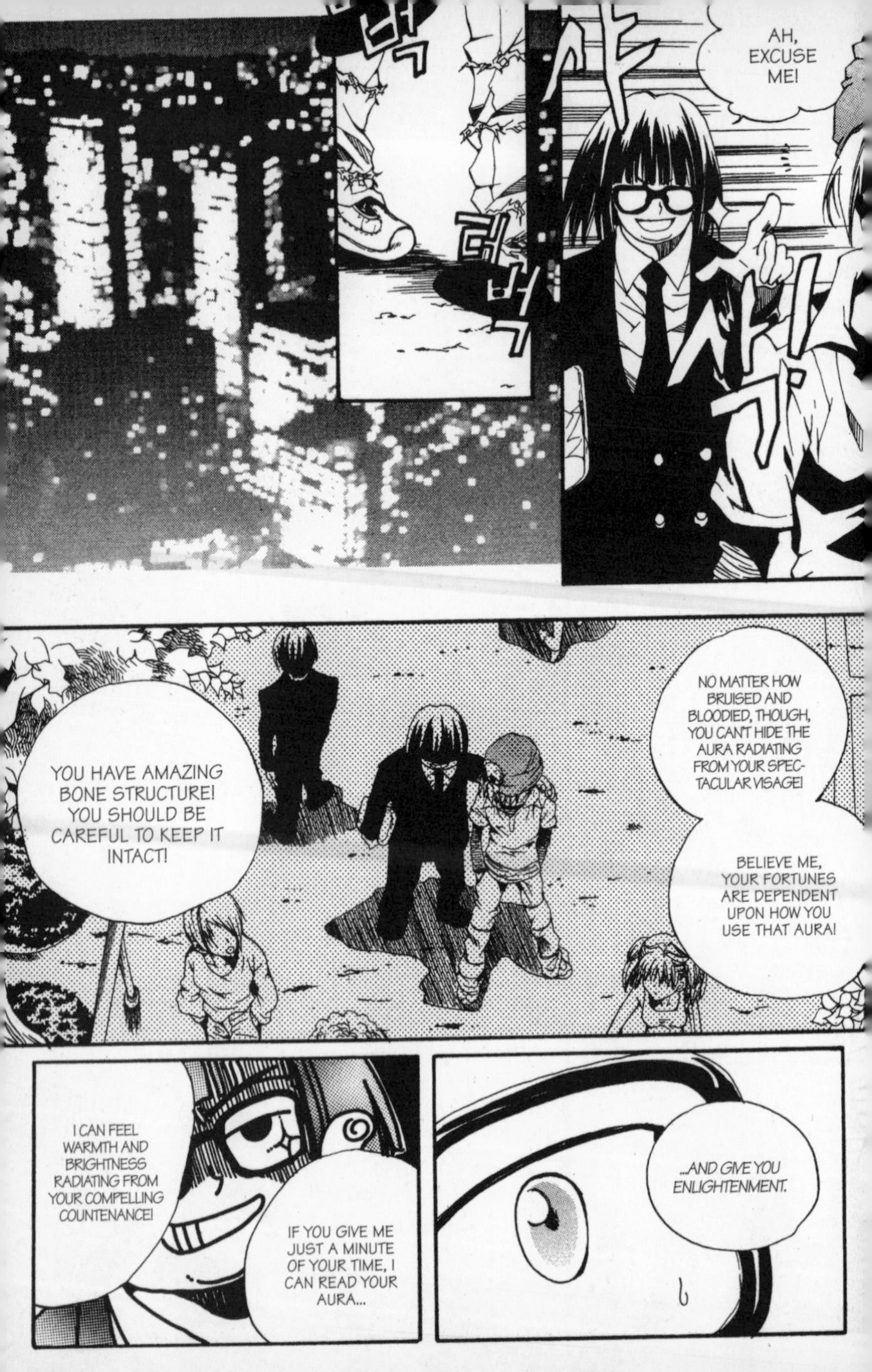
AH, EXCUSE ME!
YOU HAVE AMAZING BONE STRUCTURE! YOU SHOULD BE CAREFUL TO KEEP IT INTACT!
NO MATTER HOW BRUISED AND BLOODIED, THOUGH, YOU CAN'T HIDE THE AURA RADIATING FROM YOUR SPECTACULAR VISAGE!
BELIEVE ME, YOUR FORTUNES ARE DEPENDENT UPON HOW YOU USE THAT AURA!
I CAN FEEL WARMTH AND BRIGHTNESS RADIATING FROM YOUR COMPELLING COUNTENANCE!
IF YOU GIVE ME JUST A MINUTE OF YOUR TIME, I CAN READ YOUR AURA...
...AND GIVE YOU ENLIGHTENMENT.

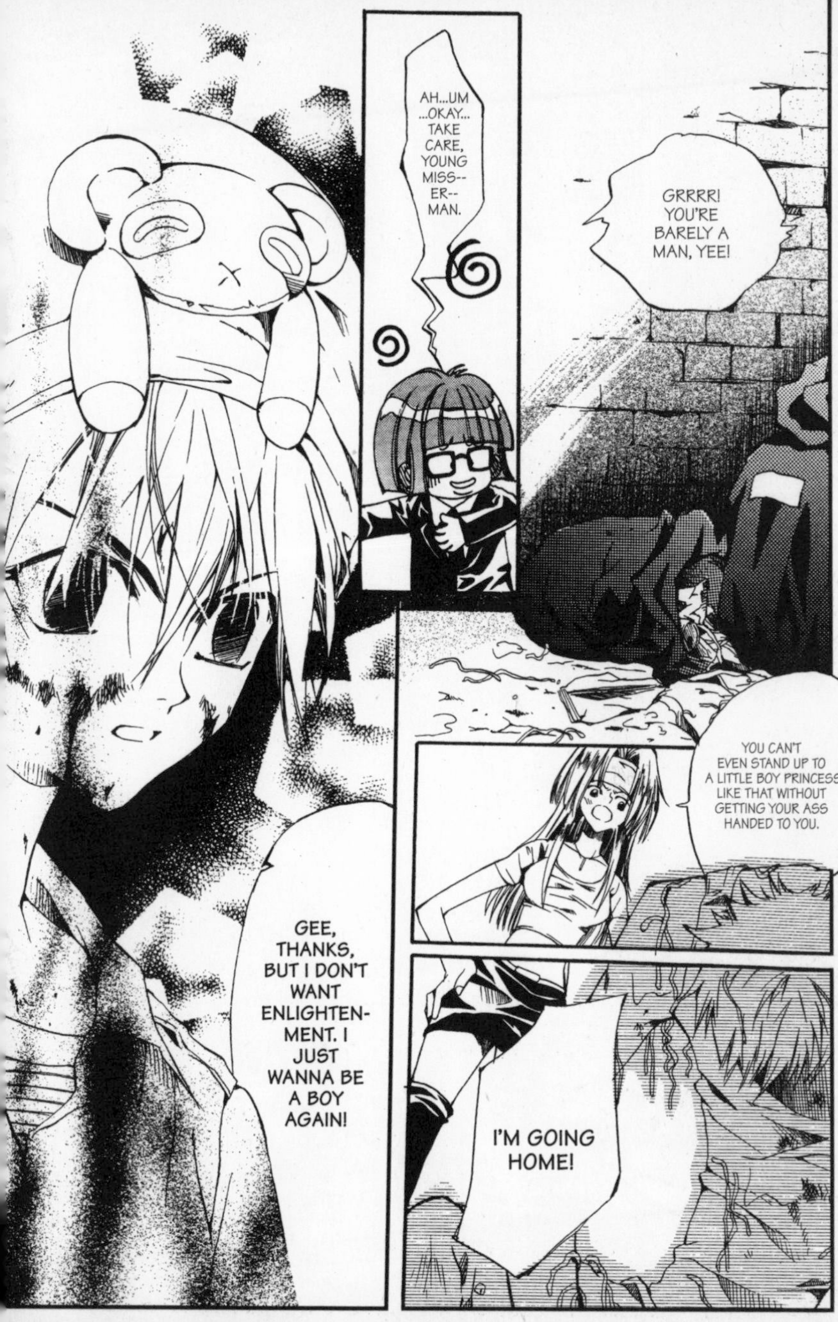
AH...UM ...OKAY... TAKE CARE, YOUNG MISS-- ER-- MAN.
GRRRR! YOU'RE BARELY A MAN, YEE!
YOU CAN'T EVEN STAND UP TO A LITTLE BOY PRINCESS LIKE THAT WITHOUT GETTING YOUR ASS HANDED TO YOU.
GEE, THANKS, BUT I DON'T WANT ENLIGHTENMENT. I JUST WANNA BE A BOY AGAIN!
I'M GOING HOME!

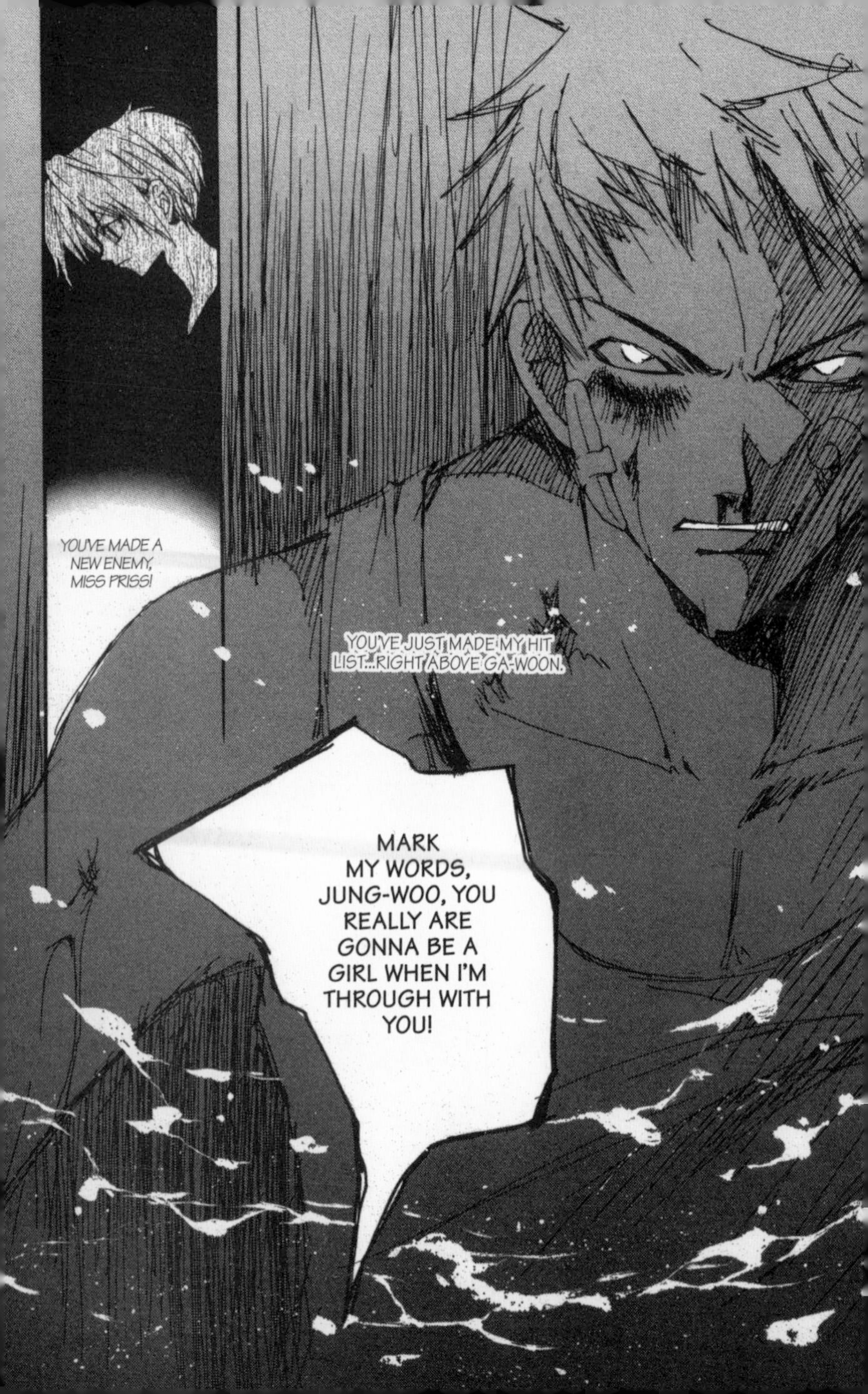
YOU'VE MADE A NEW ENEMY, MISS PRISS!
YOU'VE JUST MADE MY HIT LIST...RIGHT ABOVE GA-WOON.
MARK MY WORDS, JUNG-WOO, YOU REALLY ARE GONNA BE A GIRL WHEN I'M THROUGH WITH YOU!

KUN WAS SUCH A LITTLE TERROR BACK THEN. BUT SINCE HE WAS SO CHARISMATIC, I WAS DRAWN INTO HIS WORLD OF MISCHIEF AND MAYHEM.

WE PROMISED TO BE THE BADDEST BOYS IN ALL OF KOREA.

AND LOOK AT US TODAY. I'M STILL A DELINQUENT, BUT KUN'S EVERY TEENAGE GIRL'S BIGGEST FANTASY!

WELL, WHATEVER. HE CAN BE ON THE COVER OF AS MANY MAGAZINES AS HE WANTS. IT WON'T CHANGE ONE SIMPLE FACT--WE'LL ALWAYS BE BEST FRIENDS.

NOW AND ALWAYS.

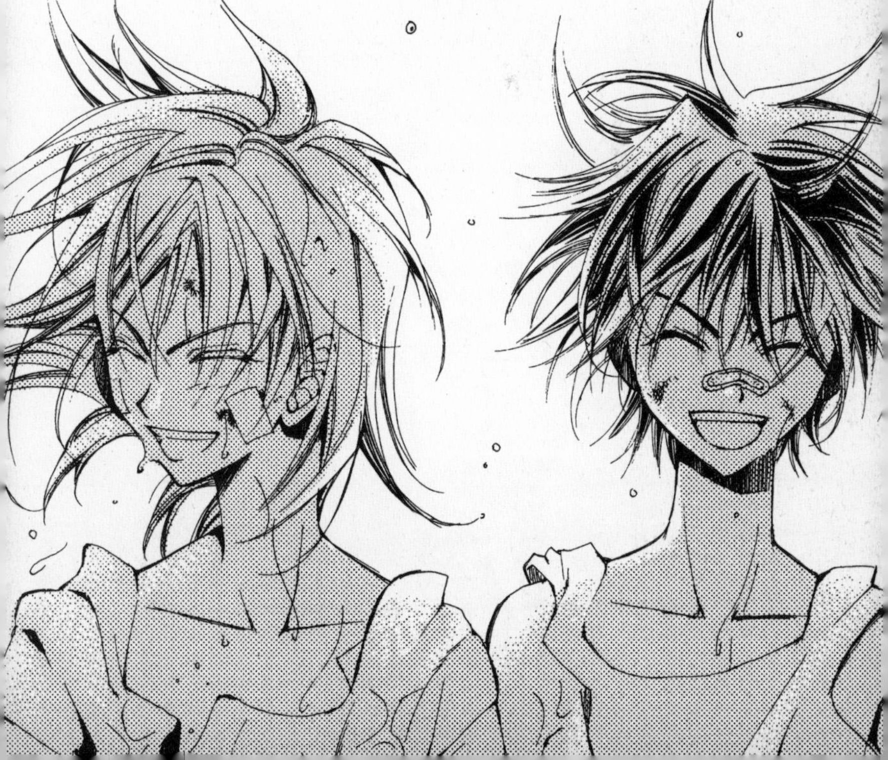

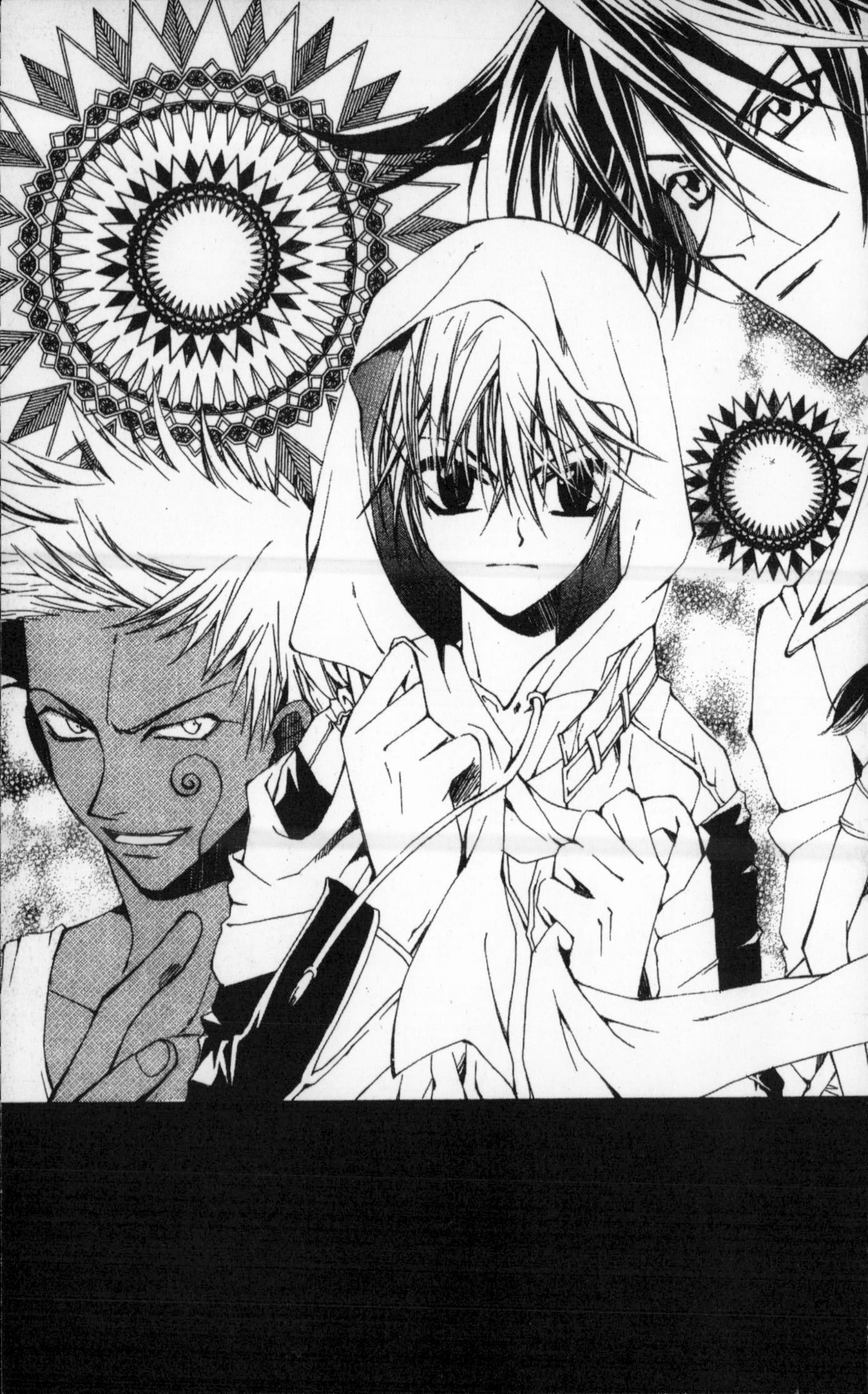

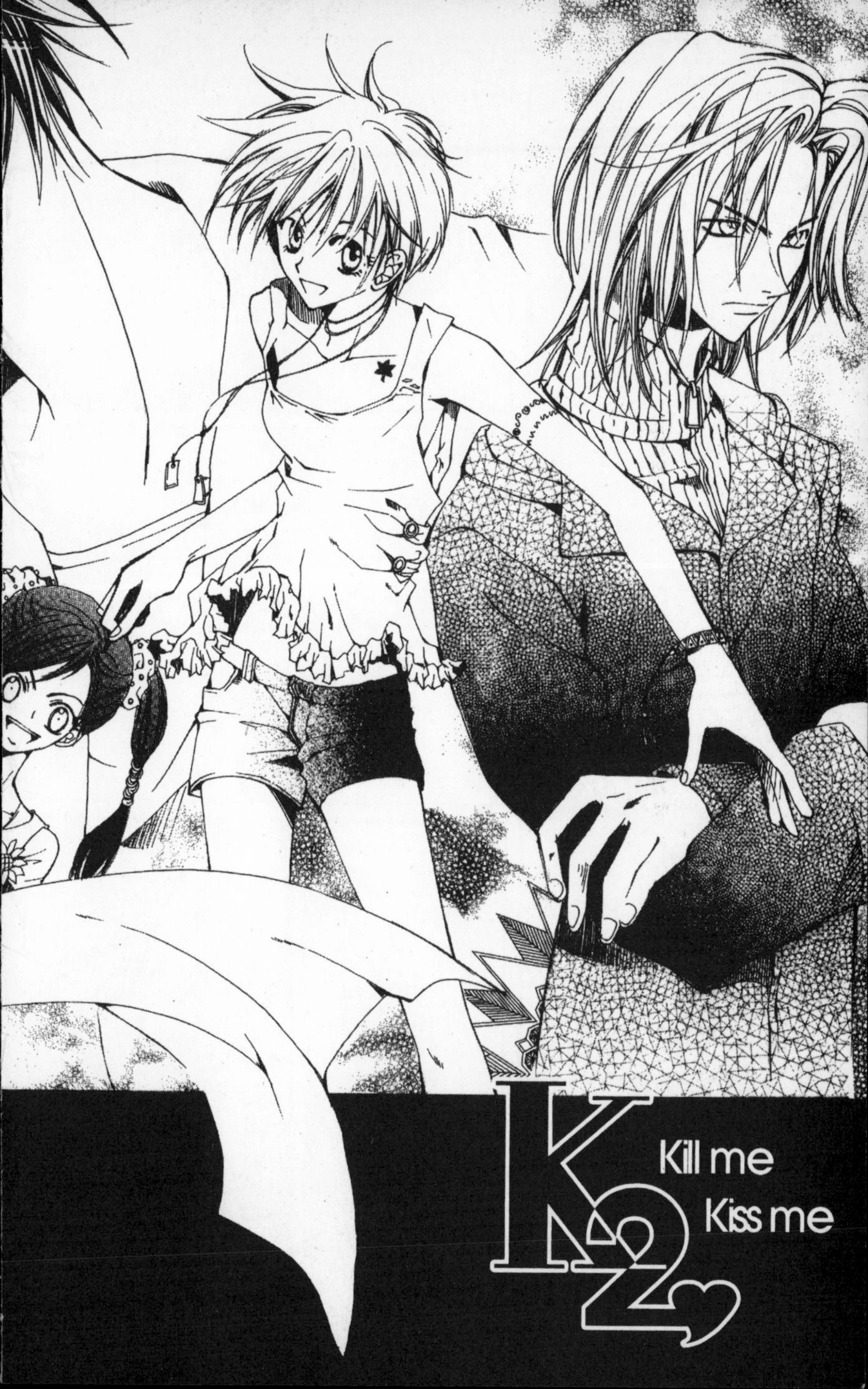
K2
Kill me
Kiss me

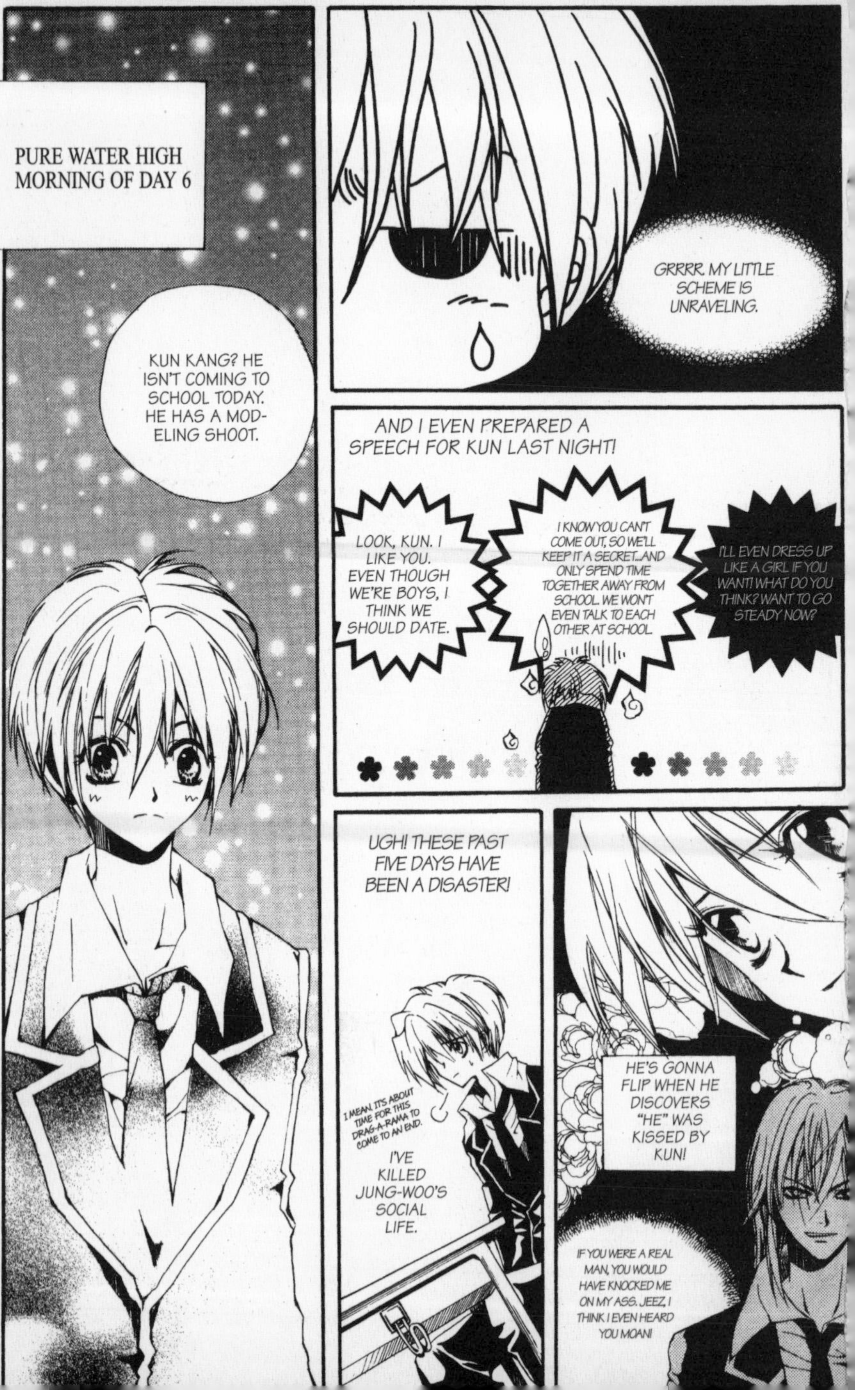
PURE WATER HIGH MORNING OF DAY 6
KUN KANG? HE ISN'T COMING TO SCHOOL TODAY. HE HAS A MOD-ELING SHOOT.
GRRRR. MY LITTLE SCHEME IS UNRAVELING.
AND I EVEN PREPARED A SPEECH FOR KUN LAST NIGHT!
LOOK, KUN. I LIKE YOU. EVEN THOUGH WE'RE BOYS, I THINK WE SHOULD DATE.
I KNOW YOU CAN'T COME OUT, SO WE'LL KEEP IT A SECRET...AND ONLY SPEND TIME TOGETHER AWAY FROM SCHOOL. WE WON'T EVEN TALK TO EACH OTHER AT SCHOOL.
I'LL EVEN DRESS UP LIKE A GIRL IF YOU WANT! WHAT DO YOU THINK? WANT TO GO STEADY NOW?
UGH! THESE PAST FIVE DAYS HAVE BEEN A DISASTER!
I MEAN, IT'S ABOUT TIME FOR THIS DRAG-A-RAMA TO COME TO AN END.
I'VE KILLED JUNG-WOO'S SOCIAL LIFE.
HE'S GONNA FLIP WHEN HE DISCOVERS "HE" WAS KISSED BY KUN!
IF YOU WERE A REAL MAN, YOU WOULD HAVE KNOCKED ME ON MY ASS. JEEZ, I THINK I EVEN HEARD YOU MOAN!

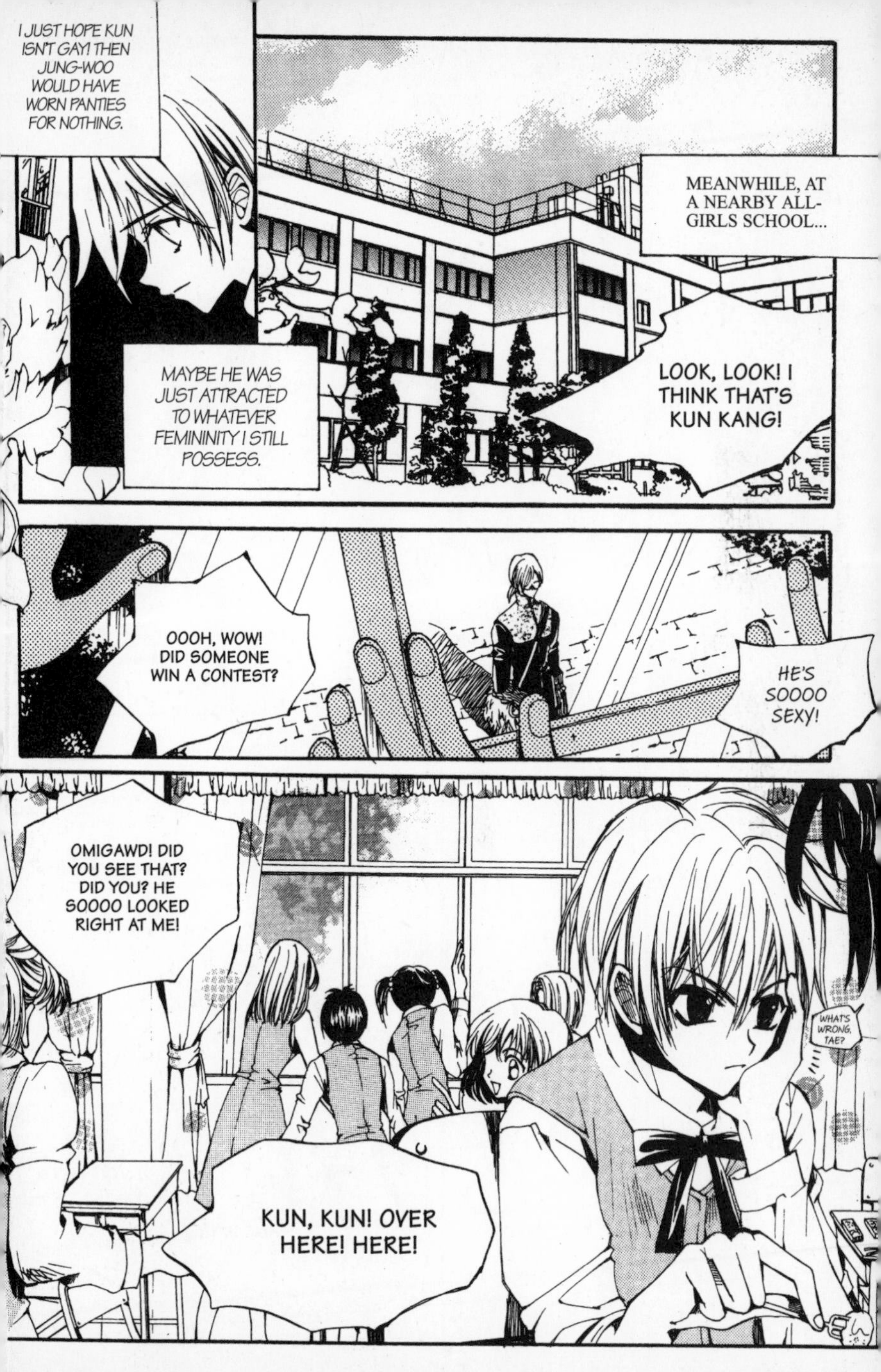
I JUST HOPE KUN ISN'T GAY! THEN JUNG-WOO WOULD HAVE WORN PANTIES FOR NOTHING.
MAYBE HE WAS JUST ATTRACTED TO WHATEVER FEMININITY I STILL POSSESS.
MEANWHILE, AT A NEARBY ALL-GIRLS SCHOOL...
LOOK, LOOK! I THINK THAT'S KUN KANG!
OOOH, WOW! DID SOMEONE WIN A CONTEST?
HE'S SOOOO SEXY!
OMIGAWD! DID YOU SEE THAT? DID YOU? HE SOOOO LOOKED RIGHT AT ME!
WHAT'S WRONG, TAE?
KUN, KUN! OVER HERE! HERE!

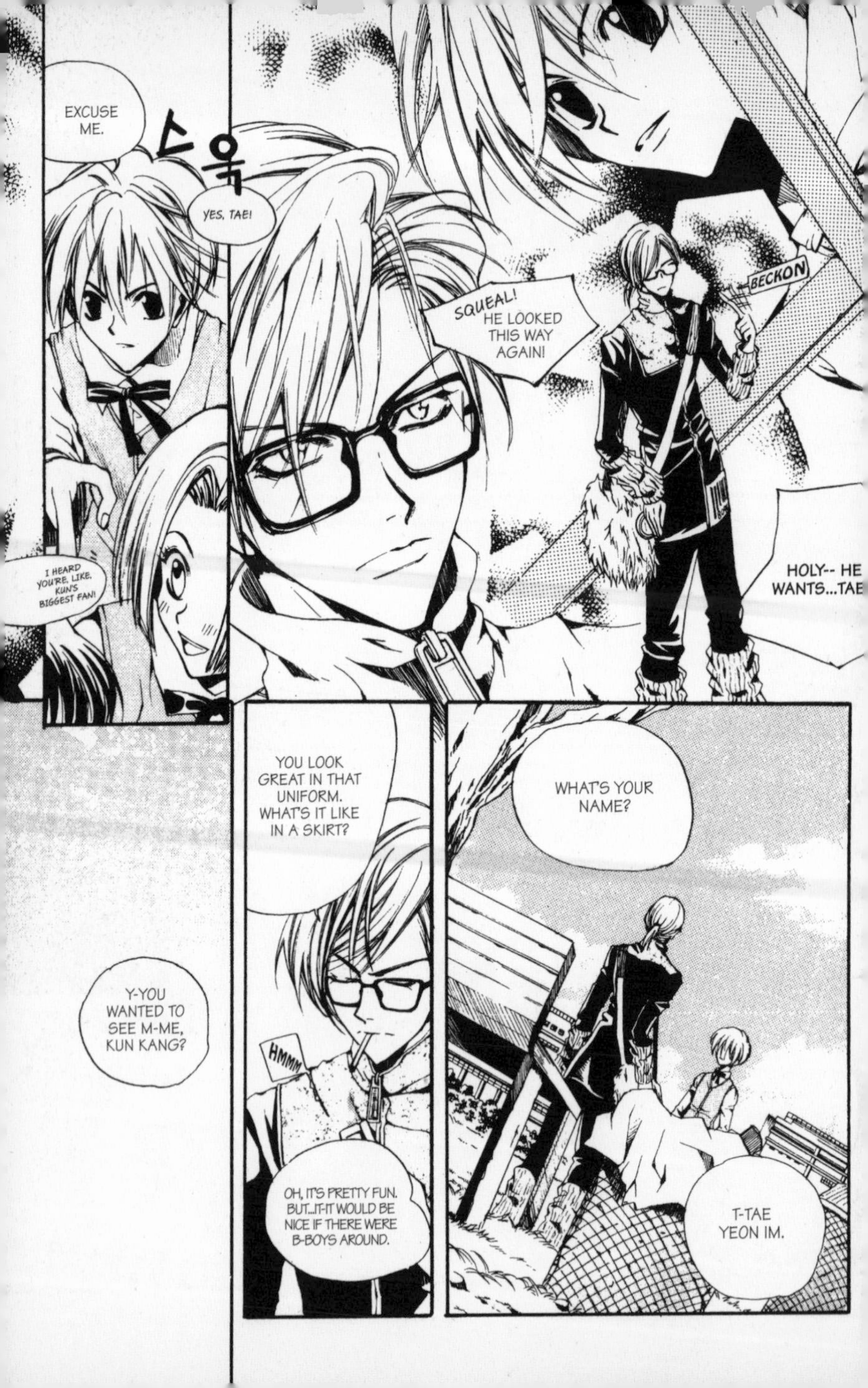
EXCUSE ME.
스욱
YES, TAE!
I HEARD YOU'RE, LIKE, KUN'S BIGGEST FAN!
SQUEAL! HE LOOKED THIS WAY AGAIN!
BECKON
HOLY-- HE WANTS...TAE
Y-YOU WANTED TO SEE M-ME, KUN KANG?
YOU LOOK GREAT IN THAT UNIFORM. WHAT'S IT LIKE IN A SKIRT?
HMMM
OH, IT'S PRETTY FUN. BUT...IT-IT WOULD BE NICE IF THERE WERE B-BOYS AROUND.
WHAT'S YOUR NAME?
T-TAE YEON IM.

I-I'M A HUGE FAN!

WHAT DID YOU SAY? IM...?

YOU KNOW WHAT'S FUNNY? I KNOW THIS GUY, RIGHT? AND HE LOOKS EXACTLY LIKE YOU. SAME LAST NAME, TOO. ODD, HUH? WELL, THIS GUY IS KINDA FEMMY, BUT HE'S GOT MOXIE. ONLY HE'S GOING AROUND ALL BEAT UP, SEE? HE'S RUNNING WITH A ROUGH CROWD...

HEARD OF JUNG-WOO IM,?

YEAH, YEAH. UM...SHE--ER-- HE'S MY COUSIN, AND...UM...HE'S A TOUGH ASS...?

LET'S CUT THE CRAP...JUNG-WOO. HAVE YOU TWO LOST YOUR MINDS?

IT WAS TAE'S IDEA. SHE JUST WANTED TO BE CLOSE TO YOU.

AND WHY THE HELL ARE YOU GOING ALONG WITH IT?

107

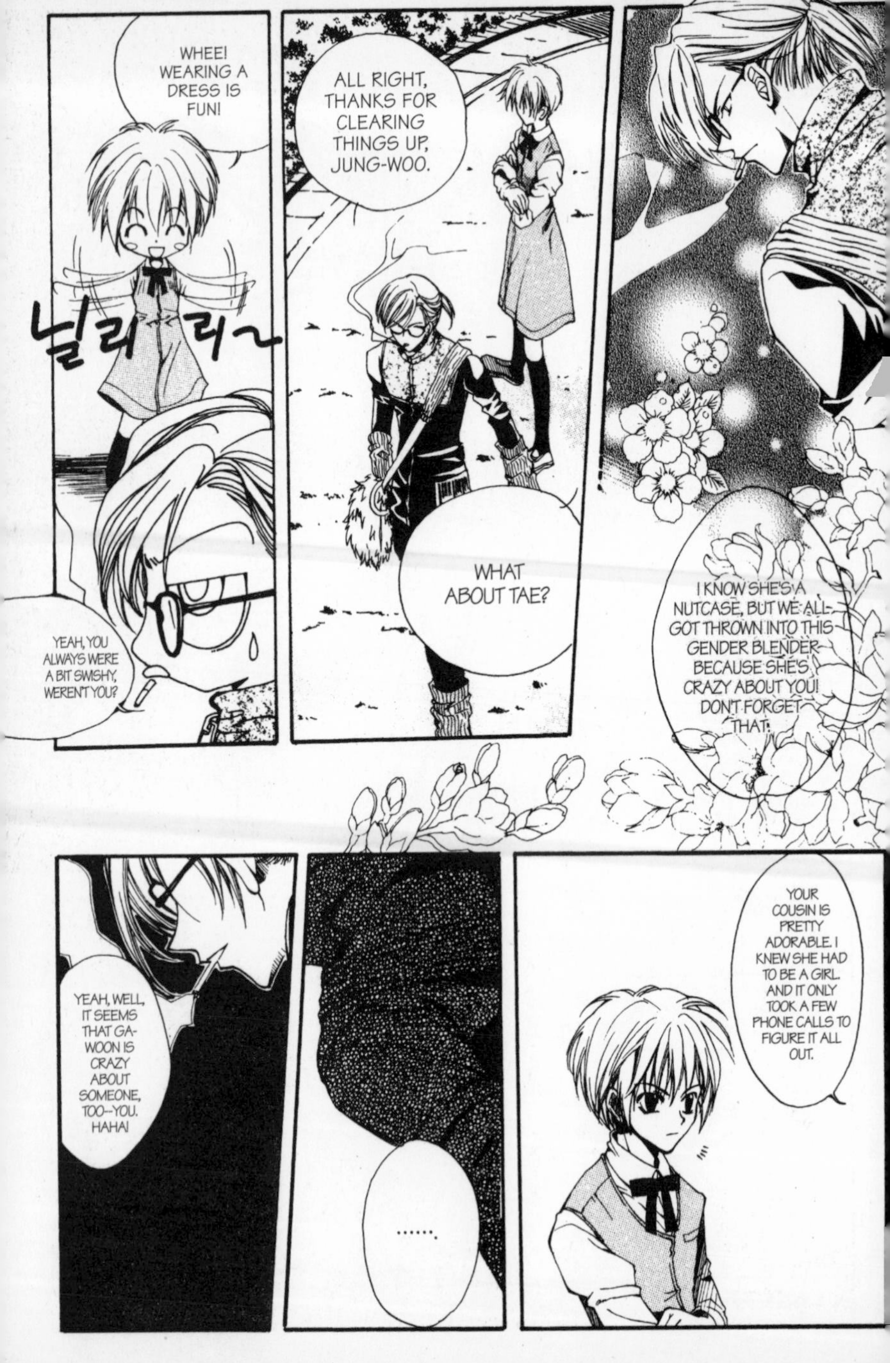
WHEE! WEARING A DRESS IS FUN!
널리리~
YEAH, YOU ALWAYS WERE A BIT SWISHY, WEREN'T YOU?
ALL RIGHT, THANKS FOR CLEARING THINGS UP, JUNG-WOO.
WHAT ABOUT TAE?
I KNOW SHE'S A NUTCASE, BUT WE ALL GOT THROWN INTO THIS GENDER BLENDER BECAUSE SHE'S CRAZY ABOUT YOU! DON'T FORGET THAT.
YEAH, WELL, IT SEEMS THAT GA-WOON IS CRAZY ABOUT SOMEONE, TOO--YOU. HAHA!
......
YOUR COUSIN IS PRETTY ADORABLE. I KNEW SHE HAD TO BE A GIRL. AND IT ONLY TOOK A FEW PHONE CALLS TO FIGURE IT ALL OUT.

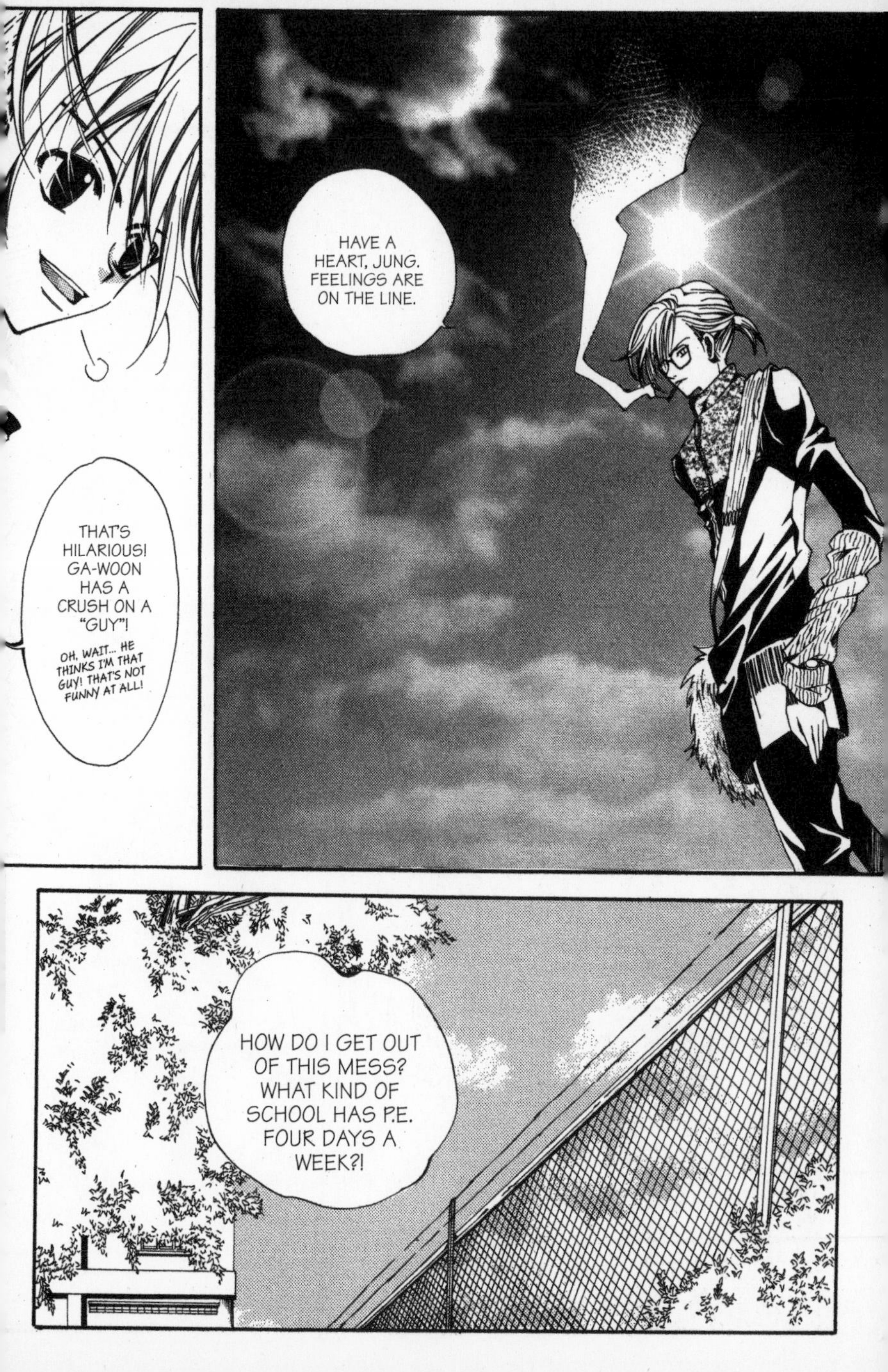
THAT'S HILARIOUS! GA-WOON HAS A CRUSH ON A "GUY"!
OH, WAIT... HE THINKS I'M THAT GUY! THAT'S NOT FUNNY AT ALL!
HAVE A HEART, JUNG. FEELINGS ARE ON THE LINE.
HOW DO I GET OUT OF THIS MESS? WHAT KIND OF SCHOOL HAS P.E. FOUR DAYS A WEEK?!

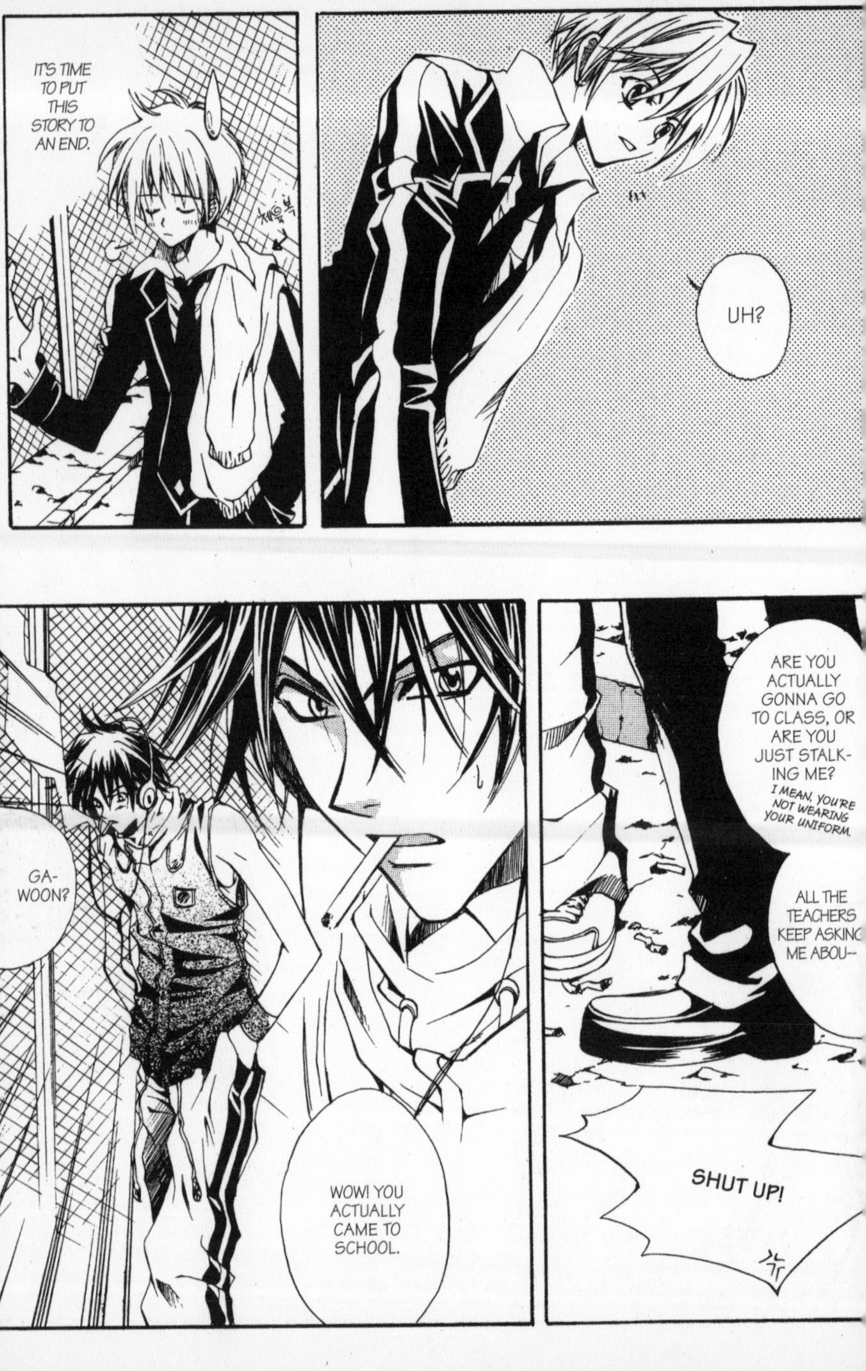
IT'S TIME TO PUT THIS STORY TO AN END.
체육복
UH?
GA-WOON?
WOW! YOU ACTUALLY CAME TO SCHOOL.
ARE YOU ACTUALLY GONNA GO TO CLASS, OR ARE YOU JUST STALKING ME?
I MEAN, YOU'RE NOT WEARING YOUR UNIFORM.
ALL THE TEACHERS KEEP ASKING ME ABOU--
SHUT UP!

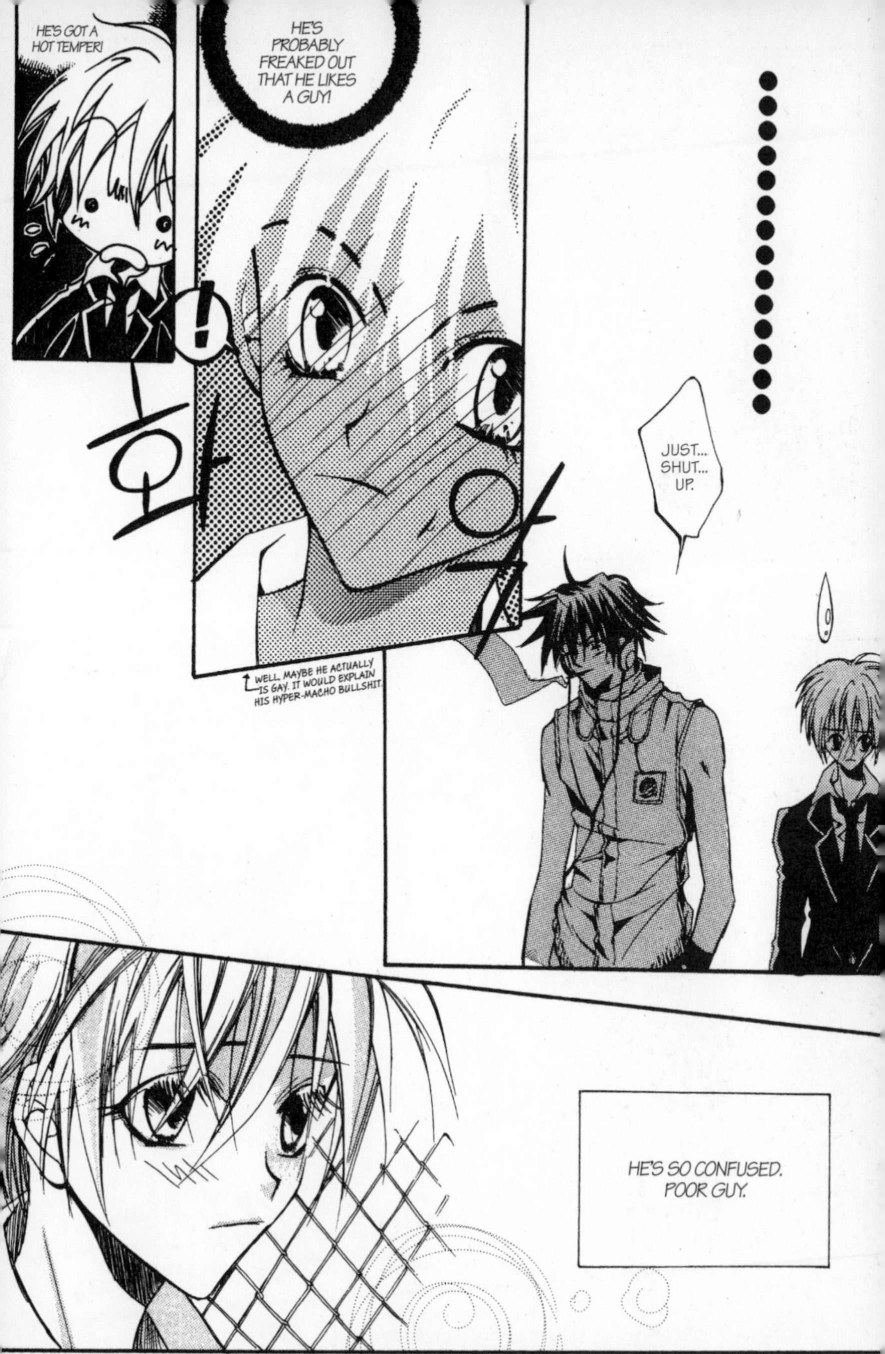
HE'S GOT A HOT TEMPER!
!
HE'S PROBABLY FREAKED OUT THAT HE LIKES A GUY!
WELL, MAYBE HE ACTUALLY IS GAY. IT WOULD EXPLAIN HIS HYPER-MACHO BULLSHIT.
JUST... SHUT... UP.
HE'S SO CONFUSED. POOR GUY.

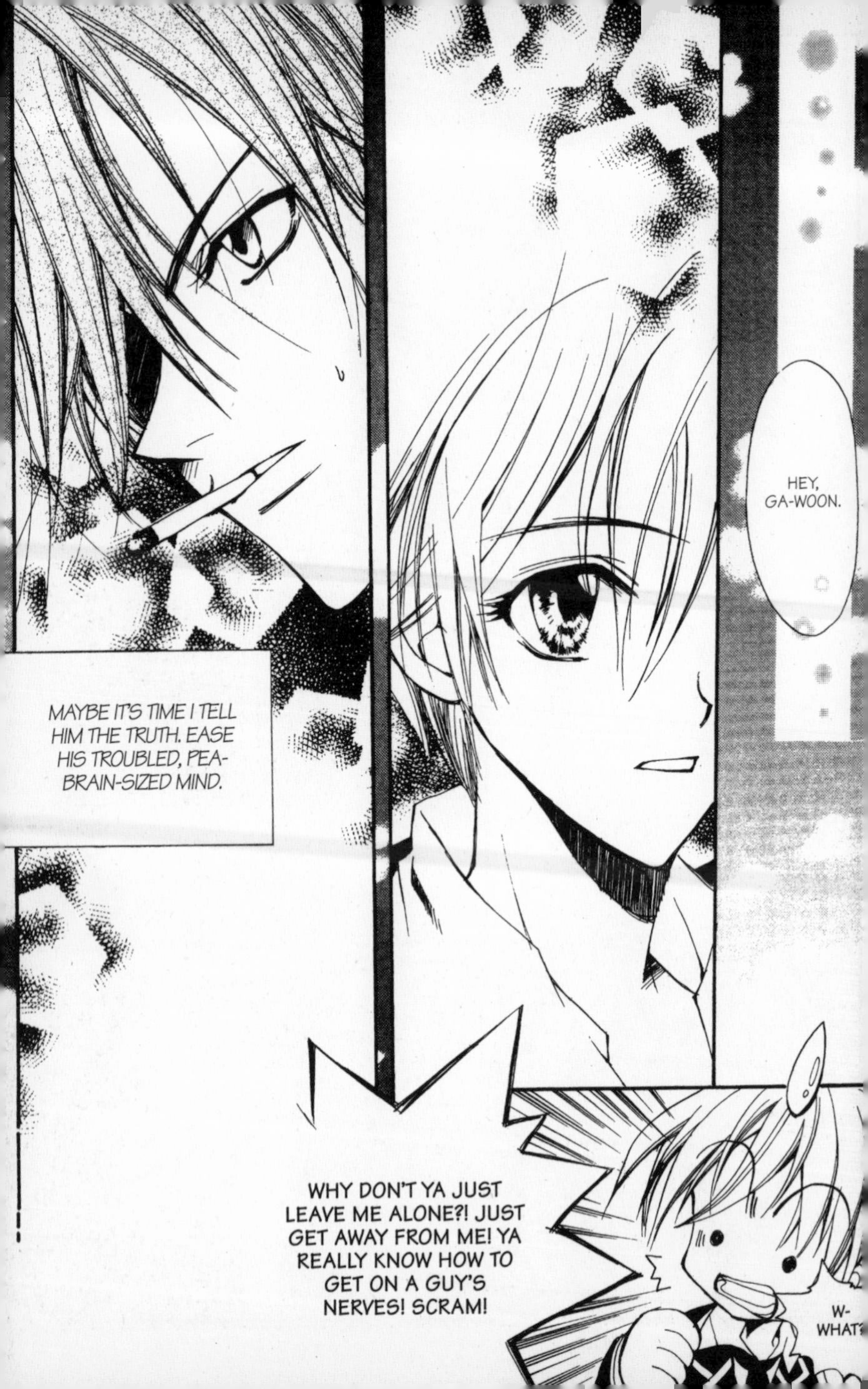
MAYBE IT'S TIME I TELL HIM THE TRUTH. EASE HIS TROUBLED, PEA-BRAIN-SIZED MIND.
HEY, GA-WOON.
WHY DON'T YA JUST LEAVE ME ALONE?! JUST GET AWAY FROM ME! YA REALLY KNOW HOW TO GET ON A GUY'S NERVES! SCRAM!
W-WHAT?

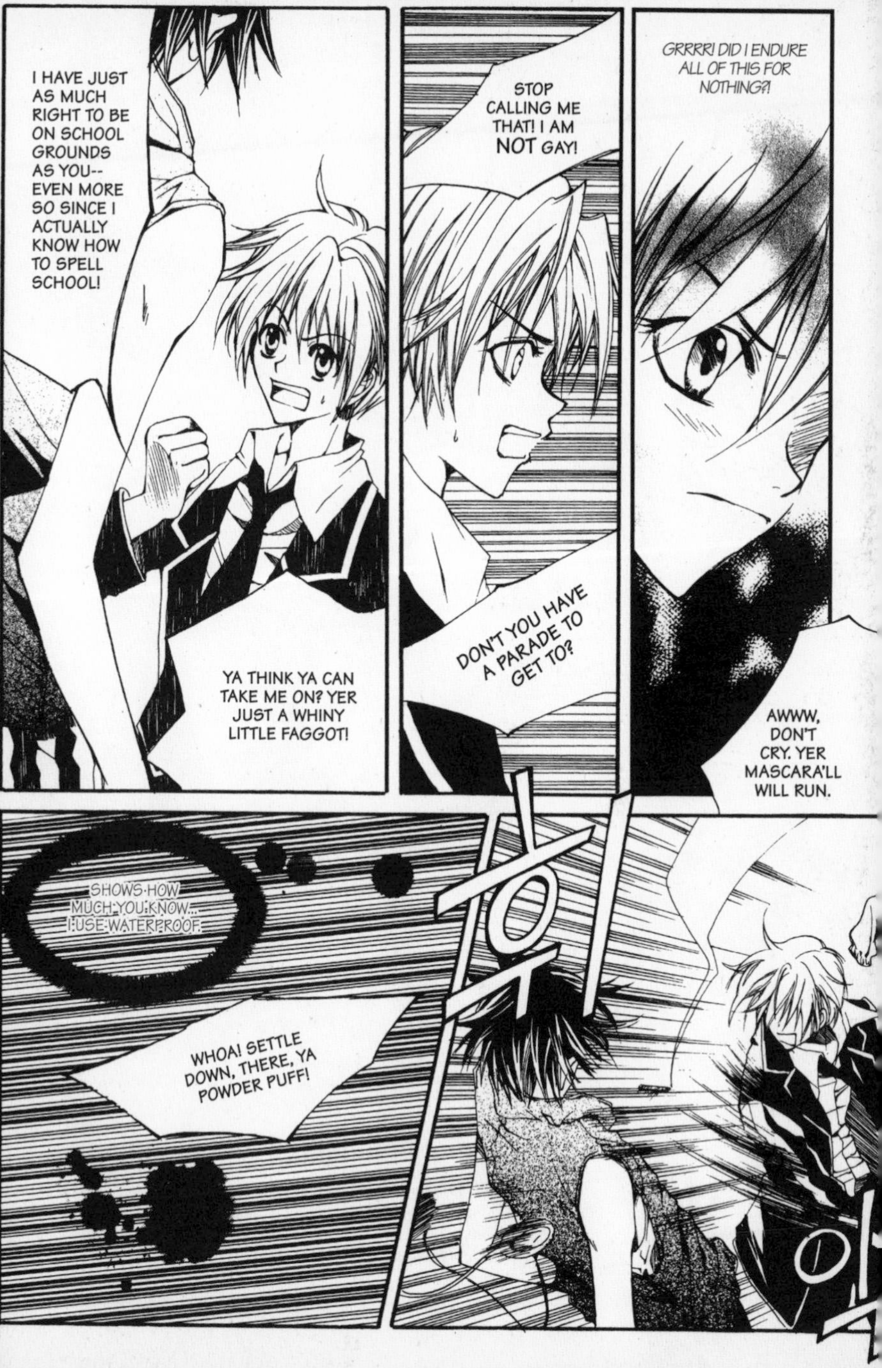
I HAVE JUST AS MUCH RIGHT TO BE ON SCHOOL GROUNDS AS YOU-- EVEN MORE SO SINCE I ACTUALLY KNOW HOW TO SPELL SCHOOL!
YA THINK YA CAN TAKE ME ON? YER JUST A WHINY LITTLE FAGGOT!
STOP CALLING ME THAT! I AM NOT GAY!
DON'T YOU HAVE A PARADE TO GET TO?
GRRRR! DID I ENDURE ALL OF THIS FOR NOTHING?!
AWWW, DON'T CRY. YER MASCARA'LL WILL RUN.
SHOWS HOW MUCH YOU KNOW... I USE WATERPROOF.
WHOA! SETTLE DOWN, THERE, YA POWDER PUFF!

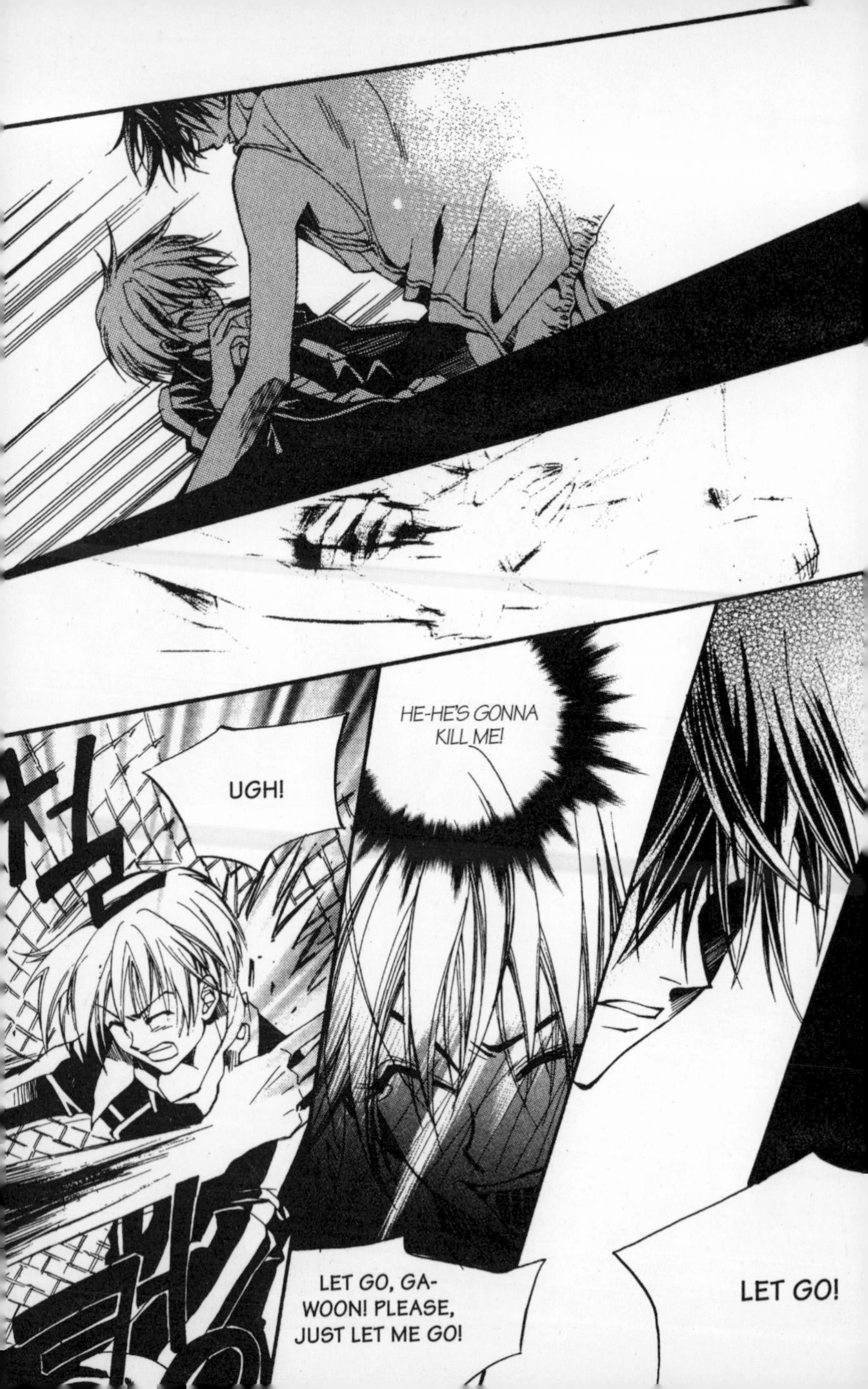
UGH!
HE-HE'S GONNA KILL ME!
LET GO, GA-WOON! PLEASE, JUST LET ME GO!
LET GO!

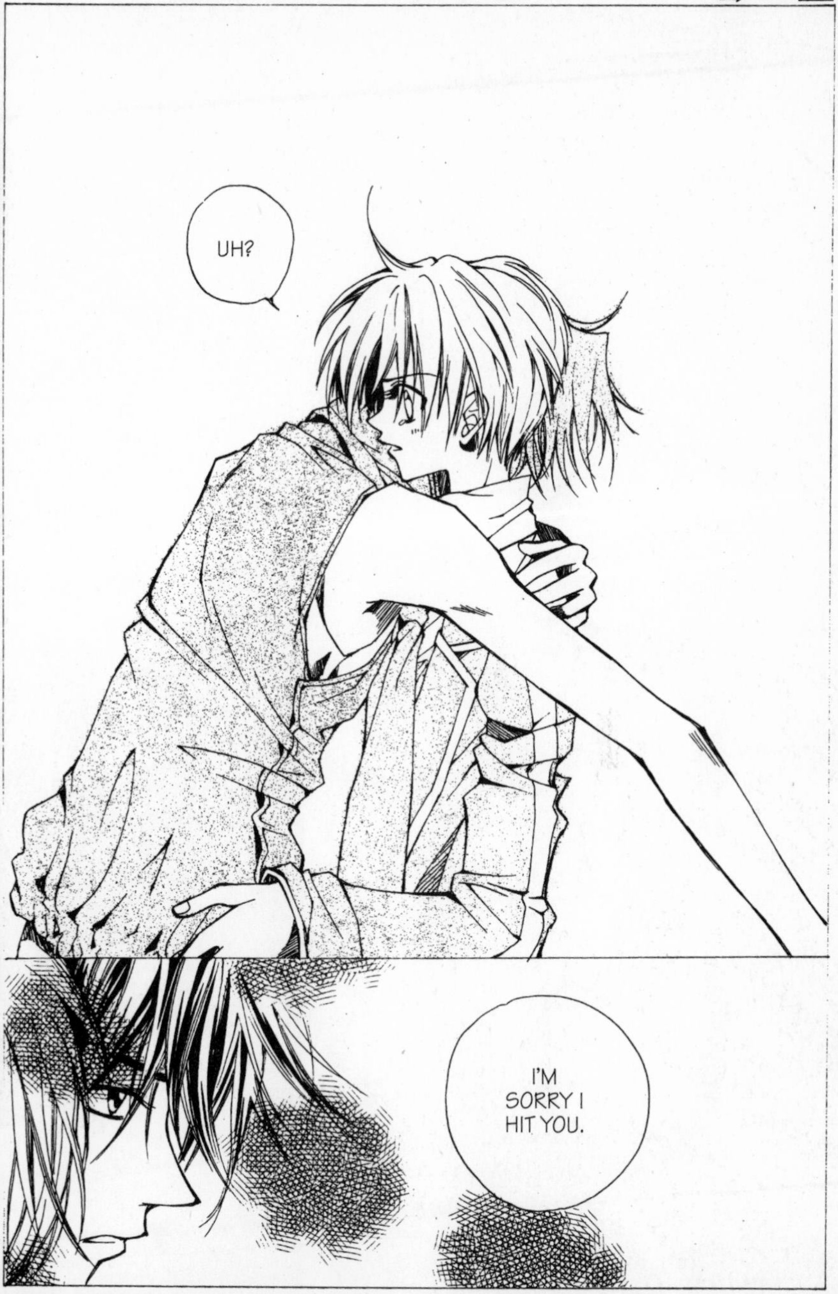
UH?
I'M SORRY I HIT YOU.

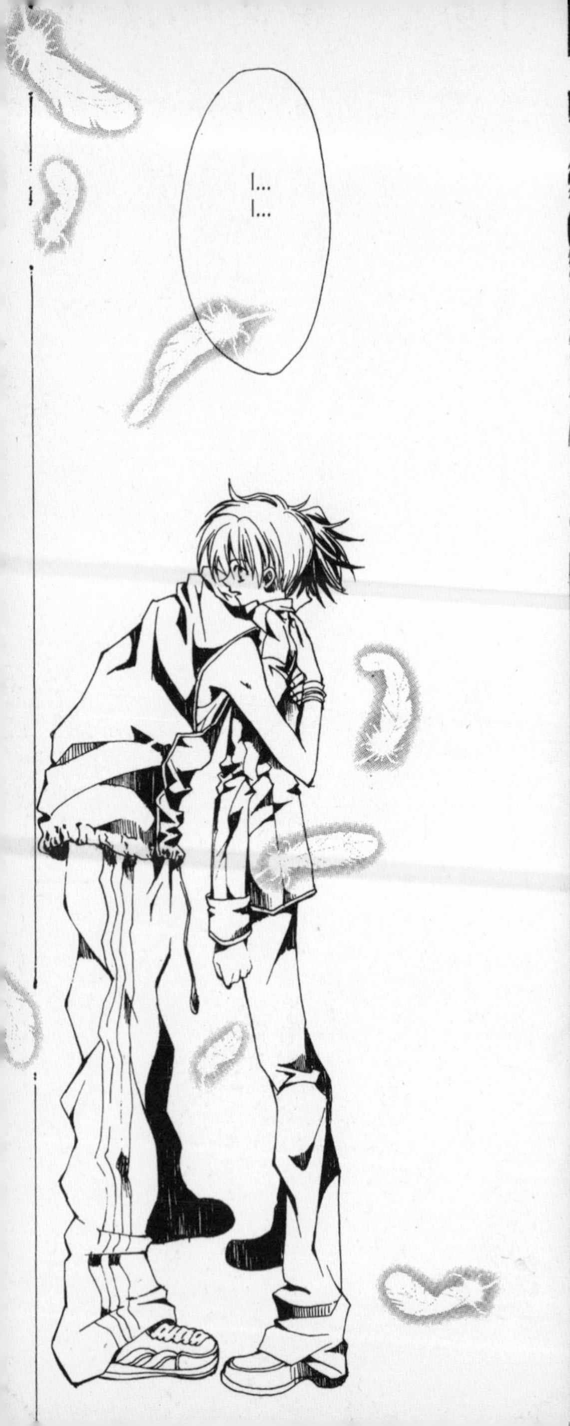
I...
I...
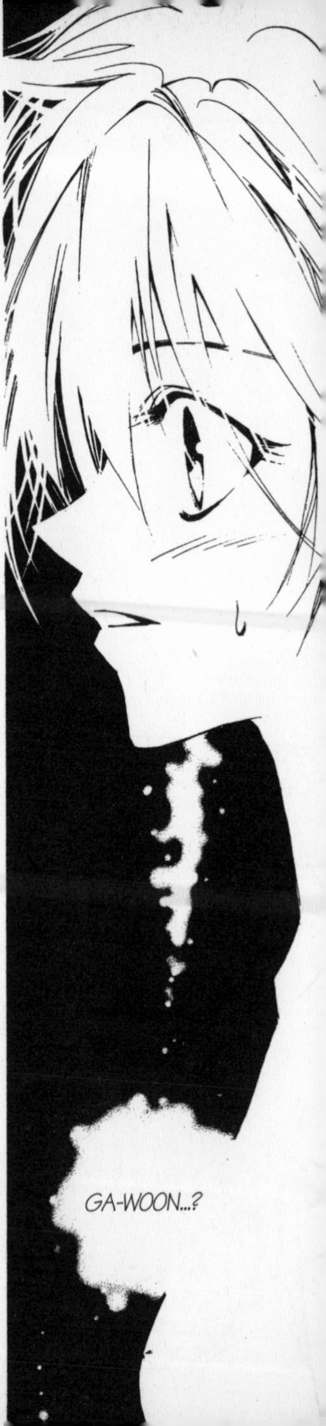
GA-WOON...?

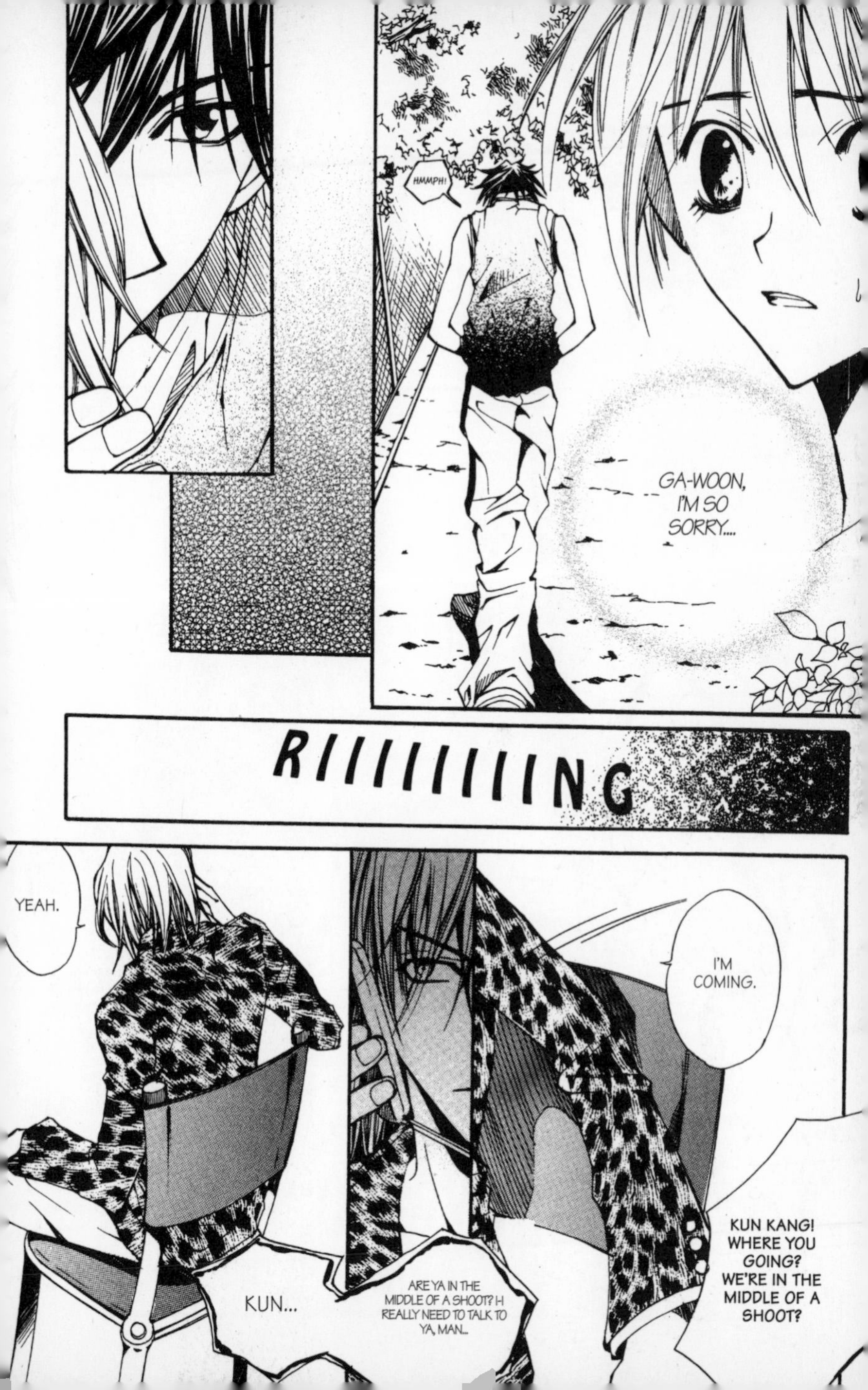
HMMPH!
GA-WOON, I'M SO SORRY....
RIIIIIIING
YEAH.
KUN...
ARE YA IN THE MIDDLE OF A SHOOT? H REALLY NEED TO TALK TO YA, MAN...
I'M COMING.
KUN KANG! WHERE YOU GOING? WE'RE IN THE MIDDLE OF A SHOOT?

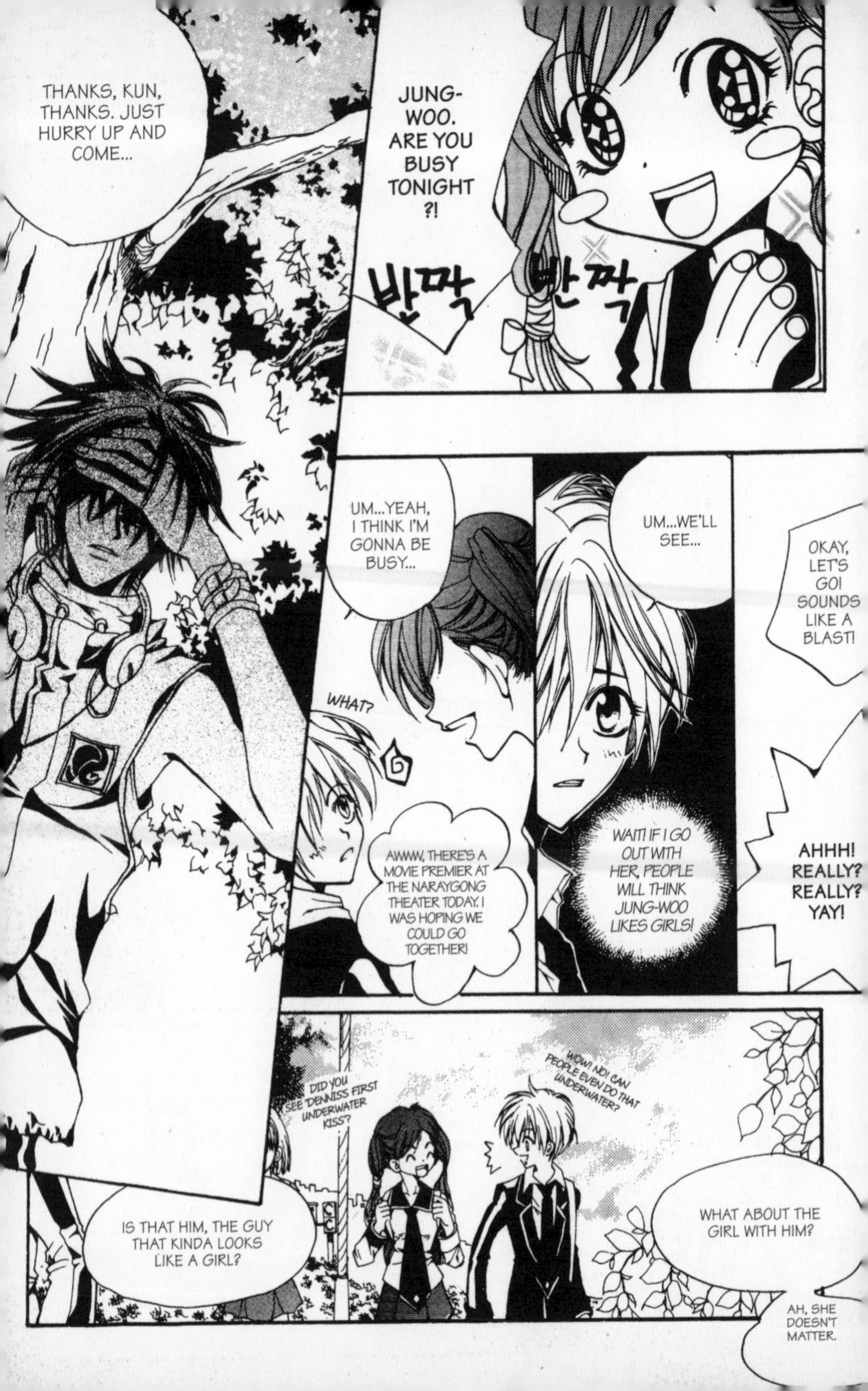
THANKS, KUN, THANKS. JUST HURRY UP AND COME...
JUNG-WOO. ARE YOU BUSY TONIGHT?!
반짝 반짝
UM...YEAH, I THINK I'M GONNA BE BUSY...
WHAT?
AWWW, THERE'S A MOVIE PREMIER AT THE NARAYGONG THEATER TODAY. I WAS HOPING WE COULD GO TOGETHER!
UM...WE'LL SEE...
WAIT! IF I GO OUT WITH HER, PEOPLE WILL THINK JUNG-WOO LIKES GIRLS!
OKAY, LET'S GO! SOUNDS LIKE A BLAST!
AHHH! REALLY? REALLY? YAY!
IS THAT HIM, THE GUY THAT KINDA LOOKS LIKE A GIRL?
DID YOU SEE DENNISS FIRST UNDERWATER KISS?
WOW! NO! CAN PEOPLE EVEN DO THAT UNDERWATER?
WHAT ABOUT THE GIRL WITH HIM?
AH, SHE DOESN'T MATTER.

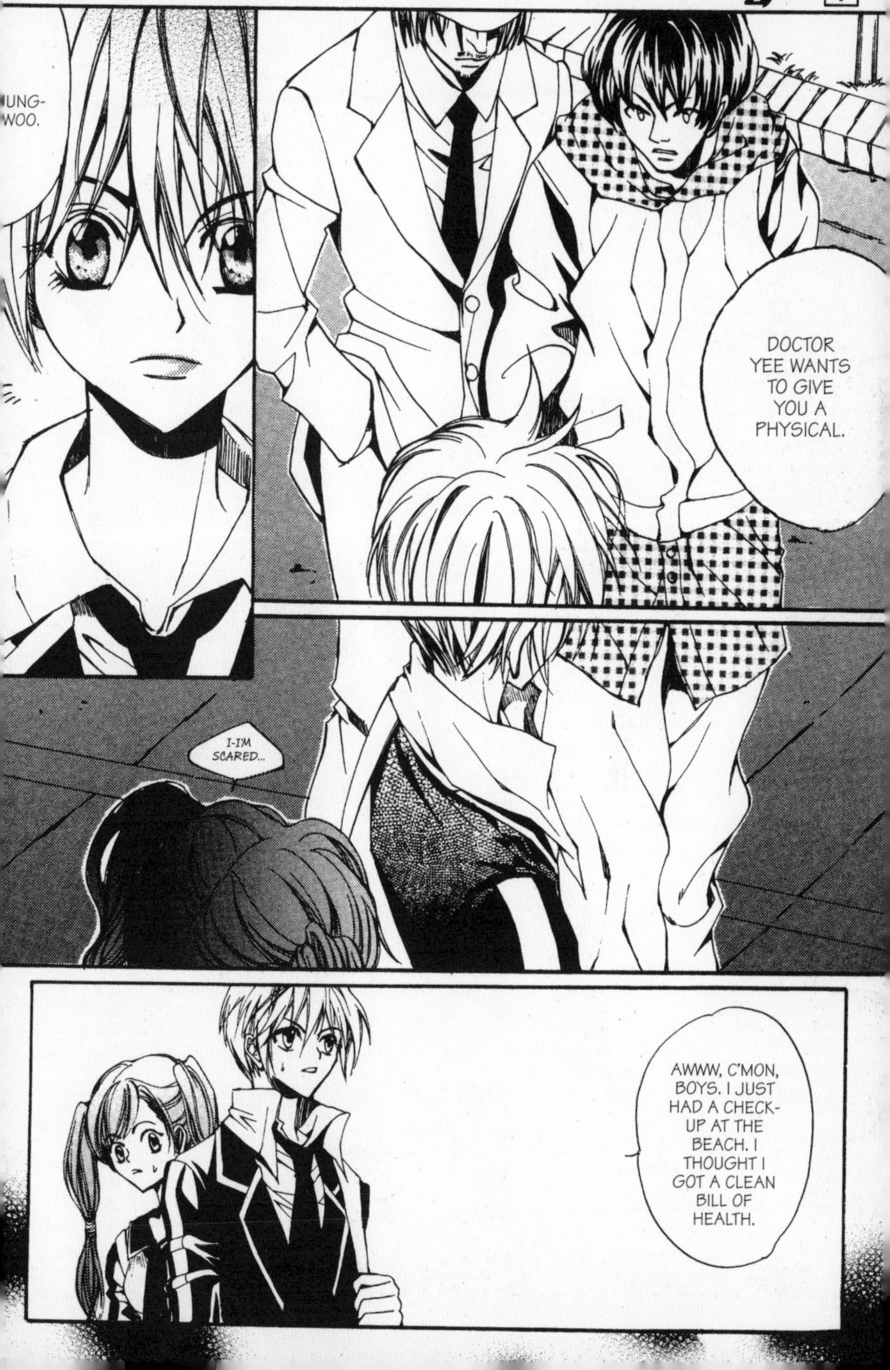
UNG-WOO.
DOCTOR YEE WANTS TO GIVE YOU A PHYSICAL.
I-I'M SCARED...
AWWW, C'MON, BOYS. I JUST HAD A CHECK-UP AT THE BEACH. I THOUGHT I GOT A CLEAN BILL OF HEALTH.

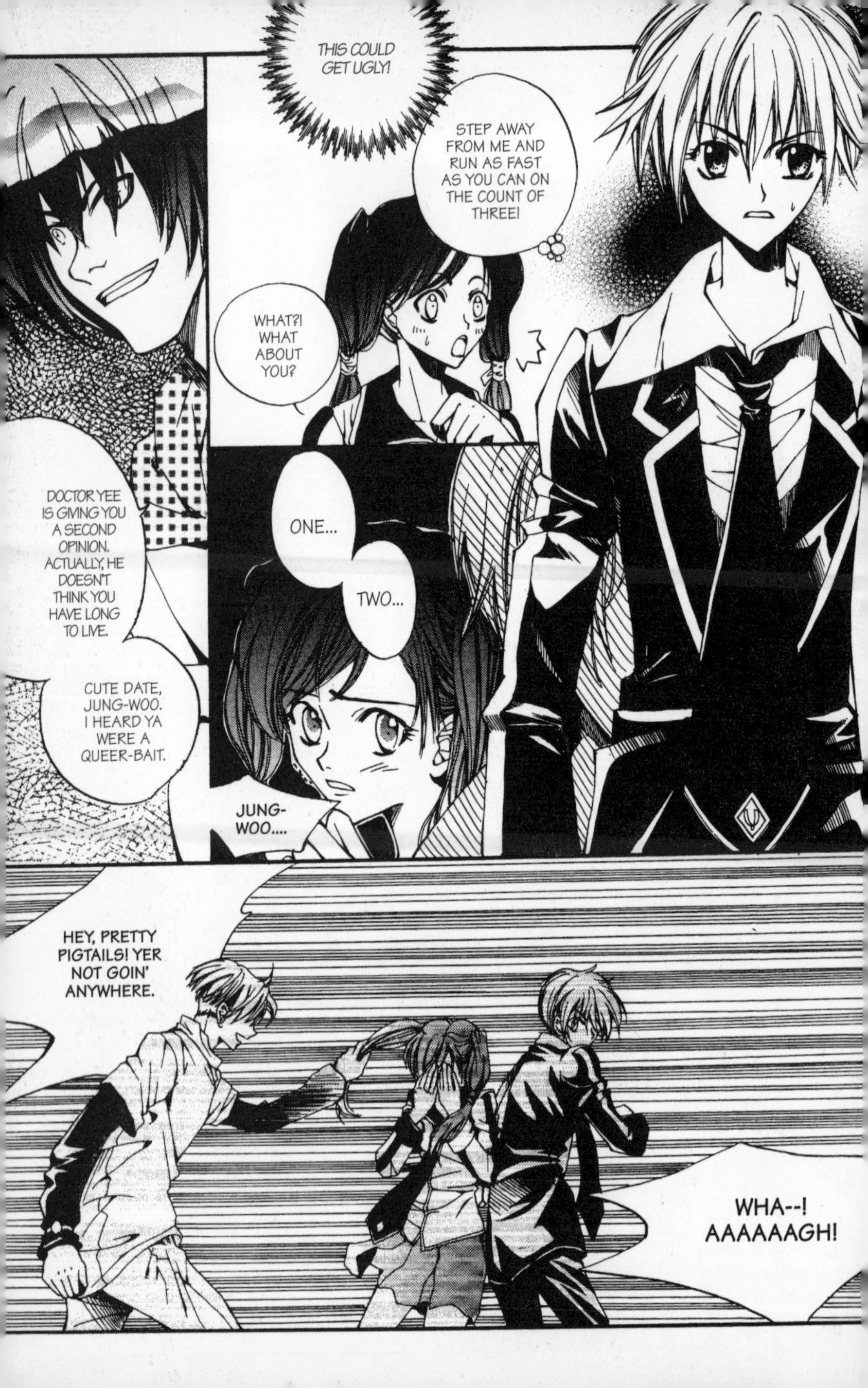
DOCTOR YEE IS GIVING YOU A SECOND OPINION. ACTUALLY, HE DOESN'T THINK YOU HAVE LONG TO LIVE.
CUTE DATE, JUNG-WOO. I HEARD YA WERE A QUEER-BAIT.
THIS COULD GET UGLY!
STEP AWAY FROM ME AND RUN AS FAST AS YOU CAN ON THE COUNT OF THREE!
WHAT?! WHAT ABOUT YOU?
ONE...
TWO...
JUNG-WOO....
HEY, PRETTY PIGTAILS! YER NOT GOIN' ANYWHERE.
WHA--! AAAAAAGH!

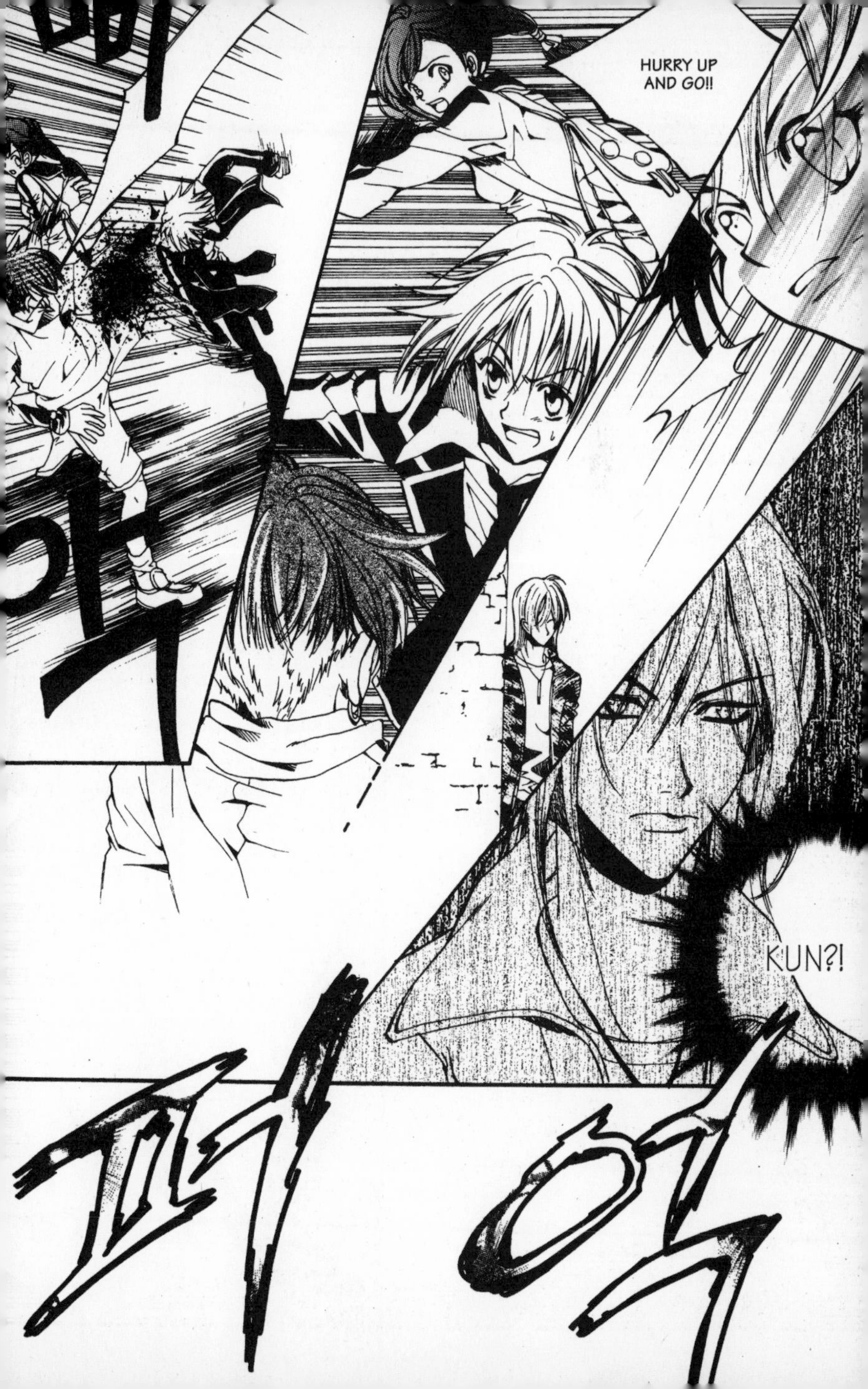
HURRY UP AND GO!!
KUN?!

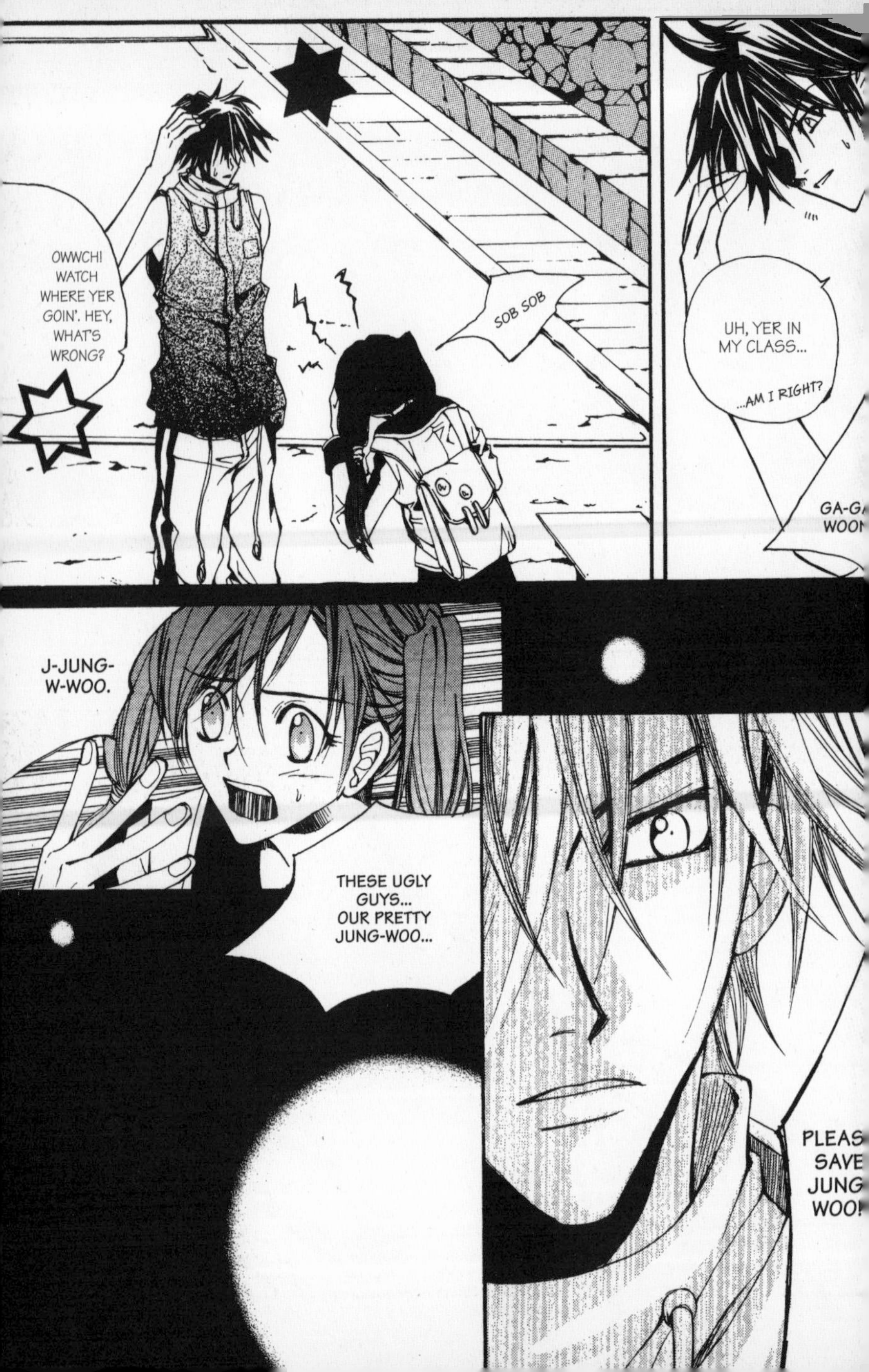
OWWCH! WATCH WHERE YER GOIN'. HEY, WHAT'S WRONG?
SOB SOB
UH, YER IN MY CLASS...
...AM I RIGHT?
GA-GA WOO
J-JUNG-W-WOO.
THESE UGLY GUYS... OUR PRETTY JUNG-WOO...
PLEAS SAVE JUNG WOO!

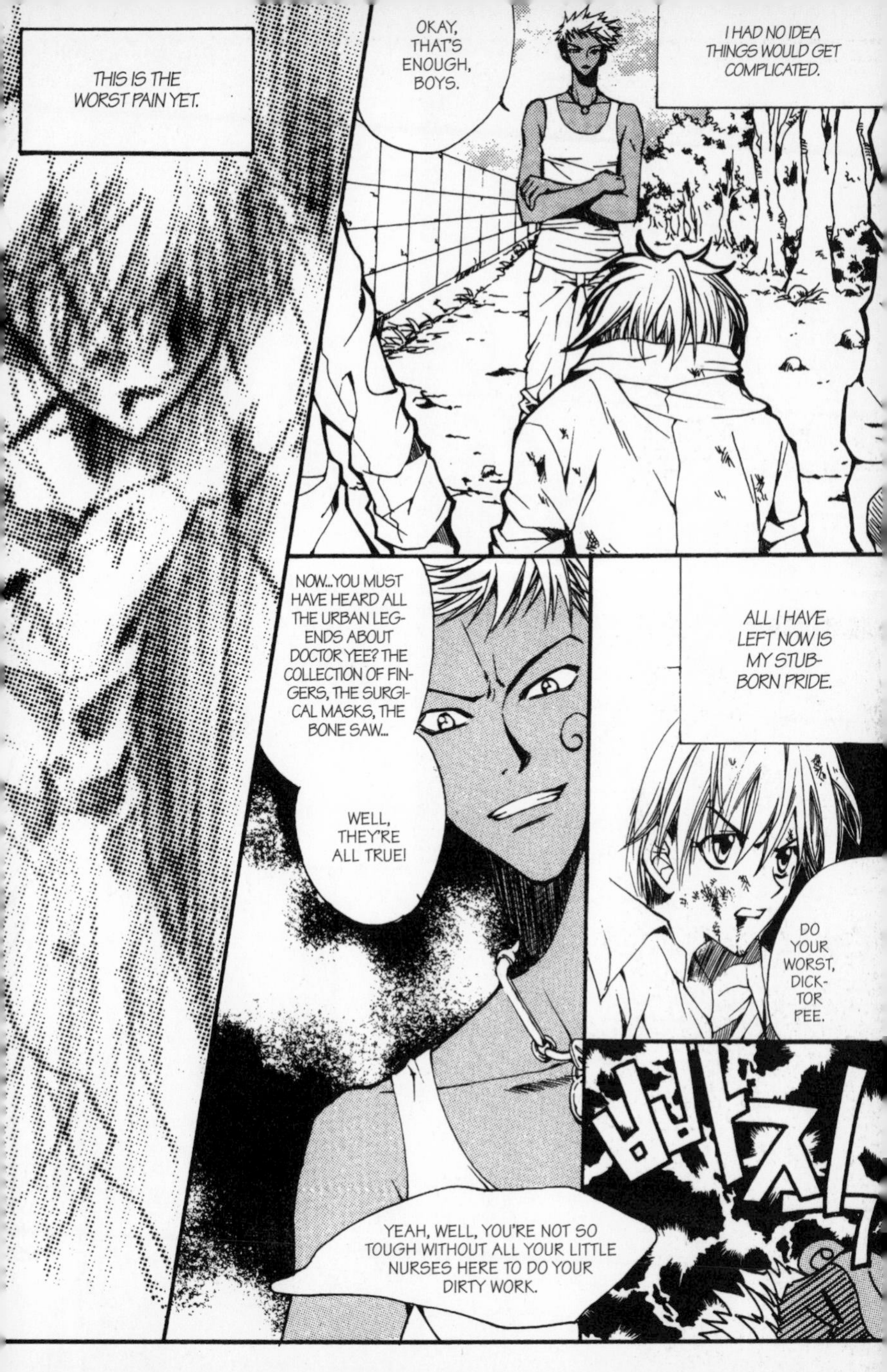

THIS IS THE WORST PAIN YET.
OKAY, THAT'S ENOUGH, BOYS.
I HAD NO IDEA THINGS WOULD GET COMPLICATED.
NOW...YOU MUST HAVE HEARD ALL THE URBAN LEG-ENDS ABOUT DOCTOR YEE? THE COLLECTION OF FIN-GERS, THE SURGI-CAL MASKS, THE BONE SAW...
WELL, THEY'RE ALL TRUE!
ALL I HAVE LEFT NOW IS MY STUB-BORN PRIDE.
DO YOUR WORST, DICK-TOR PEE.
YEAH, WELL, YOU'RE NOT SO TOUGH WITHOUT ALL YOUR LITTLE NURSES HERE TO DO YOUR DIRTY WORK.

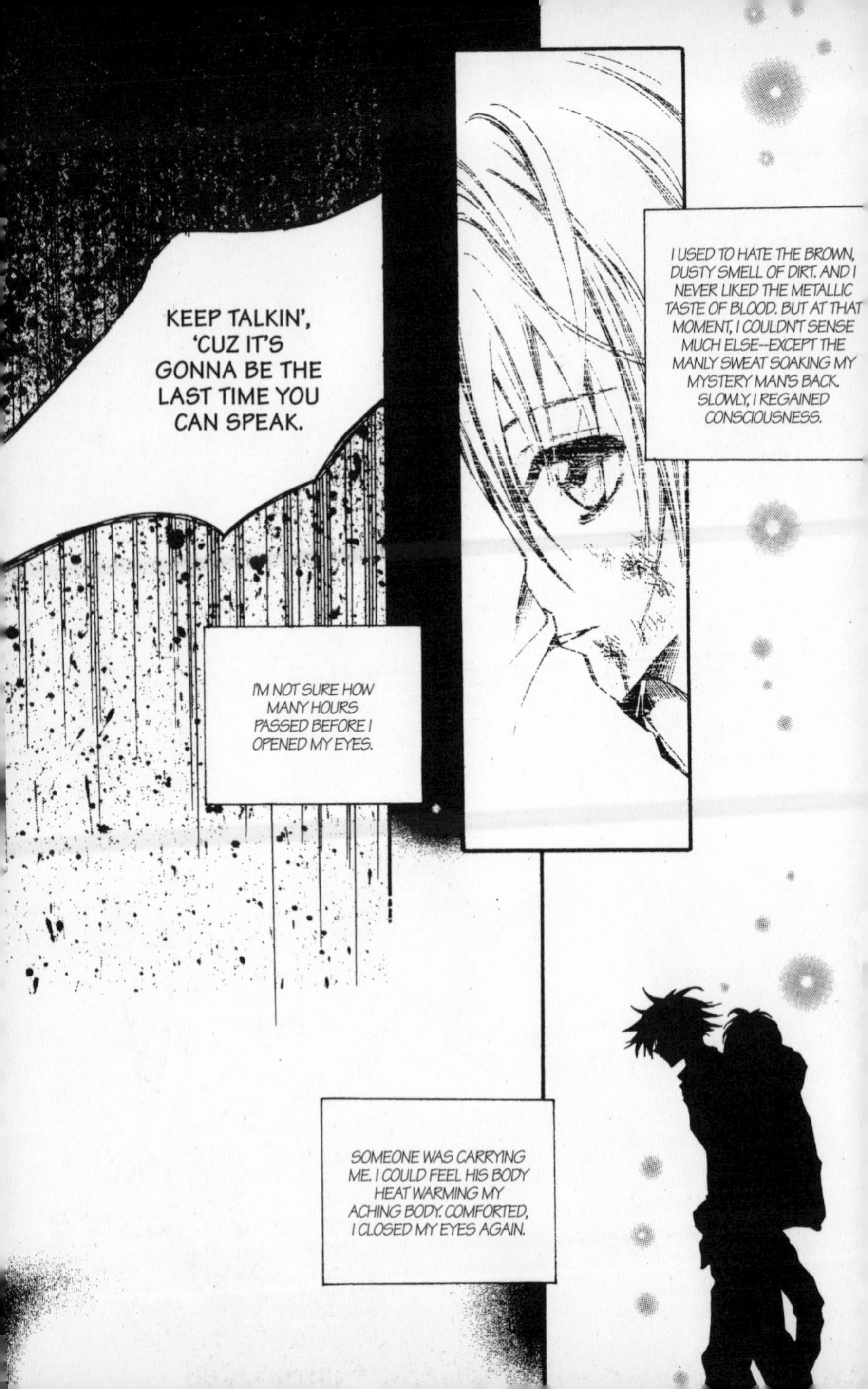
KEEP TALKIN', 'CUZ IT'S GONNA BE THE LAST TIME YOU CAN SPEAK.
I'M NOT SURE HOW MANY HOURS PASSED BEFORE I OPENED MY EYES.
I USED TO HATE THE BROWN, DUSTY SMELL OF DIRT. AND I NEVER LIKED THE METALLIC TASTE OF BLOOD. BUT AT THAT MOMENT, I COULDN'T SENSE MUCH ELSE--EXCEPT THE MANLY SWEAT SOAKING MY MYSTERY MAN'S BACK. SLOWLY, I REGAINED CONSCIOUSNESS.
SOMEONE WAS CARRYING ME. I COULD FEEL HIS BODY HEAT WARMING MY ACHING BODY. COMFORTED, I CLOSED MY EYES AGAIN.

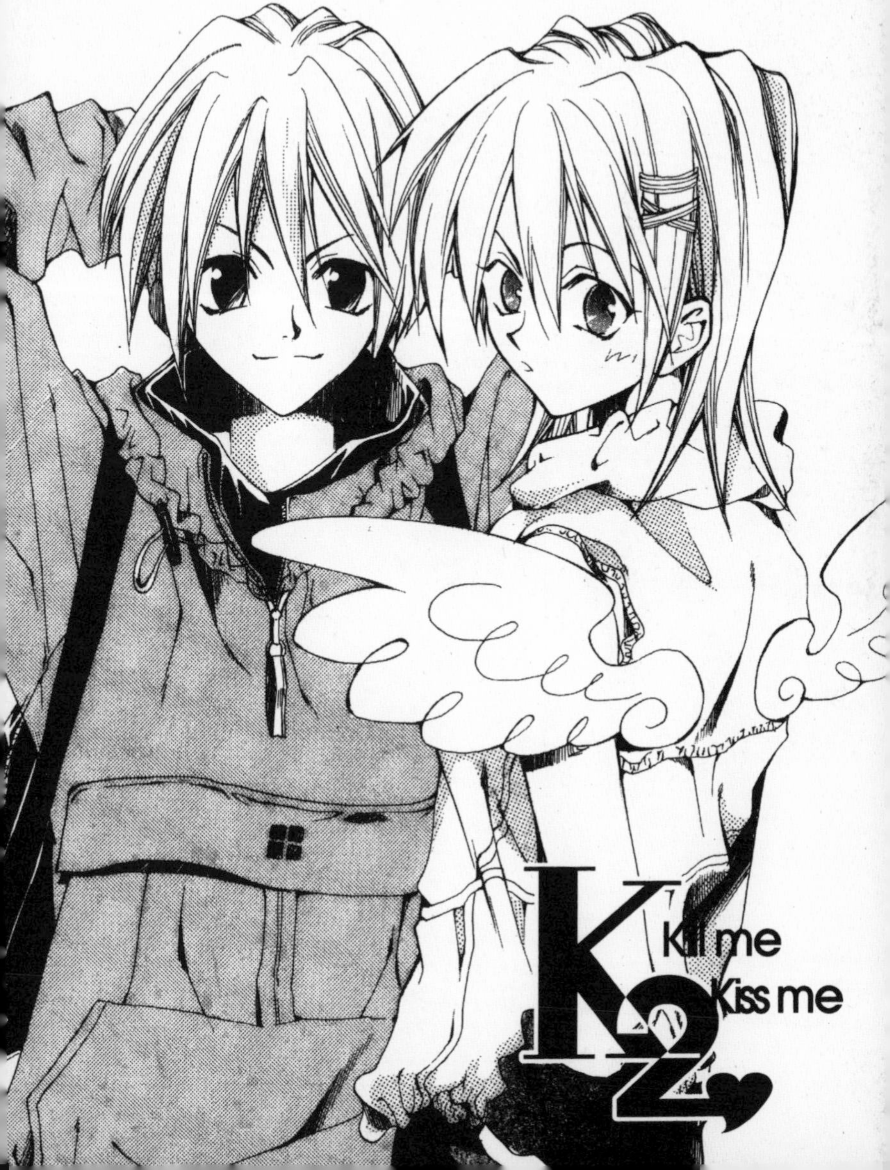
K2
Kill me
Kiss me

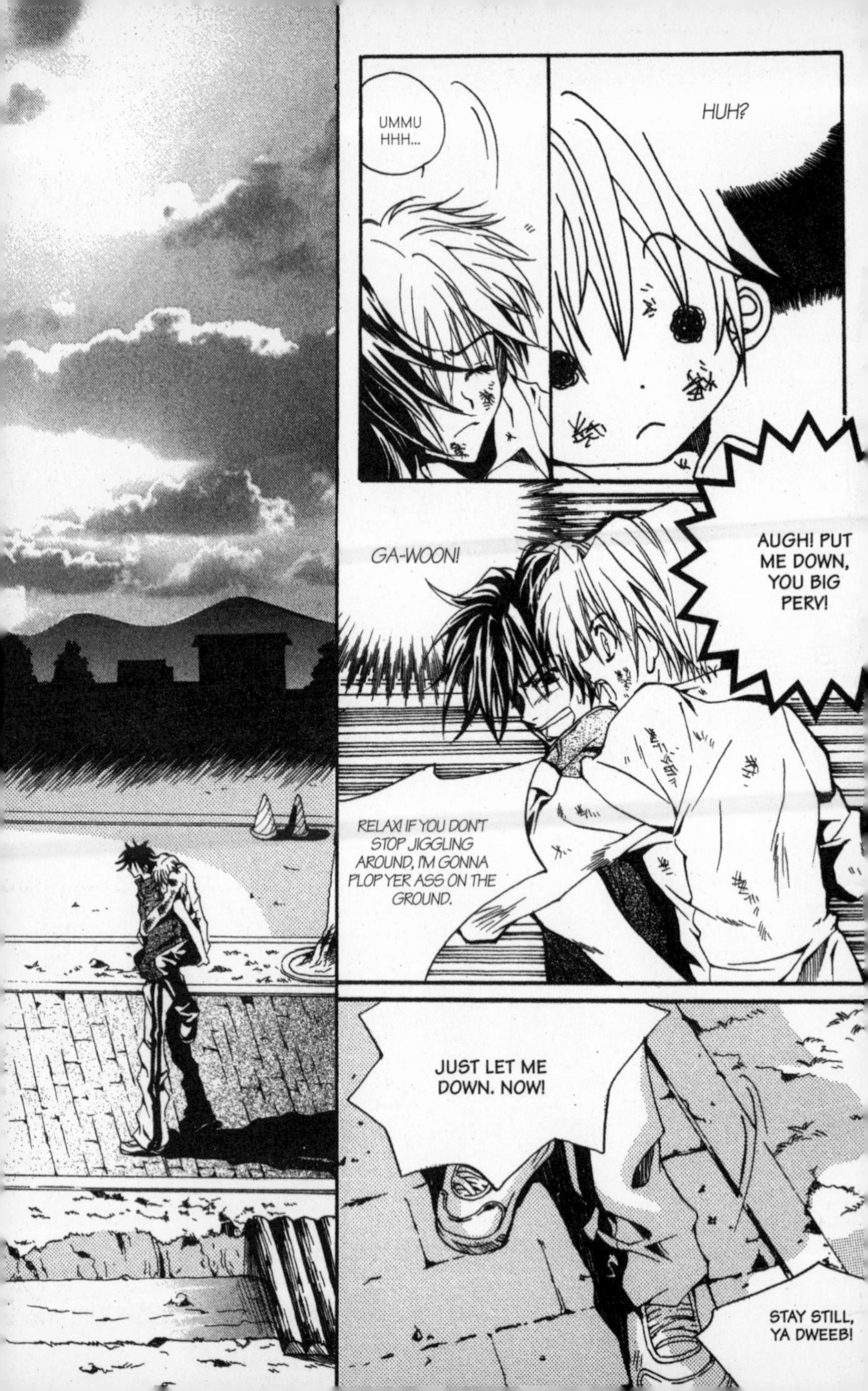
UMMU
HHH...
HUH?
GA-WOON!
AUGH! PUT ME DOWN, YOU BIG PERV!
RELAX! IF YOU DON'T STOP JIGGLING AROUND, I'M GONNA PLOP YER ASS ON THE GROUND.
JUST LET ME DOWN. NOW!
STAY STILL, YA DWEEB!

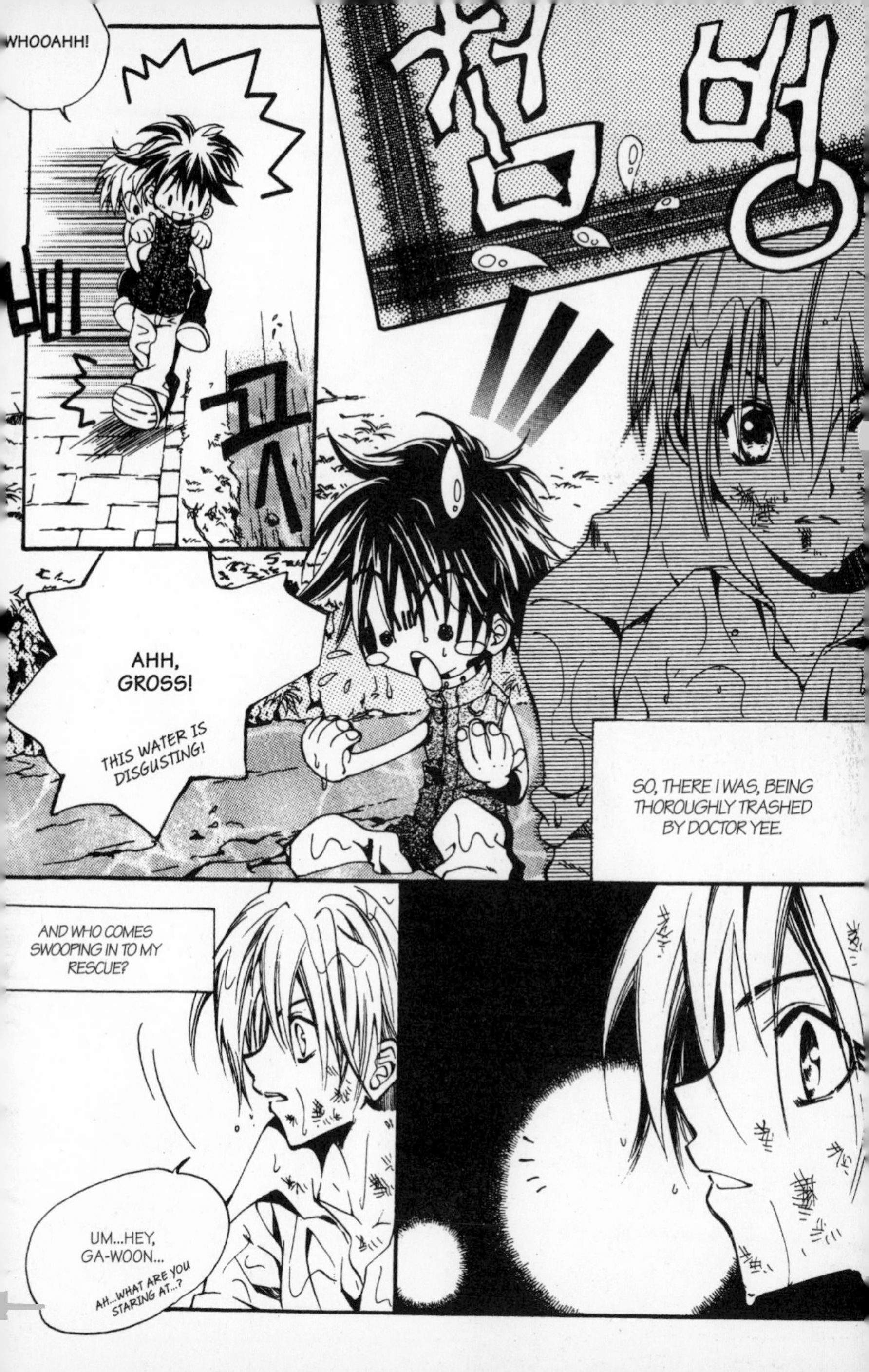
WHOOAHH!
첨벙
AHH, GROSS!
THIS WATER IS DISGUSTING!
SO, THERE I WAS, BEING THOROUGHLY TRASHED BY DOCTOR YEE.
AND WHO COMES SWOOPING IN TO MY RESCUE?
UM...HEY, GA-WOON...
AH...WHAT ARE YOU STARING AT...?

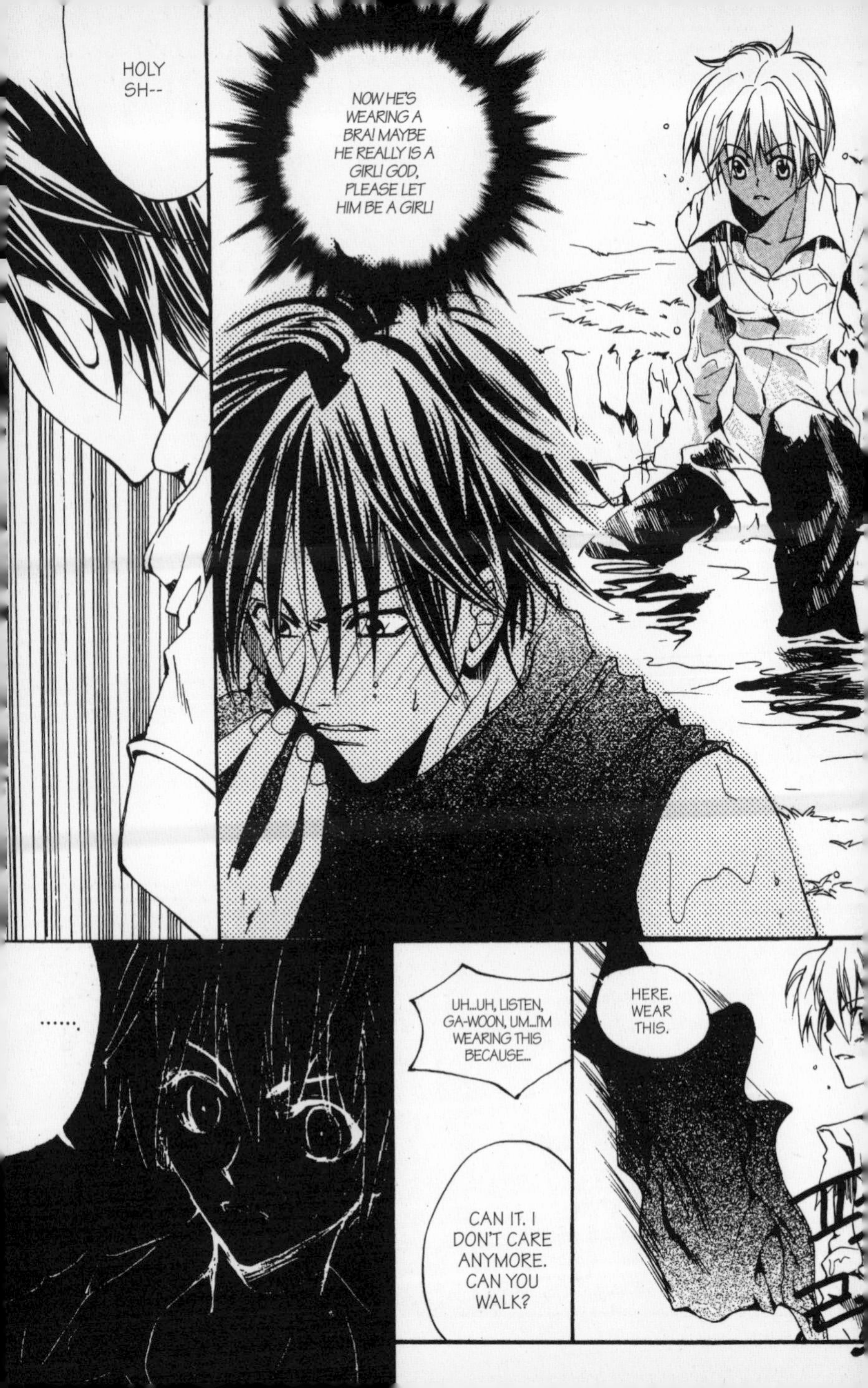
HOLY SH--
NOW HE'S WEARING A BRA! MAYBE HE REALLY IS A GIRL! GOD, PLEASE LET HIM BE A GIRL!
......
UH...UH, LISTEN, GA-WOON, UM...I'M WEARING THIS BECAUSE...
CAN IT. I DON'T CARE ANYMORE. CAN YOU WALK?
HERE. WEAR THIS.

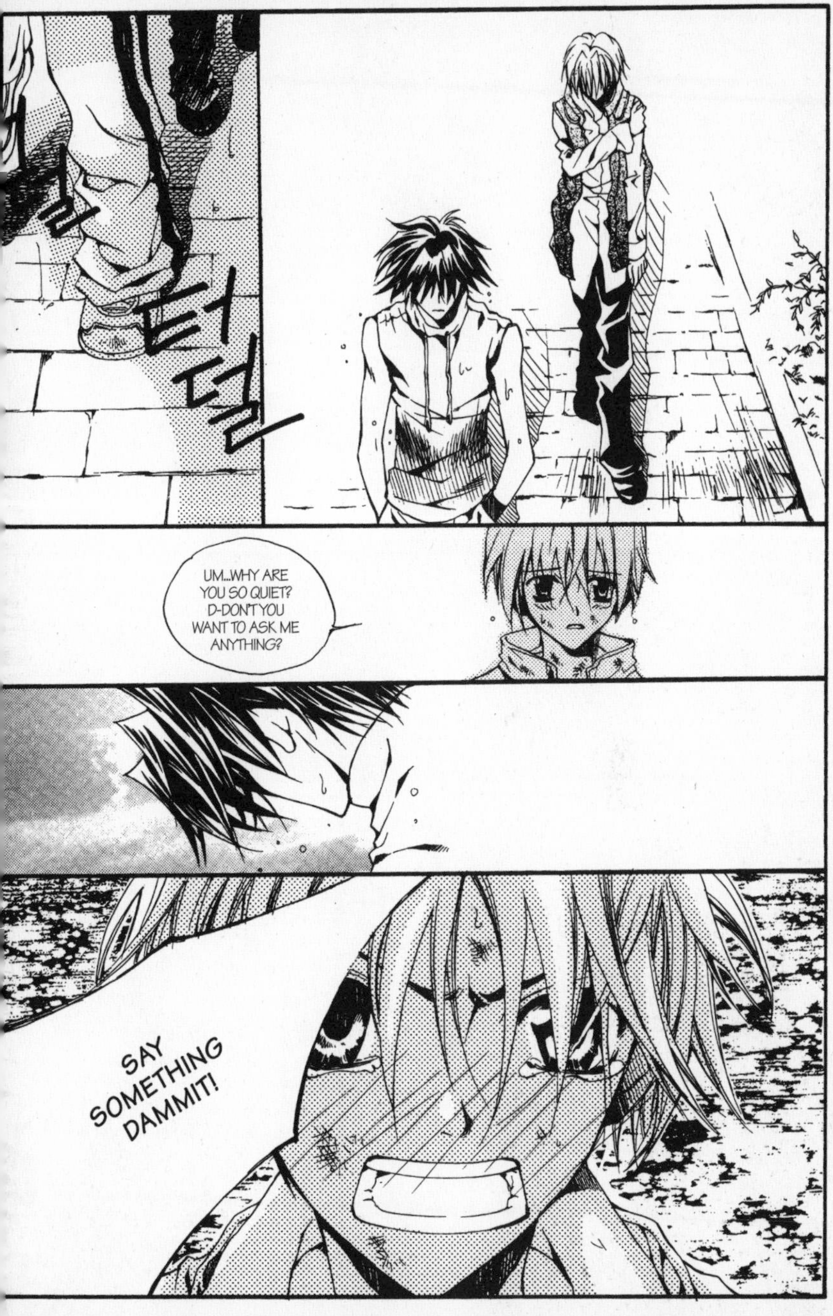
터덜
UM...WHY ARE YOU SO QUIET? D-DON'T YOU WANT TO ASK ME ANYTHING?
SAY SOMETHING DAMMIT!

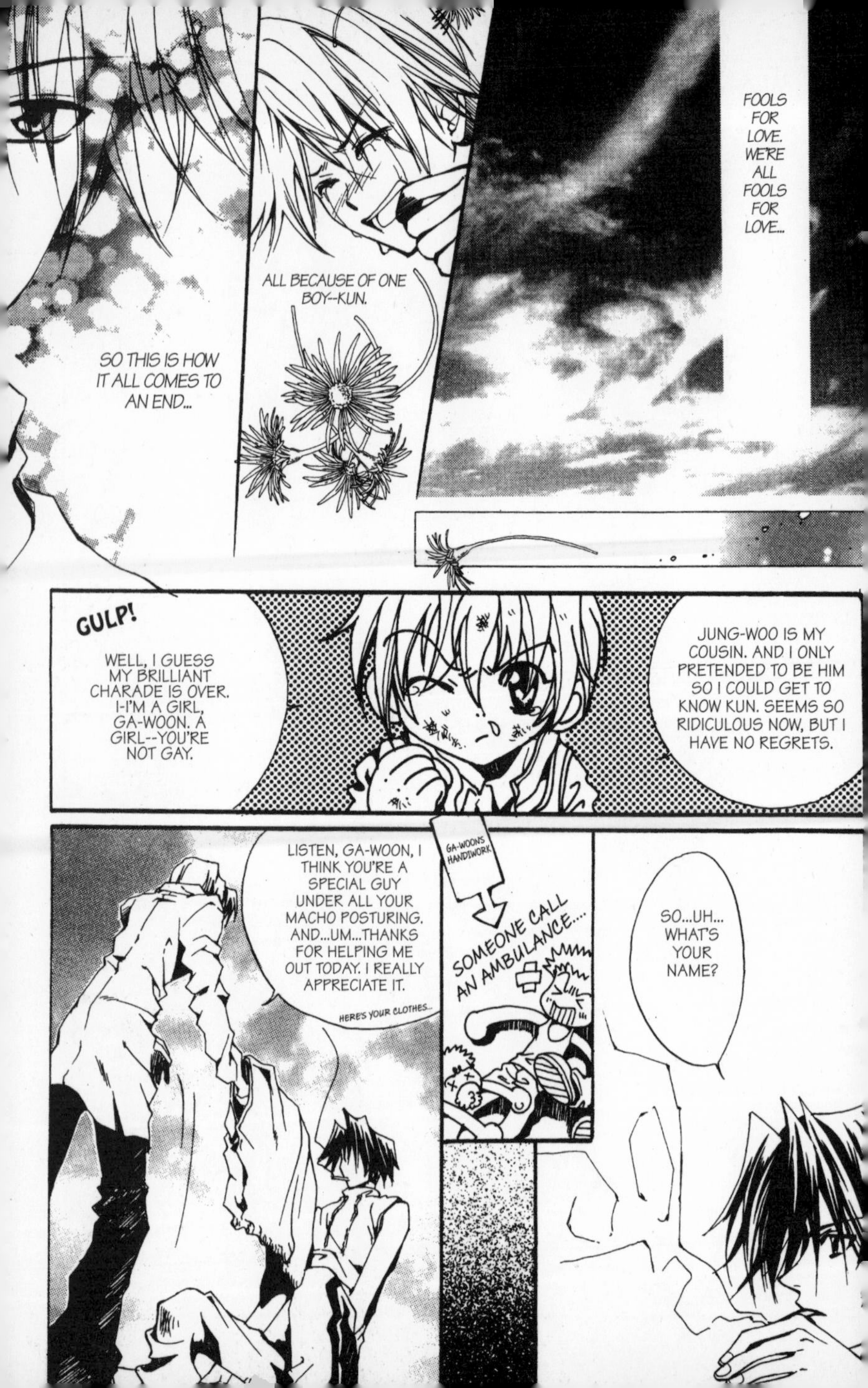
SO THIS IS HOW IT ALL COMES TO AN END...
ALL BECAUSE OF ONE BOY--KUN.
FOOLS FOR LOVE. WE'RE ALL FOOLS FOR LOVE...
GULP!
WELL, I GUESS MY BRILLIANT CHARADE IS OVER. I-I'M A GIRL, GA-WOON. A GIRL--YOU'RE NOT GAY.
JUNG-WOO IS MY COUSIN. AND I ONLY PRETENDED TO BE HIM SO I COULD GET TO KNOW KUN. SEEMS SO RIDICULOUS NOW, BUT I HAVE NO REGRETS.
LISTEN, GA-WOON, I THINK YOU'RE A SPECIAL GUY UNDER ALL YOUR MACHO POSTURING. AND...UM...THANKS FOR HELPING ME OUT TODAY. I REALLY APPRECIATE IT.
HERE'S YOUR CLOTHES...
GA-WOON'S HANDIWORK
SOMEONE CALL AN AMBULANCE....
SO...UH... WHAT'S YOUR NAME?

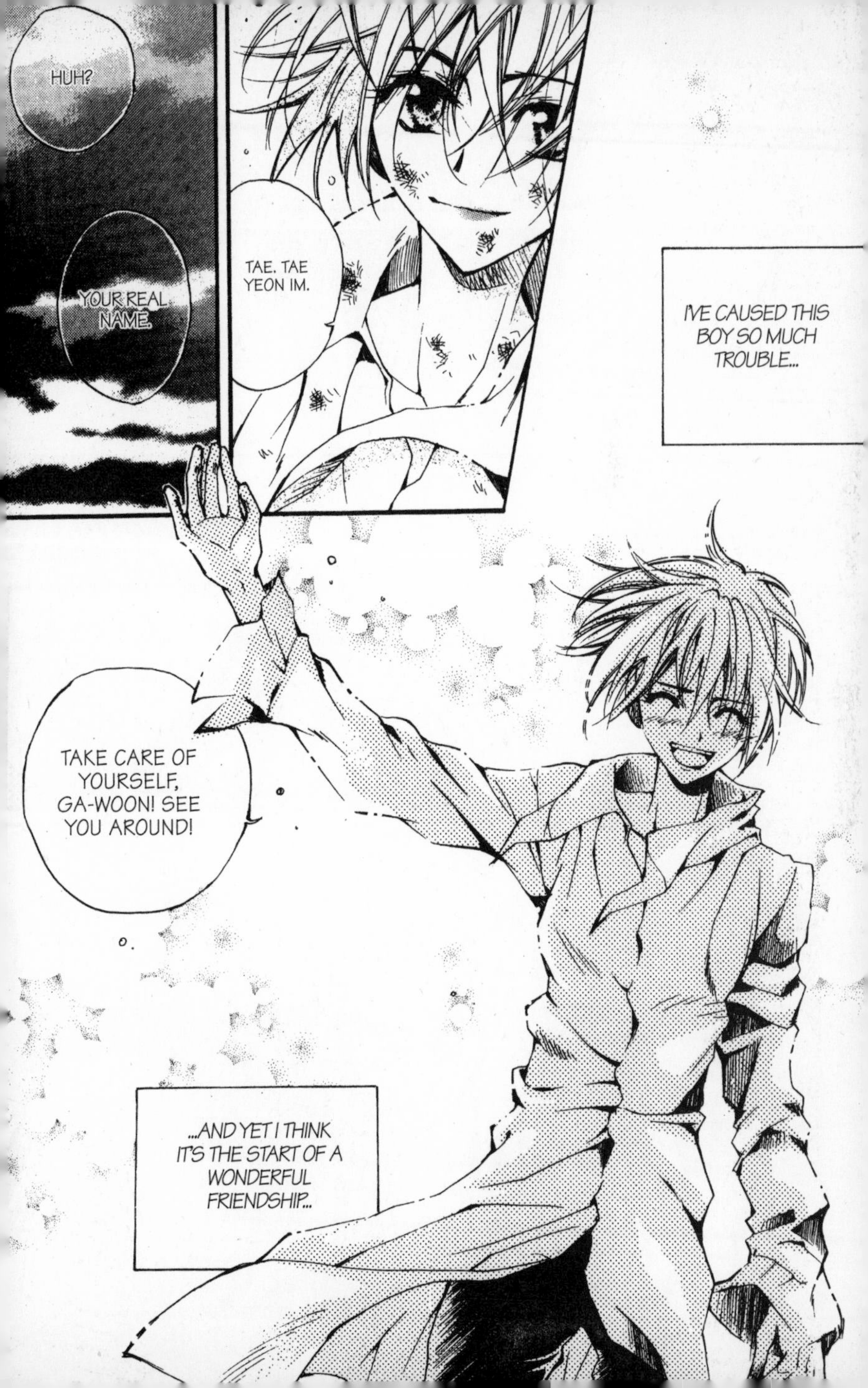
HUH?
YOUR REAL NAME.
TAE. TAE YEON IM.
I'VE CAUSED THIS BOY SO MUCH TROUBLE...
TAKE CARE OF YOURSELF, GA-WOON! SEE YOU AROUND!
...AND YET I THINK IT'S THE START OF A WONDERFUL FRIENDSHIP...

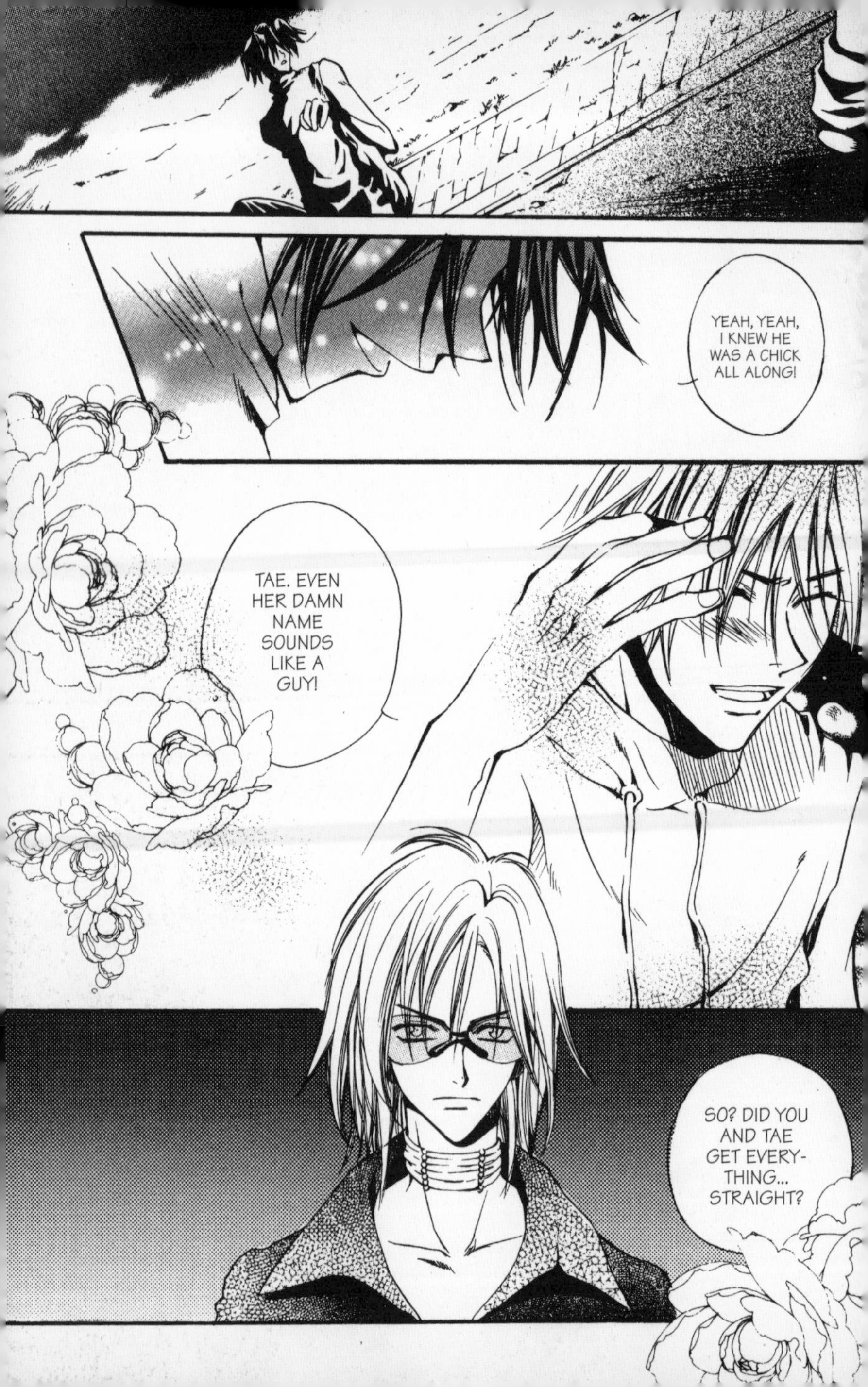
YEAH, YEAH, I KNEW HE WAS A CHICK ALL ALONG!
TAE. EVEN HER DAMN NAME SOUNDS LIKE A GUY!
SO? DID YOU AND TAE GET EVERY-THING... STRAIGHT?

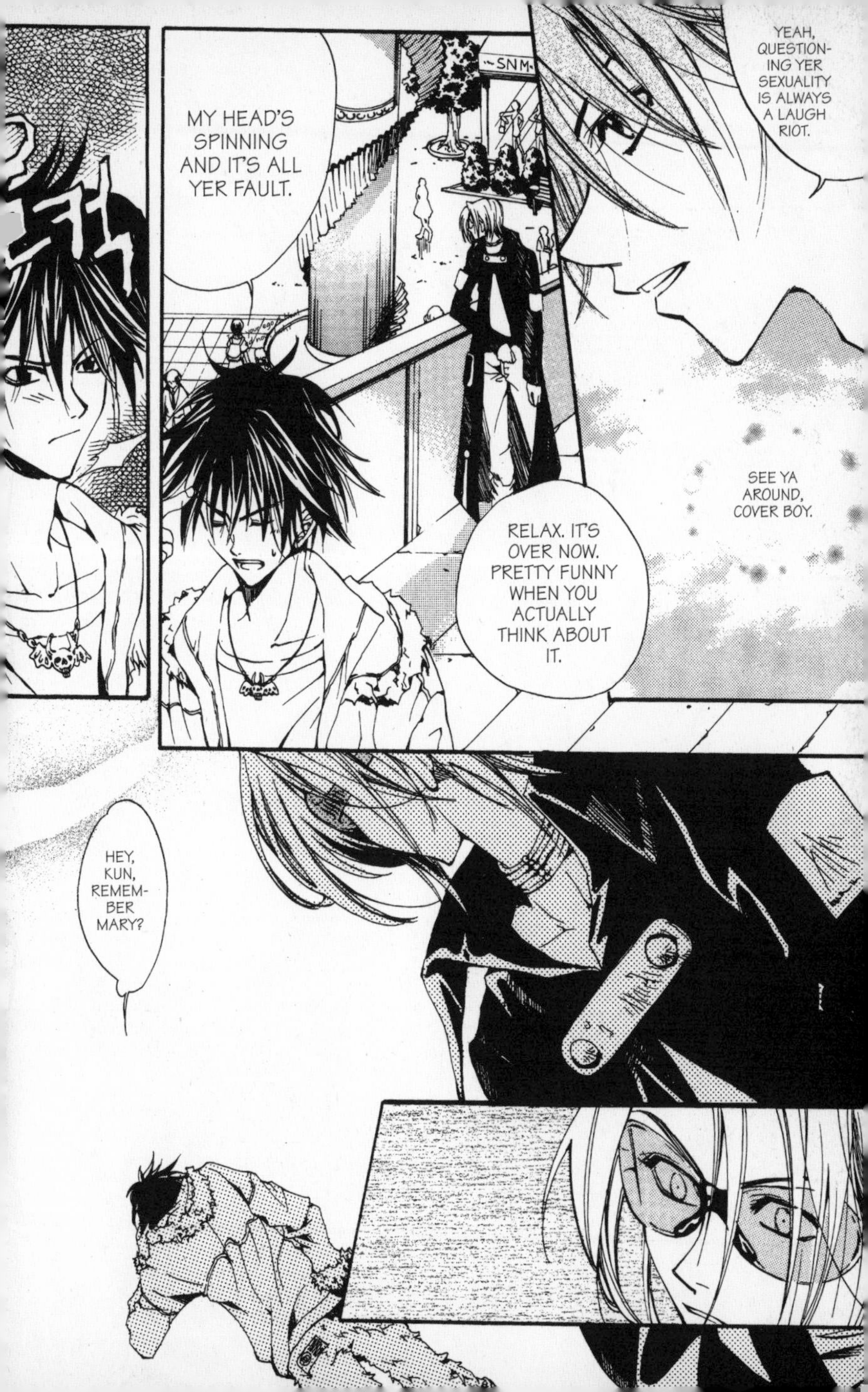
MY HEAD'S SPINNING AND IT'S ALL YER FAULT.
RELAX. IT'S OVER NOW. PRETTY FUNNY WHEN YOU ACTUALLY THINK ABOUT IT.
YEAH, QUESTIONING YER SEXUALITY IS ALWAYS A LAUGH RIOT.
SEE YA AROUND, COVER BOY.
HEY, KUN, REMEMBER MARY?

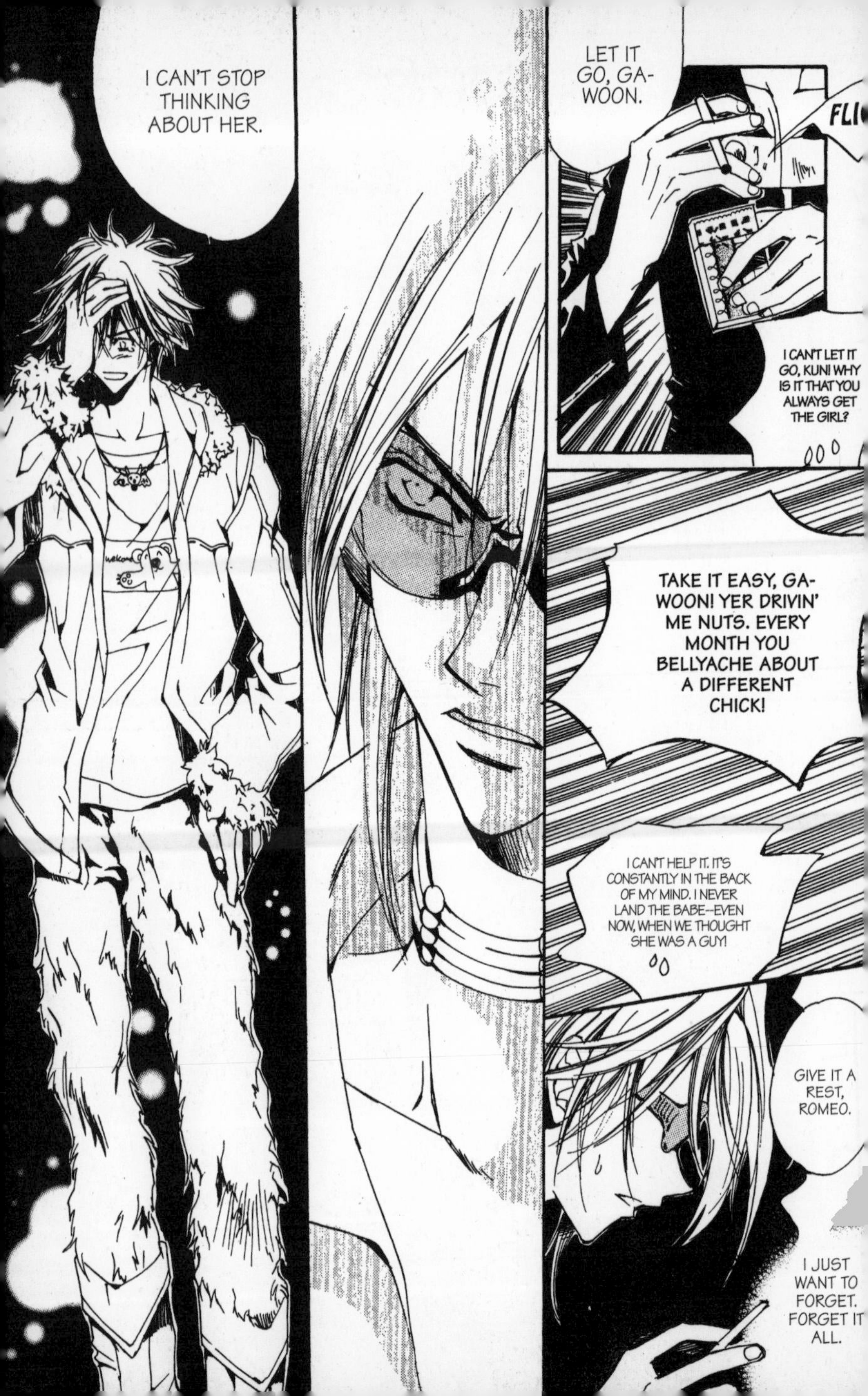
I CAN'T STOP THINKING ABOUT HER.
LET IT GO, GA-WOON.
FLI
I CAN'T LET IT GO, KUN! WHY IS IT THAT YOU ALWAYS GET THE GIRL?
TAKE IT EASY, GA-WOON! YER DRIVIN' ME NUTS. EVERY MONTH YOU BELLYACHE ABOUT A DIFFERENT CHICK!
I CAN'T HELP IT. IT'S CONSTANTLY IN THE BACK OF MY MIND. I NEVER LAND THE BABE--EVEN NOW, WHEN WE THOUGHT SHE WAS A GUY!
GIVE IT A REST, ROMEO.
I JUST WANT TO FORGET. FORGET IT ALL.

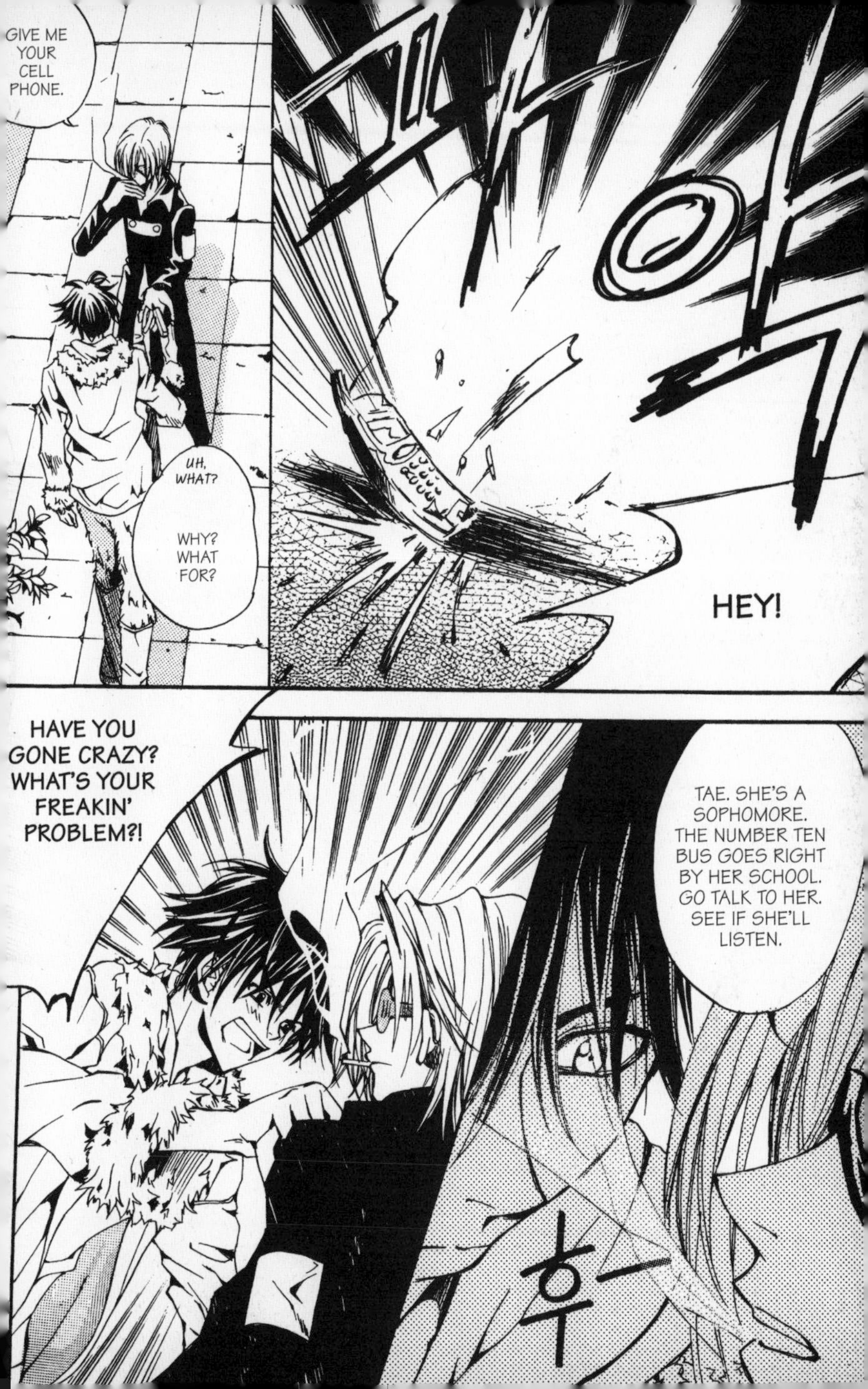
GIVE ME YOUR CELL PHONE.
UH, WHAT?
WHY? WHAT FOR?
HEY!
HAVE YOU GONE CRAZY? WHAT'S YOUR FREAKIN' PROBLEM?!
TAE. SHE'S A SOPHOMORE. THE NUMBER TEN BUS GOES RIGHT BY HER SCHOOL. GO TALK TO HER. SEE IF SHE'LL LISTEN.

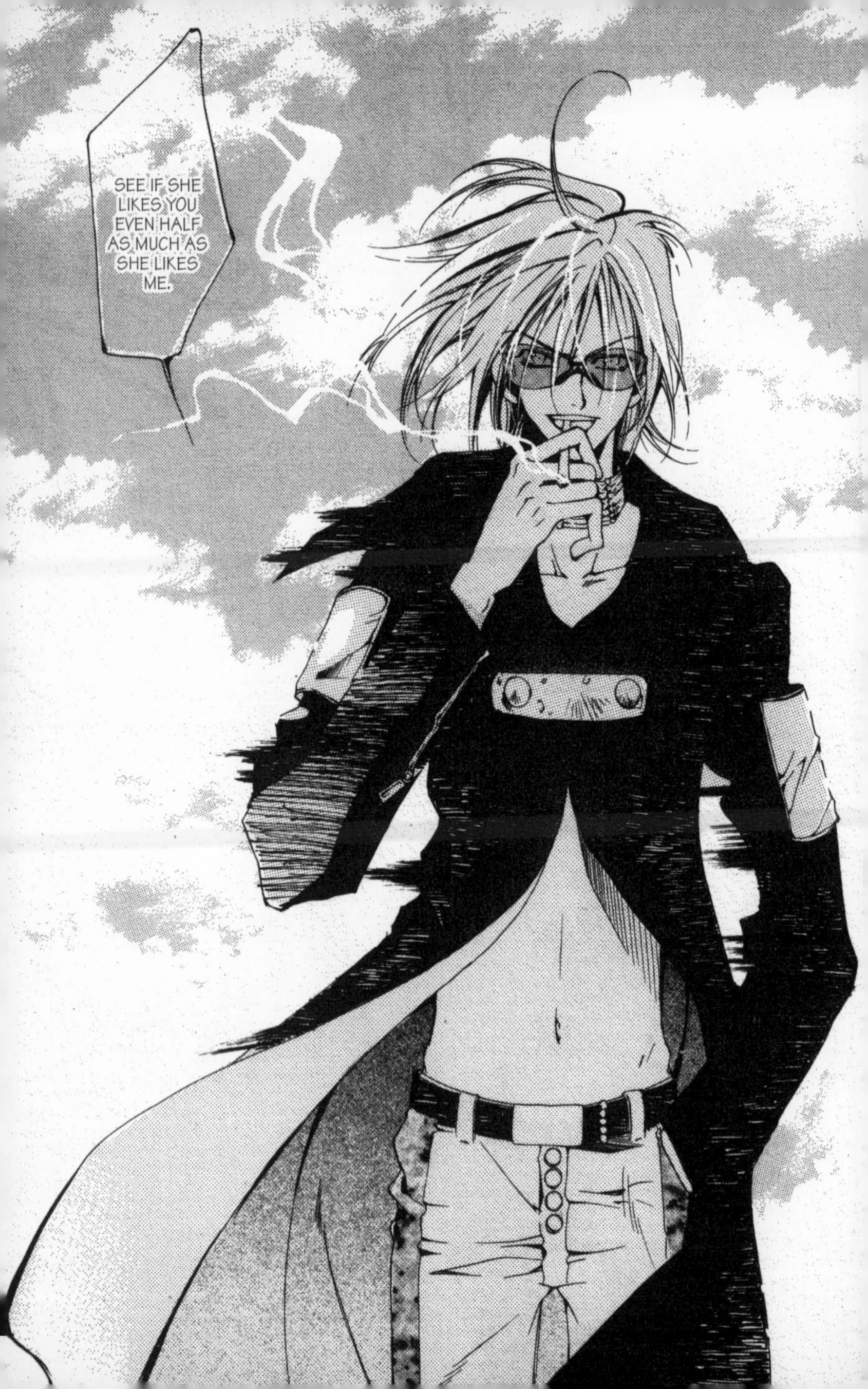
SEE IF SHE LIKES YOU EVEN HALF AS MUCH AS SHE LIKES ME.

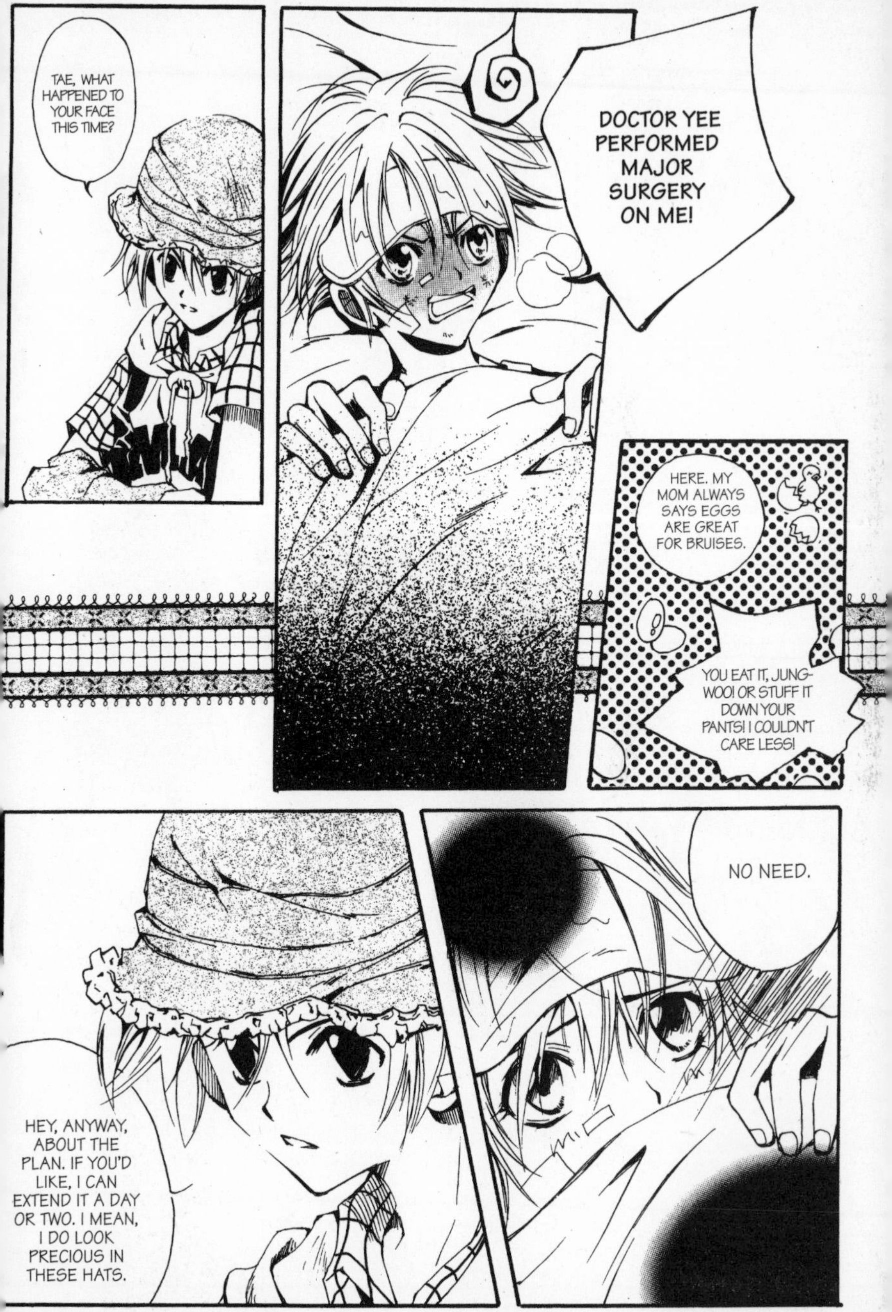
TAE, WHAT HAPPENED TO YOUR FACE THIS TIME?
DOCTOR YEE PERFORMED MAJOR SURGERY ON ME!
HERE. MY MOM ALWAYS SAYS EGGS ARE GREAT FOR BRUISES.
YOU EAT IT, JUNG-WOO! OR STUFF IT DOWN YOUR PANTS! I COULDN'T CARE LESS!
HEY, ANYWAY, ABOUT THE PLAN. IF YOU'D LIKE, I CAN EXTEND IT A DAY OR TWO. I MEAN, I DO LOOK PRECIOUS IN THESE HATS.
NO NEED.

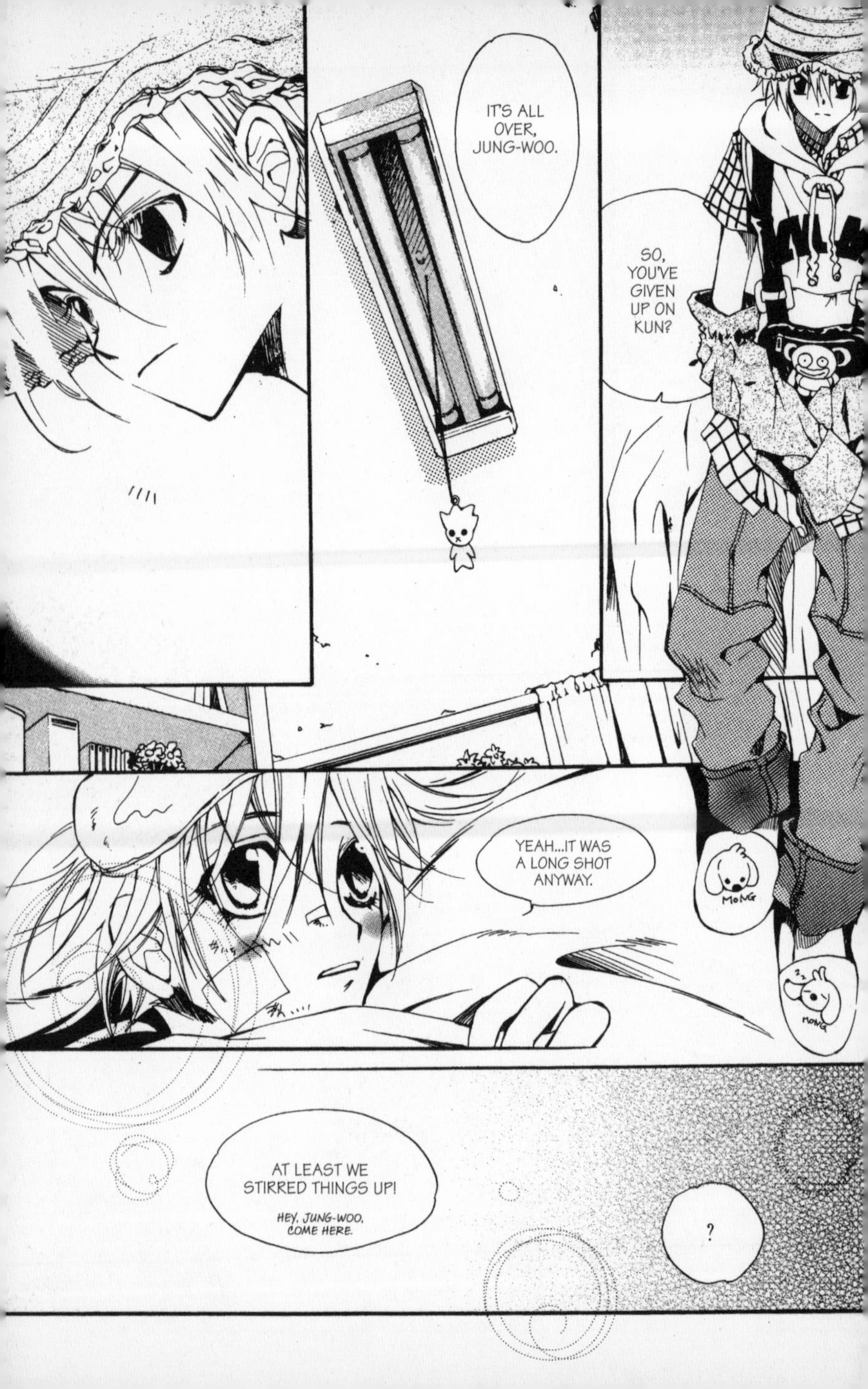

IT'S ALL OVER, JUNG-WOO.
SO, YOU'VE GIVEN UP ON KUN?
MONG
MONG
YEAH...IT WAS A LONG SHOT ANYWAY.
AT LEAST WE STIRRED THINGS UP!
HEY, JUNG-WOO, COME HERE.
?

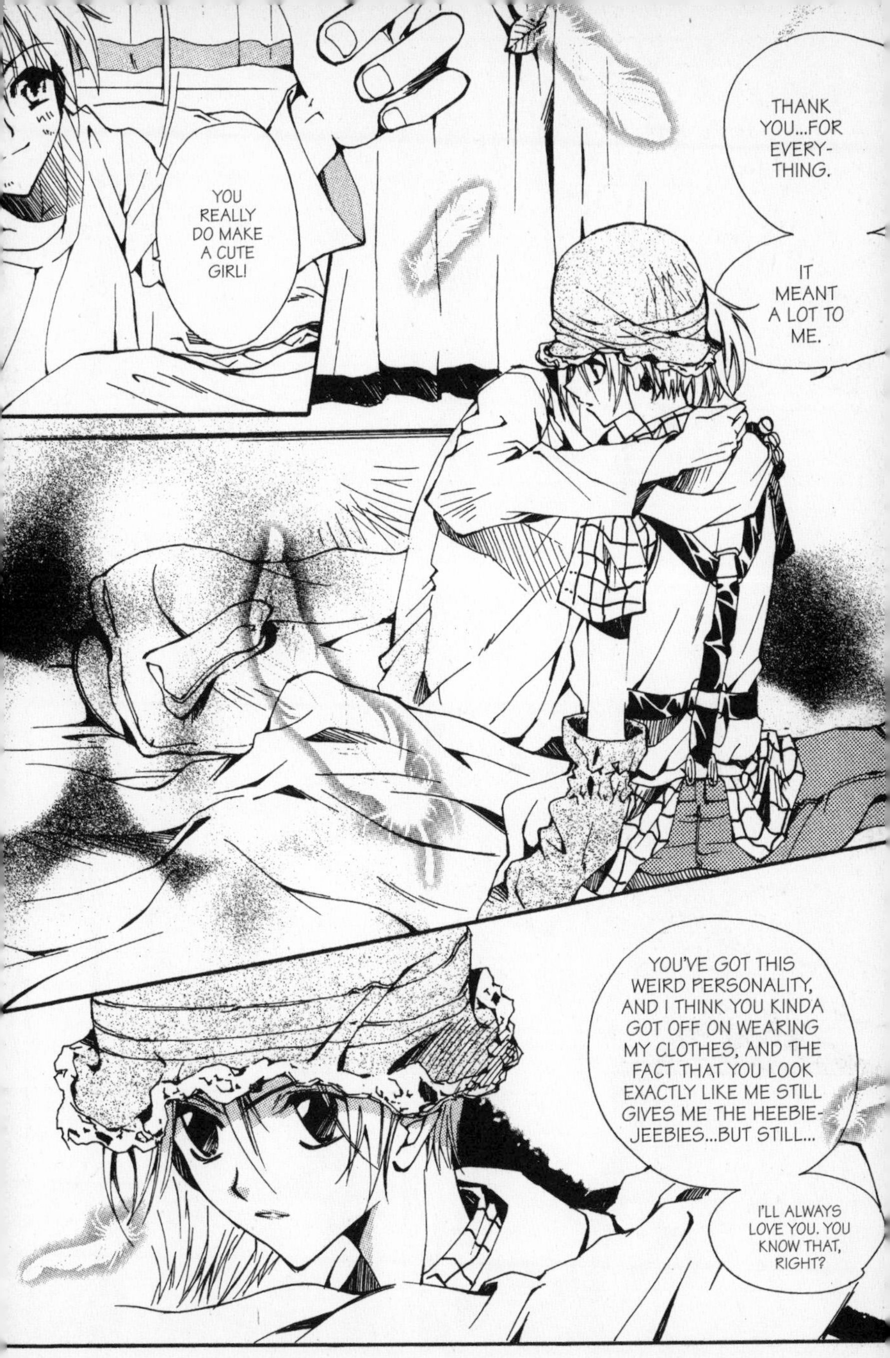
YOU REALLY DO MAKE A CUTE GIRL!
THANK YOU...FOR EVERY-THING.
IT MEANT A LOT TO ME.
YOU'VE GOT THIS WEIRD PERSONALITY, AND I THINK YOU KINDA GOT OFF ON WEARING MY CLOTHES, AND THE FACT THAT YOU LOOK EXACTLY LIKE ME STILL GIVES ME THE HEEBIE-JEEBIES...BUT STILL...
I'LL ALWAYS LOVE YOU. YOU KNOW THAT, RIGHT?

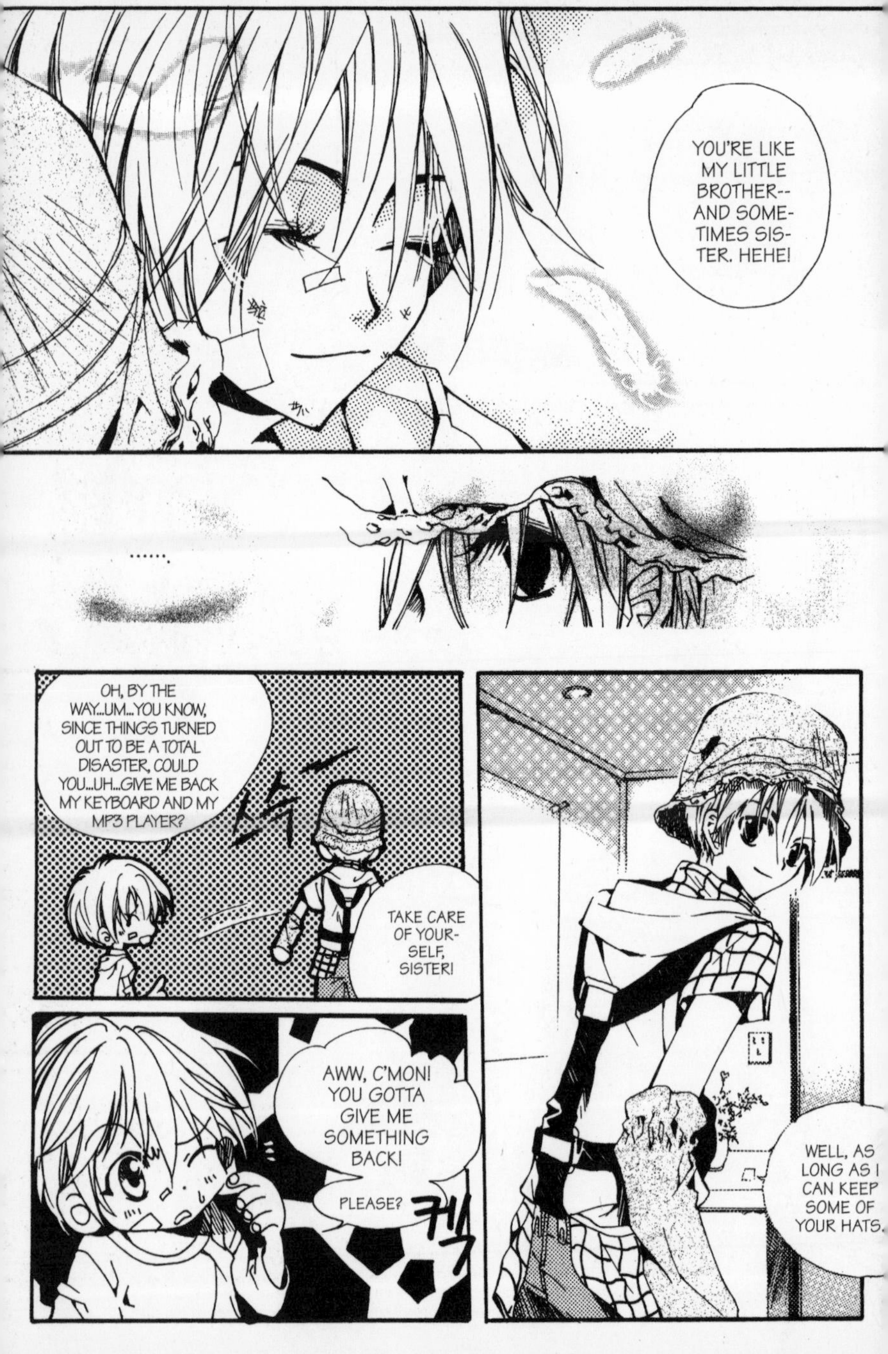
YOU'RE LIKE MY LITTLE BROTHER-- AND SOME-TIMES SIS-TER. HEHE!
......
OH, BY THE WAY...UM...YOU KNOW, SINCE THINGS TURNED OUT TO BE A TOTAL DISASTER, COULD YOU...UH...GIVE ME BACK MY KEYBOARD AND MY MP3 PLAYER?
TAKE CARE OF YOUR-SELF, SISTER!
AWW, C'MON! YOU GOTTA GIVE ME SOMETHING BACK!
PLEASE?
WELL, AS LONG AS I CAN KEEP SOME OF YOUR HATS.

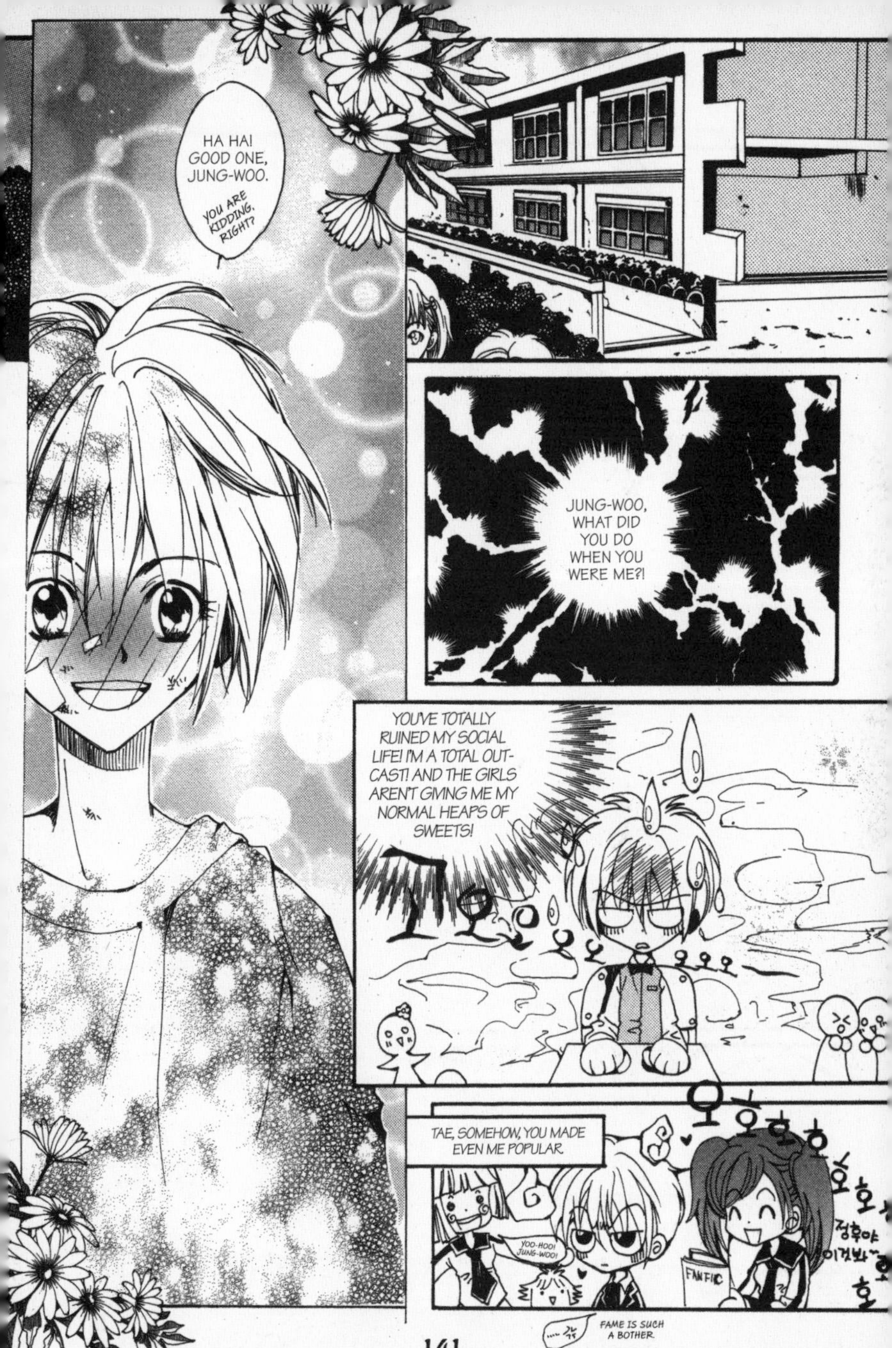
HA HA! GOOD ONE, JUNG-WOO.
YOU ARE KIDDING, RIGHT?
JUNG-WOO, WHAT DID YOU DO WHEN YOU WERE ME?!
YOU'VE TOTALLY RUINED MY SOCIAL LIFE! I'M A TOTAL OUT-CAST! AND THE GIRLS AREN'T GIVING ME MY NORMAL HEAPS OF SWEETS!
TAE, SOMEHOW, YOU MADE EVEN ME POPULAR.
YOO-HOO! JUNG-WOO!
FANFIC
정후야 이거봐~
FAME IS SUCH A BOTHER.

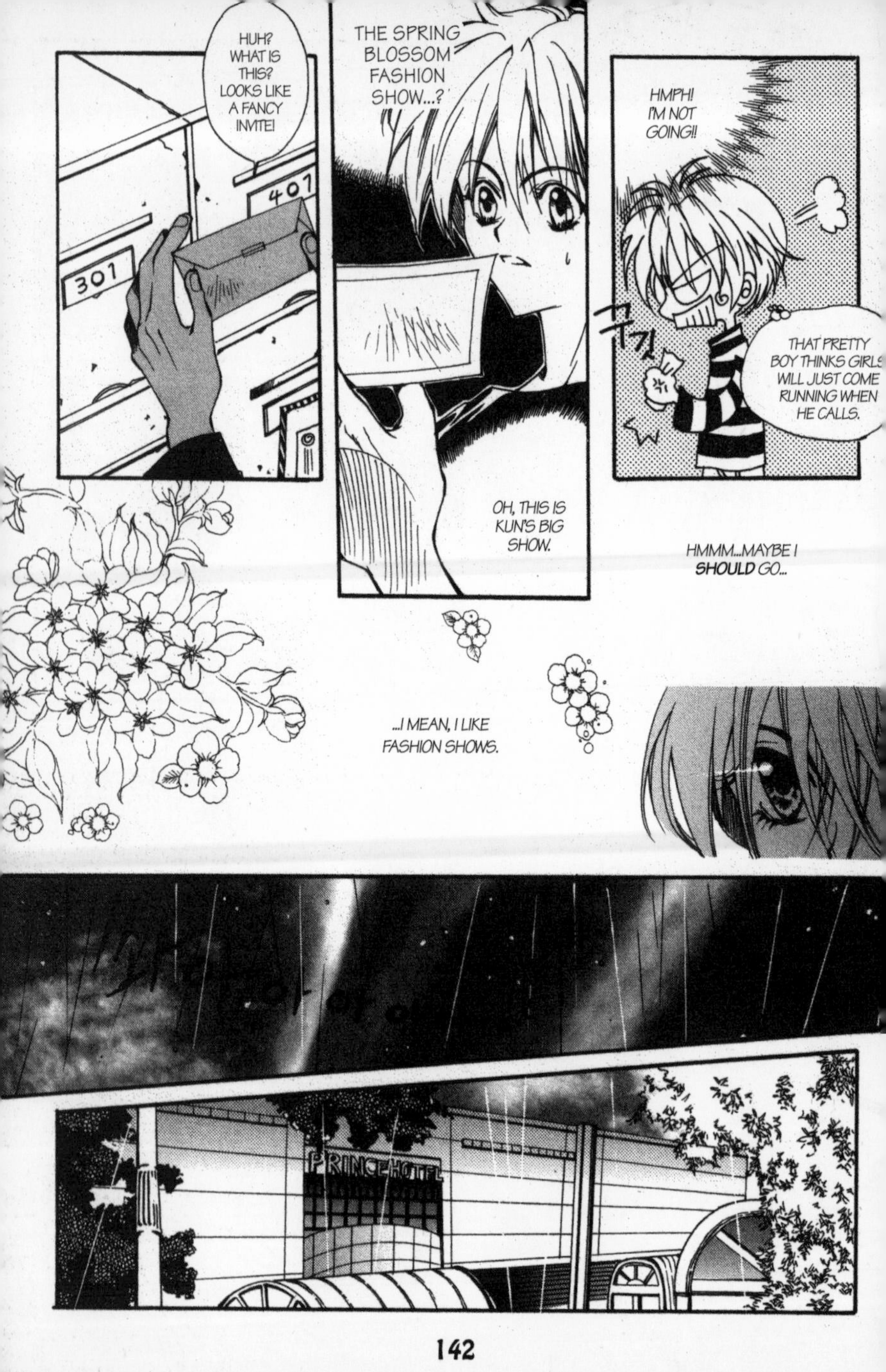
HUH? WHAT IS THIS? LOOKS LIKE A FANCY INVITE!
301
407
THE SPRING BLOSSOM FASHION SHOW...?
OH, THIS IS KUN'S BIG SHOW.
HMPH! I'M NOT GOING!!
THAT PRETTY BOY THINKS GIRLS WILL JUST COME RUNNING WHEN HE CALLS.
HMMM...MAYBE I SHOULD GO...
...I MEAN, I LIKE FASHION SHOWS.
PRINCE HOTEL

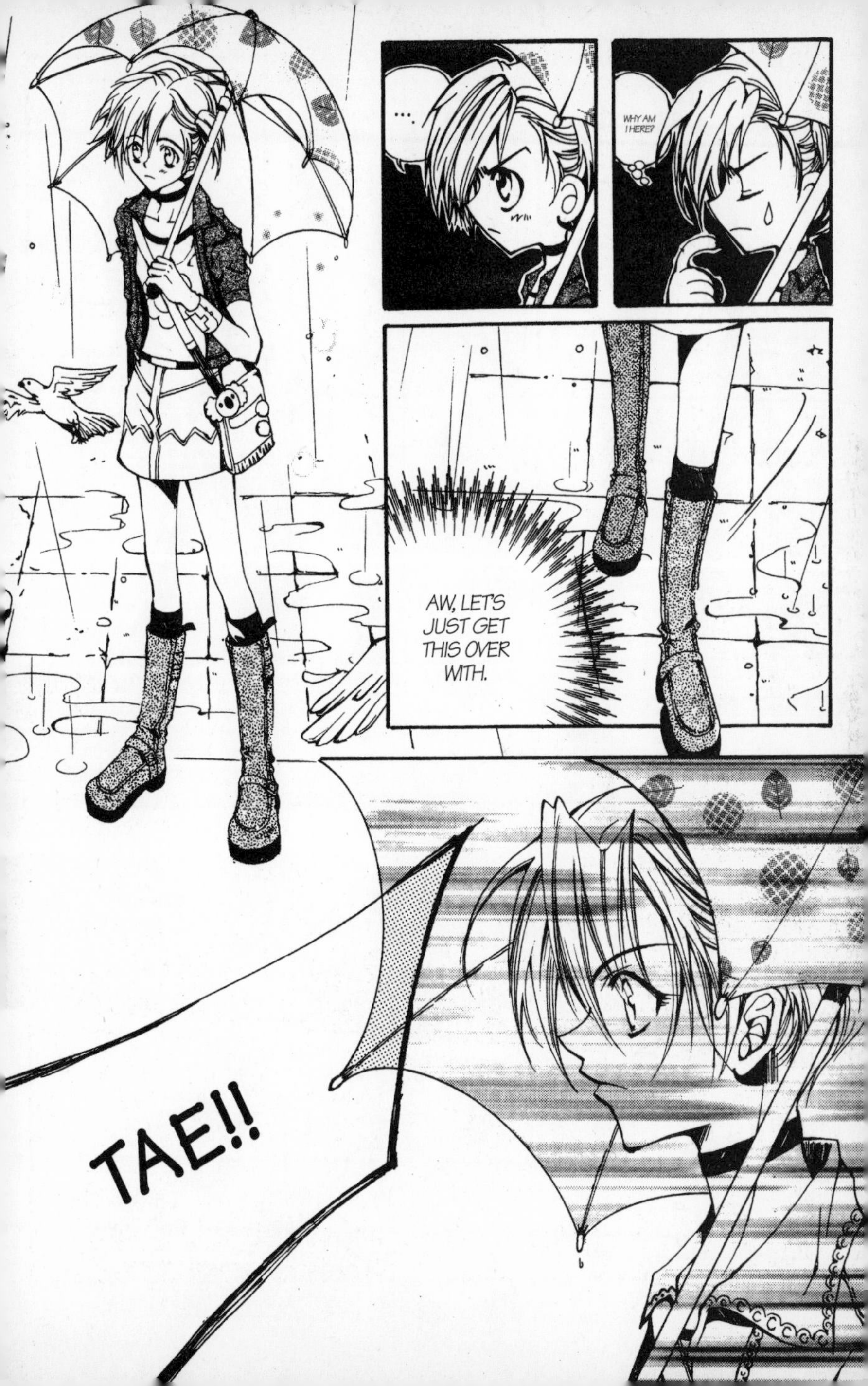
...
WHY AM I HERE?
AW, LET'S JUST GET THIS OVER WITH.
TAE!!

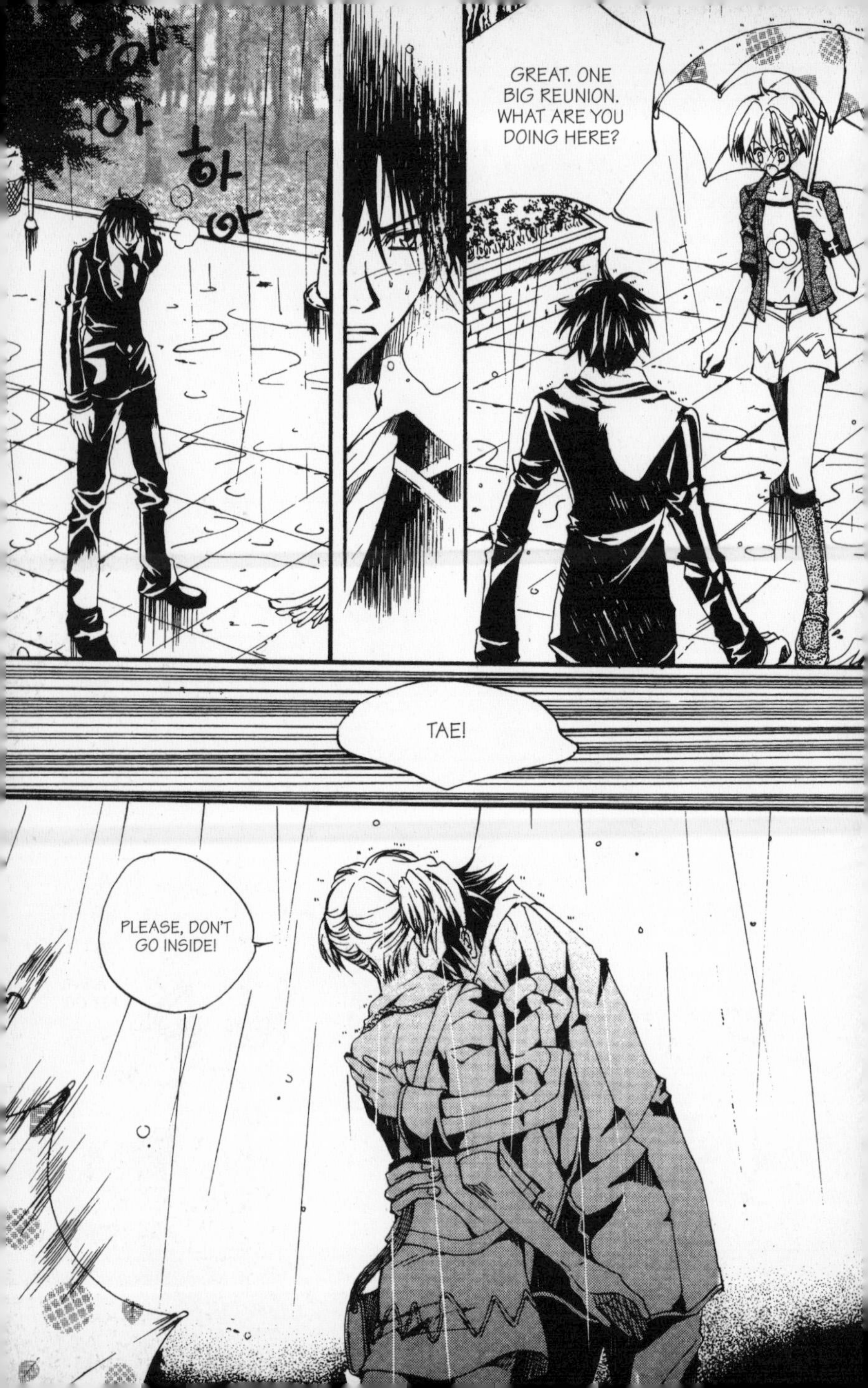
GREAT. ONE BIG REUNION. WHAT ARE YOU DOING HERE?
TAE!
PLEASE, DON'T GO INSIDE!

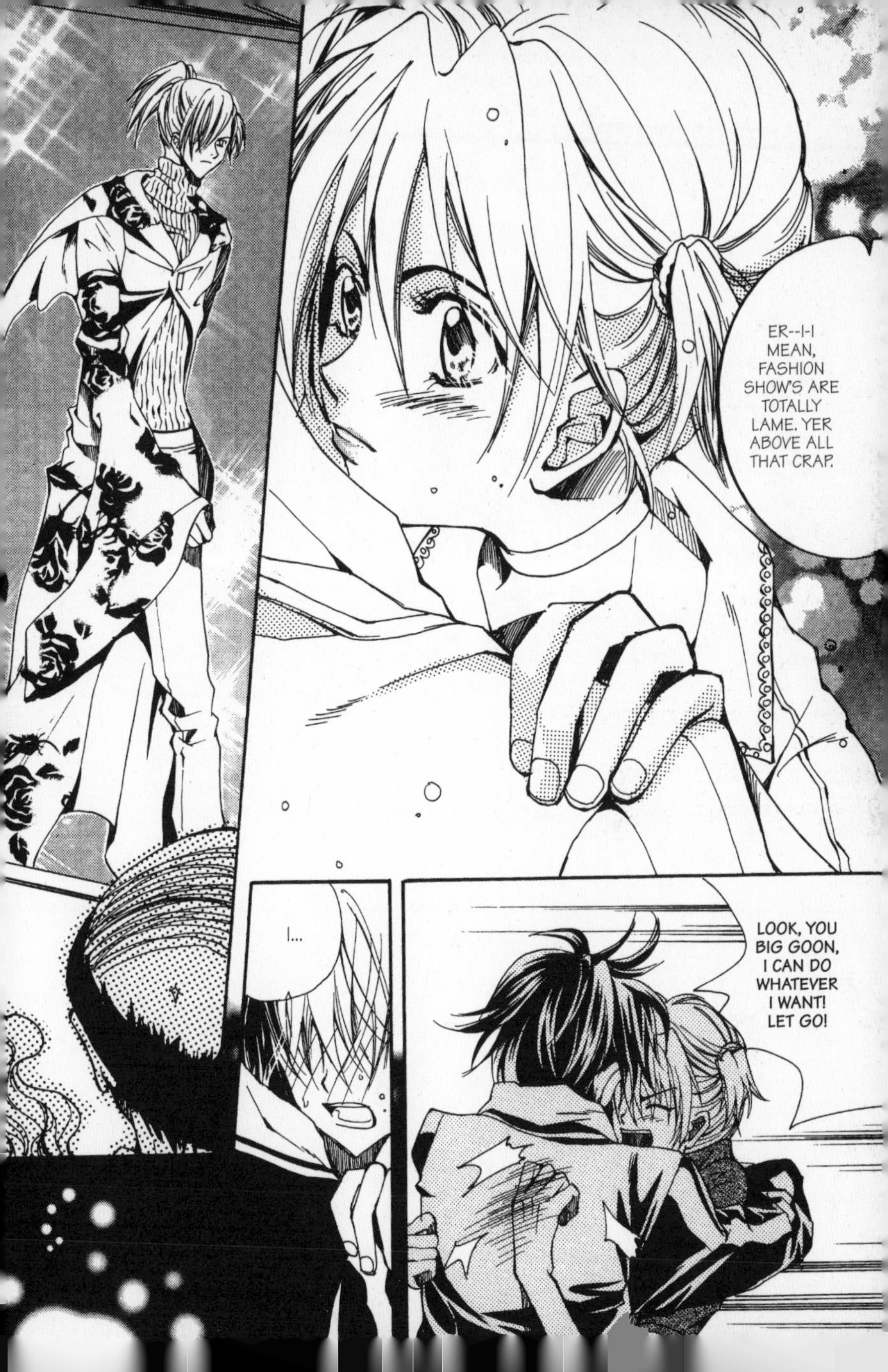
ER--I-I MEAN, FASHION SHOW'S ARE TOTALLY LAME. YER ABOVE ALL THAT CRAP.
I...
LOOK, YOU BIG GOON, I CAN DO WHATEVER I WANT! LET GO!

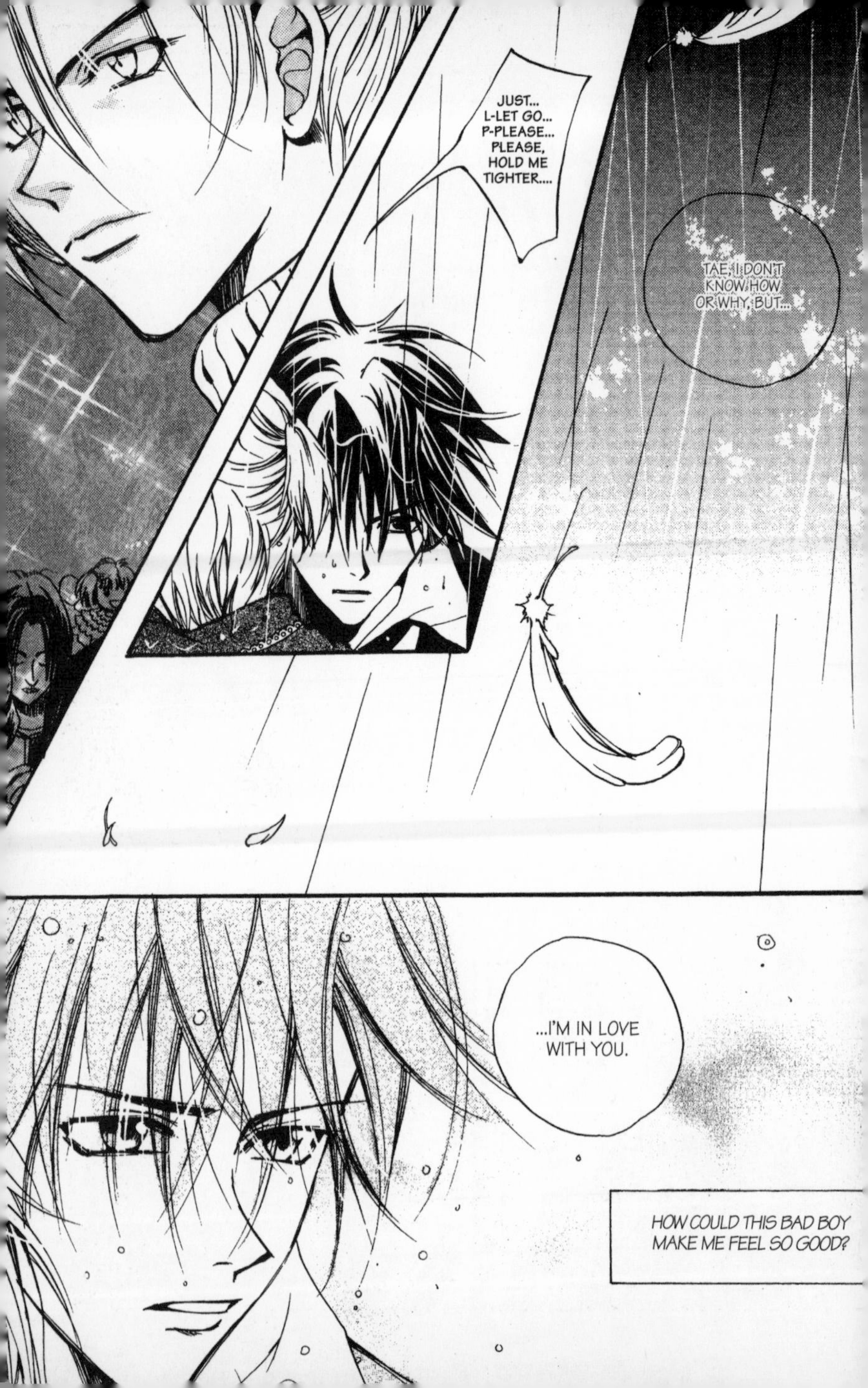
JUST... L-LET GO... P-PLEASE... PLEASE, HOLD ME TIGHTER....
TAE, I DON'T KNOW HOW OR WHY, BUT...
...I'M IN LOVE WITH YOU.
HOW COULD THIS BAD BOY MAKE ME FEEL SO GOOD?

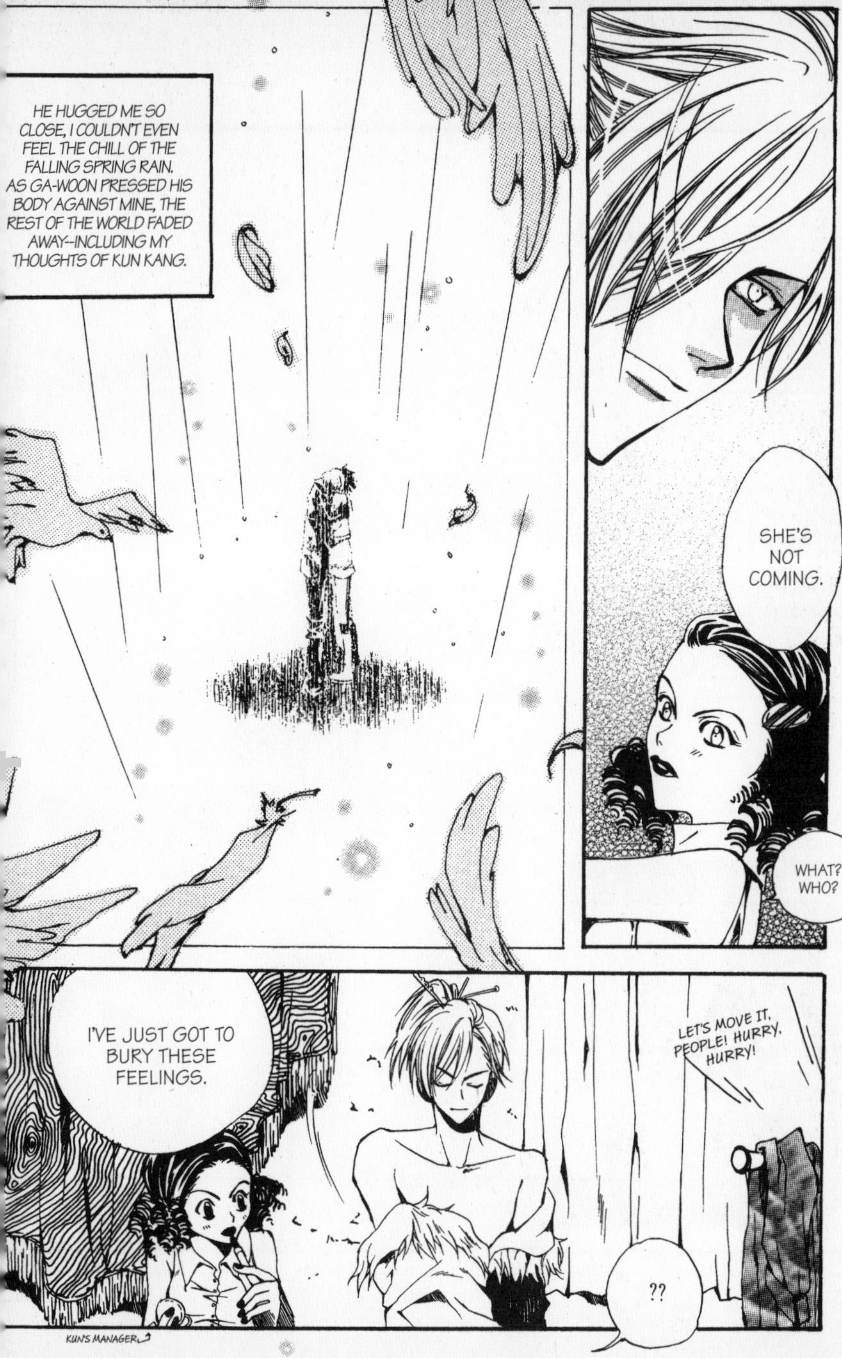
HE HUGGED ME SO CLOSE, I COULDN'T EVEN FEEL THE CHILL OF THE FALLING SPRING RAIN. AS GA-WOON PRESSED HIS BODY AGAINST MINE, THE REST OF THE WORLD FADED AWAY--INCLUDING MY THOUGHTS OF KUN KANG.
SHE'S NOT COMING.
WHAT? WHO?
I'VE JUST GOT TO BURY THESE FEELINGS.
LET'S MOVE IT, PEOPLE! HURRY, HURRY!
??
KUN'S MANAGER

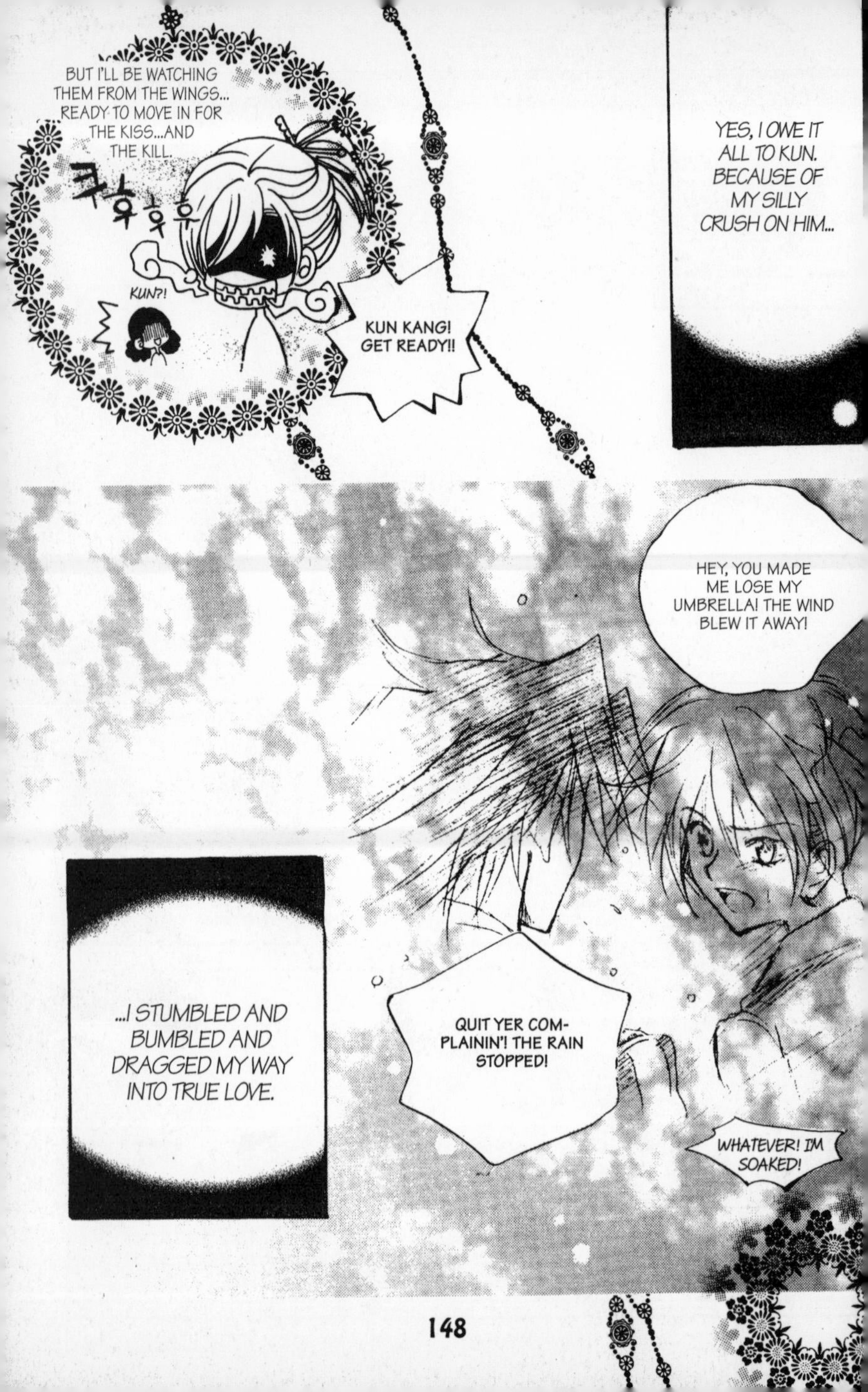
BUT I'LL BE WATCHING THEM FROM THE WINGS... READY TO MOVE IN FOR THE KISS...AND THE KILL.
KUN?!
KUN KANG! GET READY!!
YES, I OWE IT ALL TO KUN. BECAUSE OF MY SILLY CRUSH ON HIM...
HEY, YOU MADE ME LOSE MY UMBRELLA! THE WIND BLEW IT AWAY!
...I STUMBLED AND BUMBLED AND DRAGGED MY WAY INTO TRUE LOVE.
QUIT YER COM-PLAININ'! THE RAIN STOPPED!
WHATEVER! I'M SOAKED!

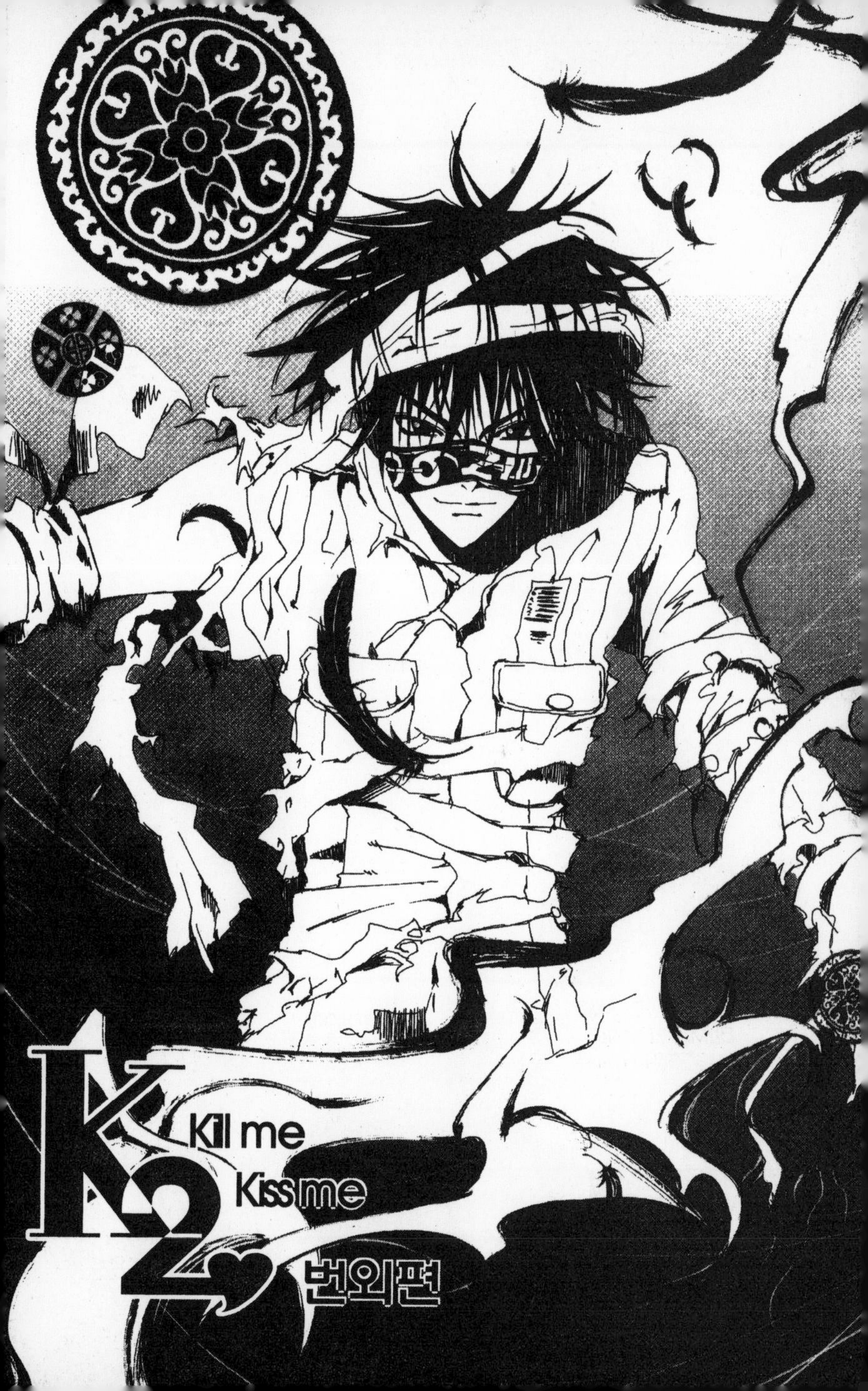
K2
Kill me
Kiss me
번외편

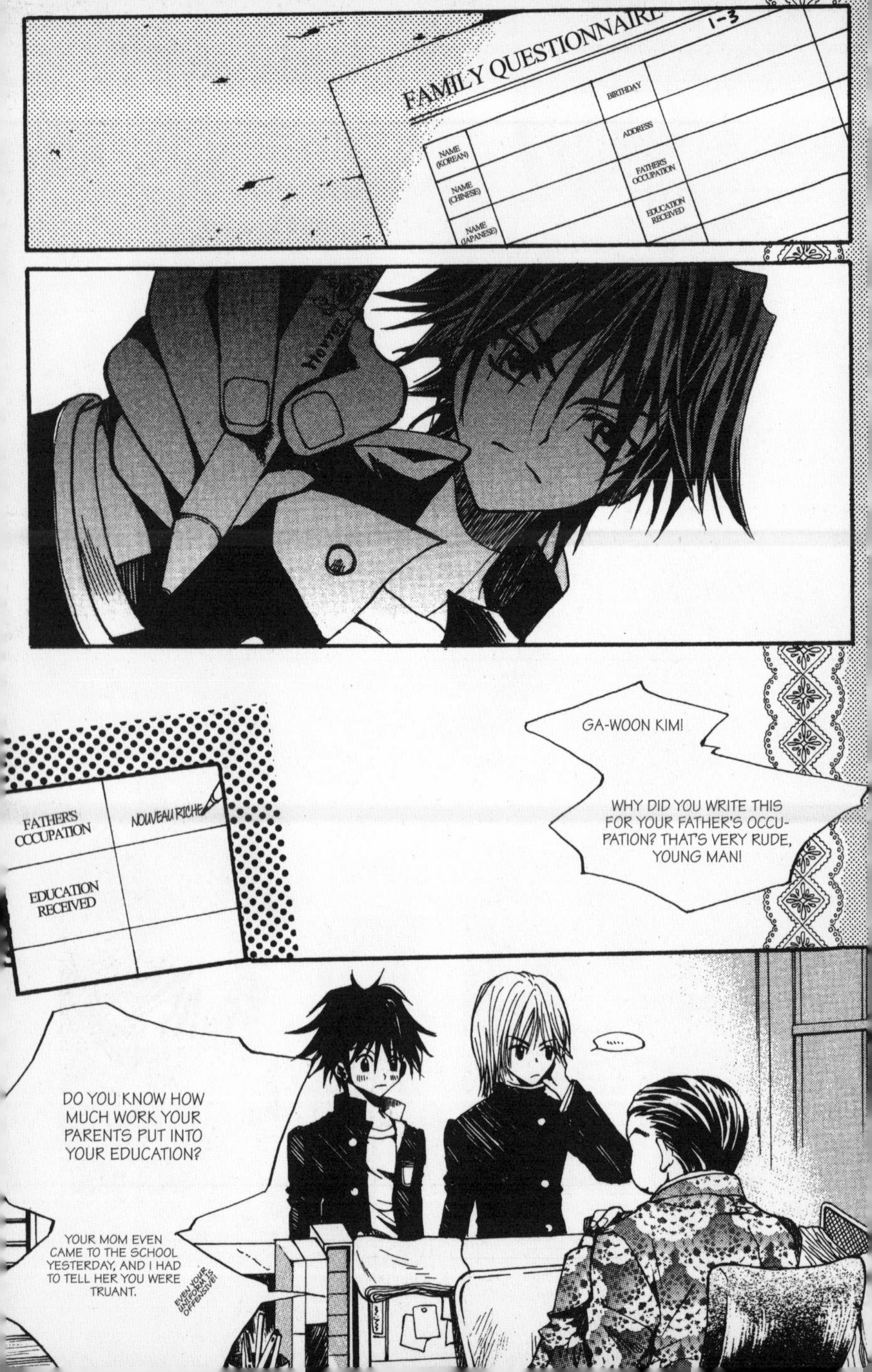
FAMILY QUESTIONNAIRE
1-3
NAME (KOREAN)
NAME (CHINESE)
NAME (JAPANESE)
BIRTHDAY
ADDRESS
FATHER'S OCCUPATION
EDUCATION RECEIVED
FATHER'S OCCUPATION
NOUVEAU RICHE
EDUCATION RECEIVED
GA-WOON KIM!
WHY DID YOU WRITE THIS FOR YOUR FATHER'S OCCUPATION? THAT'S VERY RUDE, YOUNG MAN!
DO YOU KNOW HOW MUCH WORK YOUR PARENTS PUT INTO YOUR EDUCATION?
......
YOUR MOM EVEN CAME TO THE SCHOOL YESTERDAY, AND I HAD TO TELL HER YOU WERE TRUANT.
EVEN YOUR UNIFORM IS OFFENSIVE!

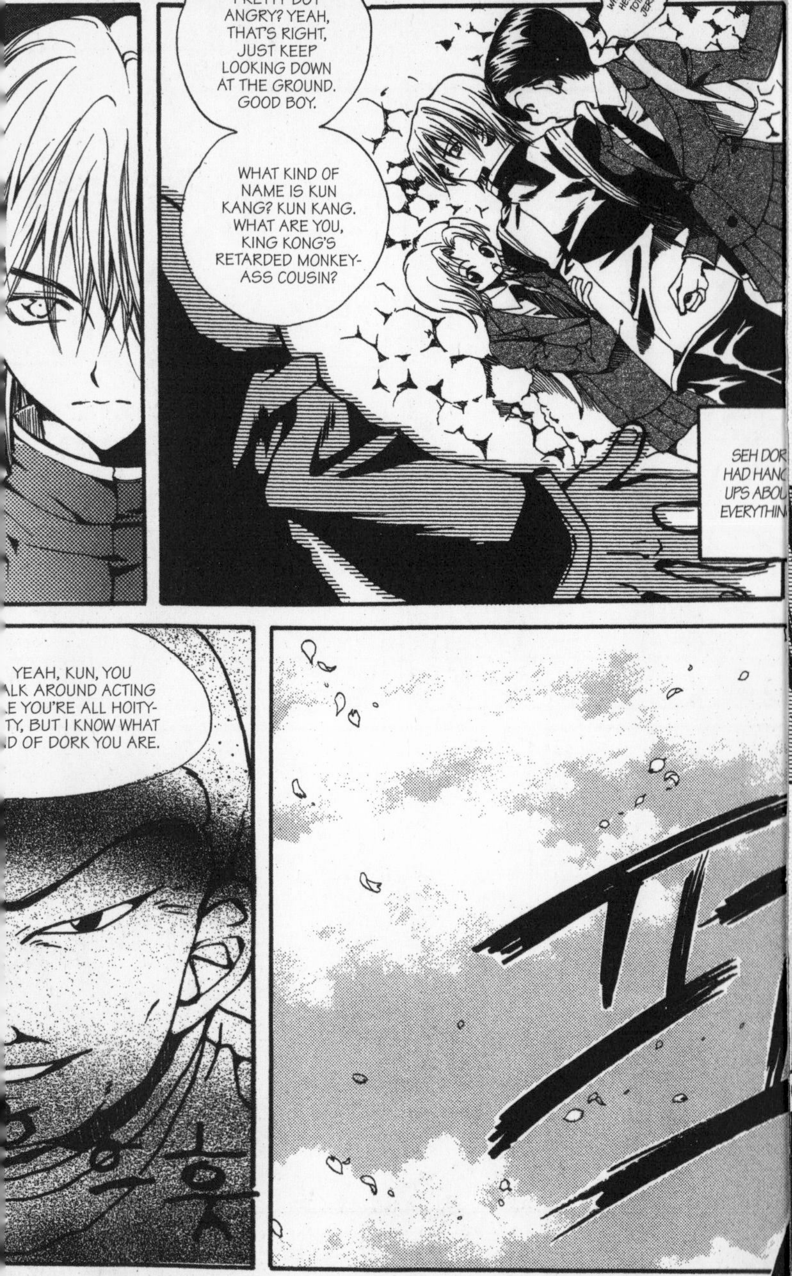
AWWW, IS THE PRETTY BOY ANGRY? YEAH, THAT'S RIGHT, JUST KEEP LOOKING DOWN AT THE GROUND. GOOD BOY.
WHAT KIND OF NAME IS KUN KANG? KUN KANG. WHAT ARE YOU, KING KONG'S RETARDED MONKEY-ASS COUSIN?
WHOS THAT? HES, LIKE TOTALLY JERKY!
SEH DOR HAD HANG UPS ABOU EVERYTHIN
YEAH, KUN, YOU ALK AROUND ACTING E YOU'RE ALL HOITY-TY, BUT I KNOW WHAT D OF DORK YOU ARE.

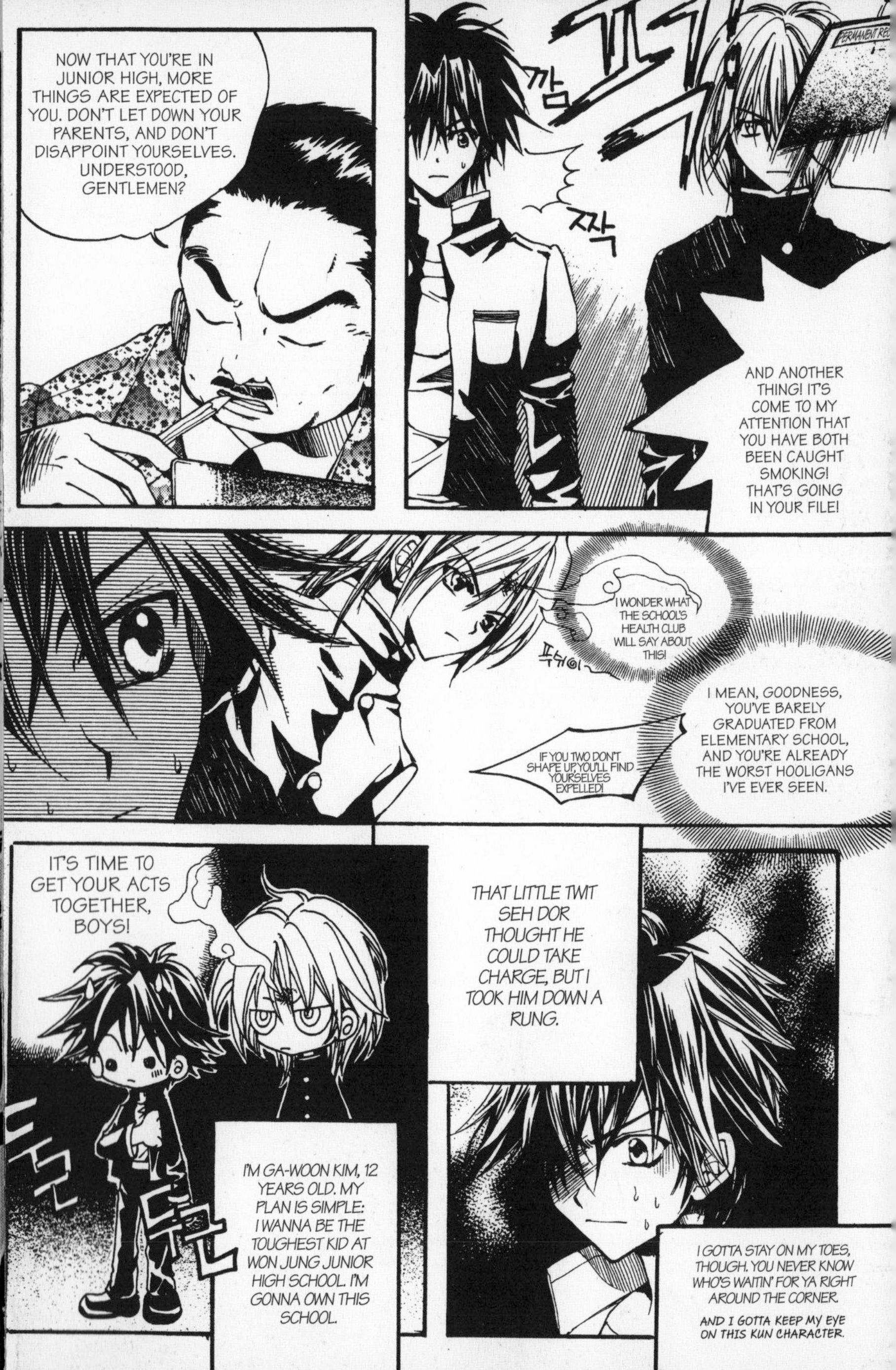
NOW THAT YOU'RE IN JUNIOR HIGH, MORE THINGS ARE EXPECTED OF YOU. DON'T LET DOWN YOUR PARENTS, AND DON'T DISAPPOINT YOURSELVES. UNDERSTOOD, GENTLEMEN?
AND ANOTHER THING! IT'S COME TO MY ATTENTION THAT YOU HAVE BOTH BEEN CAUGHT SMOKING! THAT'S GOING IN YOUR FILE!
I WONDER WHAT THE SCHOOL'S HEALTH CLUB WILL SAY ABOUT THIS!
IF YOU TWO DON'T SHAPE UP, YOU'LL FIND YOURSELVES EXPELLED!
I MEAN, GOODNESS, YOU'VE BARELY GRADUATED FROM ELEMENTARY SCHOOL, AND YOU'RE ALREADY THE WORST HOOLIGANS I'VE EVER SEEN.
IT'S TIME TO GET YOUR ACTS TOGETHER, BOYS!
I'M GA-WOON KIM, 12 YEARS OLD. MY PLAN IS SIMPLE: I WANNA BE THE TOUGHEST KID AT WON JUNG JUNIOR HIGH SCHOOL. I'M GONNA OWN THIS SCHOOL.
THAT LITTLE TWIT SEH DOR THOUGHT HE COULD TAKE CHARGE, BUT I TOOK HIM DOWN A RUNG.
I GOTTA STAY ON MY TOES, THOUGH. YOU NEVER KNOW WHO'S WAITIN' FOR YA RIGHT AROUND THE CORNER.
AND I GOTTA KEEP MY EYE ON THIS KUN CHARACTER.

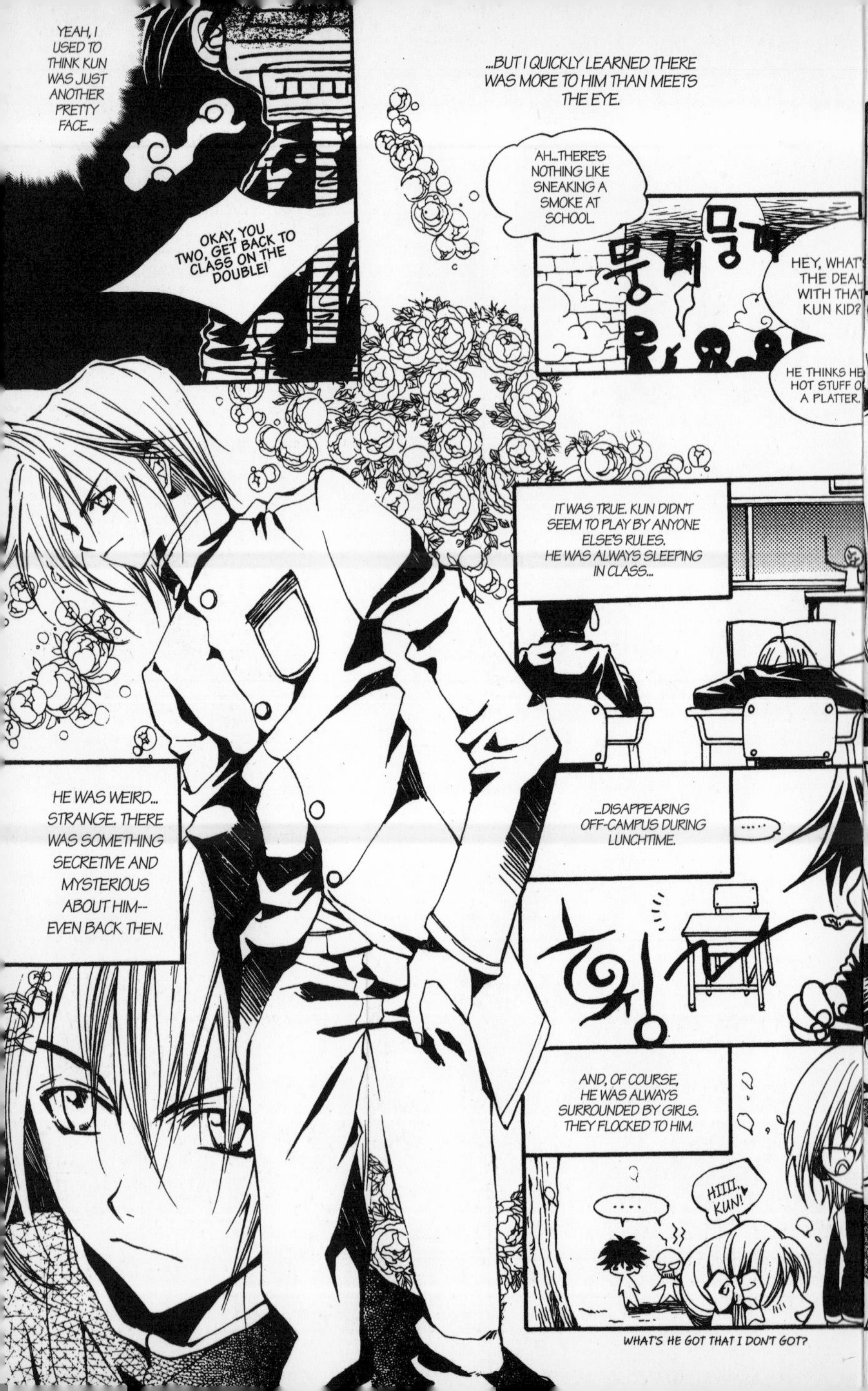
YEAH, I USED TO THINK KUN WAS JUST ANOTHER PRETTY FACE...
OKAY, YOU TWO, GET BACK TO CLASS ON THE DOUBLE!
...BUT I QUICKLY LEARNED THERE WAS MORE TO HIM THAN MEETS THE EYE.
AH...THERE'S NOTHING LIKE SNEAKING A SMOKE AT SCHOOL.
HEY, WHAT'S THE DEAL WITH THAT KUN KID?
HE THINKS HE'S HOT STUFF ON A PLATTER.
IT WAS TRUE. KUN DIDN'T SEEM TO PLAY BY ANYONE ELSE'S RULES. HE WAS ALWAYS SLEEPING IN CLASS...
HE WAS WEIRD... STRANGE. THERE WAS SOMETHING SECRETIVE AND MYSTERIOUS ABOUT HIM-- EVEN BACK THEN.
...DISAPPEARING OFF-CAMPUS DURING LUNCHTIME.
.....
AND, OF COURSE, HE WAS ALWAYS SURROUNDED BY GIRLS. THEY FLOCKED TO HIM.
.....
HIIII, KUN!♥
WHAT'S HE GOT THAT I DON'T GOT?

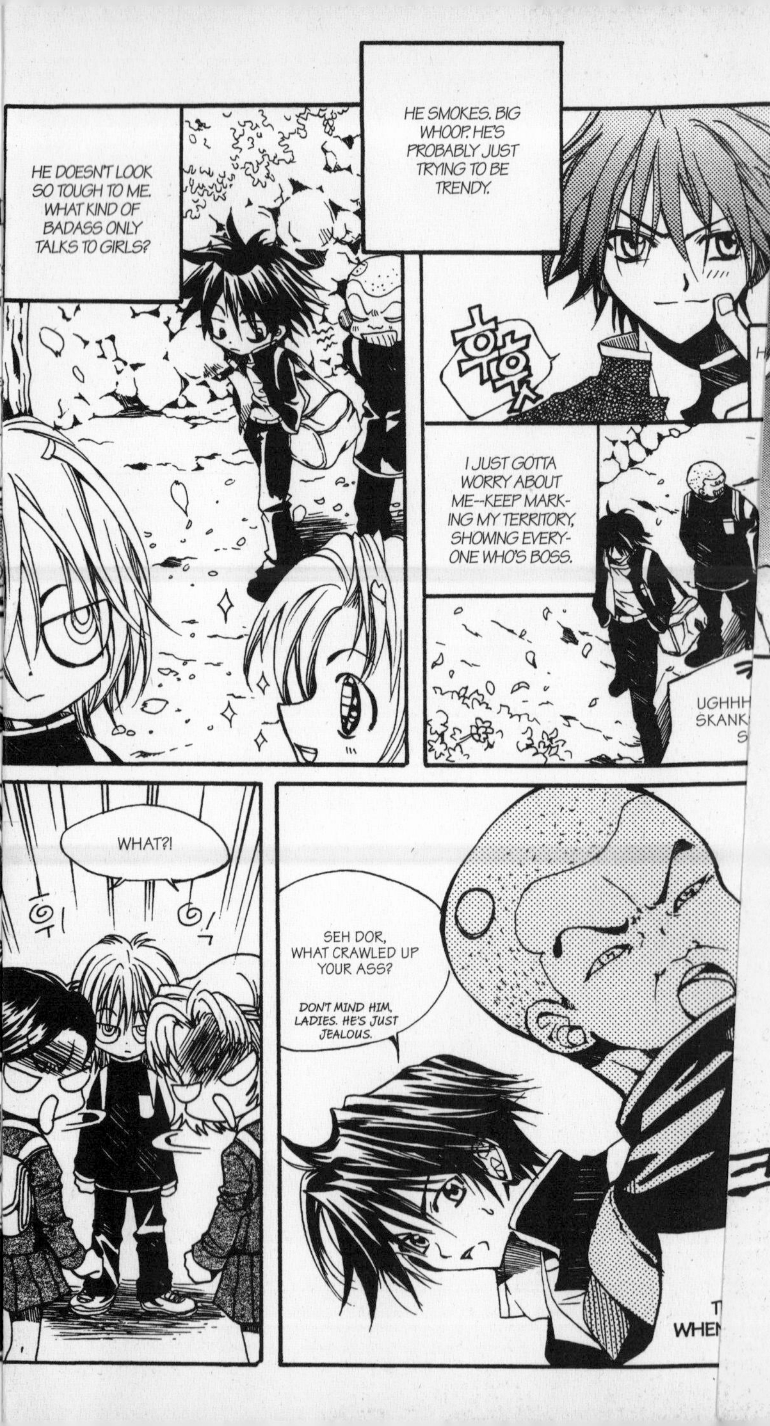
HE DOESN'T LOOK SO TOUGH TO ME. WHAT KIND OF BADASS ONLY TALKS TO GIRLS?
HE SMOKES. BIG WHOOP. HE'S PROBABLY JUST TRYING TO BE TRENDY.
I JUST GOTTA WORRY ABOUT ME--KEEP MARKING MY TERRITORY, SHOWING EVERYONE WHO'S BOSS.
WHAT?!
SEH DOR, WHAT CRAWLED UP YOUR ASS?
DON'T MIND HIM, LADIES. HE'S JUST JEALOUS.

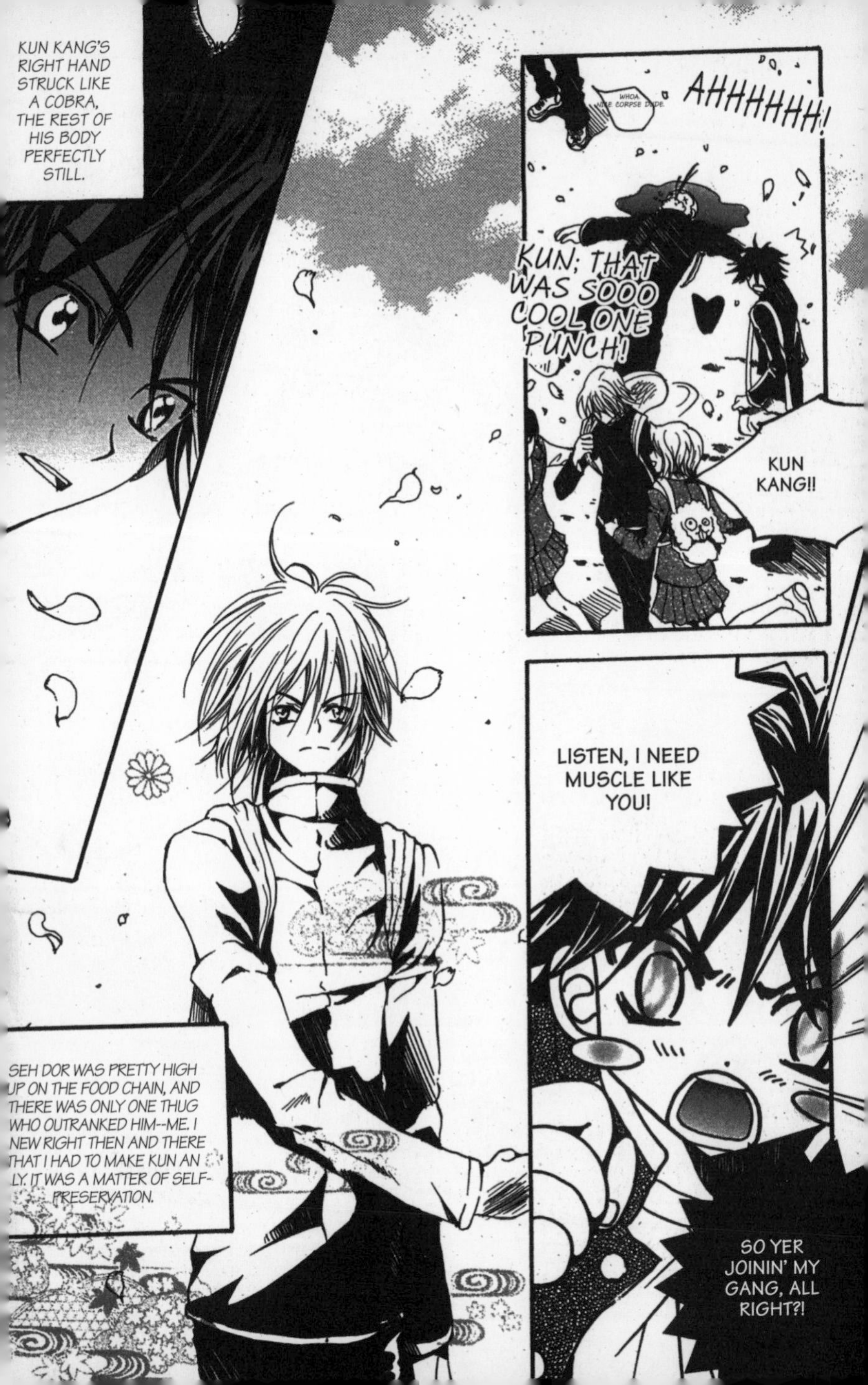
KUN KANG'S RIGHT HAND STRUCK LIKE A COBRA, THE REST OF HIS BODY PERFECTLY STILL.
SEH DOR WAS PRETTY HIGH UP ON THE FOOD CHAIN, AND THERE WAS ONLY ONE THUG WHO OUTRANKED HIM--ME. I NEW RIGHT THEN AND THERE THAT I HAD TO MAKE KUN AN LY. IT WAS A MATTER OF SELF-PRESERVATION.
WHOA. NICE CORPSE DUDE.
AHHHHHHH!
KUN; THAT WAS SOOO COOL ONE PUNCH!
KUN KANG!!
LISTEN, I NEED MUSCLE LIKE YOU!
SO YER JOININ' MY GANG, ALL RIGHT?!

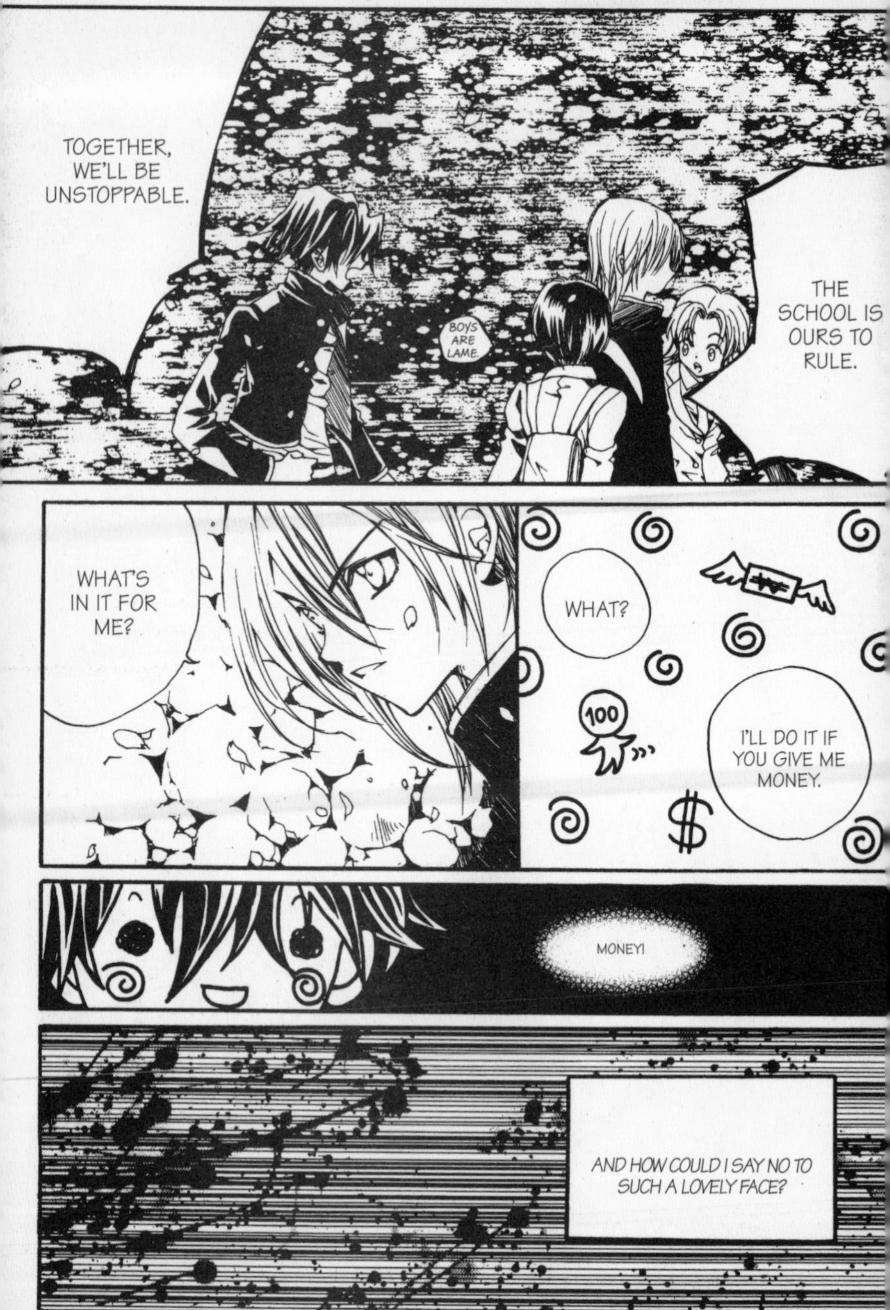
TOGETHER, WE'LL BE UNSTOPPABLE.
BOYS ARE LAME.
THE SCHOOL IS OURS TO RULE.
WHAT'S IN IT FOR ME?
WHAT?
100
I'LL DO IT IF YOU GIVE ME MONEY.
$
MONEY!
AND HOW COULD I SAY NO TO SUCH A LOVELY FACE?

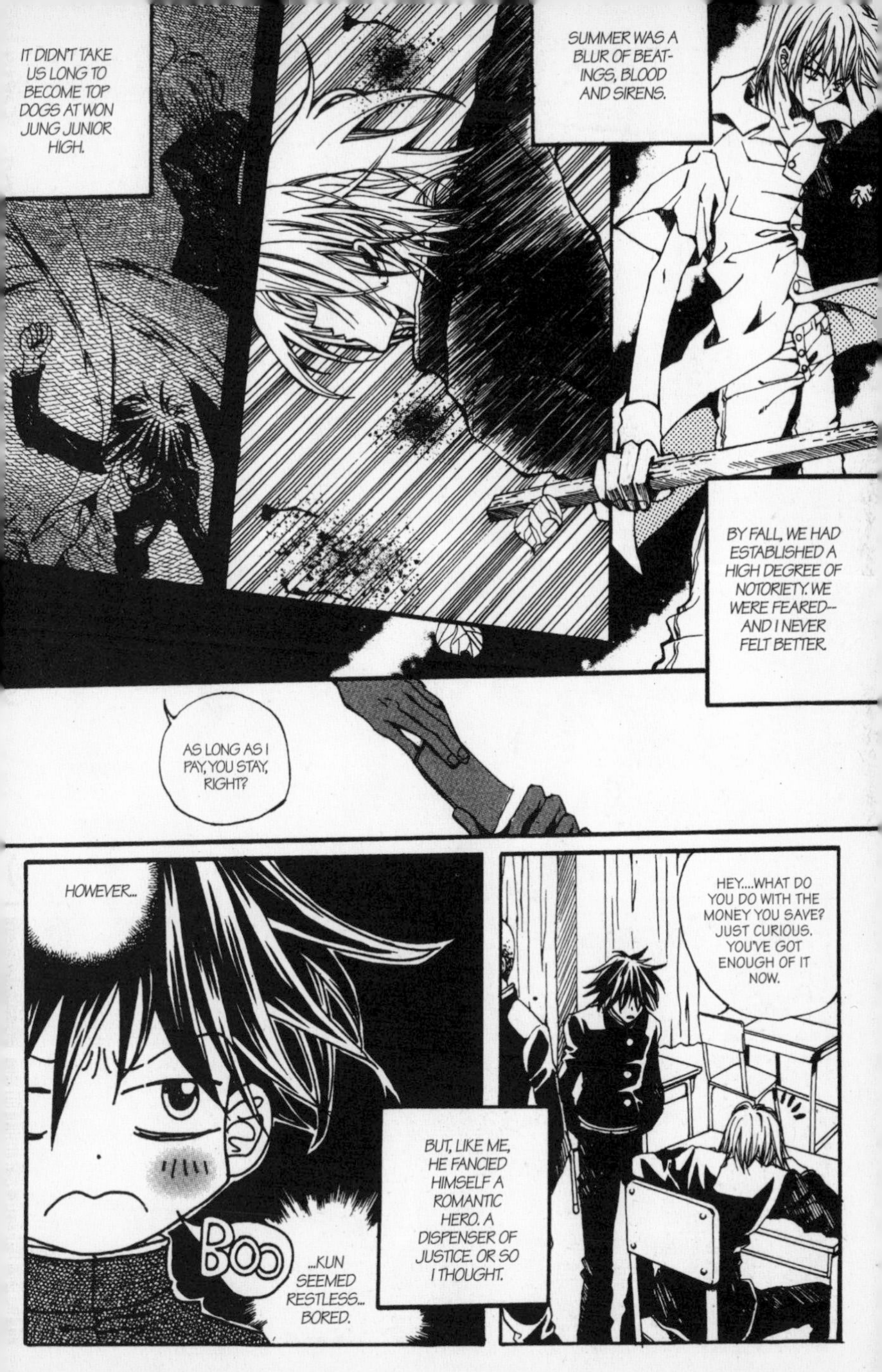
IT DIDN'T TAKE US LONG TO BECOME TOP DOGS AT WON JUNG JUNIOR HIGH.
SUMMER WAS A BLUR OF BEAT-INGS, BLOOD AND SIRENS.
BY FALL, WE HAD ESTABLISHED A HIGH DEGREE OF NOTORIETY. WE WERE FEARED--AND I NEVER FELT BETTER.
AS LONG AS I PAY, YOU STAY, RIGHT?
HOWEVER...
BOO
...KUN SEEMED RESTLESS... BORED.
HEY....WHAT DO YOU DO WITH THE MONEY YOU SAVE? JUST CURIOUS. YOU'VE GOT ENOUGH OF IT NOW.
BUT, LIKE ME, HE FANCIED HIMSELF A ROMANTIC HERO. A DISPENSER OF JUSTICE. OR SO I THOUGHT.

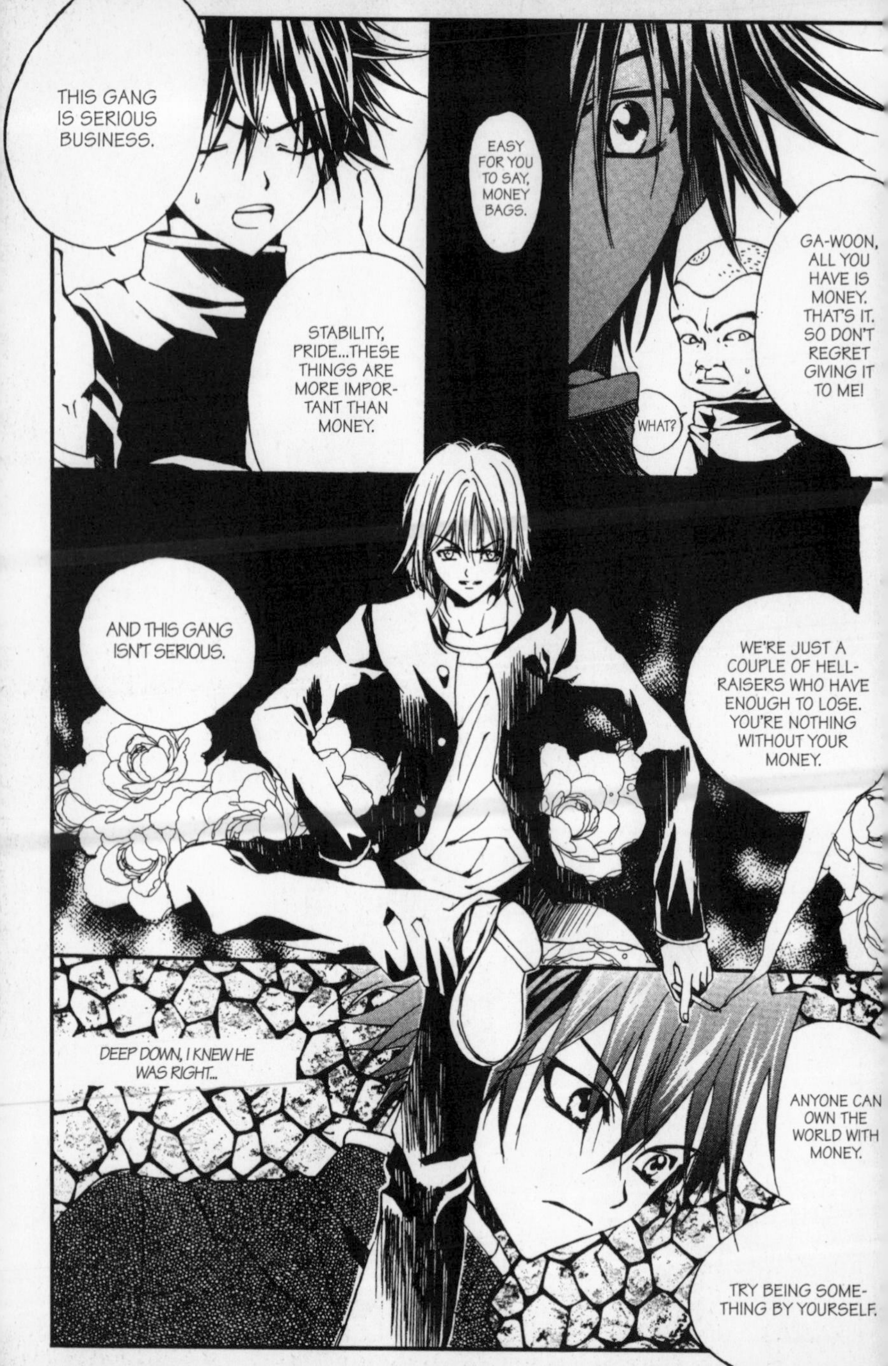
THIS GANG IS SERIOUS BUSINESS.
STABILITY, PRIDE...THESE THINGS ARE MORE IMPOR-TANT THAN MONEY.
EASY FOR YOU TO SAY, MONEY BAGS.
GA-WOON, ALL YOU HAVE IS MONEY. THAT'S IT. SO DON'T REGRET GIVING IT TO ME!
WHAT?
AND THIS GANG ISN'T SERIOUS.
WE'RE JUST A COUPLE OF HELL-RAISERS WHO HAVE ENOUGH TO LOSE. YOU'RE NOTHING WITHOUT YOUR MONEY.
DEEP DOWN, I KNEW HE WAS RIGHT...
ANYONE CAN OWN THE WORLD WITH MONEY.
TRY BEING SOME-THING BY YOURSELF.

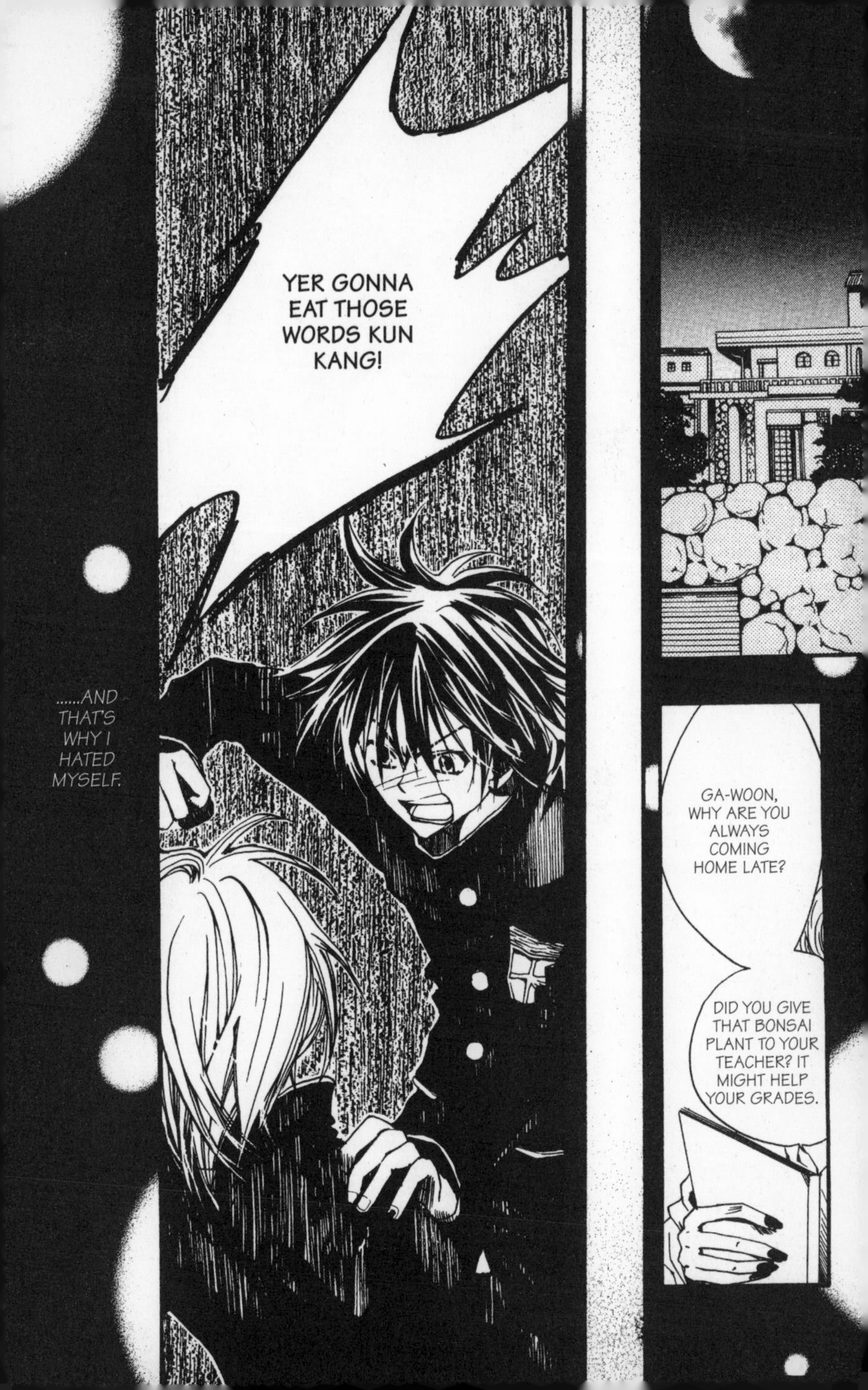
......AND THAT'S WHY I HATED MYSELF.
YER GONNA EAT THOSE WORDS KUN KANG!
GA-WOON, WHY ARE YOU ALWAYS COMING HOME LATE?
DID YOU GIVE THAT BONSAI PLANT TO YOUR TEACHER? IT MIGHT HELP YOUR GRADES.

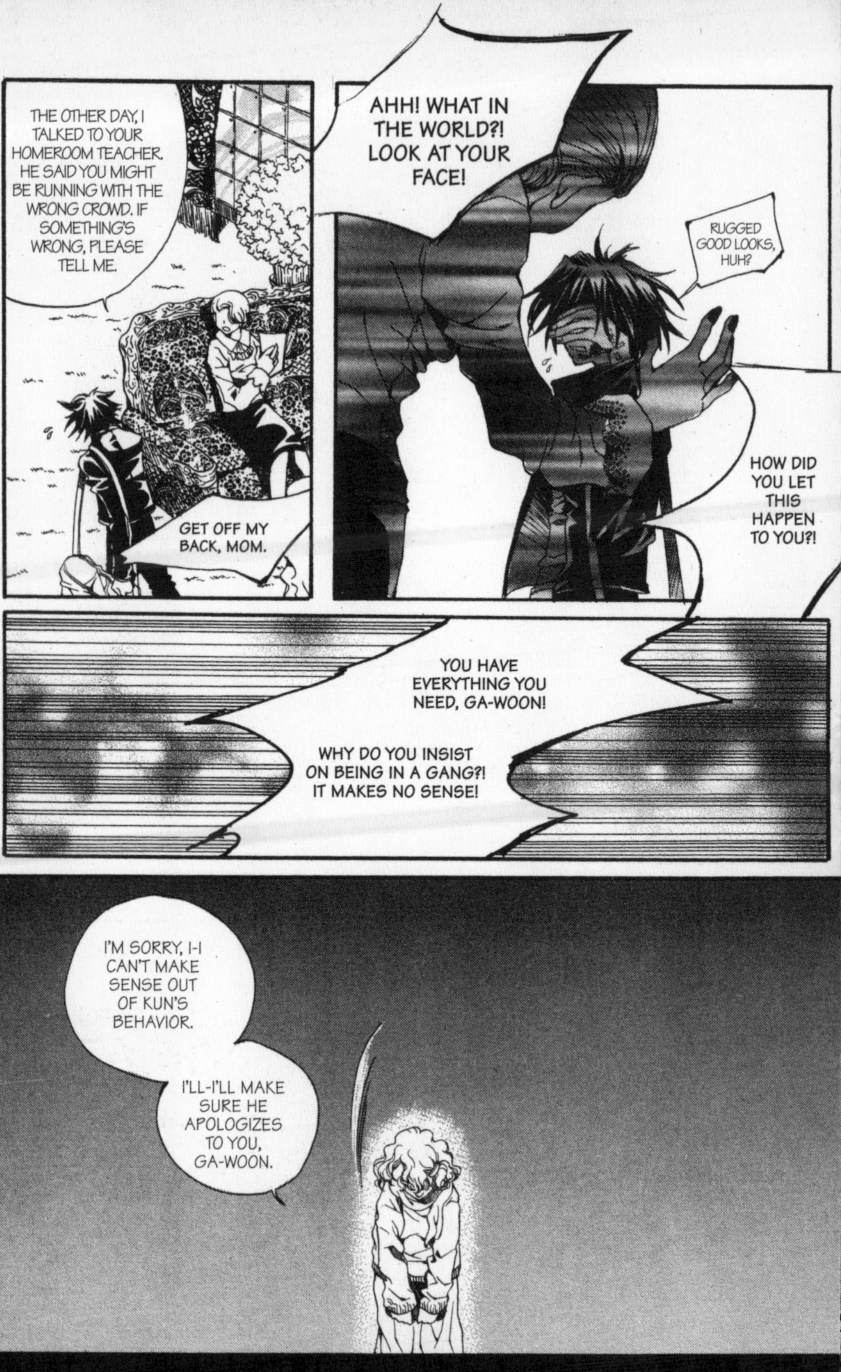
THE OTHER DAY, I TALKED TO YOUR HOMEROOM TEACHER. HE SAID YOU MIGHT BE RUNNING WITH THE WRONG CROWD. IF SOMETHING'S WRONG, PLEASE TELL ME.
GET OFF MY BACK, MOM.
AHH! WHAT IN THE WORLD?! LOOK AT YOUR FACE!
RUGGED GOOD LOOKS, HUH?
HOW DID YOU LET THIS HAPPEN TO YOU?!
YOU HAVE EVERYTHING YOU NEED, GA-WOON!
WHY DO YOU INSIST ON BEING IN A GANG?! IT MAKES NO SENSE!
I'M SORRY, I-I CAN'T MAKE SENSE OUT OF KUN'S BEHAVIOR.
I'LL-I'LL MAKE SURE HE APOLOGIZES TO YOU, GA-WOON.

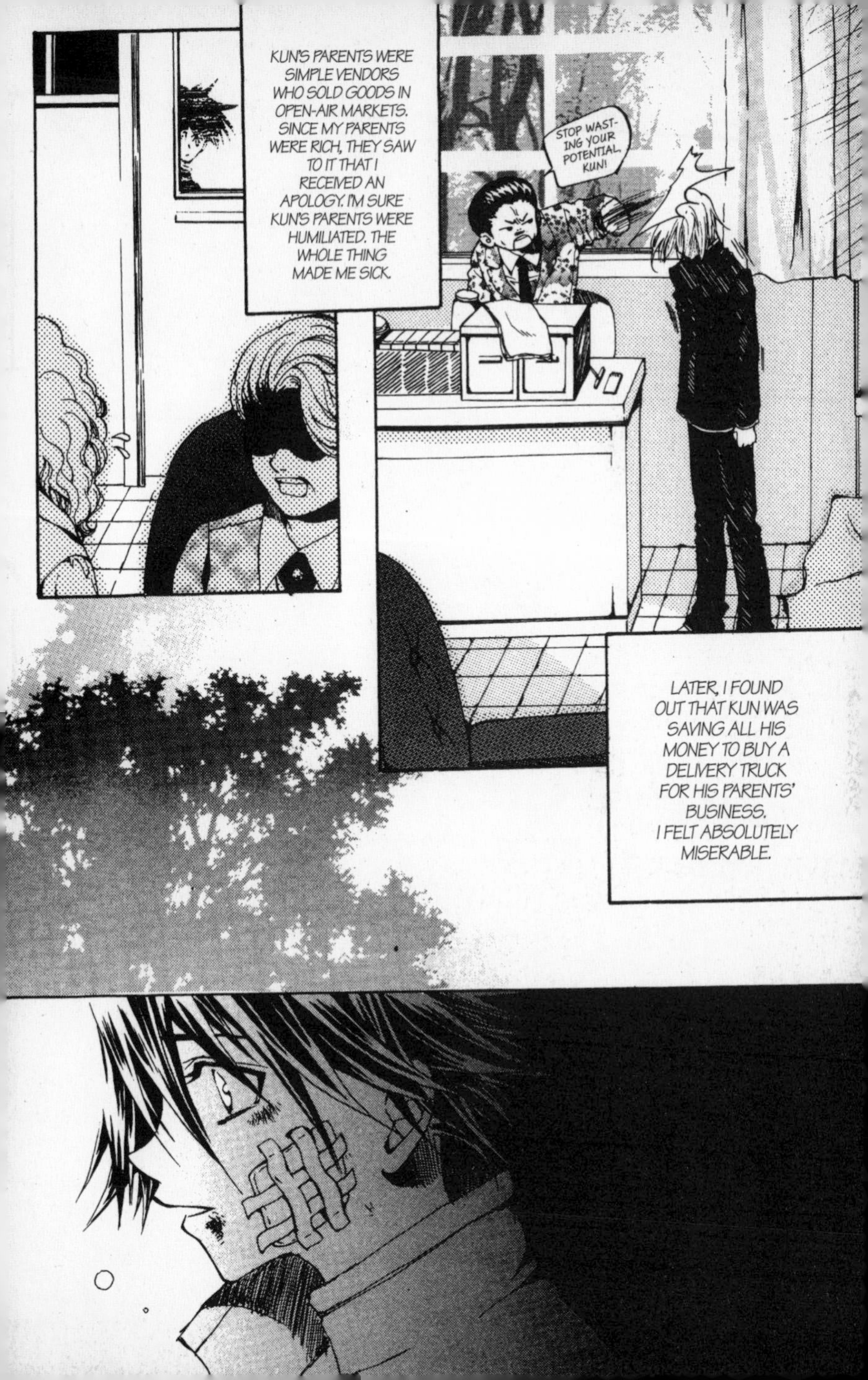
KUN'S PARENTS WERE SIMPLE VENDORS WHO SOLD GOODS IN OPEN-AIR MARKETS. SINCE MY PARENTS WERE RICH, THEY SAW TO IT THAT I RECEIVED AN APOLOGY. I'M SURE KUN'S PARENTS WERE HUMILIATED. THE WHOLE THING MADE ME SICK.
STOP WASTING YOUR POTENTIAL, KUN!
LATER, I FOUND OUT THAT KUN WAS SAVING ALL HIS MONEY TO BUY A DELIVERY TRUCK FOR HIS PARENTS' BUSINESS. I FELT ABSOLUTELY MISERABLE.

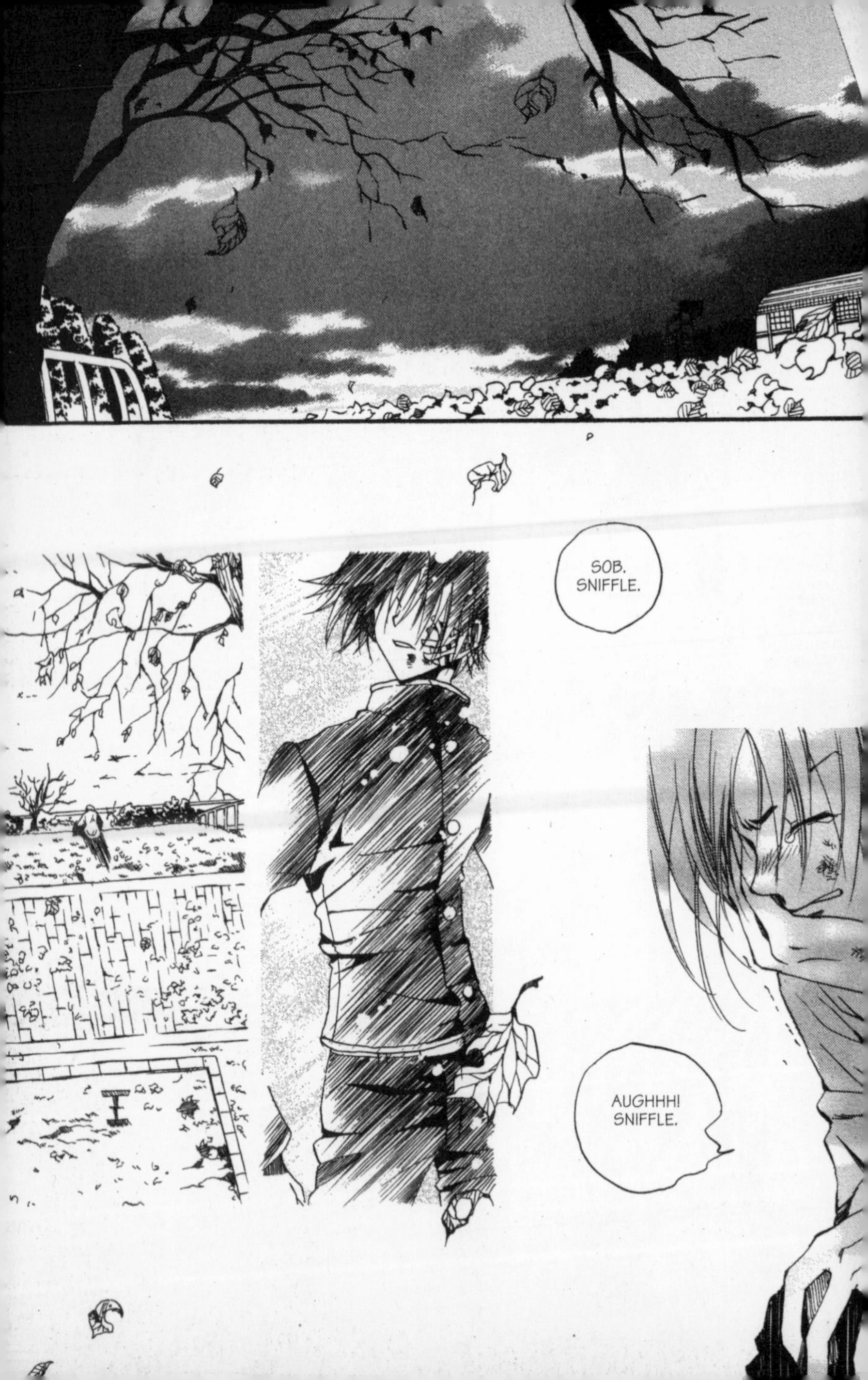
SOB. SNIFFLE.
AUGHHH! SNIFFLE.

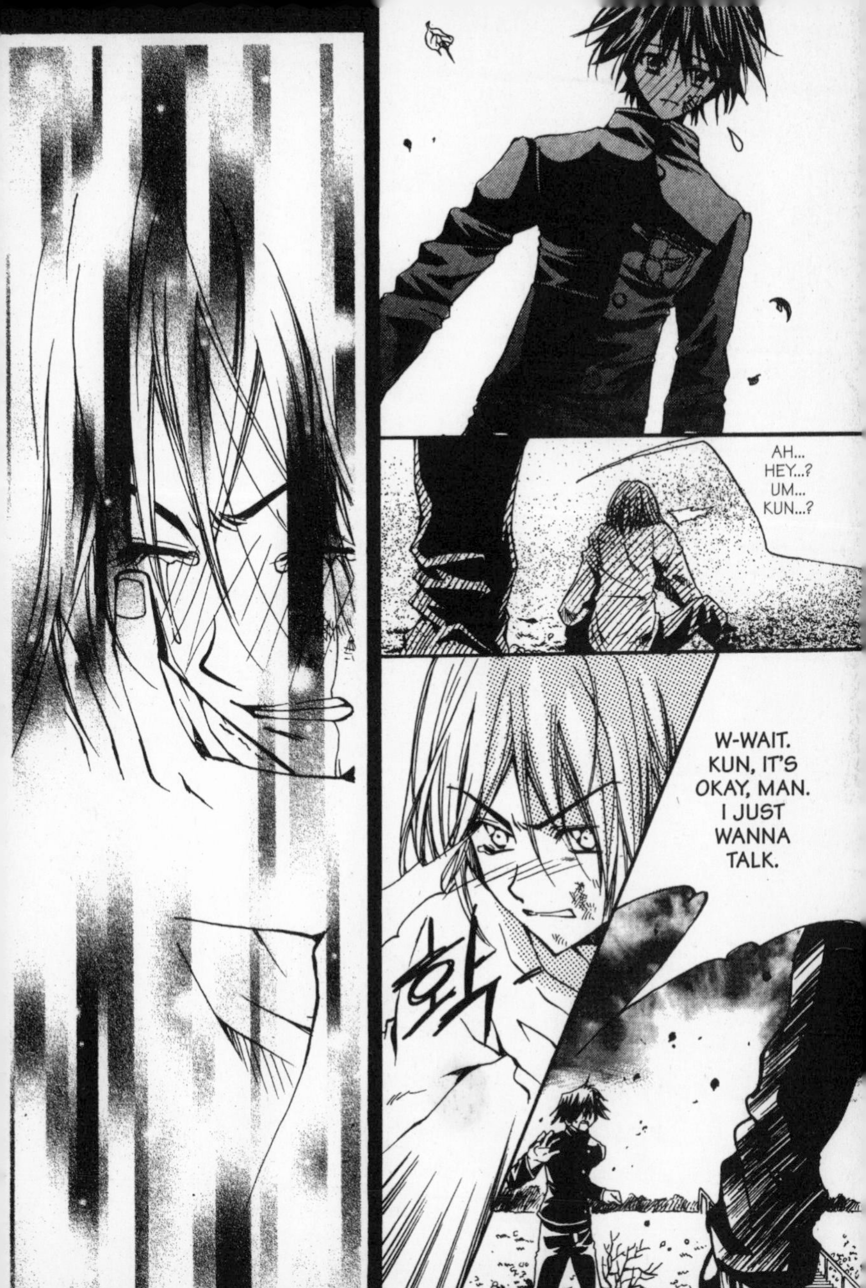
AH... HEY...? UM... KUN...?
W-WAIT. KUN, IT'S OKAY, MAN. I JUST WANNA TALK.

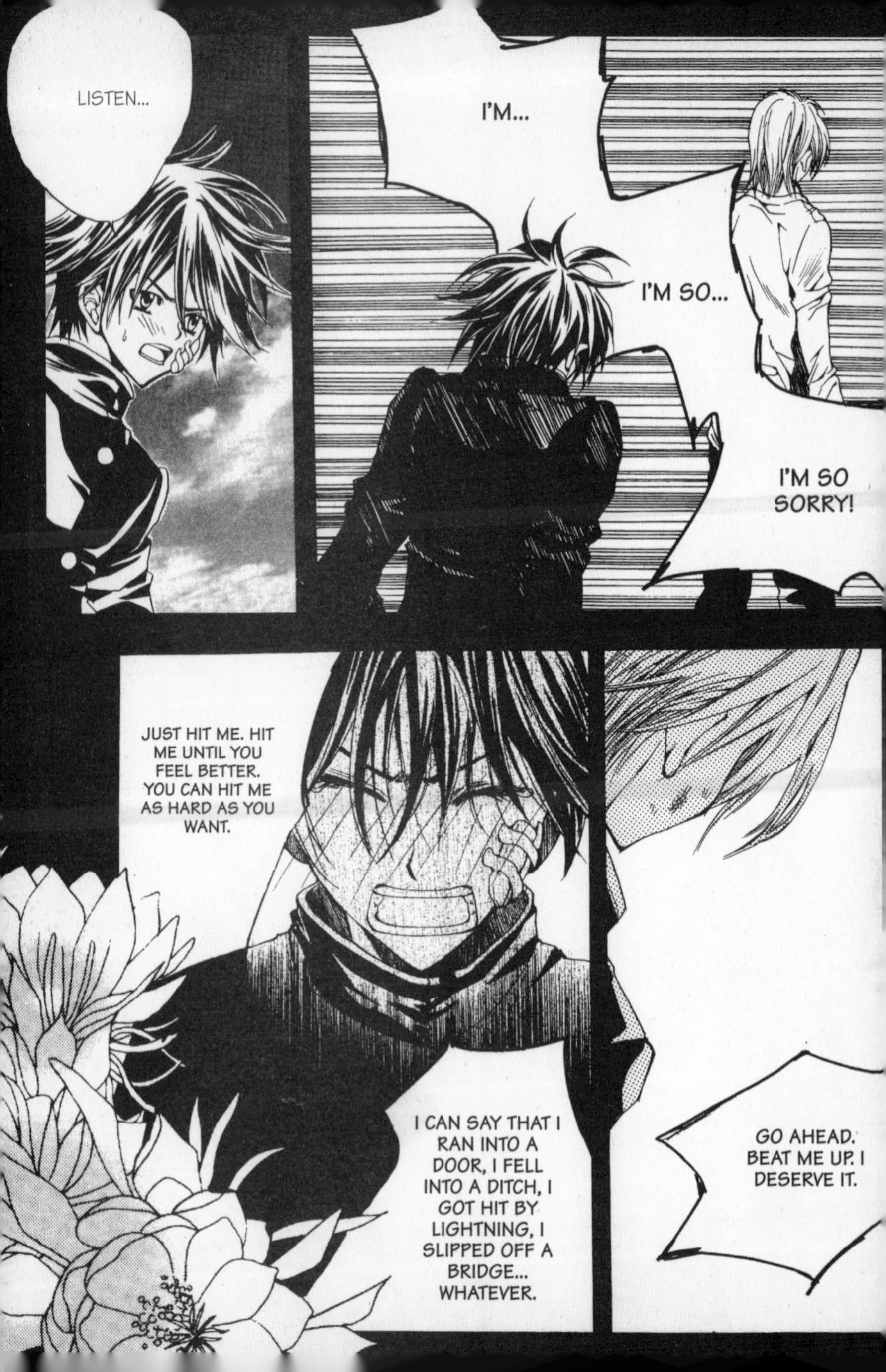
LISTEN...
I'M...
I'M SO...
I'M SO SORRY!
JUST HIT ME. HIT ME UNTIL YOU FEEL BETTER. YOU CAN HIT ME AS HARD AS YOU WANT.
I CAN SAY THAT I RAN INTO A DOOR, I FELL INTO A DITCH, I GOT HIT BY LIGHTNING, I SLIPPED OFF A BRIDGE... WHATEVER.
GO AHEAD. BEAT ME UP. I DESERVE IT.

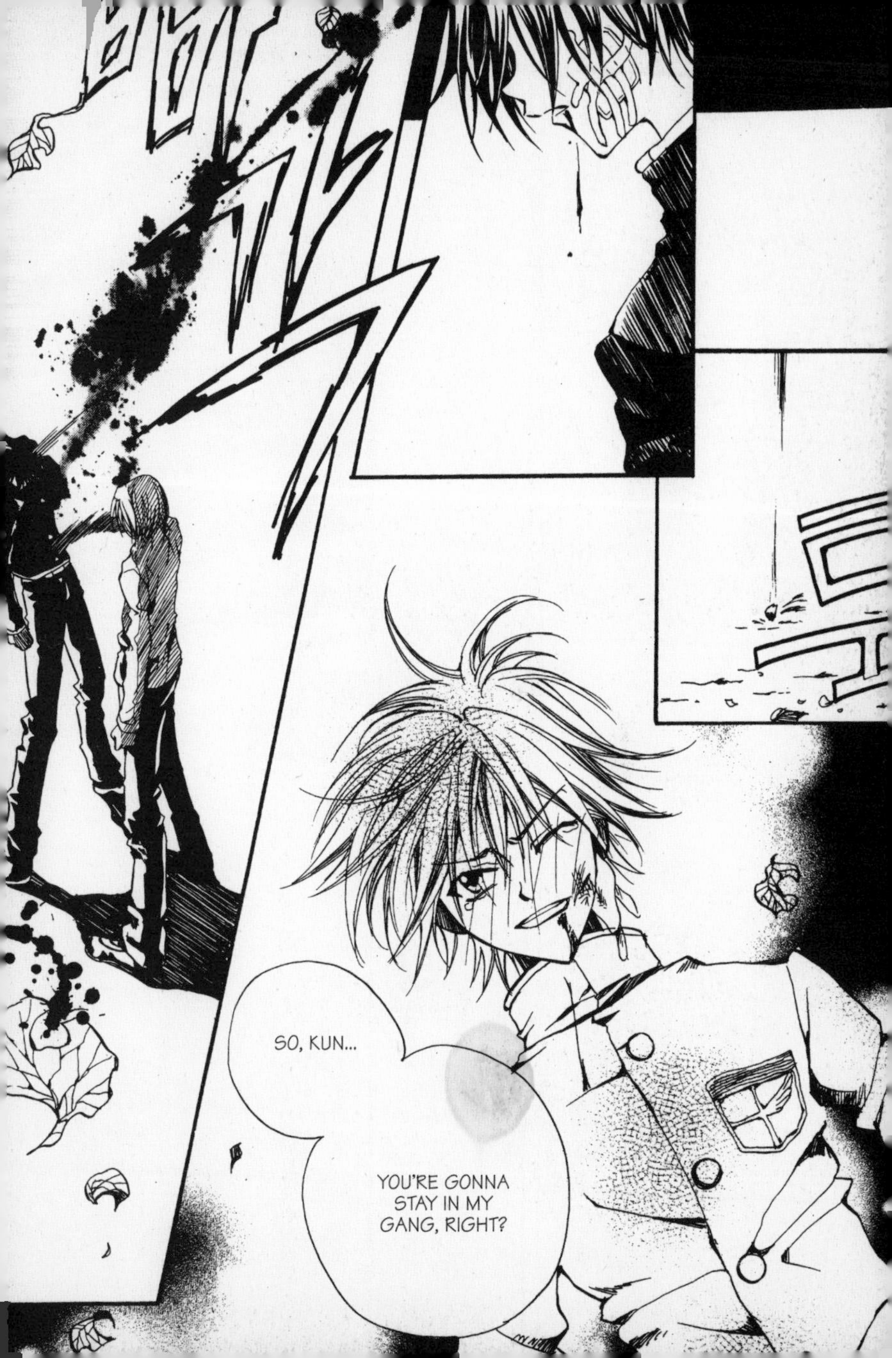
SO, KUN...
YOU'RE GONNA STAY IN MY GANG, RIGHT?

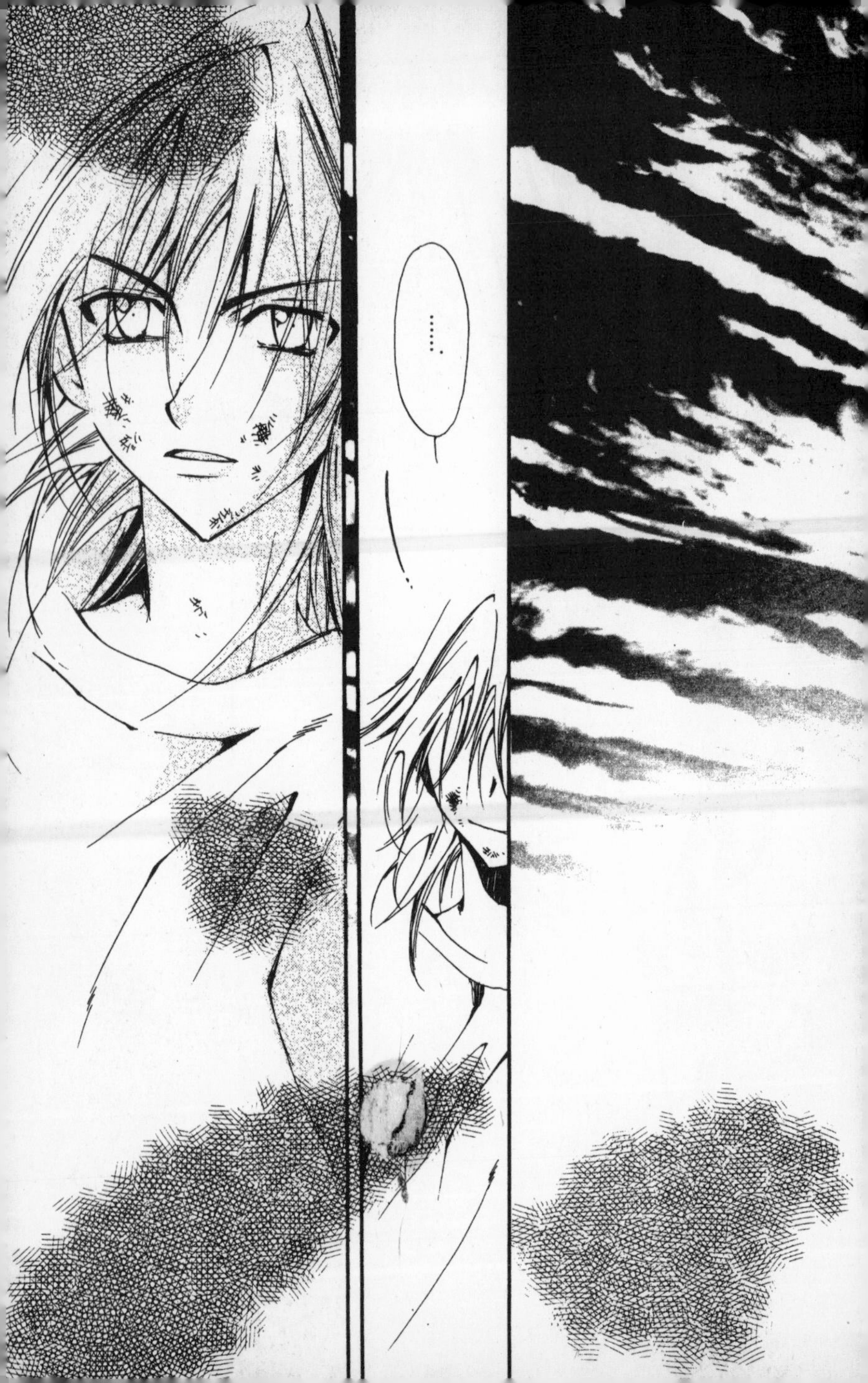
......

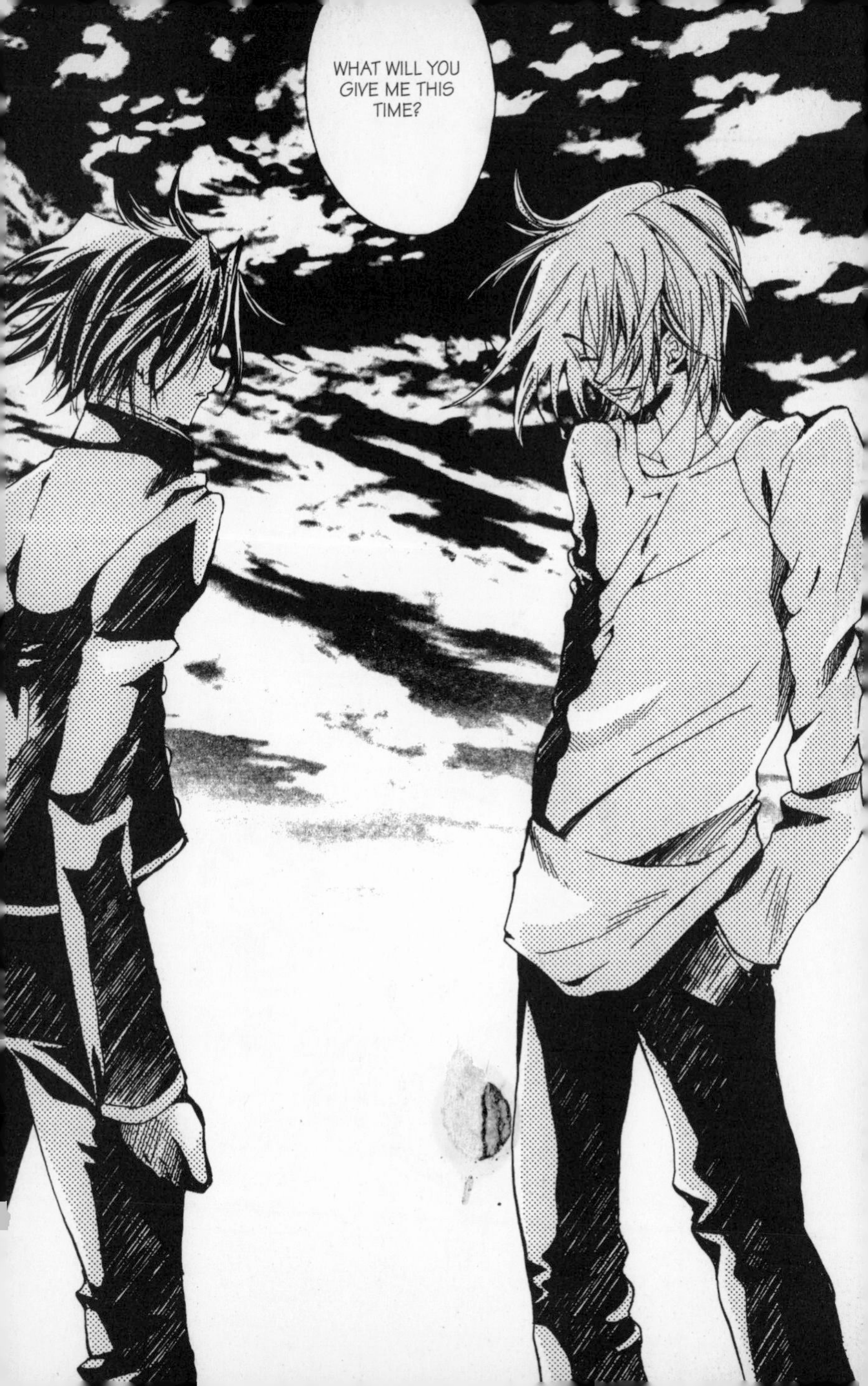
WHAT WILL YOU GIVE ME THIS TIME?

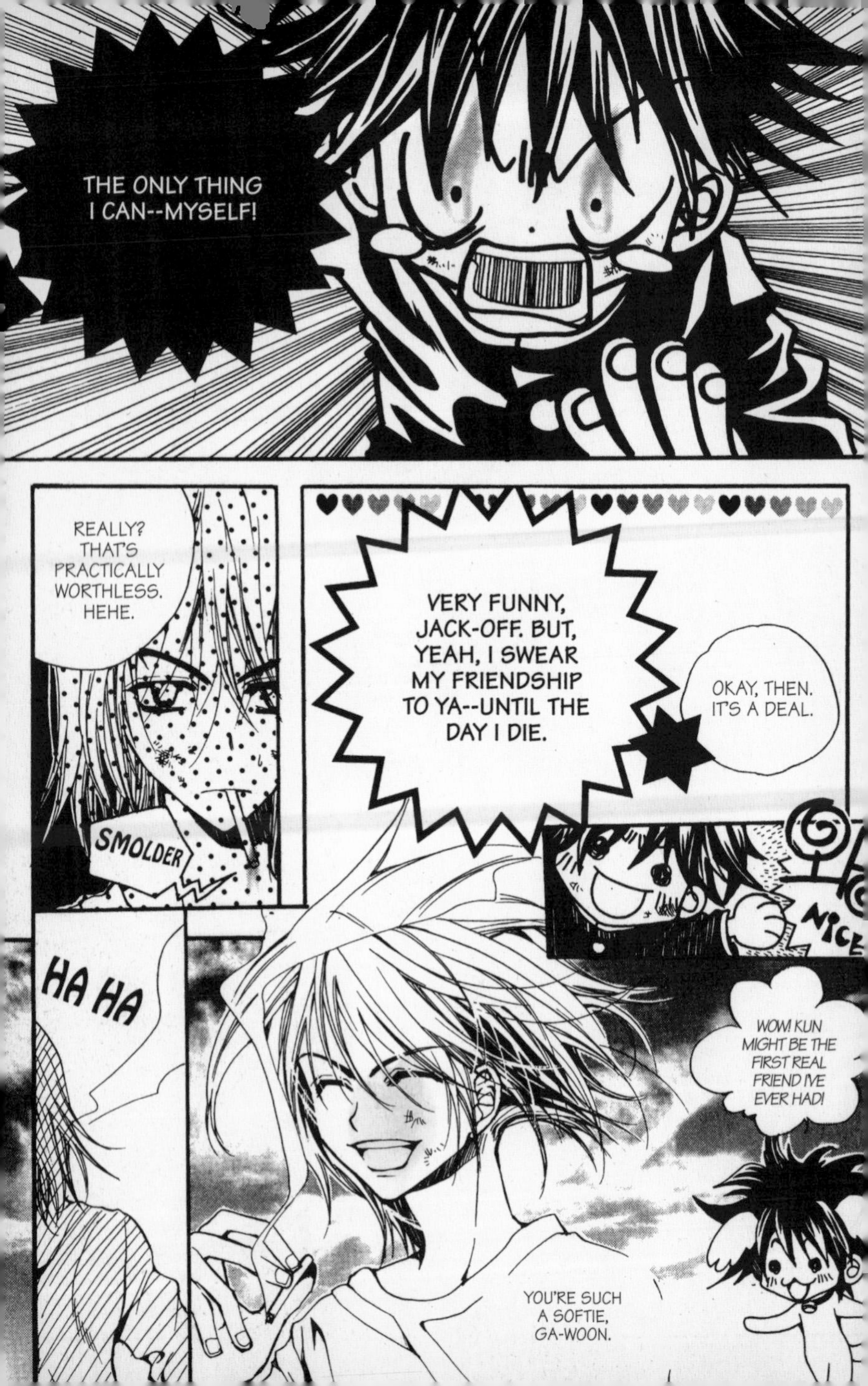
THE ONLY THING I CAN--MYSELF!
REALLY? THAT'S PRACTICALLY WORTHLESS. HEHE.
SMOLDER
VERY FUNNY, JACK-OFF. BUT, YEAH, I SWEAR MY FRIENDSHIP TO YA--UNTIL THE DAY I DIE.
OKAY, THEN. IT'S A DEAL.
NICE
HA HA
YOU'RE SUCH A SOFTIE, GA-WOON.
WOW! KUN MIGHT BE THE FIRST REAL FRIEND I'VE EVER HAD!

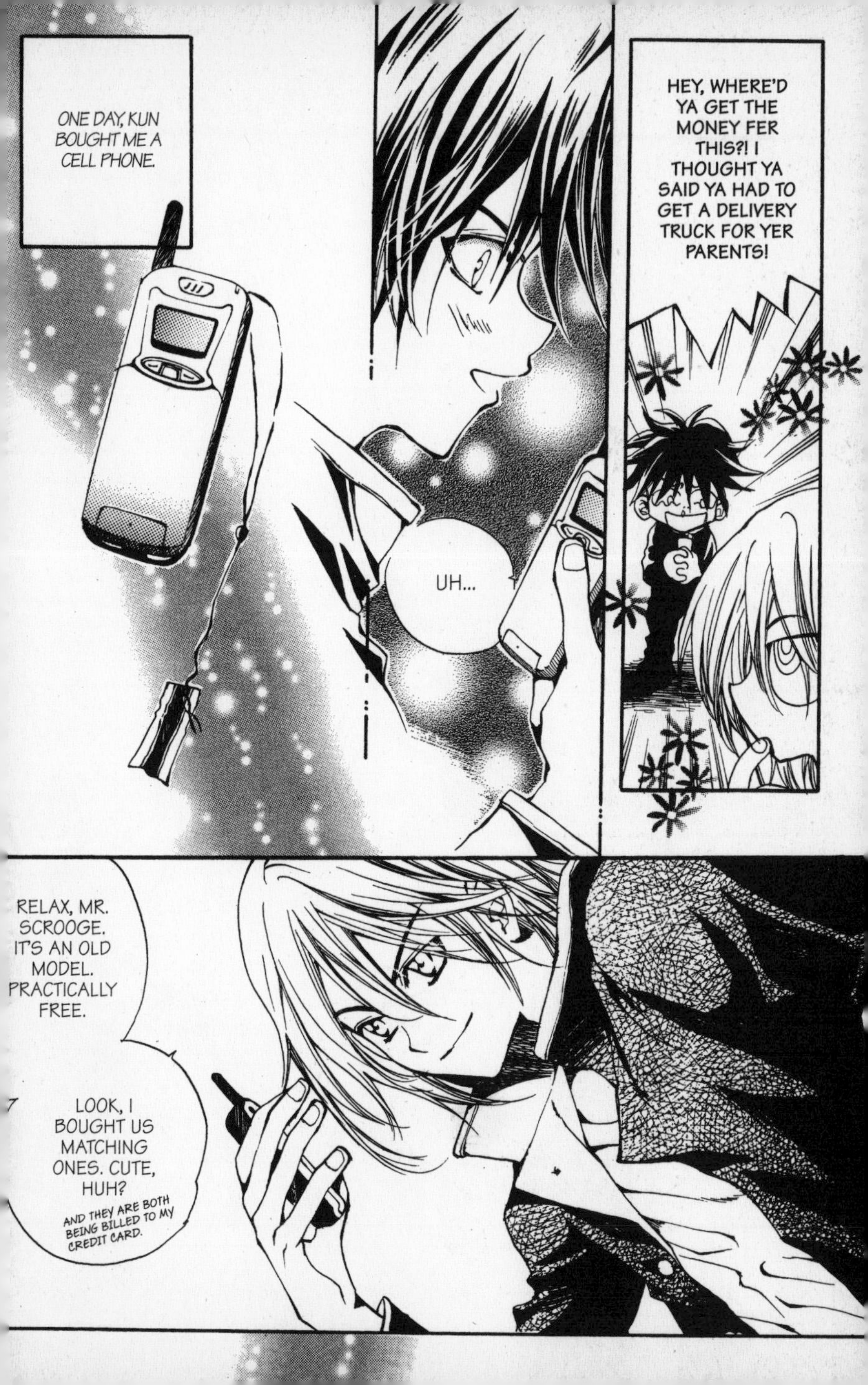
ONE DAY, KUN BOUGHT ME A CELL PHONE.
UH...
HEY, WHERE'D YA GET THE MONEY FER THIS?! I THOUGHT YA SAID YA HAD TO GET A DELIVERY TRUCK FOR YER PARENTS!
RELAX, MR. SCROOGE. IT'S AN OLD MODEL. PRACTICALLY FREE.
LOOK, I BOUGHT US MATCHING ONES. CUTE, HUH?
AND THEY ARE BOTH BEING BILLED TO MY CREDIT CARD.

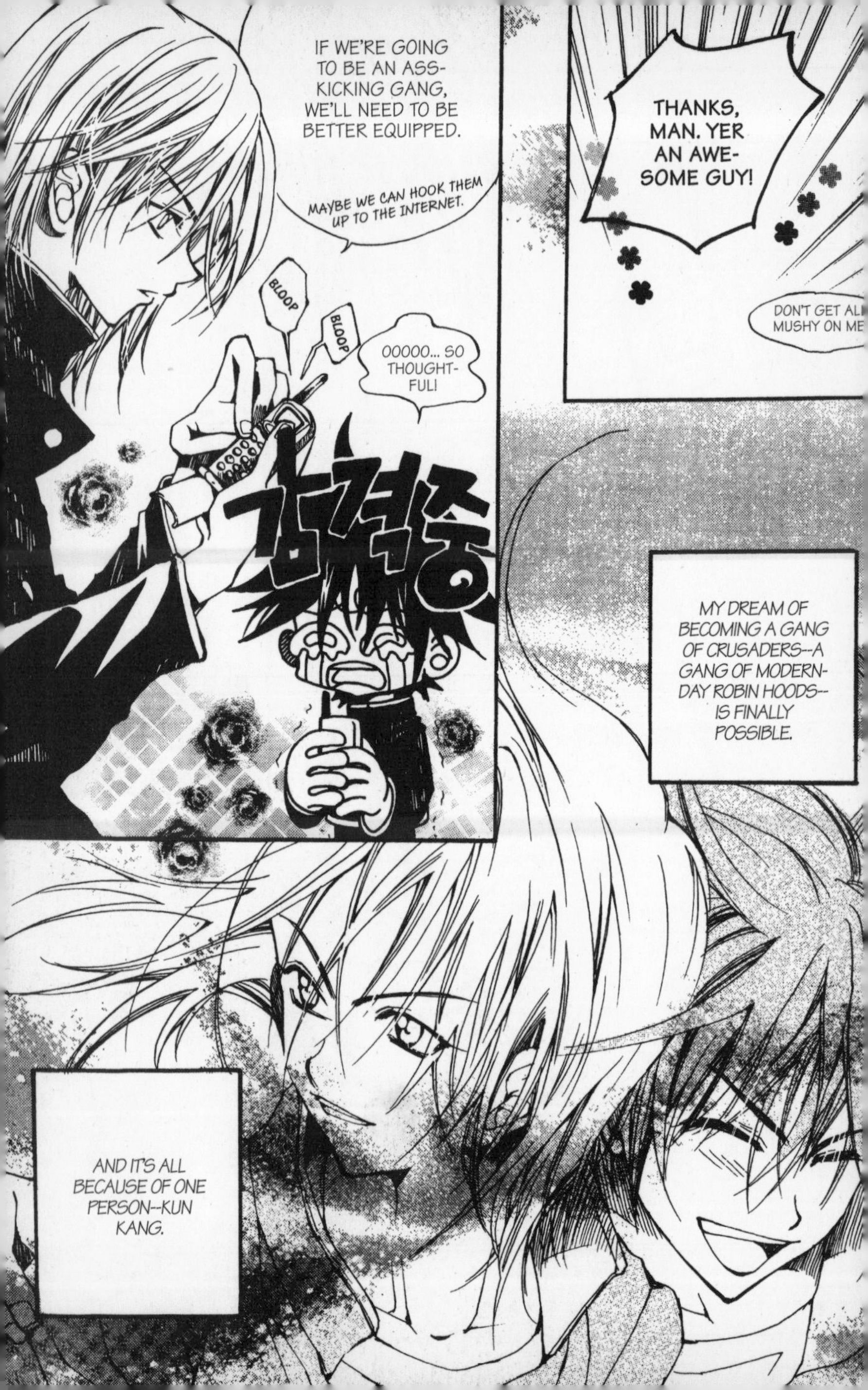
IF WE'RE GOING TO BE AN ASS-KICKING GANG, WE'LL NEED TO BE BETTER EQUIPPED.
MAYBE WE CAN HOOK THEM UP TO THE INTERNET.
BLOOP
BLOOP
OOOOO... SO THOUGHT-FUL!
감격중
THANKS, MAN. YER AN AWE-SOME GUY!
DON'T GET ALL MUSHY ON ME
MY DREAM OF BECOMING A GANG OF CRUSADERS--A GANG OF MODERN-DAY ROBIN HOODS--IS FINALLY POSSIBLE.
AND IT'S ALL BECAUSE OF ONE PERSON--KUN KANG.

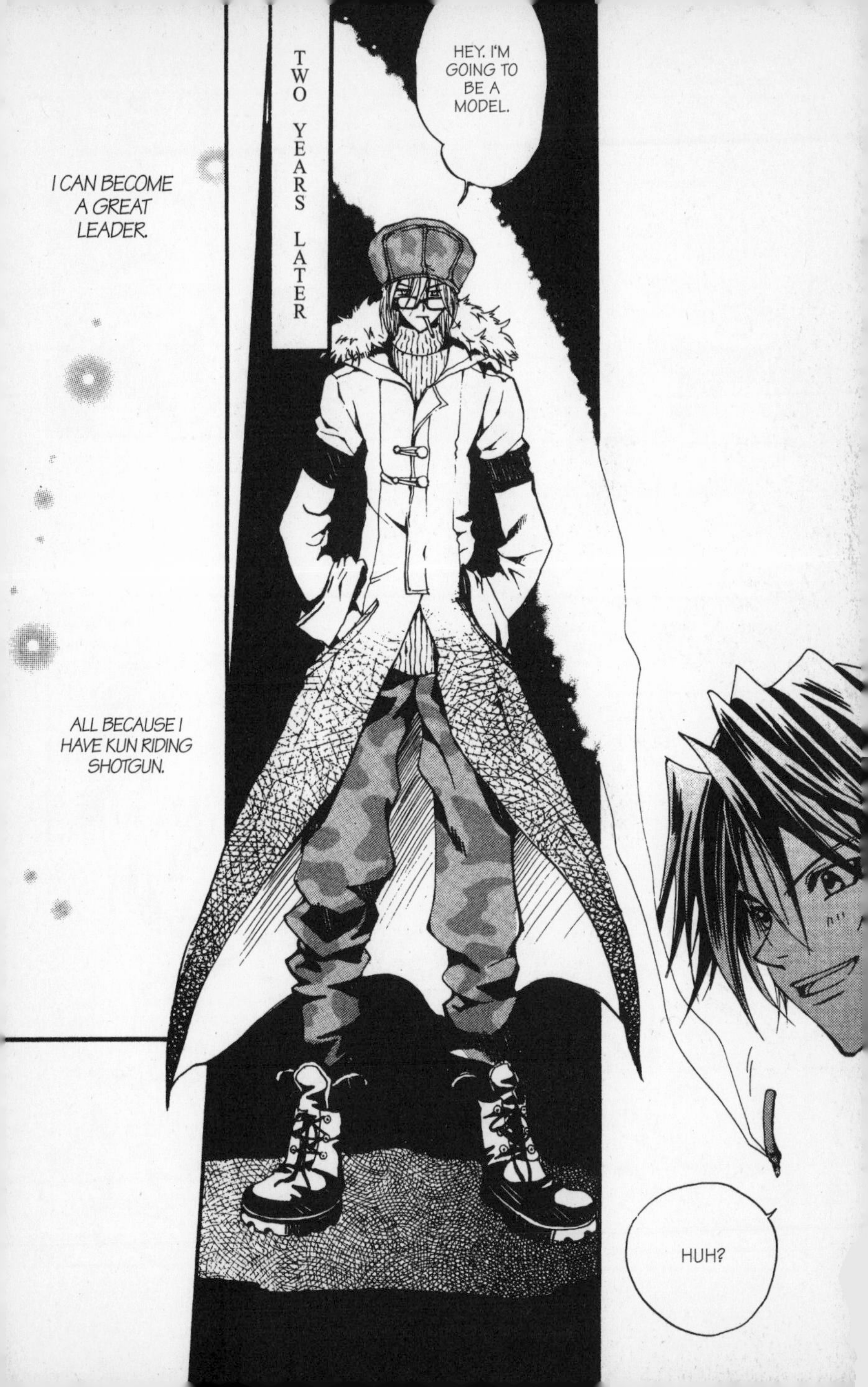
I CAN BECOME A GREAT LEADER.
ALL BECAUSE I HAVE KUN RIDING SHOTGUN.
TWO YEARS LATER
HEY. I'M GOING TO BE A MODEL.
HUH?

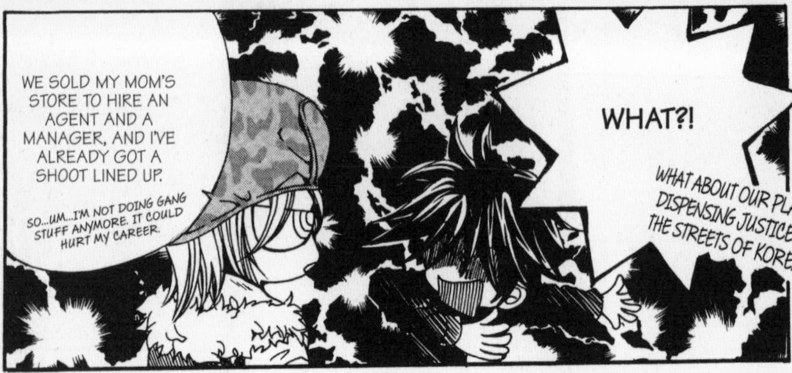
WE SOLD MY MOM'S STORE TO HIRE AN AGENT AND A MANAGER, AND I'VE ALREADY GOT A SHOOT LINED UP.
SO...UM...I'M NOT DOING GANG STUFF ANYMORE. IT COULD HURT MY CAREER.
WHAT?!
WHAT ABOUT OUR PLANS?! DISPENSING JUSTICE ON THE STREETS OF KOREA?!

AND HOW WILL THE PUBLIC REACT TO KUN'S NEW PROFESSION?

LET'S FIND OUT FROM TAE AND JUNG-WOO!

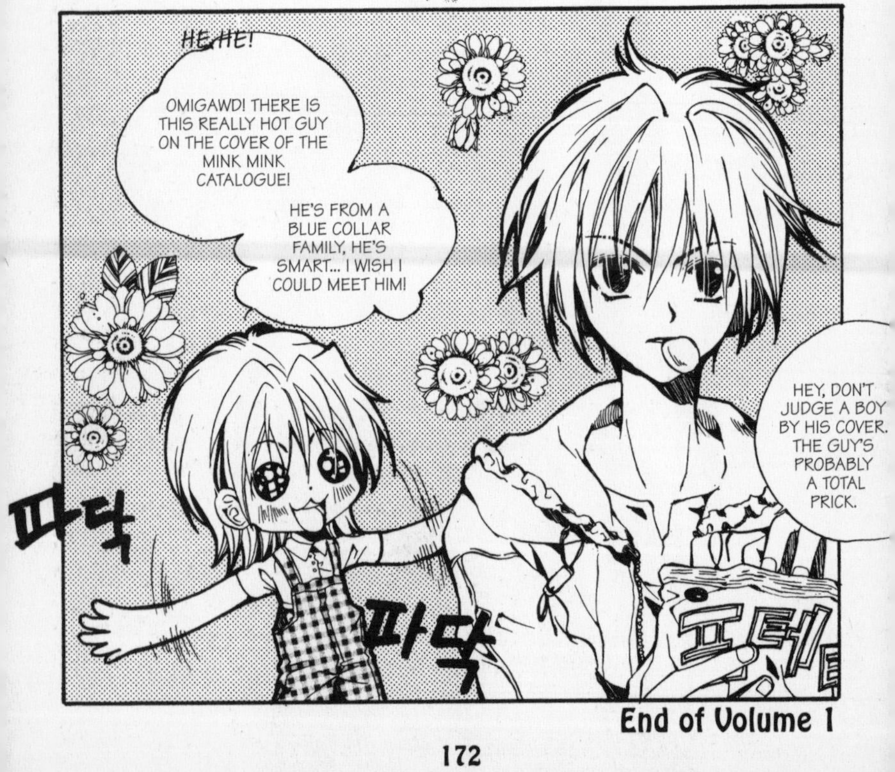
HE HE!
OMIGAWD! THERE IS THIS REALLY HOT GUY ON THE COVER OF THE MINK MINK CATALOGUE!
HE'S FROM A BLUE COLLAR FAMILY, HE'S SMART... I WISH I COULD MEET HIM!
파닥
파닥
HEY, DON'T JUDGE A BOY BY HIS COVER. THE GUY'S PROBABLY A TOTAL PRICK.

End of Volume 1

K2 WAS ORIGINALLY PUBLISHED INDEPEND-
ENTLY. (BY ME!) WOW! CLAP CLAP CLAP!
I AM SO THANKFUL TO THOSE WHO
BOUGHT AND READ THIS BOOK!
YOU'RE OKAY IF YOU JUST
BORROW IT AND READ IT, BUT
I'VE BEEN TOLD IT'S EVEN
BETTER IF YOU BUY IT! IT'S GOOD KARMA, TOO!

THIS WAS MY FIRST SERIES, AND WHILE WRITING IT,
I BECAME AWARE OF MANY UNFOLDING THINGS IN
MY OWN LIFE. IN TURN, I THINK THIS MADE K2 A
MORE MEANINGFUL WORK. LET'S JUST SAY I TASTED
THE SWEET AND BITTER.

FOR IN JUNG, WHO LABORED HARD ON MY BEHALF
DURING THE CREATION OF THIS, AND TO THOSE WHO
WROTE TO ME (THOUGH I DID NOT WRITE BACK--HOPE
YOU DIDN'T THINK I WAS DEAD) I SEND REALLY JUICY
KISSES. (C'MON! YOU KNOW YOU
WANT TO KISS ME!)

GA-WOON BECAME THE
MOST POPULAR CHARAC-
TER FROM K2'S FIRST
INSTALLMENT. I GUESS YOU
GIRLS (AND SOME GUYS!)
REALLY LIKE THE BAD BOYS!
GA-WOON CERTAINLY HAS THE ABILITY TO STIR UP
TROUBLE! AND IT SEEMS SOME OF YOU GIRLS REALLY
DISLIKE OUR PRECIOUS TAE! WHY? BECAUSE YOU
WANT GA-WOON ALL TO YOURSELVES! WELL, GET IN
LINE, YOU HUSSIES! I HOPE TO SEE YOU ALL AGAIN
WHEN THE SECOND VOLUME OF K2 HITS THE
SHELVES! WELL THEN, I WILL SEE YOU IN
SECOND ISSUE.

Free Talk

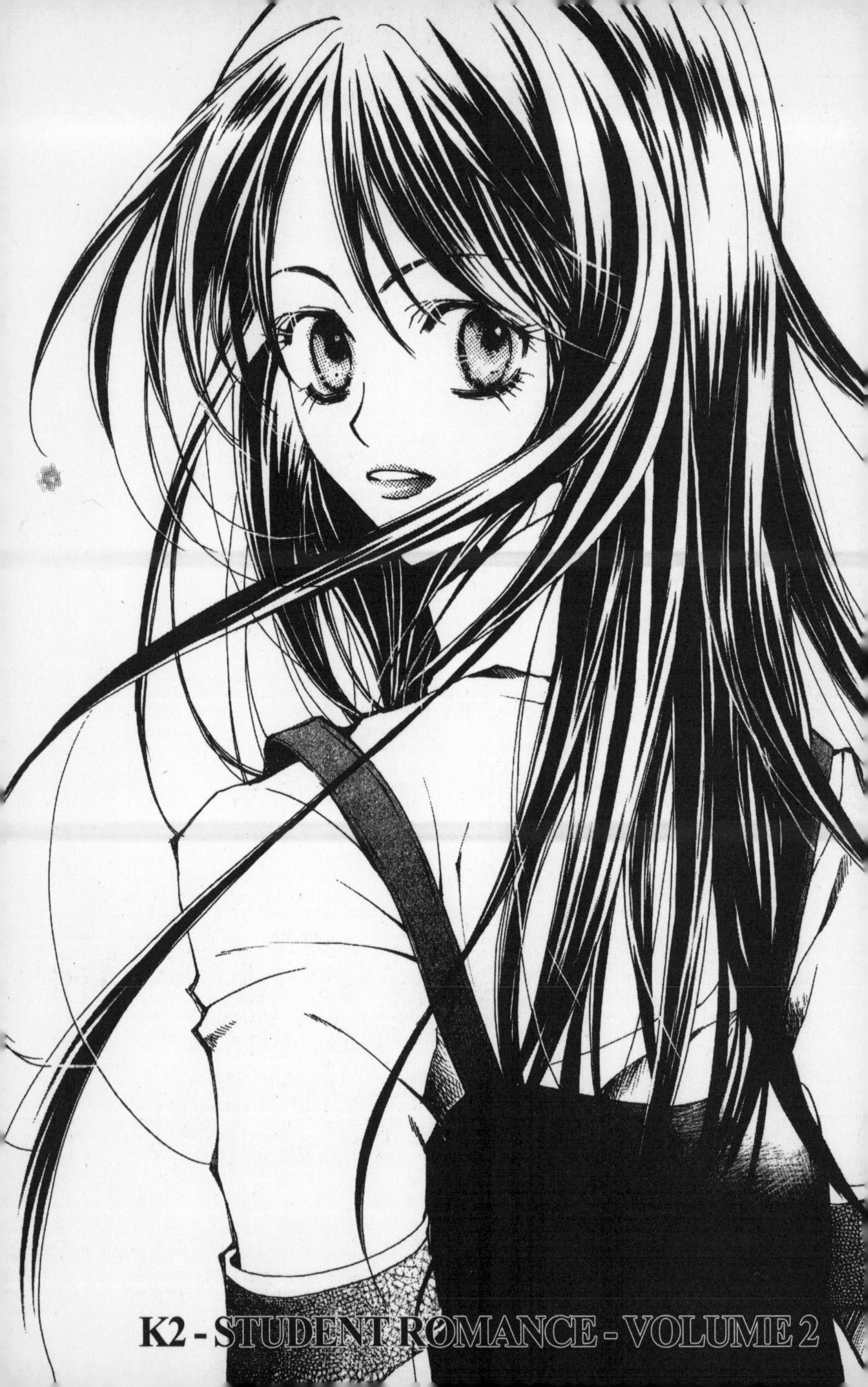
K2 - STUDENT ROMANCE - VOLUME 2

ANOTHER K APPEARS!

ANOTHER K APPEARS!

WHO IS THE MYSTERY

WHO IS THE MYSTERY

WOMAN WHO STIRS THE PASSIONS OF

N WHO STIRS THE PASSIONS OF

POKER FACED JUNG-WOO?

OKER FACED JUNG-WOO?

Vol.2

K-2

Kill me
Kiss me

IF YOU'RE A GOOD BOY, SHE MIGHT COME LOOKING FOR YOU! LOOK FOR HER IN VOLUME 2 OF *KILL ME, KISS ME*!

ALSO AVAILABLE FROM ⚙TOKYOPOP®

MANGA

.HACK//LEGEND OF THE TWILIGHT
@LARGE
A.I. LOVE YOU
AI YORI AOSHI
ANGELIC LAYER
ARM OF KANNON May 2004
BABY BIRTH
BATTLE ROYALE
BATTLE VIXENS April 2004
BRAIN POWERED
BRIGADOON
B'TX
CANDIDATE FOR GODDESS, THE April 2004
CARDCAPTOR SAKURA
CARDCAPTOR SAKURA - MASTER OF THE CLOW
CARDCAPTOR SAKURA AUTHENTIC May 2004
CHOBITS
CHRONICLES OF THE CURSED SWORD
CLAMP SCHOOL DETECTIVES
CLOVER
COMIC PARTY June 2004
CONFIDENTIAL CONFESSIONS
CORRECTOR YUI
COWBOY BEBOP
COWBOY BEBOP: SHOOTING STAR
CRESCENT MOON May 2004
CYBORG 009
DEMON DIARY
DEMON ORORON, THE April 2004
DEUS VITAE June 2004
DIGIMON
DIGIMON ZERO TWO
DIGIMON SERIES 3 April 2004
DNANGEL April 2004
DOLL - HARDCOVER May 2004
DRAGON HUNTER
DRAGON KNIGHTS
DUKLYON: CLAMP SCHOOL DEFENDERS
ERICA SAKURAZAWA WORKS
FAERIES' LANDING
FAKE
FLCL
FORBIDDEN DANCE
FRUITS BASKET
G GUNDAM
GATE KEEPERS
GETBACKERS
GHOST! March 2004
GIRL GOT GAME
GRAVITATION
GTO
GUNDAM WING

GUNDAM WING: BATTLEFIELD OF PACIFISTS
GUNDAM WING: ENDLESS WALTZ
GUNDAM WING: THE LAST OUTPOST (G-UNIT)
HAPPY MANIA
HARLEM BEAT
I.N.V.U.
IMMORTAL RAIN June 2004
INITIAL D
ISLAND
JING: KING OF BANDITS
JULINE
JUROR 13 Coming Soon
KARE KANO
KILL ME, KISS ME
KINDAICHI CASE FILES, THE
KING OF HELL
KODOCHA: SANA'S STAGE
LAMENT OF THE LAMB May 2004
LES BIJOUX
LOVE HINA
LUPIN III
MAGIC KNIGHT RAYEARTH I
MAGIC KNIGHT RAYEARTH II
MAHOROMATIC: AUTOMATIC MAIDEN May 2004
MAN OF MANY FACES
MARMALADE BOY
MARS
MINK April 2004
MIRACLE GIRLS
MIYUKI-CHAN IN WONDERLAND
MODEL May 2004
ONE April 2004
PARADISE KISS
PARASYTE
PEACH GIRL
PEACH GIRL: CHANGE OF HEART
PEACH GIRL: AUTHENTIC COLLECTORS BOX SET May 2004
PET SHOP OF HORRORS
PITA-TEN
PLANET LADDER
PLANETES
PRIEST
PSYCHIC ACADEMY March 2004
RAGNAROK
RAVE MASTER
REALITY CHECK
REBIRTH
REBOUND
REMOTE June 2004
RISING STARS OF MANGA
SABER MARIONETTE J
SAILOR MOON
SAINT TAIL

11.20.03 T

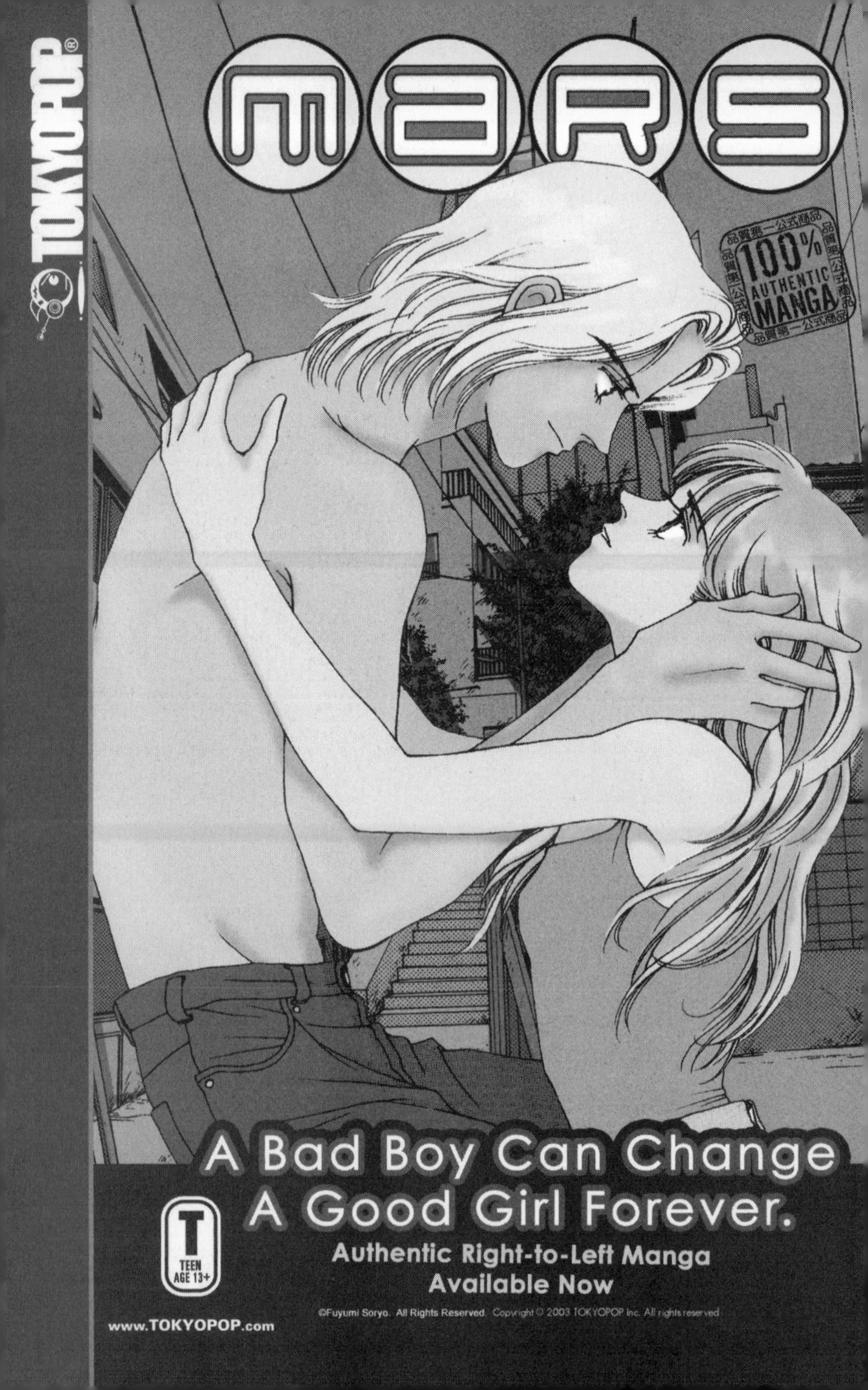
TOKYOPOP
MARS
100% AUTHENTIC MANGA
A Bad Boy Can Change
A Good Girl Forever.
T TEEN AGE 13+
Authentic Right-to-Left Manga
Available Now
©Fuyumi Soryo. All Rights Reserved. Copyright © 2003 TOKYOPOP Inc. All rights reserved
www.TOKYOPOP.com

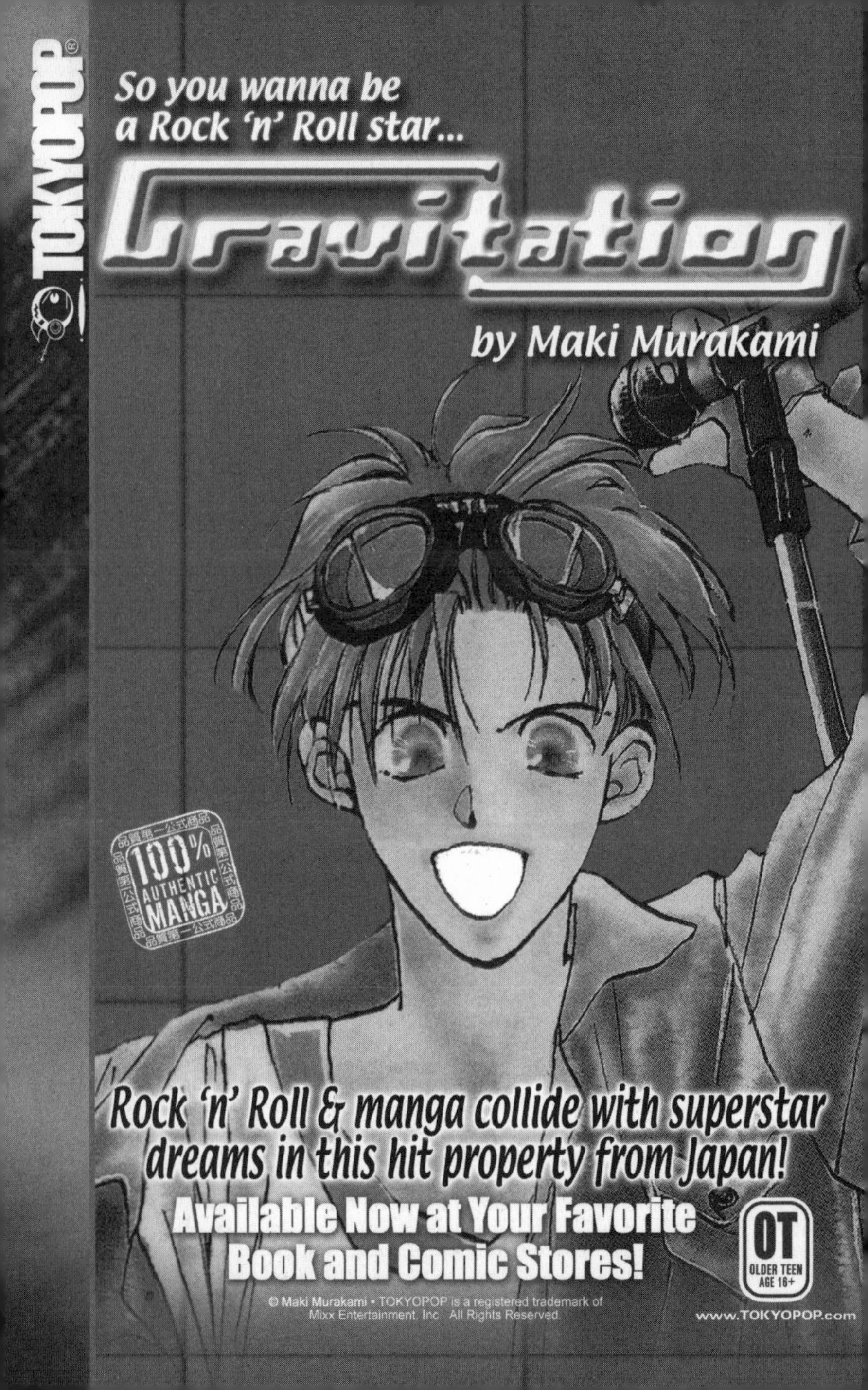
TOKYOPOP®
So you wanna be
a Rock 'n' Roll star...
Gravitation
by Maki Murakami
100% AUTHENTIC MANGA
Rock 'n' Roll & manga collide with superstar
dreams in this hit property from Japan!
Available Now at Your Favorite
Book and Comic Stores!
OT
OLDER TEEN
AGE 16+
© Maki Murakami • TOKYOPOP is a registered trademark of
Mixx Entertainment, Inc. All Rights Reserved.
www.TOKYOPOP.com

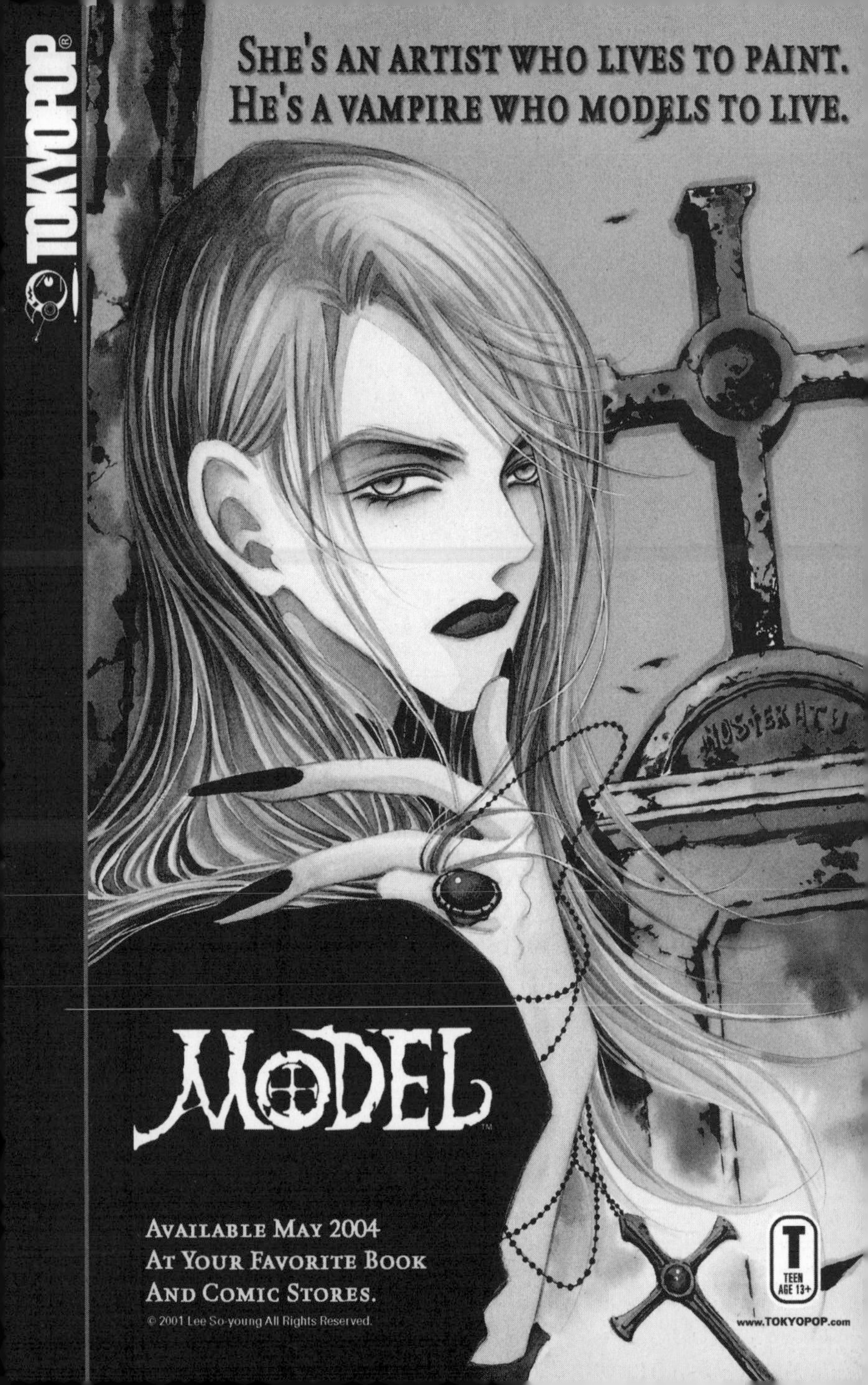
TOKYOPOP®
SHE'S AN ARTIST WHO LIVES TO PAINT.
HE'S A VAMPIRE WHO MODELS TO LIVE.
MODEL™
AVAILABLE MAY 2004
AT YOUR FAVORITE BOOK
AND COMIC STORES.
© 2001 Lee So-young All Rights Reserved.
T
TEEN AGE 13+
www.TOKYOPOP.com